DIVINITY AND
EXPERIENCE

DIVINITY AND EXPERIENCE

The Religion of the Dinka

BY

GODFREY LIENHARDT

*Lecturer in African Sociology at the
University of Oxford*

OXFORD
AT THE CLARENDON PRESS

Oxford University Press, Ely House, London W. 1

GLASGOW   NEW YORK   TORONTO   MELBOURNE   WELLINGTON
CAPE TOWN   IBADAN   NAIROBI   DAR ES SALAAM   LUSAKA   ADDIS ABABA
DELHI   BOMBAY   CALCUTTA   MADRAS   KARACHI   DACCA
KUALA LUMPUR   SINGAPORE   HONG KONG   TOKYO

ISBN 0 19 823119 9

First published 1961
Reprinted 1967, 1970, 1976

Printed in Great Britain
at the University Press, Oxford
by Vivian Ridler
Printer to the University

TO

E. E. EVANS-PRITCHARD

PREFACE

THIS book is based upon two years' work among the Dinka, spread over the period 1947–50. A generous gift from my college in Cambridge, Downing College, enabled me to make essential preparations, but the study itself was entirely financed by the Sudan Government, and this book is now published with its support. It would be difficult to imagine a Government which provided happier conditions for disinterested research than the Government of the Sudan, and I cannot here thank all those to whom I am indebted. For some indeed, like the late Chief Kuanyin Agoth and the late Dr. Mamoun Hussein el Sherif, these acknowledgements have been too long delayed.

, Sir James Robertson, then Civil Secretary, encouraged my work and showed great personal kindness to me. Of the many officials who gave me hospitality, I can mention only those in whose homes I was most frequently a visitor: Mr. T. R. H. Owen, then Governor of the Bahr-al-Ghazal Province, and Mrs. Owen; Mr. and Mrs. B. A. Lewis; Dr. and Mrs. P. P. Howell; Mr. J. M. Hunter and Mr. R. H. M. Boyle in Gogrial; Mr. and Mrs. J. H. T. Wilson in Tonj; Mr. and Mrs. Keith Williams in Rumbek; and Mr. David Fyfe and Mr. Gordon Hickson in Aweil. I have benefited greatly also from the writings, most of them unpublished, of many administrators among the Dinka.

I owe a great deal to the Verona Fathers, and especially to the missionaries in Wau and Kwajok. Without Fr. Nebel's work on Dinka language and thought, my own would have been made immensely more difficult. I hope that the numerous references to him in this book will be accepted as a tribute to his authority, and to the work of the Congregation of Verona.

The manuscript was read at various stages by many friends— Dr. J. G. Peristiany, Dr. J. H. M. Beattie, and Dr. D. F. Pocock who helped me greatly throughout, all colleagues at the Institute of Social Anthropology, Oxford; Professor A. G. O'Connor, formerly at the College of Arts and Sciences, Baghdad, where I was given the opportunity for more reflection; my brother

Peter Lienhardt; and Mr. I. Talog Davies whose comments on points of detail were helpfully astringent. Mrs. Laurence Sutcliffe accepted the labour of compiling the index. To all these I am most grateful.

My final acknowledgements are to the Dinka themselves, and to Professor E. E. Evans-Pritchard, who between them really made this study possible. The Dinka gave hospitality and friendship, and shared the knowledge in which they alone are really expert. I think of the Gogrial Council, of Chief Benjamin Lang Juk, the Rehan family, Akille Deng Aghou, Chief Akol Morkec, Chief Gir Kiro, Ambrose Wol, Frediano Dhol Yuot and Samuel Agany Kuanyin and their families, and many others—*koc kok kajuec*.

It will be very obvious that I am indebted to Professor Evans-Pritchard's Nilotic studies, and particularly to his work on Nuer religion. But personally my debt to him is greater, and I dedicate this book to him in gratitude for his teaching and friendship.

Oxford, 1961   G. L.

CONTENTS

LIST OF PLATES

LIST OF TEXT-FIGURES

INTRODUCTION

(i)

THE Dinka may number some 900,000 people in all,[1] and as can be seen from the sketch-map (Fig. 1) they are spread over a very wide area. In these circumstances their cultural and linguistic homogeneity is striking; and despite regional variations in dialect, custom, and some aspects of social structure, they may here be treated on the whole as a single people. Those who know the Dinka will, however, observe that this study is orientated towards the Western Dinka of the Bahr-al-Ghazal Province of the Sudan, and particularly the Rek tribal group, with whom I first learnt the Dinka language.

Dinkaland lies in a vast arc around the swamps of the central Nile basin in the Southern Sudan. It is a flat country of open savannah and savannah forest, intersected by many rivers and streams converging upon the central basin of the Nile. For part of each year heavy rains and river-flooding render much of the land uninhabitable and impassable. Communications become difficult between the higher stretches which remain above the flood, and where alone it is possible to build permanent homesteads and cultivate gardens around them.

Dinkaland is poor in natural resources, and the material culture of the people is simple. Stone is rare, and natural iron is available only on the fringes of the country. The Dinka in any case are not iron-workers on any considerable scale.[2] At the present day iron hoe-blades and spearheads of foreign manufacture are acquired from Arab and Greek merchants. Western Dinka say that in the past they obtained these necessities from the iron-working Luo to the south, and that at one time they used weapons and digging-sticks fashioned of horn, bone, and

---

[1] This figure is taken from *The Equatorial Nile Project, and Its Effects in the Anglo-Egyptian Sudan*, vol. i of the *Report of the Jonglei Investigation Team*, p. 213.

[2] According to C. G. and B. Z. Seligman, *Pagan Tribes of the Nilotic Sudan,* 1932, p. 138, there are 'iron-working clans' among the Cic Dinka, but their names would seem to suggest to me that they are of non-Dinka origin.

wood, though I have never seen in Dinkaland a spearhead or hoe made of these materials.[1] The absence of metal would certainly have increased the difficulties of agriculture and fishing, and hence made the Dinka even more materially dependent on their cattle than they are today.

Imported metal is now used extensively for personal adornment as well as tools and weapons, and is taken for granted as a necessity of life; but in the past its value must have been much greater than it is today, and this is perhaps significant for understanding the value attached to the ancient sacred spears from which the priests of the Dinka, the 'masters of the fishing-spear', get their title. These are said to have been metal spears, which must have long antedated the general introduction of iron into the country.

Apart from imported metal and beads, there is nothing of importance in Dinka material culture which outlasts a single lifetime. The labours of one generation hence do not lighten, or make a foundation for, those of the next, which must again fashion by the same simple technological processes and from the same limited variety of raw materials a cultural environment which seems unchanging and, until the extensive foreign contacts of modern times, was unchangeable. The only form of wealth which can be inherited is livestock; and the vicissitudes of herding—murrain and bad seasons—work against the secure transmission of this wealth in any particular family over the generations. The egalitarianism of the Dinka goes with their general insecurity, on the margins of subsistence; and this insecurity, coming from an exposure to a harsh environment against which their technology and material culture insulate them but little, is connected with features of their religion which we later describe. Further, the absence of any tradition of historical development, or any evidence of the accumulation, growth, and change of cultural possessions, throws into relief the one major mythical event, the establishment of the masters of the fishing-spear.

The material necessities of Dinka life are made from grass, mud, and wood, with the addition of materials derived from wild and domestic animals. The homestead of a typical middle-aged

---

[1] They used to be found among the Nuer, however, and horn and ebony spears are illustrated in E. E. Evans-Pritchard, *The Nuer*, 1940, p. 115.

man, such as may be glimpsed in some of the plates in this book, consists of two or three circular huts of wattle and daub with conical thatched roofs, and a cattle-byre of the same shape and materials. Each wife has her own hut, with its low mud

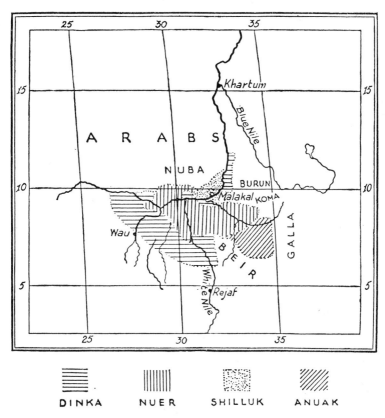

FIG. 1. The Dinka and neighbouring peoples

windscreen for her fire and mud supports for cooking-pots. A rough shelter of stakes and millet-stalks protects this woman's hearth—the *mac thok*—from sun and rain, and provides a platform upon which domestic utensils can be stored out of the way of dogs and children. At this fire a wife feeds her own children, and takes her turn, in a polygynous household, in preparing food for her husband. In the cattle-byre is a dung-fire, the *gol*, which is the centre for the men of the home when they are together in the homestead.

At these two hearths, the woman's hearth and the men's hearth, Dinka children get their first practical lessons in the principles of Dinka social organization. The relationship between the several hearths of the separate elementary families and the central hearth of the men and the cattle is the simple paradigm of the different lineages (also called 'cooking-hearth') which form segments of a Dinka subclan, the *gol* or cattle-hearth.

The furnishings of such a home may be briefly mentioned. They include clay pots for cooking, water-carrying, and brewing; gourds of various shapes and sizes, some for serving the staple millet-porridge, some for storing oil and butter, and some for milking and drinking milk; plaited baskets in which grain is stored and plaited-grass winnowing-trays; wicker fish-traps and baskets, and perhaps a wicker cradle for carrying babies on long journeys; simple nets for scooping fish out of the river when it is shallow; sleeping-skins of oxhide or skins of game, and large reed mats in which the Dinka when abroad roll themselves to protect themselves from rain and sun; cattle-pegs and bells, ropes of plaited grass and ox-collars and ropes of plaited strips of hide; a few hoes and simple adzes; head-rests and stools made by utilizing naturally forked branches of suitable shape, and hollowed parrying-sticks, which also serve as purses and pouches, made of ambatch. For the rest there are the personal trinkets of members of the household, the goatskin or sheepskin skirts of the married women, the fishing- and hunting-spears of the men, and today various small trade goods. Each homestead also contains a mortar made from a hollowed tree-trunk set in the ground, in which grain is pounded with a long pestle which figures importantly in a myth later recounted. Some families own a simple canoe, and in each settlement the dance drums which are used by everyone are privately owned by some family which has made or acquired them, though they are treated more or less as public property.

Millet-porridge with various sauces or milk is the basic food, with roast or boiled meat and fish as they are available. The products of cattle are of particular importance, though they do not in themselves provide a complete diet. Soured milk and curds form a high proportion of the food taken, especially by young men when they are in the cattle-camps, and boiled butter is both a food and an unguent. When cattle die or are sacrificed their flesh is eaten, and their hide provides rope, sleeping-skins, and shields. Their urine disinfects the milk gourds and curdles the milk, to Dinka taste, and their dried dung is the fuel for the smudge-fires with which the Dinka try to protect themselves and their herds from biting insects. Dung ashes are rubbed over the body, both for decoration and as a partial protection against flies by day and mosquitoes by night. This covering of ashes is a sign that a Dinka is actively engaged in looking after a herd, with which it identifies him. In parts of Dinkaland cattle-dung is also used as a mulch for the gardens.[1] Even in those parts of the country where conditions are most favourable for cultivation, it is doubtful if any alternative to the mixed economy of fishing, cultivating, and herding would be a practical possibility; but in any case the attachment of the Dinka to pastoral pursuits is not to be explained only by the practical value of their herds.

Conditions of land and weather accompanying the cycle of the seasons make transhumance inevitable. Each year the Dinka have to move to and fro between their permanent homesteads, of the kind we have briefly described, and riverain pastures where permanent building is impossible owing to the floods of the wet season.

The year is divided into clearly marked wet and dry seasons. The first rains of the year start in March or April, and by May have become sufficiently regular and frequent to soften the ground for cultivation. Most Dinka are then in their permanent homesteads hoeing and sowing. The cattle are grazing near home by day and tethered to their individual pegs in family herds near or in each homestead at night. In July, with heavier and more frequent rains, the numerous depressions of the country begin to fill with water, and rivers begin to rise and overflow their banks, flooding the lower-lying land about them and at their confluences. Then, leaving the older people and the girls to watch the growing crops, the young men of several re-lated families take many of the cattle away from the homesteads

---

[1] This is fully described in J. M. Stubbs and C. G. T. Morison, 'The Western Dinka, Their Land and Agriculture', *S. N. & R.*, vol. xxi, part 2, 1938.

and form camps in unsettled savannah forest. In some parts of Dinkaland this territory is close to permanent settlements and the herdsmen are never far away from home. Many of the Dinka of Aweil District, on the other hand, move into a large tract of forest between the Lol and the Bahr-al-Arab, at one or two days' journey from home, and which cannot be permanently settled because it is too far from supplies of drinking-water for most of the dry season.

As the wet season advances, the herdsmen of each subtribe converge on a few established centres within the subtribal territory, in response to the increasing severity of the season and the limitation of pastures and movement. Here larger camps are formed, and mushroom-shaped shelters are erected on stout piles to protect the men and young animals at night. By day the occupants of such camps fan out with their cattle in their several different family groups to take advantage of the best grass in the neighbourhood.

The rainy season ends in October or thereabouts. By then some of the herdsmen will have returned to their homes to help with the harvest, and when this is well under way and the rains cease all the wet-season camps disperse and return to their homes. There the cattle graze the millet leaves and stalks left from the harvest, while the preparation and clearing of new cultivations is undertaken. As the dry season proceeds and the floods recede fishing becomes possible. This autumn period is also the main ceremonial season, when much beer is brewed and sacrifices are made, and when boys are initiated into manhood.

By January, or in some places earlier, the grass near the permanent homesteads is drying out completely, and the floods in the riverain pastures have receded. People then begin to move towards the main rivers, where they build shelters and wind-breaks and spend the dry months, until they return to cultivate their gardens again with the coming of the rains. Each tribe has its own traditional dry-season pastures, and within these areas each subtribe also has its customary positions, though there is much intermingling of individuals and families from different subtribes in these camps.

Though the cycle of the seasons is regular in outline as here described, there is considerable and significant variation from year to year and from place to place. The first rains particularly are uncertain and capricious, and may be accompanied by a dry spell, in Dinka *yak*, which can seriously impair the harvest. *Yak* is a dry period when rain is needed and could reasonably be expected. It may occur at the end of an unusually protracted dry season, when the rains are late, or in the middle of the early rains. Grazing problems also may then become acute, since only grasses with long roots which reach down to moisture can produce fresh shoots at such a time. The characteristic grass of this type in Dinkaland is *awar* (*vetiveria nigritana*) which, like the killing drought which it survives, figures importantly in Dinka myth and symbolism.

In view of the fact that the permanent settlements of the Dinka contain all their members at two seasons of the year only —for the sowing and around harvest time—it is understandable that political groups should be spoken of in the idiom of the cattle-herding group or cattle-camp (*wut*) and not of the homestead, village, or settlement (*baai*).

The smallest herding-group consists of a man and his children and their cattle. A number of such groups, drawn together by kinship, friendship, and neighbourhood, form the small camps which assemble for savannah-forest camping in the beginning of the main wet season. A number of these camps together make up what I have called a subtribe, which has its own name and persists through time beyond the lives of its individual members. Several subtribes which are regarded as having developed from a single original cattle-camp form a tribe. Tribes vary much in size, from less than 1,000 to some 25,000 members. On the whole the largest tribes have the greatest number of subtribes: the large Apuk Patuan tribe of the Rek Dinka, for example, has eight, and originally had nine, subtribes. Other tribes have three or four.

Tribes are grouped in the several regional aggregations named on the sketch-map (Fig. 2). These tribal groupings are not politically organized, but the smaller groupings have naturally a greater potentiality for a measure of common action than larger ones. These may be characterized by little more than name and peculiarities of dialect or cultural detail, though in fact dialects overlap the boundaries of tribal groups, and even such a marked cultural feature as male circumcision, for

example, cuts across the great Rek tribal group. To the west of
a line drawn through Rek territory the Dinka are circumcised,
while to the east of that line they despise circumcision.

Dinka clans are of two categories: the *bany*, or priests, whose
symbol of office is the sacred fishing-spear; and the *kic*, commoner or warrior clans. Dinka clans are very numerous, and

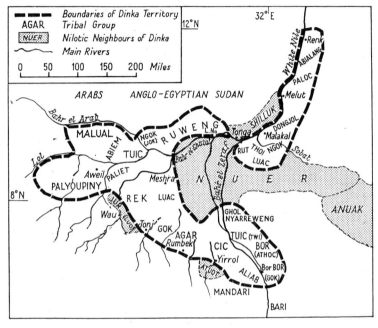

FIG. 2. The Dinka Tribal Groups

the largest are represented in many different tribes. A Dinka
does not know the whole range of his clansmen throughout
Dinkaland, and perhaps not even in his own tribe if it is a large
one.

The effective corporate descent-groups are composed of all
those who come into contact with each other who know themselves to be agnatic descendants of an original ancestor, and
these form what I have called 'subclans'. The subclan within
the tribe is understood on the model of the family within the
smallest cattle-camp, that composed only of a few different

families. Family and subclan equally are *gol*, cattle-hearth, and cattle-camp and tribe equally are *wut*, cattle-camp or herding-group. The subclans are further subdivided into lineages often named after different wives of the original ancestor.

A tribe is thus an association of subclans, with the addition of individuals or families who have attached themselves by marriage to one or another of the subclans which are thought originally to have settled together and grown into the tribe. Several different spear-master or priestly clans, and warrior clans, are represented in every tribe. Each tribe as a whole is identified with a particular subclan, almost invariably a subclan of spear-masters, who are said to 'have' the land of the tribe. Each subtribe also has a nuclear lineage of spear-masters, from which its most important master of the fishing-spear is provided. In Dinka political theory each subtribe has also its nuclear lineage of a warrior subclan, which provides its war-leaders as the nuclear spear-master lineage provides its priests. In inter-tribal warfare one of the several masters of the fishing-spear, and one of the several war-leaders, emerge as master of the fishing-spear and war-leader of the whole tribe.[1]

The theory, then, is of the dual control of war-leader and priest, in the subtribe and in the tribe. The nuclear subclans of the tribes, and the nuclear lineages of the sub-tribes, are often spoken of as 'the people of the centre of the camp', since they have first established the cattle-camps and occupy central positions on the sites, or 'the (classificatory) maternal uncles' of the subtribe or tribe, since they are the descent-groups whose women are most widely distributed through the other descent-groups of the tribe. The dual control of warrior and priest is assimilated to this uterine kinship relationship, which is one of special mutual forbearance and friendship. Ideally, the war-leaders and priests of the subtribes should stand in the relationship of nephew and maternal uncle to each other, thus creating a strong nucleus of two descent-groups related through women and with different and complementary functions for each political group.

Though this Dinka political theory is not a fully adequate

[1] It has been necessary to simplify the details, which may be consulted in my essay 'The Western Dinka', in *Tribes without Rulers*, ed. David Tait and J. Middleton, 1958.

representation of the conduct of Dinka politics, it provides a sufficient background to the present work, which aims rather at describing the structure of Dinka religious experience than analysing in detail its political concomitants.

(ii) *Cattle in Dinka Experience*

Animal sacrifice is the central religious act of the Dinka, whose cattle are in their eyes perfect victims; and therefore the chapters which follow must take for granted a full understanding of the nature of the Dinkas' interest in their herds. The economic importance of cattle to a predominantly pastoral people is readily appreciated, and has here, therefore, been touched upon only briefly; but it is their wider social importance which particularly fits cattle for the part of victim in the blood sacrifices later described.

There is a vast Dinka vocabulary referring to cattle, and particularly to the varieties of their colouring and shading in their almost innumerable blends and configurations. The interest and, one might almost say, obsession which produces and develops this vocabulary is not primarily practical in nature; for the colour-configuration of a beast is not related to its usefulness as a source of food or other material necessities and, moreover, the rich metaphorical cattle-vocabulary of the Dinka relates primarily to oxen, which are of least utilitarian importance.

Information about this vocabulary has been published by Professor and Mrs. Seligman,[1] writing about the Bor Dinka, and by Professor Evans-Pritchard, who collected a list of terms from a Ngok Dinka and published them with their Nuer equivalents.[2] Father P. A. Nebel has also published a list of some of the cattle-colour names of the Western Dinka.[3] The first two of these authorities give examples of complex metaphorical associations between configurations of colour in cattle and features of the natural and social environment which these colours call to mind. These metaphors show to what extent and

---

[1] *Pagan Tribes of the Nilotic Sudan*, 1932, pp. 169–70. The information was provided by Archdeacon Shaw.

[2] E. E. Evans-Pritchard, *Imagery in Ngok Dinka Cattle Names*, Bulletin of the School of Oriental Studies, London Institution, vol. vii, part 3, 1934.

[3] P. A. Nebel, *Dinka Dictionary*, Verona, 1948, p. 51.

in what detail Dinka thought is orientated towards their herds, and how each configuration of colour can form the centre of a whole field of diverse experience, linking one apperception with another.[1]

Cattle are described by many composite terms, each indicating by a prefix or suffix the sex and stage of maturity of a beast, combined with a term for its particular kind of colour-configuration. Bulls and oxen have the prefix *ma*, and if it is necessary to distinguish between the whole and the castrated beast the former takes as a suffix the term *thon*, meaning 'whole male', and the latter the term *bwoc*, castrated. A short-horn bull is further distinguished by the term *acoot*. Heifers have the prefix *nya*, 'young female', and cows the prefix *a*. Bull-calves may have the prefix *manh*, from *meth*, child, added to their other names.

There is a general parallelism between the prefix for 'bull' and 'ox', and for men's personal names, and between that for 'cow', and women's personal names, so that on the whole personal names with the prefix *ma*, for 'bull', are likely to be the names of men, and those with the prefix *a*, for 'cow', are likely to be the names of women. Though some personal names have no connexion with cattle-names, many of the personal names, and all the cattle-names, which occur later in texts and descriptions may be understood to be formed in this way.

The following is an example of the terms for beasts of the configuration *ma kuei*, which are black with white on the head. The basic term for this configuration is *kuei*, the word for the fish-eagle, a striking bird of similar black and white marking. A bull of this configuration is *ma kuei(n) thon*; an ox, *ma kuei(n) bwoc* or merely *ma kuei*; a bull-calf, *manh ma kuei*; and a cow-calf or heifer, *nya(n) kuei*. A cow is *a kuei*. A short-horn bull would be *ma kuei(n) acoot*, and there are other terms which might be added to indicate different shapes of horns and stages of growth.

In most cases the term which denotes the colour-configuration has also another meaning, as the name of something of similar configuration in nature or Dinka culture, and the Dinka

[1] Professor Evans-Pritchard first indicated something of the wider sociological interest of these colour-names and metaphors in writing: '. . . little is known at present about Nilotic cattle-names, which are of great interest sociologically, illustrating language as a technique of economic relations, and showing the ways in which symbols referring to colours and their distribution are formed.' Op. cit., 1934, p. 628.

explicitly connect the basic colour-terms for their beasts with
the source from which they derive. So, in the example above,
the connexion between the *kuei* colouring in cattle and the
kuei, the fish-eagle, is consciously made.

Almost the whole extensive colour vocabulary of the Dinka
is one of cattle-colours. A particular pattern or colour in newly
imported cloth or beads is thus necessarily referred to by the
name of the configuration of colour in cattle which it is thought
most to resemble. A black and white spotted cloth, for example,
would be *alath* (*-nh*) *ma kuac*, *ma kuac* being the term for a spotted
bull or ox, which is itself connected explicitly with the spots of
the leopard, *kuac*. A striped cloth would be *alath* (*-nh*) *ma nyang*,
ma nyang being the term for a brindled bull, which is connected
with the brindling of the crocodile, *nyang*. I think that the only
Western Dinka words for colours, other than terms connected
also with colour-configurations in cattle, are *toc*, green, which
also means rawness and freshness in vegetables, and *thith*, red,
which means also the redness of raw meat. These colours are
not in any case found in cattle.[1] *Agher*, white, which refers to
bright white light, may be connected with the term *yor* or *yar*
in the names for white cattle, and *col*, black and also 'soot',
though absent from the term for a black bull, *ma car*, is included
in the names for black cows and heifers, *a col* and *nyan col*.

The basic vocabulary of names for configurations of colour
in cattle is fixed and traditional, consisting of words for colours
and combinations of light and shade which a Dinka learns to
use from childhood, perhaps without initially having seen what
it is, in wild nature, to which they refer. Thus any spotted
pattern in which the spots generally resemble in size and distribution those of the leopard will be called *ma kuac*, and in this
and many other cases the child may well have seen the *ma kuac*
configuration in cattle before he has seen the leopard, *kuac*, to
the configuration of which the name refers. A Dinka may thus
recognize the configuration in nature by reference to what he
first knows of it in the cattle on which his attention, from childhood, is concentrated.

The Dinkas' very perception of colour, light, and shade in
the world around them is in these ways inextricably connected

---

[1] Though *thith* may be added to the term for a brown beast to indicate a strong
reddish tone—*malual thith*, 'a very red-brown ox'.

with their recognition of colour-configurations in their cattle. If their cattle-colour vocabulary were taken away, they would have scarcely any way of describing visual experience in terms of colour, light, and darkness. Other Nilotic peoples, who have lost many of their cattle and much of their material dependence upon them, have yet retained a colour vocabulary based upon cattle-colours, and develop poetic images on the basis of these cattle-colour names, as I now describe for the Dinka.[1]

When boys reach manhood they take the colour-names of oxen in addition to the personal names they have been previously known by, and are called by intimate friends and age-mates by the ox-names they have then taken at initiation. A young man then becomes in a manner identified with an ox of some particular colour, which he proudly displays before the girls. He will praise his ox in songs, delighting in inventing new ways of referring to its appearance, and in introducing into song imagery fitting to an ox of that colour. The ability to create new imagery based upon the traditional colour-names of cattle is considered a mark of intelligence in a man; and though some men are acknowledged to be more gifted than others in this respect, every Dinka can attempt a measure of poetic ingenuity and originality.

The type of imagery developed may be illustrated by the following names for a man with a black display-ox. In song, or when addressed by his age-mates, he will not be content with the basic name for a black ox (*ma car*), but will be known by one or more other names, all explained ultimately as deriving from the blackness of his ox seen in relation to darkness in other things. He may therefore be known as *tim atiep*, 'the shade of a tree'; or *kor acom*, 'seeks for snails', after the black ibis which seeks for snails; or *bun anyeer*, 'thicket of the buffalo', which suggests the darkness of the forest in which the dark buffalo rests; or *akiu yak thok*, 'cries out in the spring drought', after a small black bird (*adhjiec*), which gives its characteristic cry at this time of the year; or *arec luk*, 'spoils the meeting', after the dark clouds which accompany a downpour of rain and send the Dinka who are having a meeting (*luk*) running for shelter. The following list indicates but a few of these metaphorical

[1] The Anuak, for example, now have few cattle, but still use metaphorical praise-names based upon cattle-colour names.

cattle-names, from which the extent and direction of imaginative interest may be judged:

For a white ox (*mabior*): 'bull of the women' (*muor diar*), because the women are anxious to get white European salt; *matoordit*, after the bright scales of the *atoor* fish; 'the moon brightens the cattle camp' (*dhol pei wut*); 'the cows await the moon' (*atit ghok pei*), the white bull in the camp thus being likened to the moon, and indeed a white beast is discerned clearly in a cattle-camp on a darkish night; 'elephant tusk' (*tung akoon*).

For a red-brown ox (*malual*): 'the game rest at midday' (*col lai piny*), after the antelope of this colour; 'it shakes the clump of bushes (around an ant-hill) (*ayek but*), after the behaviour of a lion which is here seen to be of this colour, though it figures also in the metaphorical names developed around the basic term for tawny yellow beasts; 'it loves the pool' (*anhiar kol*), after the hippopotamus which is of this colour; 'it lies in the pool' (*atoc kol*), also after the hippopotamus; 'what makes women's elbows creak' (*ke dhiau tik kok*), when they grind, that is, to make beer which is reddish.

For a grey ox (*malou*) (*lou* is the bustard): 'big game' (*landit*), after the elephant which is of this colour; 'breaks up trees' (*abeng tim*), after the elephant; 'respecter of the cattle-byre' (*athek luak*), after the elephant which does not pursue people into a cattle-byre; 'game killed by the foreigners' (*lan a jur nok*), again after the elephant, as is 'spoor of the grey one' (*duopelou*).

For a black and white ox of the *majok* configuration: 'marking of the creator' (*bung aciek*), based upon an association between Divinity, and white and black, later described; *wel jok*, 'exchange *jok*' after a custom of the Dinka by which an elder brother has first claim on bulls of this configuration in exchange for some other; '*jok* ivory armlet' (*jok apyok*), emphasizing the whiteness of the white parts in contrast to the black; 'sacred ibis' (*arumjok*), after the black and white markings of this bird; 'spoiler of the marriage' (*arec ruai*), because this is one of the most valued configurations and people want it among marriage cattle, but the owners do not wish to part with it; 'flour' (*abik*), the reference being to the whiteness of flour spread out to dry against the dark earth.

For a black and white ox of the *maker* configuration: 'soldier ant' (*ajing* or *majing*), after the columns of these black ants carrying white particles, grain, ants' eggs, or termites; 'of the thicket', in reference to the leopard; 'totem of the Nuer' (*yanh Nuer*), after the monitor lizard (*agany*), in which the light and shade are seen in this pattern, and which most Nuer will not eat; 'star-ox' (*makuel*), after the brightness of the stars in a dark sky; '*ker*-fish-eagle' (*kerkuei*), referring to a bull of this configuration with a white head, like the fish-eagle and like the *makuei* configuration, which is much admired; 'brought by drizzle' (*a bei nyir*), referring to the spots of a light shower on a man's body.

For a brindled ox of the *manyang* (crocodile) configuration: 'mongoose' (*agor*), after the stripes of this creature; 'spoiler of the fish-battue' (*arec mai*), referring to the crocodile which frightens the Dinka from the river; 'striker of the canoe' (*ayup riai*), again after the crocodile, as is 'wild-dog crocodile' (*magol-nyang*), referring to the brindling of the dog and also perhaps to a story of the dog which slit open the crocodile's mouth.

For a grey ox of the *malith* (*lith*—the chanting goshawk) colour: 'it finishes the cultivations' (*athol dom*), referring to the baboon which raids the gardens and is said to be of this colour; 'wants chickens' (*kor ajith*), after the habits of the chanting goshawk; 'master of the birds' (*beny diet*), again after the goshawk; 'tree of the birds' (*matiem diet*), referring to the way in which the chanting goshawk is attacked in a tree by tiny birds on which it has been preying.

Such names are almost inexhaustible, and are clearly not all necessary for practical convenience in referring to and distinguishing different beasts. They show the interdependence of the Dinkas' perception of colour and shading in nature and in cattle, and represent a deliberate effort to link cattle with features of the natural and social environment through perceived similarities of colour and shading. In such metaphors a wide range of Dinka experience is referred to the central theme of cattle; and it will later be seen that such metaphorical associations are also the basis of a colour symbology important for an understanding of Dinka religious thought and practice.

Sometimes practical and aesthetic values may be in conflict. Some cattle-colours are preferred to others, and particularly desirable are those bold pied markings, called in Dinka *majok* and *marial*. It is said that when a bull-calf of one of these colours is born, the friends of its owner may tear off his beads and scatter them, for his happiness is such that he must show indifference to these more trivial forms of display. He is made sufficiently handsome by the beauty of his beast. But the Dinka know that a bull-calf from a dam which is a good milch-cow will be likely to produce cow-calves which will themselves give much milk. So where a bull-calf of a specially valued colour is produced by a good milch-cow, the Dinka say they may find it hard to decide whether to castrate it, and use it for display as later described, or to keep it whole for stud purposes. Their preference seems to be for keeping it for display, and to trust that its dam will later produce for stud a bull-calf of some less striking configuration. In my experience one sees few whole beasts of the most valued display-colours. Many castrated beasts are kept for display, and it is sometimes officially urged that the high proportion of these is uneconomical and prevents a rational conservation of the pastures. But for the Dinka the imaginative satisfactions provided by their herds are scarcely less important than the material benefits; and they correctly argue that in any case every beast is used, for whether it dies a natural death or is sacrificed (which in the case of bulls and oxen is more likely) its flesh is eaten.

A man's metaphorical ox-name is not expected to refer directly to anything in his personal appearance, though in some cases, especially with the ox-names given to Europeans, a distinctive feature of the appearance may also be seized upon for inclusion in the total association of perceptions of the ox-name. In songs the same man may be given several metaphorical ox-names, perhaps derived from oxen of colours and configurations which he has never owned. The object is to praise him. A Dinka's self-esteem and standing in the community are intimately bound up with cattle in this way.

Cattle and men are still further linked, in an idiom common to both, by which the Dinka explicitly conceive their own lives and the lives of cattle in some ways on the same model. Men imitate cattle. A characteristic sight in Western Dinkaland is that of a young man with his arms curved above his head, posturing either at a dance or for his own enjoyment when he is alone with his little herd. Herdsmen, indeed, spend so long alone with only cattle for company that it is understandable that they should regard themselves as identified with their herds. The curving of the arms is one of the forms of 'handsomeness' (*dheng*), a bodily attitude which the Dinka consider graceful. Such a posture may be seen in Plate I. The curve of the man's arms is associated with the sweeping horns of a display-ox, and part of the admired variety of movement which each man tries to introduce into his dance-gestures is the lowering and bending of the left arm, or of both, in imitation of the

PLATE I

Boys beginning to dance

PLATE II

Rek Dinka: unmarried man and girl

artificially deformed and trained horns of many display-oxen. A dance in which such gestures are made is known as *gar* or *agar*, and is found among the east and central Rek Dinka, and sometimes farther west.[1] It is clearly based upon the theme of the running of oxen with cows in the herd. Display-oxen are the equivalents of young warriors in the camp. The whole bull, the centre and sire of the herd, is associated with the father of a family and senior man of a camp. It is display-oxen, and not bulls, which are bedecked with tassels and hung with bells. They represent the unmated rising generation of the herd and the camp, of which the bull is the begetter and master. In the *gar* dance the men advance and retreat, guiding or driving their female partners backwards and forwards, and stamping and crying out before them. The young men regard themselves in this dance as oxen, and their girls as cows. The stamping and cries of the men are stylizations of the sounds and vigorous movements of bulls and oxen. The rhythmical repetitions of the cry '*e-yi, e-eyi*' which the men make when imitating oxen are not attempts to reproduce the actual sound which the beasts make, but they represent and express the whole rhythm of the beasts' movements, with their powerful ambling gait and swaying heads.

Self-identification with the ox, of which we have seen examples from linguistic usages, is thus exhibited in customary and common postures of the body. A young man who has no display-ox to parade will sometimes take an ox-bell and walk with it, singing his song and ringing the bell to simulate the presence of the ox. Men also identify themselves with their oxen, through their ox-names, by shouting out the ox-name (*myoc*) as a spear is thrown in a battle or a hunt, or at dances and wedding ceremonies, when one may hear men shouting their ox-names even in the rain for most of the night. In courting displays or parades, when the young men of a village or camp walk round together as the girls are milking, leading their decorated oxen and singing their songs, the attention of the girls is drawn as much to the ox as to the man. Both together form a unity which is, as a whole, pleasing to girls, and one told me that she would

---

[1] The characteristic leaping dance of the Agar Dinka from whom the Rek dance is sometimes said to have come is somewhat different, though there also the arms are held in a position which imitates the sweep of an ox's horns.

prefer a somewhat ugly young man with a fine ox to a handsome man with an indifferent ox. The decorated ox, the beads, and other finery of the man, and his song, thus all identify and recommend him to eligible girls.

The following is part of such a song, composed to be sung by a young man when he walks with his ox or is tending cattle, and which illustrates how metaphorical ox-names are included. The song is itself about composing a song, when several young men have gathered together guided by one well known for his cleverness in fitting words to rhythms and tones, and who will expect a gift for his pains. The circumstances are set out as part of the song itself, though, from a European point of view, the themes are typically disconnected:

I call to Deng 'refuser of burnt grass'[1]
'Has the composer come?'
And we go into the hut (to compose)
The hut of Adeng, daughter of Majok 'growl of the leopard'[2]
I call to Kuot 'pied-back'[3]
'Has the composer come?'
Anguec, wife of my father, I have nothing more to say . . .[4]
The composer confuses people, the song twists,
But if the song starts by going crooked
One of the listeners will straighten it out
The ox *Majak* makes the bell bought by my father tinkle
With the rings of that daughter of the Paguor clan, Adau,[5]
My father brought eight rings from the town
To tie on the neck of fat *majak*
The fat ox strikes his peg when he lies down
Great *majak*, you are not a beast brought by theft.[6]
My grandfather was a warrior, and knew no master,
And knew no master of the fishing-spear
And sought a club and struck and killed the master of the fishing-
  spear

[1] The 'refuser of burnt grass' is the giraffe, which eats leaves and is the same colour as a beast of the *malek* configuration, for which 'refuser of burnt grass' is a metaphorical name. In Dinkaland the dead growth of the pastures is burnt off in the dry season.
    [2] Referring to an ox of the *makuac* (leopard) configuration.
    [3] Referring to an ox of the *majok* configuration.
    [4] The implication is that the composer has come, and that the singer is now satisfied because his father's wife has brought food for them.
    [5] He praises his half-sister.
    [6] The implication is that this ox is intimately bound up with the family, and not a stranger.

And called upon the clan-divinity of his own father[1]
I am helped (in composing the song) by five clever people
I am helped by three of my maternal uncle's family
And a son of the Pagong clan called Guot 'swim in the river'[2]
And Jok Rial, who heard about this party
And had I known he was about, I should have sent a boy to fetch
   him. . . .[3]
And we will sing (of) *majak*, and the mother of *majak*[4]
Will become old, and walk stiffly. . . .

This is only part of the song—ox-songs are very long and repetitive—but it is enough to show again how intimately the lives of the men, and the life of cattle, are assimilated to each other. In many songs it is only by knowing the special circumstances of their composition that one can distinguish the praise of men from the praise of oxen.

Dinka cattle are integrally part of human social life in other ways also. Many of the commonest personal names given at birth to Dinka children are the names for basic colour-configuration of cattle, and they are often called after particular beasts which have been sacrificed in the past in order to bring about the birth of children. This naming is sometimes regarded as a form of compensation to the beast itself.

The ox-name which a young man takes at initiation should not coincide with that he may bear as a birth-name. A man called Majok, for example, should not take as his song-ox a beast of the *majok* configuration. He would not augment his social personality by so doing, for he would be known in his manhood by nothing additional to the name by which he was known as a child. Also a man should not eat the flesh of an ox of his colour-name, a prohibition which, though it may not always be taken very seriously, yet indicates the intimacy of its relation to himself. The Dinka frequently pointed out to me those things in nature which had the *marial* colour-configuration upon which my own metaphorical ox-name was based. The

---

[1] The implication is that he was so bold and independent that he trusted in the divinity of his own clan to help him against the theoretically more important divinity (totemic spirit) of a master of the fishing-spear.

[2] The man's ox is also of the *majak* colour, so called after the *jak*, the pelican. Hence, 'swims in the river'.

[3] That is, he would have come by invitation and not by chance.

[4] He praises the dam of his ox.

sight of such things calls to mind the ox, and the ox calls to mind the courting and other personal display in which it is a necessary companion. In contemplating such things as bear the colour-configuration of his ox, a man is in effect deriving pleasure from contemplating himself, handsome, prosperous and successful with women.

In personal display men are linguistically identified with oxen, which are primarily of aesthetic interest; but in fighting, and in relation to their women, they are thought of as bulls, begetters, and fighters, each ultimately the centre, source, and leader of his own herd. The bull represents virility for the Dinka, as clearly appears from some features of Dinka sacrifice of whole beasts, and in many songs Dinka warriors attribute to themselves the strength, aggressiveness, and sexual potency of bulls:

> If we are away, there is no bull in the camp (herd)
> The Pagong subclan of the big camp has not come:
> If we are away, there is no bull in the camp (herd)
> When we have come, the bull of the camp has come . . .[1]

is a typical war song; and in a dance song we find

Tether the *mayom* bull which has mounted all the long-horned cows, I am not afraid of marriage, I have cattle . . .

where the bull which has mounted the cows is the singer, who boasts of his affairs with the most eligible girls of the village and says that he is not afraid of getting himself into the position in which their kinsmen may insist upon marriage, or else attack him.

The Dinka words for basic social groupings—*wut*, the cattle-camp, section, subtribe or tribe, and *gol*, the agnatic descent-group, refer equally to groupings of men and to groupings of cattle. The Dinka may sometimes distinguish, in the larger groups, between a 'camp of people' (*wun koc*)—that is, a tribe or subtribe considered simply as a group of men—and a 'camp of cattle' (*wun ghok*)—that is, a number of people actually herding cattle together—but in general usage the word *wut* implies both men and cattle. Their cattle do, in fact, bring and hold the human group together; their interests meet in the herd, either

---

[1] The meaning is that a lineage of the Pagong clan regard themselves as being morally and politically at the centre of the camp or subtribe, as the bull is at the centre of the herd.

in the 'camp' or in the descent-group, the members of which are thought to share a common herd over the generations. Sacrifice is made equally for the benefit of men and of cattle, for the whole group, cattle and men together, suffers or thrives. Masters of the fishing-spear are required to pray nightly in cattle-camps, and it is from their supposed ability to multiply and protect cattle by their prayers that they derive much of their importance.

Dinka sometimes treat cattle as though the beasts had a kind of understanding of the wishes of their human guardians. They are often addressed by name, especially in invocations before sacrifice. I have heard it said that some beasts are more intelligent and responsive than others and (perhaps fancifully) that long-horned beasts understand better what is required of them than short-horns, which have a reputation for being bold and pugnacious, but stupid and obstinate. There is a large vocabulary of cries to use in herding and addressing cattle.

Yet they do not sentimentalize their relations with their beasts, imaginatively endowing them with human intelligence and affections as do some European owners of domestic pets. The moral closeness and interdependence of cattle and men is rather brought about by the human imitation of the characteristics of cattle; and it is consistent with this imitation that cattle, in many situations, should be regarded as the most fitting substitutes for human beings.

The cattle have rights according to their kind within the total society, and the Dinka look with disgust upon their non-Dinka neighbours who slaughter cattle merely for meat. Cattle, when sacrificed, are eaten, but a Dinka would be ashamed to give his appetite for meat as a reason for killing a beast. '*Ghok aciye nok epath*', they say, 'Cattle are not just killed for nothing'. The expression 'eater of cattle' is an insult which suggests that the one to whom it is applied is scarcely to be regarded as a Dinka, for it implies that he does not acknowledge the non-utilitarian value of cattle, by the presence of which Dinka judge that they are dealing with their own kind—like, for example, the similarly cattle-orientated Nuer. A beast which has been killed for no good reason and without ceremony (and the desire for meat, as distinct from the necessity of preserving life in famine, is not a good reason) may haunt (*cyen*) its killers, as may a human person unjustly slain, and I have been told that 'ghosts' of such cattle might return to reproach their owners. Though the Dinka do not always behave in practice as though they took this belief very seriously, they do often announce to a beast that is to be sacrificed the important and necessary purpose for which it is victimized. Further, in compensating the beast for its death by naming the next child after it, they are preserving its memory in a way which is very characteristic of their thought about perpetuating the names of their families' dead in naming the living. They complain that in the government herds of cattle which have been taken as fines, it is wrong that the cattle of different families should be all mixed together, for cattle 'have their own names'—their own affiliations and groupings in relation to human groupings—and are not merely so many individual 'head of cattle' as they are officially regarded.

That beasts should not be treated as just so many equivalent units in a herd is understandable when we consider how each one recalls a unique history of human relationships, and has been anxiously watched and intimately known from the time of its birth. It is by calling to mind the beasts one by one that a Dinka knows something of the extent of his herd, and he dislikes either stating in figures how many cattle there are in it, or counting them by numbers and not by names of particular beasts. Even in transactions where the number of cattle to be handed over is generally agreed in principle, there is always a good deal of vague evasion of the number itself until the negotiations are well under way, so that an offer, in marriage for example, may be of 'cattle as numerous as a flock of doves'. Even when a more modest number has been fixed, the discussions are in terms of particular known beasts, each of which is accepted or rejected on its merits. A common complaint of Dinka whose marriage negotiations have broken down is that some malicious gossip has 'numbered' his cattle, and attempts to count cattle will be likely to result in suggestions that the assessor has the evil eye. 'One does not ask a man the number of his cattle or the number of his children', I was frequently told; and although a certain reluctance to speak of cattle-wealth might be expected in discussions with Europeans, Dinka among themselves are not happy about counting their cattle or their children, which are riches of the same sort, not made and 'owned', but given into human care.

Cattle, and children, are gifts from Divinity and from the clan-divinity and they always ultimately belong to Divinity, the clan-divinity, and the whole agnatic descent-group of which the clan-divinity is the tutelary spirit. Any owner's or father's relationship to his cattle or his children is thus a mere temporary expression of a transcending relationship between a human group, its herd, and its divinity, which persists through the generations. Thus for a man to number his children or cattle would be for him morally to cut himself off, with his own specific 'possessions', from the whole group within which he should ultimately be merged. This aspect of the Dinkas' attitude towards cattle is of some importance for an understanding of the dedication of cattle to Divinity or other Powers, for in this their superior claims to 'possess' the cattle are clearly acknowledged.

Perhaps the clearest example of the way in which cattle represent not only human beings but human relationships may be seen in the division of the sacrificial meat when a beast is killed. 'The people are put together, as a bull is put together', said a Dinka chief on one occasion; an examination of the formally prescribed division of sacrificial meat suggests the explanation. It will be seen from the plan of the division on p. 24 that when the beast has been sacrificed, most of it is divided according to the division of groups within a kinship system, leaving some over for the community in general, distinguished according to sex and age.

Since every bull or ox is destined ultimately for sacrifice, each one demonstrates, potentially, the ordered social relationships of the sacrificing group, the members of which are indeed 'put together' in each beast and represented in their precise relations to each other in the meat which it provides. It will be seen that in this partition the clan-divinity too has its accustomed share, which is placed, for a time, at the foot of the shrine. Each beast represents the community of the people present at a sacrifice, though their eating of the flesh is not a communion meal or 'mystical' communion as that word has been used in anthropological literature.[1] It is a point of some

---

[1] That is, there is no explicit theory that divine life is communicated to the worshippers by the fact of sharing the flesh of the victim with the divinity, as described, for example, in W. Robertson Smith, *The Religion of the Semites*, 3rd edn., with notes by Stanley A. Cook, 1927, p. 439. An exception may be seen in the sacrifices to the divinity Flesh later described.

importance in connexion with the relations of maternal kin already mentioned and which appear as additionally significant in the sacrificial situations later described, that the right hind leg, the most honourable part of the beast, is given to the classificatory and other maternal uncles of the sacrificing group.

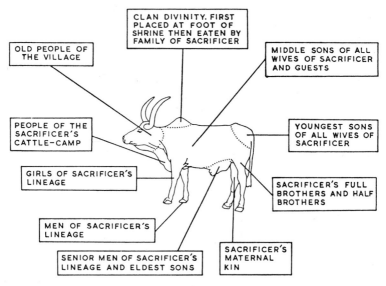

CLAN DIVINITY. FIRST PLACED AT FOOT OF SHRINE THEN EATEN BY FAMILY OF SACRIFICER

OLD PEOPLE OF THE VILLAGE

MIDDLE SONS OF ALL WIVES OF SACRIFICER AND GUESTS

PEOPLE OF THE SACRIFICER'S CATTLE–CAMP

YOUNGEST SONS OF ALL WIVES OF SACRIFICER

GIRLS OF SACRIFICER'S LINEAGE

SACRIFICER'S FULL BROTHERS AND HALF BROTHERS

MEN OF SACRIFICER'S LINEAGE

SENIOR MEN OF SACRIFICER'S LINEAGE AND ELDEST SONS

SACRIFICER'S MATERNAL KIN

Fig. 3. Distribution of sacrificial beast. *Note.* The distribution of significant organs is included in descriptions in the text.

Human beings and cattle are substituted for each other and are symbolically linked not only in linguistic usage and in other ways so far discussed, but also in a more practical way in the quasi-legal transactions of the Dinka. All important relationships between members of different agnatic descent-groups, and all important acquisitions for any particular group, may be expressed in terms of cattle. Relationships between human beings and the divine are regulated by the transfer of cattle in dedication and sacrifice, as conflicts between different human groups are resolved by the simple transfer of cattle from the offending to the offended group.

Sheep and goats and other creatures and commodities may sometimes be substituted for cattle in these transactions, for 'people do not play with cattle'—cattle are an important matter. They are then understood, however, to be mere substitutes for cattle. It is particularly in minor crises which yet demand sacrifice that inferior creatures may be made to represent cattle. There is a hierarchy of values in Dinka society—in the total domestic society of men and beasts—at the top of which are human beings, beneath them cattle, and beneath them sheep and goats. To a quite inferior order belong chickens, and commodities such as fish, grain, canoes, and tobacco. As cattle may be substituted for human beings, so sheep and goats may sometimes be substituted for cattle, while on occasion chickens may be substituted for sheep and goats, though here the disparity in value between the superior and inferior creature is greater than in the higher ranks.

In any part of Dinkaland a man will be able to state an ideal number of cattle suitable for making a marriage, or for compensation for homicide and adultery. The larger compensations, in bridewealth and homicide payments, always ideally include both cows or heifers and oxen; whole bulls are usually not handed over, for they are in a very intimate way associated with the virility and fertility of their human owners. There are also scales of compensation for minor injuries, though there is little machinery by which a man can effectively claim his theoretical entitlements, and in cases of payment of compensation it is not ideal fixed entitlements which are in question, but histories of actual relations between the contracting groups. Each case of transfer, then, has its own unique merits which materially affect agreement upon an equitable settlement. Sheep and goats are not directly equated with human beings in such transactions. Only cattle can really restore to a person or a group what has been lost in the value of a human member. The Dinka say that in the troubles of their past they were reduced to marrying for sheep and goats and even still inferior media of exchange, indicating thereby the depths of poverty and misery to which they think they at that time sank.

In compensation for homicide, and in marriage payments, which are the most important occasions of substitution outside the sacrificial situation, it is expected that the cattle handed over in place of the dead man, or in place of the girl, will multiply for the lineage of people who have lost a member, the

continuity of generation in cattle thus being balanced against
the continuity of human generation which has been broken by
the loss of a member to the lineage. The cattle which are
received for a daughter given in marriage are used for the
provision of wives for her brother; the cattle handed over in
compensation for homicide are used for the provision of a
woman who will bear members into the lineage of the deceased,
and thus restore to them what they have lost in him. All Dinka
are deeply concerned with the continuity of generation in their
line, and social continuity—the continuity of their formal
descent-groups and of the political groups of which they form
parts—cannot, in their traditional society, be assured without
cattle. Without them there is no public demonstration and
validation of paternity, and the acknowledgement and definition of the *pater* is one of the mainstays of the Dinka lineage
system, and thus of the social order. A man's wealth in cattle
directly affects the likelihood of the remembrance of his name
by a large posterity, and the fertility of his cattle is intimately
bound up with the number of children he can expect. Dinka
greatly fear to die without issue, in whom the survival of their
names—the only kind of immortality they know—will be
assured. Since cattle are the means to legitimate issue, in theory
a higher rate of compensation for homicide is required for an
adult male who has no children than for one who has already
raised his own family.

To have rights in a herd is to have rights in a descent-group,
and through that in the political group to which it belongs. To
have no such rights, or to be unable to assert them effectively,
is to have no place in the main structure of Dinka society.[1] It is
for this reason that a frequent theme of complaint introduced
into songs is that of a young man denied the cattle which he
regards as his right, and forced to delay his first marriage until
a senior kinsman has taken a second wife. This theme is often
accompanied by threats of withdrawing from Dinka society to
live and work for ever with foreigners. For the Dinka, who never
doubt the superiority of their own society to all others, this
threat of withdrawal is an indication of despair only a little
removed from that of a threat of suicide.

---

[1] The few groups of Dinka who have lost their cattle and live mainly by fishing
are not significant for our account.

Cattle are thus intimately connected with human personality; a man cannot be fully a Dinka without them. On occasions they may even be valued above human life, for men must sometimes die and kill to acquire or defend them. There is a story which represents a certain hostility between men and cattle, underlying their mutual attachment, and which seems to suggest that men feel that their satisfaction in their beasts can be bought at too high a price. It is said that Buffalo and Cow vowed to take revenge on Man, who had killed their mother. Buffalo said that he would kill Man in the forest, and thus constantly avenge his mother's death; Cow elected to live in the home of men so that men might kill each other for her sake.

The moral and imaginative significance of cattle to the Dinka in these ways complements their utilitarian importance. Their value is that of something to which men have assimilated themselves, dwelling upon them in reflection, imitating them in stylized action, and regarding them as interchangeable with human life in many social situations. It is with this in mind that the victimization and death of cattle, in the sacrifice later described, is to be understood.

PART ONE

I

DIVISION IN THE WORLD

I

WITHIN the single world known to them (for they dwell little upon fancies of any 'other world' of different constitution) the Dinka claim that they encounter 'spirits' of various kinds, which they call generically *jok*. In this account I call them 'Powers'. These Powers are regarded as higher in the scale of being than men and other merely terrestrial creatures, and operate beyond the categories of space and time which limit human actions; but they are not imagined to form a separate 'spirit-world' of their own, and their interest for the Dinka is as ultra-human forces participating in human life and often affecting men for good or ill. They emerge in the interpretation of events, and hence the broad Dinka division of the world into 'that which is of men' and 'that which is of Powers' is in part a classification of events into two kinds. Man and that which shares his terrestrial nature may be contrasted in thought to Powers, considered collectively as exhibiting a different nature. Dinka religious notion and practice define and regulate the relations between beings of these two different natures in the single world of human experience which is their common home.

I have not found it useful to adopt the distinction between 'natural' and 'supernatural' beings or events in order to describe the difference between men and Powers, for this distinction implies a conception of the course or laws of Nature quite foreign to Dinka thought.[1] When, for example, the Dinka attribute lightning to a particular ultra-human Power, it would

[1] Cf. E. Durkheim, *The Elementary Forms of the Religious Life* (trans. J. W. Swain), 1915, pp. 26 ff.

falsify their understanding, and indeed exaggerate its difference from our own, to refer to a *supernatural* Power. The force of lightning is equally ultra-human for ourselves as for the Dinka, though the interpretation we place upon that fact is very different from theirs. It is part of my later task to demonstrate how many features of Dinka religious thought and action are connected with their experience of what we call 'Nature', and of the scope and limits of human control within their particular environment.

The word which any inquirer into Dinka religion will first and most frequently hear is *nhialic*. Literally, the word is the locative form of *nhial*, meaning 'up' or 'above', and *nhialic* is the word used in many contexts in which we should speak of 'the sky'. Part of the meaning of *nhialic*, then, is conveyed by 'sky' and 'in the above'.

But further, *nhialic* is addressed and referred to as 'creator' (*aciek*) and 'my father' (*wa*), and prayers and sacrifice are offered to it. It then has a masculine and a personal connotation, and is used in contexts where, for ordinary purposes, it would be suitably translated as 'God'. Yet the attributes of our 'God' and their *nhialic* are not identical, and I have thought that the advantages of using the obvious translation are eventually outweighed by disadvantages. To use the word 'God' in translating some Dinka statements about *nhialic* would raise metaphysical and semantic problems of our own for which there is no parallel among the Dinka and in their language. Perhaps the extent to which it would be permissible to translate *nhialic* by 'God' is something of which theologians might judge at the end of an account of Dinka religion.

It would be easy, it is true, to translate *nhialic aciek* and *nhialic wa* as 'God the creator' and 'God (my) father', for the attributes of *nhialic* and 'God' there closely coincide, as do many others— unity (of a kind), power, justice, 'highness', for example. When, however, numbers of 'spirits' later discussed are all said in Dinka to be *nhialic*, it would not make similar sense in English to say that they were 'all God'. The word *nhialic* is meaningful in relation to a number of Dinka terms with which our 'God' has no such association. *Nhialic* is figured sometimes as a Being, a personal Supreme Being even, and sometimes as a *kind* of being and activity which sums up the activities of a multiplicity of beings, while the word 'God' has no such extended meaning in our common speech.

So the word *Divinity*, thus written with the capital letter and without definite or indefinite article, is here used to translate *nhialic*. 'Divinity', like *nhialic*, can be used to convey to the mind at once *a* being, a *kind* of nature or existence, and a quality of that kind of being; it can be made to appear more substantive or qualitative, more personal or general, in connotation, according to the context, as is the word *nhialic*.[1] It saves us too, despite its occasional clumsiness, from shifting our attention from a Dinka word to undefined, yet for everyone fairly definite, conceptions of our own.

The most important Powers recognized by the Dinka are called collectively *yeeth* (sing. *yath*)—a word, it will be observed, of which there are singular and plural forms. *Nhialic*, Divinity, has no plural; it is both singular and plural in intention. In some senses discussed later all the existences called *yeeth* may be equated with Divinity, and in this account I have found it fitting to refer to them as *divinities*, thus written without the capital letter.

The divinities are of two kinds which for clarity of exposition are here distinguished, though the Dinka use the one word *yath* for both. There are first those which are the tutelary spirits, or genii, of Dinka descent-groups, which in some ways resemble the 'totems' of anthropological literature. Here they are called *clan-divinities*; and when, as is usually but not invariably the case, they are represented in material forms—in animal and other species—I call these forms their *emblems*.[2] So, for example, a clan which has Lion as its clan-divinity will in various ways respect lions, the emblems of that divinity.

There are other *yeeth*, divinities, which are not in special relationships with descent-groups; they establish relationships with individuals, and through them with their families, which then adopt towards them some of the attitudes adopted towards clan-divinities by whole clans. I call these *free-divinities*, or by

---

[1] I should have preferred throughout to refer to Divinity in the third person by the neuter pronoun. In some sentences, however, such a usage would appear extremely forced, and I have consequently written of Divinity as 'it' or 'he' according to what the context seems to demand.

[2] This usage approximates to that of Durkheim in *The Elementary Forms of the Religious Life*, though for him the 'totemic' species is the emblem of the clan also.

their Dinka proper names, as DENG, GARANG, MACARDIT, and others later described.

Divinity and divinities belong to that widest class of ultra-human agency collectively called, in Dinka, *jok*, Power. *Jok* is less specific in connotation than *nhialic* or *yath*, Divinity or a divinity. *Jok* as a noun may refer to a particular ultra-human Power. It then has the plural form *jaak* when several distinct individual existences of this kind are in mind. It has also, however, like *yath*, a qualitative sense, indicating the kind and quality of ultra-human power, rather than any particular Power. So when they see some surprising example of European ingenuity the Dinka may say that *turuk ee jok*, 'the European is ultra-human Power'. The implication is merely that Europeans' power is of that quality or order: they would not state this in the plural, *turuk aa jaak*, 'the Europeans are ultra-human Powers', for they are, clearly, only men. Again, confronted with unexpected behaviour in an animal, Dinka might say 'it is Power' (*ee jok*) or 'it is Divinity' (*ee nhialic*). The implications would be, not that the animal itself was *a* Power, or was identical with Divinity, but that its behaviour manifested a Power or Divinity.[1]

Though if asked for 'definitions' Dinka may say that Divinity and divinities are *jok*, Power or Powers, they normally distinguish clan-divinities and free-divinities from other Powers which concern them less by referring to them as *yeeth*, which, according to Dinka definition, are 'Powers which are related to people'. The relationship is often figured in the idiom of kinship, as when Divinity and the free-divinities are called 'fathers' of men, and clan-divinities are called the 'grandfathers' or ancestors of their descent-groups. The emblems of clan-divinities, the species in which they are now manifest, are hence called 'paternal cousins' or half-brothers of their human clansmen.

---

[1] The way in which the word *jok* may be used is suggested by the following trifling example. I once took out to Dinkaland a little mechanical crawling doll to amuse the children. It at first caused some consternation among older people, who said that had they encountered it in the forest they would certainly have regarded it as a Power, and made some sacrifice to protect themselves from its possibly harmful import. Those who had learnt its mechanism amused themselves by frightening others with it, until all came to know that the grounds of its behaviour were merely mechanical.

The Dinka do not suppose that all the Powers which may exist in their world have been encountered by men, and their numbers are theoretically unlimited. Some are known as the grounds of sicknesses, and others, figured with varying degrees of distinctness and individuality, are associated with particular places, especially streams and woods. There they occasionally manifest themselves to human beings, and Dinka folk-tales are peopled by such, often anonymous, Powers, described as 'a Power of the wood' or 'a Power of the stream', much like sprites in our own fairy-tales.

Divinities are altogether more clearly figured as individuals, and are of much greater importance. They manifest themselves to men, and in men, more commonly and purposefully, and are given distinct characteristics by being each associated with its own colours and natural species, as I later describe.

Dinka religion, then, is a relationship between men and ultra-human Powers encountered by men, between the two parts of a radically divided world. As will be seen, it is rather phenomenological than theological, an interpretation of signs of ultra-human activity rather than a doctrine of the intrinsic nature of the Powers behind those signs.

2

The Dinka, of course, do not know the sky as ultimately a mere appearance, as we do, conditioned as we are by a knowledge of facts unknown to them. For them, the sky is fixed in space at a vast distance from the earth, and could in theory be reached and touched if a man were to go far enough. Divinity is 'in the above', and what rises into the sky thus approaches Divinity. I have been asked whether an aeroplane ever touches the sky, and if Divinity can be seen from it. This is a clear indication that the Dinka can regard Divinity as distinct from the 'physical' sky, for the sky itself can obviously be seen from the earth. The way in which terrestrial being may approach Divinity is by going high, by levitation, or sometimes by building a mound or 'pyramid'. There are many reports of the rising of holy men into the sky, and levitation also figures in the dreams of Dinka. It is referred to sometimes by those who claim that special relations have been established between Divinity and themselves. Conversely, Divinity makes contact with the earth by falling, or by letting something fall, or hurling something down. Such contacts are made in rain, lightning, comets, and meteorites, and also in the free-divinities which 'fall' and possess men. All these are manifestations of Divinity.

Although the sky is thus regarded as a distinct fixed region or place, the Dinka do not seriously picture some sort of 'land above', made in the image of what they know on earth. They may speak sometimes of the stars as the cattle-fires of people with their herds in the sky, and I have heard it said that rain is grain falling from the millet of Divinity when birds peck it; but these are conscious flights of fancy, and anyone who took them literally would be considered childish.

Logically, and for the Dinka historically, their relations with Divinity begin with a story of the supposed conjunction, and then division, of the earth and the sky—the emergence of their world as it is. All the Western Dinka know much the same version of the myth of this original situation, which is their representation and ultimate explanation of some of the conditions of human life as they now find it.

A myth tells how Divinity (and the sky) and men (and the earth) were originally contiguous; the sky then lay just above the earth. They were connected by a rope, stretched parallel[1] to the earth and at the reach of a man's outstretched arm above it. By means of this rope men could clamber at will to Divinity. At this time there was no death. Divinity granted one grain of millet a day to the first man and woman, and this satisfied their needs. They were forbidden to grow or pound more. Divinity here clearly emerges as a person, with the attributes of father and creator, and conceptually distinct from the observable sky; in this context we can thus refer to Divinity with the personal pronoun, as 'he'.

The first human beings, usually called Garang and Abuk, living on earth had to take care when they were doing their little planting or pounding, lest a hoe or a pestle should strike Divinity, but one day the woman 'because she was greedy' (in this context any Dinka would view her 'greed' indulgently) decided to plant (or pound) more than the permitted grain of

[1] I was told that the rope was stretched parallel to the earth, though some Dinka may imagine it to have been dangling vertically (as do the kindred Nuer).

millet. In order to do so she took one of the long-handled hoes (or pestles) which the Dinka now use. In raising this pole to pound or cultivate, she struck Divinity who withdrew, offended, to his present great distance from the earth, and sent a small blue bird (the colour of the sky) called *atoc*[1] to sever the rope which had previously given men access to the sky and to him. Since that time the country has been 'spoilt', for men have to labour for the food they need, and are often hungry. They can no longer as before freely reach Divinity, and they suffer sickness and death, which thus accompany their abrupt separation from Divinity.

This myth is also known in the land of the Agar Dinka, some two hundred miles to the west of the Rek among whom it was recorded. I also found there another story, which enables us to suggest which are the central themes of the first, though almost all the details are quite different.

According to this second version, in the beginning the earth was already *created*, but there was no light, and hence it could not 'appear'.[2] In this darkness Divinity created men, and he created one called Aruu Pabek.[3] He pushed Aruu forwards, and then pushed him back, to what is called in the Dinka text 'the opening in the fence, or dike', and the sense is here that Divinity made as though to let the man out, and then forced him back. Then Aruu twisted a rope, and Divinity gave him eyes so that he could see that he was in darkness. Aruu caught a game-animal with his rope, and gave the foreleg to the wife of Divinity, who suggested that Aruu should be rewarded. Divinity asked Aruu what gift he would like, and Aruu replied, 'My father, if there is a little chink to see through, that is what I would like.' Divinity refused this request, and offered him instead a spear, which he refused, and then an axe, which he accepted. Then, to quote a text:

My grandfather Aruu Pabek took the axe, and he struck the

---

[1] According to Fr. P. A. Nebel, *Dinka Dictionary with Abridged Grammar*, 1936, this is 'a kind of sparrow'. I thought it looked like the cordon-bleu.

[2] In Dinka *piny aci bak*, literally 'the world has divided', means 'it is dawn'. Here, though the earth (*piny*) was created, it was not separately distinguishable from the sky in the darkness.

[3] This is the name of the founder of an Agar Dinka clan. Aruu is connected with the word *ruu*, dawn. The whole story is, in a way, about the first dawn.

earth, and said 'Why do you not light up?'[1] And a part went above and a part below, and the earth lit up. And Divinity said to Aruu 'Why do you do so?' I gave you a tiny little thing before and why have you now done this? Now you are a prisoner.' And Divinity pushed Aruu down to earth, and closed up the earth. And he gave people a path, one path, for them to walk in, and he stuck reeds (in the form of a fence made to catch fish)[2] in the way. And when a man came along the way, he struck him in the head with a fishing-spear, and said 'Let a man come out if he can!' He waited there, and he killed people.[3]

And people came to Aruu Pabek, and said 'People are being fin-ished—what shall we do?' My grandfather said, 'Do not be anxious, I will see to it.' And he took a stone and put it on his head and went to where Divinity was waiting with his fishing spear. Divinity struck him on the head with the spear, and the stone deflected it and bent the point. He said 'I shall have to have my spear straightened'. He seized my grandfather by the neck and said 'Why are you like a man?'

Among the Cic Dinka there is another story to account for the separation of Divinity from men below. It tells how there was once a wall in the sky, which held a man in until he ate part of the wall, and was therefore pushed below by Divinity.

In my experience the notion of an original conjunction of earth and sky, which also necessarily refers to the relation be-tween men and Divinity, is found among all Dinka; and all I know are acquainted with the first version of the story of separation above, in which a rope is severed so that the two become separated.

These myths in part account for physical realities. Earth and sky obviously do form parts of the whole world we know, and within this whole, men on earth are separated from the sky. But the myths also represent an original state of the physical universe less differentiated than that which is now known, and they represent that state as a moral state. The first man and woman then had security and physical ease; death was

---

[1] The text here plays on the associations between *bak*, to separate, used with *piny*, earth, to mean the coming of daylight (*bak piny*), and *bak* or *abak*, a division of something. The division of the world into earth and sky, and the daily differen-tiation of earth and sky at dawn, are here associated.

[2] The story here merges with a version of the myth of the first masters of the fishing-spear given in Chap. V.

[3] The imagery here is of the type of fishing described in Chap. V, p. 173.

unknown; 'Divinity stayed with people and was good to them'.[1]
Complete integration gave security, but that very security
involved a closeness to Divinity which Man also found an irksome and restricting dependence. Man came to his present
human stature in relation to Divinity only by leaving the confinement in which Divinity had placed him. This point is made
very clear in a myth which I did not hear, but which Father
Nebel collected and published in Pater Schmidt's comprehensive work:[2]

> The creator created people in the East under a tamarind tree—
> or others say, on the bank of a great water. Their names were Abuk
> and Garang. He made them so small—only half the length of a
> man's arm—of clay, and laid them in a pot which he then covered.
> When he uncovered it, the two stood up and were complete and
> fully-grown. In the morning, Garang was grown and carried the
> spear (the penis), and the breasts of Abuk were big, and they mar-
> ried. And they bore children. And the creator said 'Your child will
> die, but after only fifteen days he will return.' Garang disagreed
> and said 'If people return again they will be too numerous. Where
> will they build their homes? There will not be enough land.'

Here the equating of the spear, the mark of the adult male,
with the penis, appears in the text as given. The connexion
between leaving the confinement in which humans were placed
by the creator and becoming adult is explicit. This connexion
is of importance for our later discussion of the parallelism between the separation of Man from Divinity and the separation of men from their fathers when the time comes for them to
marry. Further, it is implied that Divinity intended that men
should not die, and that Man in a sense chose death by his
arguments, as in the other myths it was a human act by which
death was introduced into the world.

Man is thus represented as having been originally confined
and constricted by his closeness to Divinity. He might not eat
more than a permitted grain of millet each day, and had to
move carefully (this cautious movement is sometimes enacted
by the Dinka when telling the story, and resembles in spirit the
quiet and modest demeanour they adopt in situations in which

---

[1] A quotation from a text collected by Fr. P. A. Nebel, and published by P. W.
Schmidt in *Der Ursprung der Gottesidee*, 1949, vol. viii, p. 132.
[2] Ibid., p. 131.

they must now customarily show formal respect); or he was enclosed within a fence or wall or pot, from which he eventually came out; or, in the Agar version, he could not 'see' properly.[1] There were thus no independently human affairs until Man had 'come out', or become separated from Divinity. But freedom then brought with it toil, suffering, and death which he had not previously known. When Man was with Divinity, he wanted freedom. When he became independent, he was still dependent, in that he had to accept suffering and death.

The total situation represented in the myths is one of conjoined opposition between men and Divinity, a relationship in which, at once together and apart, they are held in a tension which it is part of the function of religious rites to regulate and maintain, as will be seen. It is to be noted also that the separation is represented as accidental, not essential. The stories do not begin with the state of affairs now known, but assume (or create) an original conjunction for which there is no basis in the simple natural observation of earth and sky as they now are, except, perhaps, at night, when they merge into each other more than by day.

The Dinka try to bring together the parts of their world which were once united when they suffer the misfortunes (death and sickness) following from the separation. The following song, for example, is a representation of this desire:

. . . the strangers came with muskets
and the aeroplane flew and evil followed
Does Divinity laugh and injure?[2] Alas, ants of the earth (human
    beings)
Divinity laughs, Creator, alas!

---

[1] The themes of sight, sexual activity, and Divinity's control of Man are linked also in an account of Divinity's dealings with the founder of another Agar Dinka clan, as recounted in a text apparently written by a literate Dinka and preserved in the files at Rumbek. In this story the founding ancestor of the clan, Padhieu Mator, is made head of all creatures by Divinity, when all are living in a very cold place covered with mist. Padhieu hides the creatures when Divinity comes to inspect them, and Divinity therefore removes one of his eyes, one of his testicles (hence his name *Mator*), and fixes his right foot to the ground with a fishing-spear. The story at this point is clearly a version of the Rek Dinka account of the founding ancestor of the clan Padheou given on pp. 179–81.

[2] The aeroplane, coming from above, is associated with Divinity, and yet brings suffering. The singer asks if Divinity is indifferent. For the laughter of Divinity, cf. the 2nd Psalm: 'He that sitteth in the heavens shall laugh; the Lord shall have them in derision.'

> DENG brings the rope of the finch[1]
> That we may meet on one boundary[2]
> We and the moon and Divinity
> Give the rope of the finch
> That we may meet on one boundary with the moon. . . .

And in a song of complaint in which a young man has referred to the failure of his marriage plans, he relates the separation of earth and sky to his misfortune:

> The finch *atoc mayol* cut the rope truly
> The finch *atoc mayol* severed the rope on the right[3]
> The land was ruined in a single day
> Alas, alas, alas. . . .

In prayers and sacrifices Divinity, the free-divinities, and the clan-divinities are sometimes asked to come near to men to help them, and sometimes to remain away from men and not to trouble them. One hymn, collected independently in a slightly different version by Fr. Nebel, explicitly refers to a paradox of the nearness and farness, the conjunction and division, of the above and the below:

> Great DENG is near, and some say 'far'
> O Divinity
> The creator is near, and some say 'he has not reached us'
> Do you not hear, O Divinity?
> The black bull of the rain has been released from the moon's byre[4]
> Do you not hear, O Divinity?

It was explained that the intention of the singers in suggesting that *some* said that Divinity was far away, was that it should come near and help men.[5] Another Dinka hymn in which the 'nearness' of Divinity is in question has the lines:

> I pray the white one[6]
> Is Divinity not near?

---

[1] DENG is the free-divinity discussed below, Chap. II, pp. 90–97. The rope is the rope connecting earth and sky in the stories recounted above.

[2] The image is of neighbouring homesteads whose occupants help each other.

[3] I could find no explanation for the cutting 'on the right'.

[4] The image is of the clouding over of the penumbra of the moon.

[5] Fr. Nebel, in P. W. Schmidt, op. cit., 1949, explains this as a dialogue between believers and sceptics.

[6] In Dinka *mabyor*, which is literally 'the white ox'. Here it was said to mean *nhialic*, Divinity. Fr. Nebel's version of the hymn replaces this line by 'Kill the white ox, so that God may be near' (P. W. Schmidt, op. cit., 1949, p. 143).

Does my father not give us life?
DENG son of ABUK[1] pray for life
Life of cattle, life of men.[2]

These hymns show the most important and most frequently mentioned attributes of Divinity: creativity and fatherhood. When the Dinka ask Divinity to be near them in misfortune, or when they ask him to leave them in peace, it is as a creator and father that they appeal to him, and it is from a Power with these attributes that they are separated by the events of the myths already quoted.

In Dinka there are important interconnexions between notions of creation and of fatherhood, though the verb 'to create' is never interchangeable with the verb 'to beget'. Divinity created (*cak*) men in the beginning, and the men he created begot or bore (*dhieth*) children. Divinity did not 'beget' or 'bear' men, and it would be a linguistic mistake in Dinka either to use this expression for the creation of men by Divinity, or to say that father and mother 'created' their child. Yet the notions are linked. *Dhieth* means both 'to beget' and 'to give birth to', so that verbally the activities of men and women in procreation are not distinguished from each other. When a man was asked to explain what happened in coitus, he described the physical act, and added 'And that is called begetting (*dhieth*), and Divinity will then slowly create (*cak*) the child in the woman's belly.' Divinity thus has a creative function in the formation of every human being, and when human beings are barren their barrenness is explained by reference to it; when a woman fails to bear a child despite intercourse with a man known to be able to beget children, it is commonly said that Divinity has 'refused' her a child, and at sacrifices masters of the fishing-spear or prophets commonly ask that Divinity may allow women to bear children. Men, therefore, beget children in association with the creative operation of Divinity, which is thus the real and ultimate

Husband (man) of the cattle
Husband of the women . . .

as it is expressed in a Dinka hymn. The ideas of 'creator' and

[1] These are free-divinities described in Chap. II.
[2] In Dinka this 'life' is *wei*, which means also 'breath' and is later discussed at length (Chap. V; pp. 206-7).

'father' are fused with each other when Divinity is thought of as the active source of life for his 'children', men.

Dinka stories of the original creation of man are shorter than those of the separation of men from Divinity, and seem more simply aetiological. One man said with amusement that he had heard that Divinity blew his nose. From one nostril came mucus which turned into tall Dinka, and from the other mucus which turned into the dwarfs whom one still occasionally sees in Dinkaland. A commoner story is that Divinity fashioned men from mud, as pots and toys are now fashioned by the Dinka, and in this story the same word, *cuec*, is used of the fashioning of men as is used of the fashioning of pots. One of the myths of the separation of earth and sky already given shows that the Dinka also have the idea that Divinity originally created a pair, Garang and Abuk, from whom all men are descended. According to some versions of this story, Abuk bore a black and a 'red'[1] son, from whom men of the colours they know are all descended. It is further sometimes held that men were created in the sky,[2] and then put into the river, from which they finally emerged, or that Divinity created them first in the river. This is consistent with the Dinka custom of disposing of malformed children by placing them in a river, or 'returning' them to the river, as I have heard it called; for such monsters are held not to have been well and completely created. They are called *aciek*, which is probably connected with the verb *cak*, to create, and is the word not only for Divinity as Creator, but for prophets and composers also, with whom the idea of divine creative activity is strongly associated. The malformed and monstrous seem congruently, by default, to be referred in their incompleteness to a partially performed creative act; and so there is an intrinsic appropriateness in returning them to the river, the medium in which, according to some Dinka, creation took place. Still another story is that Man was created at the foot of a tamarind tree;[3] again, there is no elaboration of detail about the creation itself. The stories of it seem to be little more than points of departure for the events of greater human significance which follow, and in which Divinity emerges as a being, a person, and

---

[1] For the Dinka, Europeans are *jur thith*, 'red foreigners'.
[2] Again assuming an original closeness of men and Divinity.
[3] This is current particularly among the Agar Dinka, as it is among the Nuer.

a father, with will and intentions towards human beings. The creation is often spoken of as the work of Divinity's hand. In a version of the myth of the Dinka demiurge and prototypical master of the fishing-spear, Longar, it is said that

> Longar the great, when people were created, he was the first to be created . . . he was the first created in the beginning. He had just come from the hand of Divinity, he was at the head (source) of life. . . .

The implications of this are left for later discussion; but it should not be supposed that the Dinka think of Divinity as a 'being' with a nose or hands. The reference to the hand of Divinity is as metaphorical for them as the expression 'the hand of God' is for ourselves. When they say that he fashioned men, as women fashion pots and children fashion toy oxen of mud, the implication is that Man belonged to Divinity to do as he liked with, as those things which a man makes with his own hands in Dinka society belong fully to him. Man, as we have seen, then asserted a life and will of his own which brought him into opposition to his maker.

The only circumstances in which it is possible to use the verb to create, *cak*, of a *human* activity are those in which what is created is the product of the imagination or of thought, that is in songs, prophecies, and the naming of things and children.[1] Composers and prophets are equally *aciek*, 'creators'. A man skilled in fashioning material things is not a 'creator' but a craftsman (*atet*). As creator, Divinity may also be spoken of as having created human dispositions to lust, malice, and so on.

Divinity, as father, is needed to look after, or bring up (*muk*), his people, like a human father with his children. The Dinka speak of themselves as being resigned in the same way to the 'word'—that is, decision or will—of their fathers, and to the will of Divinity. For example, a father allowed his son, whom I knew, to be imprisoned rather than consent to his marriage

---

[1] Fr. Nebel, op. cit., 1936, gives as two separate words, '*càk*, v.: create, creare' and '*cák*, v.: to give a name, educate, correct; dare un nome, educare, correggere'. He gives as an example of the latter usage the sentence *wun aci mahnde cak*, 'the father named his child'. It is almost impossible to assess satisfactorily the common content of meaning in two very similar Dinka words, and the usages are clearly related, as they seem to be in Nuer according to Fr. Kiggen's *Nuer Dictionary* (1948). It is the father's prerogative to name his son, and in naming him Majok, for example, he is in fact making him into Majok and nobody else.

with a girl whom he had persistently pursued, and whose father might have accepted a few cattle as an earnest of the youth's serious intentions. In speaking to the son I was rather critical of the father's refusal to help him, which would seemingly have cost him little. The son replied, 'Why, is not your father like Divinity? Does he not bring you up and look after you? And if he injures you or helps you, is it not his affair? How should you be angry about it?'

The Dinka form of the argument by analogy here is consistent with the fact that the ancestors and the clan-divinities, which stand in the relationship of 'the fathers' to their descendants and descent-groups, are more closely assimilated in thought to Divinity than is the living human father, and the authority of the living father is for the Dinka connected with their transcendent fatherhood. In the case just described, what the son accepts, in principle at least, is the authority of the Father—of all the fathers—an authority associating them with Divinity. The associations of one sort and situation of fatherhood are carried over to the others, and the transcendent fatherhood represented by Divinity reinforces the position and authority of the actual human father. So Divinity images fatherhood in general, as he images creativity in general.

The Divinity/man : father/child analogy of the Dinka may go further than this. The son–father relationship is not simply one of submissiveness, obedience, and resignation on the one side, and unquestioned authority on the other, despite the ideal of filial piety which Dinka subscribe to in theory. On the contrary, sons are often in conflict with their fathers, and are not slow in urging their just claims upon them. The conflict of wills between son and father occurs particularly at the time when the son wishes to marry, and the father refuses his permission, wanting to keep the son longer under his own roof and in tutelage. Though the sons of such fathers have ultimately little alternative but resignation or leaving home to find work, they do not pretend to be satisfied with their lot, and a very common theme of ox-songs is oblique criticism of a father or guardian who has thus refused to let his child marry when he wishes and is old enough to do so.

Here again the Divinity/man : father/child analogy is reinforced. Both are relationships with a source of existence and its support; but the support given by the father, or by Divinity, demands also submission, and exacts a control over the dependent son in ways which he may come to find irksome. This situation appears in the stories of Man's initial closeness to Divinity, where he was secure as long as he remained passive, and lost that security by a bid for freedom; it is found in many Dinka families today. Fathers want to have their sons remain dependent on them, while the sons, when of suitable age, are anxious to detach themselves sufficiently from their fathers to set up their own homes and start their own lines of descent. In starting or hoping to start his own lineage, a man is in effect hoping for the day when he himself will be known as 'the father of so-and-so', rather than as 'the son of so-and-so': he is hoping, that is, for separation, but it is separation which cannot escape conjunction, as in the myth.

Children incur an obligation to their parents, and especially to their father, by the very fact of their birth. This obligation is often stressed, and 'heartless' children who neglect the wishes of the parents who bore them are much criticized. Bringing up, which involves caring for, feeding, protecting, and instructing— all included in the Dinka word *muk*—is the second source of dependence. Bridewealth is the third, and marriage brings the childish dependence of the son to an end; but he remains always religiously dependent upon his father, as his link with Divinity, the clan-divinities, and the chain of his ancestors. Between son and father there are thus relations of dependence, conjunction, and opposition, which feature in the relations of human beings with Divinity, their common father.

The theme of *opposition* to Divinity which will later appear more fully is shown in an extreme form in a curious record in the official government records in Tonj, Bahr-el-Ghazal Province, where it is reported that the young men of one subtribe, fat with milk and spoiling for a display of their strength, once decided that only Divinity himself was a great enough adversary for them. They therefore attacked (how they did so is not recorded) the rain (*deng*), which is in the report described as the 'symbol of God'. In fact, what was probably intended was the free-divinity DENG. All were killed except one man, who, it is reported, was left with a hole pierced through his thigh, through which visiting Dinka would pass a stick. The father of an older man who is still alive is said to have seen, in his childhood, this rebel against Divinity with the hole in his thigh.

With father and son, as with Divinity and men, the relations of conjoined opposition must be harmoniously adjusted by the weaker party for his benefit. A serious breach with his father is one of the worst things that can happen to a man of any age; but on the other hand, the complete dominance of the father when the child is grown denies him a legitimate freedom. If a son has offended his father, or a man has offended Divinity or one of the divinities, he must attempt to appease and propitiate them. We find in the hymn of which two lines have already been quoted the statement:

> You [Divinity] protect the homestead
> Shall I not propitiate you with a cow?
> Divinity, father, you protect the home
> Husband of the cows,
> Husband of the women,
> It is you who protect the home.

Here Divinity is clearly represented as the head of a homestead, a husband and father barring the door of his huts (*gar-gar ghot thok*) against the dangers of the night. 'To bar the door', which is metaphorically used for this protective action, and 'Divinity (who) bars the door, (who) protects', represent the father's care for his home and children. The old man of the Awan (Pajok, or Kon Pioth) tribe of the Rek Dinka who sang this song said that it might be sung when people were afraid, in a thunderstorm, and that it was for this reason that the theme of propitiating Divinity came in. 'It is what a man does when he has quarrelled with his father or his elder brother', he said, 'he will give him something *bi ye wac puou*, to wash away the anger from his heart.'

It is not, then, merely a European psychological interpretation of the relations of the Dinka with Divinity to compare them in some detail with the relations of Dinka father and son; it appears spontaneously in the context of Dinka religious thought itself. As complaints are obliquely addressed to the human father in songs, and are also often intermingled with pleasing praise (*lec nhom*, literally 'to praise the head'), so hymns to Divinity and divinities also include the complaint of an anxious child. The following is part of such a hymn:

I have been left in misery indeed,
Divinity, help me!
Will you refuse [to help] the ants of this country?[1]
When we have the clan-divinity DENG[2]
Our home is called 'Lies and Confusion'.[3]
What is all this for, O Divinity?
Alas, I am your child.

Such a tone of complaint, which, if resigned, is not without an element of resentful accusation, is a common feature of Dinka prayers and hymns.[4] The divinities in particular are asked why they treat their 'children' so badly, why they are unresponsive, on occasions, to prayer and sacrifice, and whether they love suffering. To say 'I am your child' is a usual way of urging one's claims upon a superior of any sort, and the father–son relationship is that upon which all relationships of dependence upon a controlling authority are modelled.

It is usual, on the death of the father of a Dinka family, for his eldest son to take his place as the head of the family, and thus to assume his social personality in relation to the other members of it. Even in life, in relation to the other children, the father is closely associated with his eldest son, and the mother with the youngest. The eldest son, further, is usually the one to marry first and set up his own household, and is thus the first of the children to pass out of the father's control and become independent. Similarly the Dinka sometimes speak of their prototypical master of the fishing-spear and culture-hero Longar as 'the eldest son' of Divinity. As such he shares something more of the 'father's' nature than do other men, and is for that reason a point at which men and Divinity meet. Further, as some of the details of myths recounted later show, he is both in a manner opposed to, and in a manner conjoined with, Divinity. He represents men to the divine; he mediates the divine to men. This mediation of Dinka spear-masters and

---

[1] In religious contexts the Dinka often speak of themselves as 'ants' in the sight of Divinity, thus looking at themselves as they may be supposed to appear in the eyes of Divinity.

[2] In Dinka DENG yath, a clan-divinity discussed in Chap. II.

[3] Meaning that everything is going wrong, since people deceive and distrust each other.

[4] Two hymns suggesting that Divinity has forsaken men are given in P. W. Schmidt, op. cit., 1949, p. 149, though on the whole the valuable hymns presented there express the more positive devotion of the Dinka.

prophets, made possible by a combination analogous to that in the eldest son of the dual roles of son and father, is one of the most important concomitants, for Dinka social structure, of the attribution of transcendental fatherhood to Divinity.

Some people claim to have had visions of Divinity. Two youths, at different times, told me that their mothers had once seen Divinity (*nhialic*). Both were proud of these special revelations, for as will be seen frequently in this account Dinka are inclined to treasure any claim to special insight into divine matters, as conferring on them a special importance. In one vision Divinity was seen as an old man, with a red and blue pied body and a white head. In the other he appeared as a huge old man, with a blue-green body (the colour of the sky) and again a white head. Other Dinka who have heard of such visions seem usually to be agreed that in them the body of Divinity is strikingly pied, but with a white head, a mark of age and venerability. White, the colour of light, is an auspicious colour, and white oxen or oxen boldly marked with white are especially appropriate for sacrifice to Divinity. In a Sudan government file at Rumbek it is reported that one of the ox-names of the important Agar Dinka priest and prophet, Gol Mayen, was *atenakuei*,[1] there explained as meaning 'build a white head on a black body', the white head 'signifying wisdom and goodness'.

If creativity and fatherhood are the attributes of Divinity most commonly referred to, justice (despite the complaints in hymns mentioned earlier) follows them closely. Divinity is held ultimately to reveal truth and falsehood, and in doing so provides a sanction for justice between men. Cruelty, lying, cheating, and all other forms of injustice are hated by Divinity, and the Dinka suppose that, in some way, if concealed by men they will be revealed by him. In the line from a hymn quoted above,[2] 'Our home is called "Lies and Confusion"', lies (*lueth*), and the misunderstandings, suspicions, hostilities, and malice[3]

---

[1] The ox-colour from which this name is derived is the *makuei*, with its black body and white head-markings. The fishing-eagle (*kuei*) from which this ox-colour name in turn derives, is esteemed as a lordly bird.

[2] p. 45.

[3] In Dinka the single word *aliab* has all these connotations. It is in my experience the vice which the Dinka most frequently mention and criticize.

which accompany them, are mentioned to show that Divinity is specially needed to intervene in human affairs, to put them straight by making the truth appear. *Wet nhialic*, the 'word' of Divinity, is the truth, or what really and absolutely *is* so; and the Dinka think that in certain circumstances men may speak this totally objective 'word', representing to others the true nature of things, whether of present, past, or future situations. *Cit nhialic*, 'like Divinity' or 'as Divinity', is one of the common expressions men use to guarantee the truth of what they say, and 'Divinity will see' is what any Dinka will say if he suspects another of lying or cheating him and can take no further action of his own in the matter. In some of the invocations reproduced later it will be seen that Divinity is made the final judge of right and wrong, even when men feel sure that they are in the right. Divinity is thus the guardian of truth—and sometimes signifies to men what really *is* the case, behind or beyond their errors and falsehoods. The Dinka have no problem of the prospering sinner, for they are sure that Divinity will ultimately bring justice. Since among them every man at some time must meet with suffering or misfortune, death or disease among his family or his cattle, there is always evidence, for those who wish to refer to it, of divine justice. It is a serious matter when a man calls on Divinity to judge between him and another, so serious that only a fool would take the risks involved if he knew he was in the wrong, and to call upon Divinity as witness gives the man who does so an initial presumption of being in the right.

Dinka often interpret accidents or coincidences as acts of Divinity distinguishing truth from falsehood by signs which appear to men. Two examples will suffice to show the conviction which such arguments can carry in some cases. A young man accused his classificatory sister's son of stealing his beads. The suspect denied it; and although his accuser tried to prevent him from doing so (fearing that the results would be more serious than the mere loss of beads warranted) he insisted upon calling Divinity to witness that he had not stolen them, accompanying this by touching metal with his tongue as the Dinka do in one sort of oath. Within a few hours the suspect had acute nose-bleeding which could not be stanched. Eventually he admitted to having taken the beads. On another occasion a dispute arose between a boy and a man of the village in which we were staying. The boy had a chisel in his possession—not a usual implement to find in a Dinka village—which the man claimed had been originally his. He could not prove this by any mark upon the chisel or by producing any witness, and the boy claimed that he had owned it for a long time. It seemed impossible to be quite sure of the rights and wrongs of the matter, though most Dinka were disposed to believe that the boy was lying. The man who claimed that he had been robbed went away saying that Divinity would see and decide the matter. Shortly afterwards the boy's wooden box, which was locked, was seen to be smoking, and when it was opened his blanket, clothes, and other possessions were found smouldering away inside it. (A spark from the fire had presumably blown in through a chink in the box.) The boy at once supposed that this occurrence would suggest to others that he had been lying, though he maintained still that the chisel belonged to him. Other Dinka, however, were clearly convinced that Divinity had intervened to reveal his lies, and made no secret of their satisfaction at such a demonstration of divine justice.

Similar incidents might be multiplied. Once a man has left his cause to Divinity, any misfortune which befalls his opponent is easily interpreted as the result of divine action. The higher the religious reputation of a man—a master of the fishing-spear or a prophet—the more careful people are not to offend him, and similarly, the more consistently and strikingly such coincidences occur 'on the word' (as the Dinka say) of a man, the higher his religious reputation. It is said that a famous prophet, Arianhdit, could kill those who offended him by simply breaking straws representing them, and masters of the fishing-spear will give examples of misfortunes which have befallen people who have done them small injuries.

Events which are out of the ordinary course of things are thus taken as signs of divine activity; and creatures which behave in some way differently from the rest of their kind, and seem to transcend the ordinary nature of their kind, are especially associated with Divinity. It would be easy to suggest that, in this matter, the Dinka were more superstitious than is in fact the case; but one or two examples must be given in illustration of this very characteristic feature of Dinka religious thought.

PLATE III

Women's Dance

The Seligmans,[1] for example, write:

... there is no happening or event however little out of the common
that is not regarded as of religious significance and an occasion for
sacrifice. The outlook of the Dinka may, as it seems to us, be summed
up in a passage from the Psalms, cxviii, 23 'This is the Lord's doing;
it is marvellous in our eyes.' As a concrete example we may cite the
behaviour, as related to us by the Rev. H. Lea Wilson, of a Cic
Dinka who noticed an unusually large pumpkin in his garden. The
vegetable was not cut; on the contrary the owner, saying '*jok aci loin*'
('the spirit has fallen'), prepared to sacrifice a goat. . . .[2]

They later comment that

The religious attitude of the Dinka is further illustrated by their
behaviour near Tonj when aeroplanes first appeared. Mr. Richards
informs us that some fifty bulls were slaughtered, while one old man
confessed to a murder committed several years before.

The following example concerns the behaviour and treatment of a black goat, which appeared one day in spring, when
the crops were a few inches high, in the central Rek (Apuk
Patuan) village of Lony Aker. I was told that a creator, or prophet (*aciek*), or a creator-goat (*nyong aciek*), had arrived in the
village, and I went to visit it where it was staying at the homestead of an important elder, a master of the fishing-spear.
A small party, mostly composed of women and girls, was in
progress there, and they were dancing the women's dance and
making the high-pitched quavering cries which mark the cele-
brations of women. In the centre of the homestead were several
bowls of flour and grain, and a little germinating grain laid out
for future beer-making. The 'prophet' was in a hut given to it
for its stay, and there, among a group of older women and one
or two men, I met it—a black billy-goat, with a large bundle of
finger-rings and bangles attached by a cord to its neck, and
a gourd filled with further bangles and rings (including one or
two government chiefs' signet rings) and a few coins of small
denominations beside it. These were offerings made to the
'prophet' by those who sought benefits from it. Such gifts are
also made to human prophets, and are worn in large numbers

[1] C. G. and B. Z. Seligman, *Pagan Tribes*, 1932, p. 178.
[2] It is likely that the man belonged to a clan respecting gourds.

by some of the prophets of the free-divinities, as described in the next chapter.

The goat had its own sleeping-skin, like those used by human beings, and its own wooden pillow, which it was said to use like a human being, though at the time of my visit it was standing on the skin and fearlessly eyeing the crowd. More visitors kept arriving and each one crouched in the doorway of the hut and proffered the goat his two hands in a Dinka gesture of respect, and murmured the word *beny*, 'master'. It was a festive occasion.[1] People laughed at my surprise as the goat, in response to my similar greeting, lifted one of its hooves as a trained dog among ourselves may offer a paw. The Dinka said that this goat did not like grass, but lived on porridge, beer, flour, and milk, 'like a human person'; and it did in fact make special demands in receiving its food. It would not take milk from any of the men (as they demonstrated) but only from old women, and it would often refuse to eat a titbit unless it were held in the hand at a convenient distance from the ground.

I was told to make a gift to this 'prophet', and gave it a bangle and a handful of sugar which it ignored when it was placed on the ground before it, but ate when it was held under its nose, after it had pushed my hand down with its hoof to a convenient height. The Dinka said that it might like to come to visit me in my hut, and it was brought along later and accepted a dish of tea and a little Dinka tobacco.

The goat retired to its hut to rest. The next day the women had another little party (see Plate III) in its honour. A few men attended as spectators. Among other songs, the women sang a begging hymn to the female free-divinity ABUK, the patroness of women and of women's produce, the produce of the gardens:

> I did not taste beer last year;
> If ABUK my mother is told [that this is so]
> Then I may find a great pot of beer.
> You ABUK O!
> Mix sesame with grain,
> Mix sesame with beer and beans.

It will be remembered that goats and sheep are more closely identified with women, who tend them, than with men.

---

[1] It is a point of some importance that the goat was as much a source of entertainment as of wonder. The Dinka were not filled with 'awe'.

The goat, with a rope round its neck, was brought out of its hut to see the feast prepared in its honour, but it turned away from its feast and, jerking its rope out of the hand of the man who held it, ran into the garden and started to nibble grass. This behaviour caused consternation and amusement, and the women sang a little song about the 'prophet's' being displeased, and offering to propitiate it with a heifer. This was almost certainly a purely formal gesture, for among the Dinka a heifer is not lightly disposed of. People went to fetch the goat back into the cultivation, where a small flock of goats was tethered. As the 'creator-goat' approached them, they pulled and tugged vigorously at their tethering ropes in fright. The goat did not attempt to join its kind, as do most goats when they are being chased, but continued on its way. A Dinka who was travelling with me said, 'It is a creator-goat indeed! Did you ever see a goat behave like that?'

The animal was brought back, and the feast and dance of the women went on while it remained in its hut. It was then decided that since it did not pay any attention to the feast in its honour, it now wanted to be on its way to another village. A small party of old women formed up. Four of them carried its sleeping-skin, which had been washed and anointed with oil, one carried its gourd of rings and bangles, and another carried a gourd of flour for it. They moved off in procession, holding the sleeping-skin over the animal to protect it from the sun, and set off to the next village a few miles away, there to hand it over to its new hosts. The shielding from the sun with a skin (*geng biok*) is a sign of regard and respect for that which is shaded. It is also a Dinka image for the protective action of Divinity, who 'shields with a skin' the world. The sun can be very fierce, and the Dinka suppose that travellers may easily be injured by it.

It was said that this black goat had been thus travelling round the country for many years. In the course of each year it visited many villages from one end of Rek Dinkaland to another, and sometimes even went as far as the Western Twij Dinka. It was said to have started to travel when it was a kid, claimed by nobody, and yet miraculously preserved from the hyaenas and other wild beasts which normally seize any stray kid. It was found that those villages which entertained it had good harvests and for these reasons it was recognized as a 'creator-goat' (perhaps 'goat of the creator' would equally serve as a translation), for only Divinity could thus enable a goat to transcend the normal conditions of goat-life. It will be remembered that *aciek* means a monster or a monstrous birth as well as a prophet, and in calling this strange animal *aciek* the Dinka showed the blend of ideas of strangeness and uniqueness which this word, whether applied to prophets or to monsters, contains. In being apparently different, in its inner being, from its own kind, it was assimilated to the other kind of being which the Dinka apprehend in their world, Divinity. Like Divinity, and like the human prophets of the free-divinities also, this goat distributed its favours where it would throughout the land, irrespective of any tribal or descent-group affiliations.

Some of those things and beings which are regarded as being specially close to Divinity (*kene nhialic*, 'of Divinity') are again those that strike the imagination by possessing certain unusual characteristics. Plants which grow without human aid on graves or shrines are associated with divine action. The tree *akier*, or *acier* (unidentified), which loses its leaves in the wet season and, unlike all other trees, brings forth leaves in the dry, is regarded as *tim nhialic*, the tree of Divinity. The inderab tree (*akoc, Cordia Rothii*), which plays an important part in religious rites later described, is also a tree of Divinity, since it stores water and is sappy at the end of the dry season when other trees are dormant. It is also said to be the first tree to put forth leaves at the end of the dry season, and to grow of itself in the homes of masters of the fishing-spear. All very large and old trees have associations with Divinity, and people should not lightly break off their branches or otherwise damage them. Among beasts, the largest, the elephant and giraffe, are spoken of as *lan nhialic*, animals of Divinity. Among artifacts, those with associations with Divinity or divinities are often surpassingly large. In describing their sacred spears of the past, Dinka always emphasize the length of the metal heads of the spears. I have seen sacred fish-spears with heads 4 ft. in length—much longer than those of the modern fishing-spears now often used as substitutes for sacred spears which have been lost.[1]

---

[1] A sacred spear which functions as a clan-divinity of the Gwalla group of Bor Dinka, and called *Lirpiou*, 'cool-heart', is as far as I know unique in size, and

Much of the description so far has represented the Dinka Divinity as a unitary being, endowed with some features of human personality. That this is not the whole meaning of the term *nhialic*, some later chapters will more fully indicate; but I must mention here that despite the quasi-human form in which Divinity is sometimes imagined to appear in visions, the figurative references to parts of his 'body', and the attribution to him of a kind of universal fatherhood, the Dinka understanding of Divinity is in important respects the reverse of anthropomorphic. Indeed, it is precisely as contrasting with men—their judgements, ways, and powers—that *nhialic* is most frequently heard.

The attitude of the Dinka towards the stories of Divinity's withdrawal from Man is of some interest here. Those who have commented upon these stories have sometimes made it clear that their sympathies lie with Man in his plight, and draw attention to the smallness of the fault for which Divinity withdrew the benefits of his closeness. The image of striking Divinity with a hoe or pestle often evokes a certain amusement, almost as though the story were indulgently being treated as too childish to explain the consequences attributed to the event. But it is clear that the point of the story of Divinity's withdrawal from men is not to suggest an improving moral judgement on human behaviour. It is to represent a total situation known to the Dinka today. Men now are—as the first man and woman then became—active, self-assertive, inquiring, acquisitive. Yet they are also subject to suffering and death, ineffective, ignorant, and poor. Life is insecure; human calculations often prove erroneous, and men must often learn by experience that the consequences of their actions are quite other than they may have anticipated or consider equitable. Divinity's withdrawal from Man as the result of a comparatively trifling offence, by human standards, presents the contrast between equitable human judgements and the action of the Powers which are held ultimately to control what happens in Dinka life. It is true that misfortune is associated by the Dinka with some offence; but

appears to be an elephant-spear with a shaft some 194 cm. long and 19 cm. in circumference, with a blade over 50 cm. long and proportionately broad. Among the Eastern Twij Dinka, also as clan-divinities, there are several very large drums, one of which I saw. It was fully 15 ft. in length, and quite unlike Dinka drums in normal use. See p. 264.

often the seriousness of the offence is not known until the results then attributed to it have been experienced.[1] To the Dinka, the moral order is ultimately constituted according to principles which often elude men, which experience and tradition in part reveal, and which human action cannot change—is given, that is, in much the same way as for practical purposes we regard the physical order to be given. The myth of Divinity's withdrawal then reflects the facts of existence as they are known. The Dinka are in a universe which is largely beyond their control, and where events may contradict the most reasonable human expectation. The Divinity who is sometimes a kindly father is also the Divinity which is manifested in the non-rational forces of nature and hence has non-rational as well as rational and moral attributes.

The concept *nhialic* reflects Dinka experience of both the social and the natural world and hence, though Divinity is spoken of as though its actions were to some extent predictable according to moral principle, particularly in eventually making justice between man and man appear, it is also a term for what is unpredictable. When the word *nhialic* is murmured as an adequate account of accident, luck, disaster, triumph, hope, or disappointment, it often represents a type of adjustment to the uncertainties and chances of human life, a recognition of real ambiguities in experience rather than a pious aspiration towards resignation to the will of an ultimately benevolent personal God. The attitude to which I draw attention is well represented in the following hymn:

Spring rain in a dry spell, strikes the ants on the head with a club[2]
And the ants say: My father has seen[3]

---

[1] Examples are given later.
[2] The hymn is one collected by Fr. Nebel and quoted in P. W. Schmidt, op. cit., 1949, p. 161. There the German translation is as follows:
> Frühlingsregen schlug mit der Keule dem Volk auf dem Kopf.
> Und das Volk sagt: Der Vater wußte darum.
> Und man weiß nicht, ob er den Clan (freundlich) besuchte.
> Und man weiß nicht, ob er den Clan züchtigte.

The idea of the first line is that in the storms of spring, men are struck by lightning, the 'club of DENG'. DENG is a free-divinity particularly connected with rain (*deng*) and lightning, as described in Chap. II.
[3] An idiom which implies that 'it is the work of Divinity', much like the expression 'God knows . . . !'

> And they do not know whether he helps people
> And they do not know whether he injures people.

If any question as to why things happen or have happened is pressed home, the Dinka answer will eventually refer them to *nhialic*, a point in explanation beyond which further questioning is meaningless. In the ordinary course of life, however, and not in such an artificial questioning from cause to cause, Divinity is spontaneously referred to primarily when men have to adjust themselves to situations in which they involuntarily find themselves, and where clear oppositions and ambiguities of thought and experience occur. This evocation of the notion of Divinity by paradoxes and contrarieties of experience, which relate to the major theme of the division of earth and sky, is further considered in later chapters. First, other ways in which Divinity and divinities are grounded in knowledge of the social and physical environment must be described.

II

DIVINE UNITY AND MULTIPLICITY: (i) FREE-DIVINITIES

I

ALL Dinka assert that Divinity is one, *nhialic ee tok*. The implications of this affirmation are that their *nhialic* is the same Divinity as that which different peoples know under different names, the Divinity the Nuer call '*kwoth*', the Muslims 'Allah', the Christians 'God', and so on. Yet *nhialic* is also a comprehensive term for a number of conceptions which differ considerably from each other. Powers, of which the most important religiously are those I have called free-divinities and clan-divinities, are distinct from each other, though of most of them the Dinka may say simply *ee nhialic*, 'it is Divinity'. This unity and multiplicity of Divinity causes no difficulty in the context of Dinka language and life, but it is impossible entirely to avoid the logical and semantic problems which arise when Dinka statements bearing upon it are translated, together, into English.

The most important and active of the free-divinities known in western Dinkaland are DENG, GARANG, MACARDIT, and ABUK. Deng, Garang, and Macar are common personal names for men, and Abuk is probably the commonest name for women, so here the names of the free-divinities appear in capital letters to distinguish them from human personal names. Among the Agar and Cic Dinka, another free-divinity called LOI is also important, but knowledge of this divinity had not spread farther westwards during my visits to Dinkaland, ending in 1950.[1] Elsewhere in Dinkaland there are others, which are unknown in the west, or have been forgotten in all but name because they are thought no longer to be active there.[2]

---

[1] As will appear, it is characteristic of these free-divinities that they should extend the range of their activities, and it would not be surprising if LOI were now more widespread.

[2] Such are ADIM, a free-divinity said to have originated in Agar country, and connected with hyaena and the protection of stock against hyaena; AYAK, the

None of the free-divinities, with the possible exception of MACARDIT, also sometimes called COLWIC, is thought to exist independently of the particular name by which the Dinka know it. That is, unlike Divinity, who is thought to be universal and known by various names to different peoples, the free-divinities are active only where their specific names are known and where effects in human life can be attributed to them.

Free-divinities make their presence known by causing illness, by possessing human beings and announcing through their mouths their names and demands, and sometimes by speaking in dreams. They do not, strictly speaking, *appear*, for in themselves they are held to be formless, though each has a set of colour- and other associations. Before describing these, like the Dinka I first explain the free-divinities by the effects they produce, beginning with a description of a typical example of possession of a man attributed to one of them.

The subject of this possession was a youth, Ajak, younger son of a master of the fishing-spear. He had left home for the town at an early age and had found various poor kinds of work there, which distressed his father and caused a breach between son and father. The son still much admired his father, often spoke of him, and was very distressed when the old man died while he was with me, away from home and before they had been reconciled. The family was then left in the hands of a brother, whom the youth thought incompetent, and he was often anxious about the future of the family, which might now disintegrate. From time to time he had news from home which fed his anxiety, but he preferred to work, travelling and earning money, rather than to go back and see what he could do. On the occasions of his possession, Ajak had started by becoming maudlin with beer.

Ajak always hinted with pride that Divinity had formed a special relationship with him. He had been told by his mother that he had been born without testicles, and that his father, according to the custom, had intended to put him into the river. Instead, he had been prevailed upon by the mother and others to offer a white sheep in sacrifice to Divinity, and pray that the

mother perhaps of ABUK, known among the Bor Dinka; and DAYIM, also known amongst the Bor Dinka and the subject of a hymn translated by Archdeacon Shaw, 'Dinka Songs', *Man*, vol. xv, 1915, p. 20.

child might become normal. After this sacrifice first one and
then the other testicle had appeared. Ajak, like his mother,
interpreted this as a special intervention of Divinity on his behalf, and trusted in further such interventions to save him from
later difficulties in his life. He sometimes hinted that he had
special gifts of insight and clairvoyance, and that he could
strongly affect the lives of others for good or evil by his attitudes
and prayers. He was a cheerful and pleasant person but, as we
should say, very highly strung, and given to extremes of melan-
choly and gaiety.

Late one night it was announced that Ajak 'had the creator
(or prophet) in his body' (*lo guop aciek*), or 'had a ghost in his
body' (*lo guop atiep*). These are the usual expressions used where
we should use the word 'possessed', and the possession now
described is the characteristic behaviour of men when they are
thought to be in very close personal contact with Powers. The
free-divinities or clan-divinities are also said to 'seize' (*dom*)
men, or to 'wake up' (*pac*) in their bodies, or to appear in them
like the shimmering of a heat-haze.

Ajak was running round and round outside a hut, breathing
heavily and panting and grunting. He did not appear to hear
when addressed. It was said that this outburst had been pre-
ceded by a period of sitting alone, during which he chanted
and muttered to himself. This is often a sign of impending
possession. Nobody knew the songs he had been singing; they
were said to be hymns to Divinity (*diet rok nhialic*), and one
which I later heard included the expression 'Power(s) of sky
and earth' (*jong nhial ku jong piny*), which was the only time
among the Dinka that I heard Power(s) (*jak*) thus generally
dichotomized.[1] Ajak ran about for some twenty minutes, apparently quite unaware of spectators. As he gradually tired his
movements became clumsier and less vigorous, and his breathing was deeper and quicker. Although he seemed to be gazing
straight ahead, without care for where he was going, he avoided
bushes and stumps of wood in his path. Eventually his legs
began to give way beneath him, and he staggered and eventually fell sprawling on the ground, where he stayed, rolling
about and lashing out with his arms and legs.

He lay there for some time. Bursts of frenzied movement

[1] They are so dichotomized among the Nuer and the Anuak.

were interspersed with quieter periods, when he sang snatches of songs which nobody could understand. By this time a few spectators from the village had gathered round. Some smiled at the performance. The situation is a familiar one to all Dinka. Even a small boy can give a convincing imitation of possession of this sort, though I think that children do not become possessed. 'It is a Power (*jok*) of his home,' one of the spectators said, while another said, 'he has a ghost (*atiep*, a 'shade' or the ghost of a man) in his body'. Then a minor master of the fishing-spear came and, addressing what he said to the threshing form of Ajak, asked whatever it was which troubled him to tell its name and say what it wanted. In his address he tried to elicit answers from several potential sources of possession, saying, 'You, Power' (*yin jok*), 'You, divinity' (*yin yath*), and 'You, ghost' (*yin atiep*). No reply, however, came from Ajak, who continued to moan and roll about. The master of the fishing-spear then began to take to task the Power which troubled Ajak, as follows: 'You, Power (*jok*), why do you seize a man who is far away from his home? Why do you not seize him there at home where the cattle are? What can he do about it here? He is travelling in a foreign place, and he is with this European. Why do you seize a man who works for the Government?'[1]

Ajak mumbled unintelligibly; the spectators were clearly expecting something to speak through his mouth, and to tell us its name and business. They explained that in due course it would leave him (*pal*). When I asked what 'it' was, I was told variously that it would be his (clan) divinity (*yath*), or the ghost of his father, or the free-divinity DENG, or 'just a Power' (*jok epath*). Since it would not announce itself, how could one know? By this time Ajak had become quieter and seemed to be becoming aware of his surroundings. The master of the fishing-spear, who had previously been speaking to the Power in the body of Ajak, now began gently to admonish him personally, as a man. Why had this happened? What secret wrong had he done, or what had he failed to do that he should have done? And why did he behave in this way when he was far away from his home, where it was impossible to deal with the matter by

[1] The Dinka tend to think that anyone who is not a trader or a missionary must be some kind of government official.

bringing out a calf, invoking over it, and either dedicating or sacrificing it to the Power which troubled him?

Ajak, who seemed dazed and exhausted, gave no reply. He got up and went to bed without a word, showing by this time the presence of mind to adjust his mosquito-net carefully. The next morning he either feigned not to remember anything of what had happened, or he really had forgotten. He denied with irritation that what we described had occurred, though he said later that on one previous occasion his father's ghost had seized him when he was away from home, and had flung him on a fire. He used to dream about his father, and felt guilty about the death of the old man and his absence from home at that time.

He became possessed for a second time some months later. After some preliminary singing Ajak again began to run about. Since here there were cattle-pegs—stakes—in the ground, over which he stumbled occasionally, I thought it better to secure him loosely lest he fell on one. He rolled about as before, and again there were periods of comparative calm, alternating with bursts of singing and more frenzied movements.

Spectators arrived, and at once objected to his being prevented from running. I asked them if he might not fall and be trans-fixed on a cattle-peg. They said that if a Power wanted to kill him, it would; otherwise, he would be safe. I asked how they knew that the Power did not intend that he should be saved from more serious injury by being prevented from running, and they laughed and agreed that it might be so.

As before, an old man began to question the source of the possession: 'Who are you that seize this man far from his home? If you are a divinity (*yath*), speak and say what you want.' He asked the name of the clan-divinity of Ajak's clan, and then questioned it by name, specifically demanding if it was this Power which wanted attention. Ajak still moaned and uttered occasional snatches of song. 'Are you then the divinity DENG?' asked the old man. Some Dinka clans have the free-divinity DENG as a special clan-divinity also; and I asked how it could be DENG which troubled Ajak, since, as far as I knew, his clan did not possess this. I was told abruptly that all Dinka possessed or venerated (*mac*), and might be possessed by, DENG. The old man, getting no reply to any of these questions, then asked if it was the free-divinity GARANG which was troubling Ajak. Ajak still did not reply, though he was becoming more composed and calm, and sang a hymn which I could not understand, except that DENG was mentioned in it. He then became quite rational, and quietly spoke a few words in his own voice to the man who was questioning him. He said that he had never killed a man, and that it was not something at home which was troubling him—that is, that he had nothing on his conscience as far as home was concerned. He then became possessed again.

One of the spectators said that the source of his possession could not be his clan-divinity. That would have announced itself and what it wanted through his mouth, and then left the man, for 'the clan-divinity is respectful (considerate)'. The old man, however, returned to the clan-divinity and, addressing it in the body of Ajak, told it that in Ajak's home they would dedicate a calf to it, and that Ajak would return to attend to this as soon as possible. Ajak again became quieter, and I spoke to him by name. Someone said: 'It is no use speaking to Ajak; it is *not* Ajak.'

After a while he sat up, saying that his head was confused (*ci nhom liab*). Some of the spectators took a gourd of water, and the old man blew a little saliva into it and on to Ajak's head. Water from the gourd was then poured over his hands, feet, chest, and back, and the source of possession, addressed simply as 'You, Power' (*yin jok*), was told to leave the man in peace and not to trouble him when he was travelling far away from home. People patted Ajak's back and lifted his hands above his head to make him expel breath, and he got up and went off to bed. The next day he was again sceptical about what had occurred, but said that on the previous day he had not felt at all well—his body had been 'heavy' (*thiek guop*)—whereas now it had become light, or well.

The third and last occasion of possession was one which I could not observe in detail. The man ran out into the forest in the middle of the night, where the darkness and the floods made it impossible to find him. One could hear his voice singing somewhere in the distance, and eventually someone caught up with him just as he was about to walk into a crocodile-infested river, and redirected him towards home, where he was eventually found comfortably sleeping in his bed before the search for him in the forest had been abandoned.

This time there had been such manifest danger that everyone agreed that something was wanting to kill him, and there was some discussion about what it might be. Ajak himself was finally convinced he had been in danger, and said that he thought it was because his brother had parted with their cow dedicated to DENG (*weng atiem deng*) in marriage. Some people disagreed with this suggestion. They pointed out that whichever Power it was which wanted to harm him, it did so when he was far away from home, while DENG, though it might indeed lead people off into the forest, would not do so in order to kill them, and would more probably make them sick at home. Nor, urged some, could the grounds of possession be the father's ghost, nor the clan-divinity, for they would have made their wants known when asked, and in any case would not have troubled their man when he was in a foreign place. The grounds of the possession must be just a Power of the forest (*jong roor epath*), or the free-divinity MACARDIT (or COLWIC), which might more readily kill people in the wilds and on their travels, pointlessly and unaccountably.

No agreed solution was reached. He was never possessed again. Ajak told me a year later that he had been troubled and confused the previous year; but that he had since been home and attended sacrifices for Divinity, his clan-divinity, and his father's ghost, and since then had been well and at peace.

This example illustrates the typically diagnostic attempts to trace certain effects to one or another of a number of Powers which are, for the Dinka, the customary explanations for such effects. They show also how uncertainty is increased when possession (or illness) takes place away from home, where nobody knows well the circumstances of the sufferer and his family. For in some situations possession is expected and even desired. At sacrifices men and women also often become temporarily possessed, and nobody pays much attention. It is when a lone individual is seriously possessed that uncertainties arise. In this case it will be seen that a constant theme is that Ajak is away from his home and kin, and that he therefore should not be troubled, for neither he nor his kin can take action to satisfy or propitiate the grounds of his possession.

The argument that only MACARDIT (which literally means

'the great black one') would be likely to try to kill a man away from his home refers to a clear distinction which the Dinka make between the wilds (*roor*) and the homestead (*bai*), 'the desert and the sown'. The uninhabited forests are the homes of harmful, usually anonymous, anti-social Powers which cause suffering which has no constructive aspect. The distinction between the uncontrolled life of the wilds, without human order and reason, and the orderly and rational domesticated life of men and beasts in society, is thus reflected in a division of Powers into the non-rational and rational, the purposeless and the purposeful, those which share men's social life and those which, like the wilds with their animals and untouched scrub, are merely menacing to human beings. The free-divinity MACARDIT, as will be seen later, is related to both; the other free-divinities, the clan-divinities, and Divinity itself, which are the major concern of Dinka religion, are Powers of the homestead, of men in society, rather than of wild Nature.

A characteristic variety of individual interpretations of the situation is shown in the case described; each spectator guesses at the source of the trouble according to his own knowledge and experience. Ajak had no kinsmen near him, and therefore nobody who was deeply involved in his condition. Had he been in his own home his suggestion that he had been seized by DENG because his brother had parted with a cow consecrated to this divinity would have been a much more effective protest against his brother's act. The guilt incurred would then have been equally felt by all his close kinsmen, and what had happened to him, with all its threat of possibly worse things to come, would have appeared as a danger to all. Ajak's possession would have reminded them of a sin for which any one of them might suffer.

During the states of possession Ajak certainly was not the total personality which at other times one had known. We may be inclined to see this situation as deriving from an absence of the normal features of the personality, a temporary lack of knowledge and control of the self. The Dinka state the situation in positive terms, supposing the presence of something other than his own personality in the body of the possessed person. His body becomes host and vehicle for another *kind* of being. Once this interpretation of possession or sickness is accepted it is but logical to try to diagnose the specific source, as physicians look for positive extrinsic sources for physical sickness.

Sometimes, as in this case, unprofessional and somewhat casual attempts at diagnosis are made, and it is hoped that in some way the trouble will clear itself up. In other and more serious cases, however, a specialist in the diagnosis of such conditions is called in. Such specialists are thought to have, in varying degrees, a deeper knowledge of the grounds of sickness and possession than the ordinary Dinka has, and it is partly through them that Dinka beliefs in free-divinities are attested, and knowledge of them extended. I therefore describe these specialists here in general terms, before giving an account of what the Dinka say about the free-divinities whose wants they help to make known.

There are several categories of 'religious' specialist (I here use the term widely) in Dinka society, and the boundaries between some of them are not very clearly defined. The permanent hereditary priesthood of masters of the fishing-spear is described in later chapters. Here we consider those seers, diviners, and prophets whose powers, unlike those of the priests, are not necessarily hereditary.

I first consider and then dismiss as marginal a number of magical practitioners whose powers reside in their possession of fetish-bundles, which they may have bought or inherited. A man who possesses such fetishes is called *ran (lo) wal*, 'a person with medicine'. *Wal* is the term for grass and vegetable life generally, and hence for medicine, in the dual sense of herbal remedies and magical medicines. Among the Western Dinka the most famous of such magical medicines is one called *mathiang gok*, though the varieties of *wal* may be as numerous as the private superstitions of which individuals are capable. *Mathiang gok*, however, is the very type of potent medicine possessed by medicine men, and a brief account of it will be enough to suggest the nature of all; as I have said, they are not to be regarded as of great *religious* importance, and the Dinka themselves are quick to point out the difference between the characters and abilities of such earthly medicines and their owners, and those of priests and prophets, in their roles as such.[1] I say

---

[1] Fetishes are thought by the Dinka to be particularly characteristic of the Sudanic-speaking peoples to the south of their country.

'in their roles', because anyone may possess and use such medicines; they serve individual human ends and, as individual human beings, priests and prophets may acquire them like anyone else. I think, however, that they are less likely to do so, as although they fear them they pretend to despise them.[1]

Mathiang gok, like other medicines of a magical nature, is in the general category of Powers, *jok*. It resides in the physical fetish-bundle and can be bought with it; but its action is of a spiritual nature, and is attributed to a Power informing the fetish-bundle but which also moves outside it, to affect the consciences and fortunes of men against whom it is directed. *Mathiang gok* is called a 'black Power' (*jong col*), or sometimes an 'earth power' (*jong piny*), to distinguish it and other medicines of its kind from the higher Powers, the divinities.

I do not know what the physical constituents of a *mathiang gok* bundle are; the one I saw consisted of bits of unidentifiable wood and withered roots, and I think that roots of some kind are always included. The connexion of the medicine with the earth is thus perhaps reinforced, for I do not think that among the various material things associated with the higher Powers, the divinities, there are any which come from under the ground. The name, *mathiang gok*, is not given any consistent etymology by the Dinka. *Mathiang* indisputably means 'dark brown', but it might also be a man's name, as is supposed by Captain Fergusson.[2] *Gok* similarly may be a man's name, or the name of a tribal area. I have also been told by a Dinka that the name means 'brown dove', since, he said, the name of the medicine may really be *mathiang guk*, and *guk* is a dove. Yet I cannot think that this is more than a piece of *ad hoc* etymology, since in Dinka the adjective follows the noun and 'brown dove' would correctly be *guk mathiang*.

The circumstances in which *mathiang gok* is thought to operate, and its mode of operation, are consistently described by all Dinka. Its main function is to obtain for its possessor an

[1] Fetishes are thought by the Dinka to be particularly characteristic of the Sudanic-speaking peoples to the south of their country.

[2] V. H. Fergusson, ' "Mattiang Goh" Witchcraft', *S.N. & R.*, vol. vi, 1923, p. 112. Captain Fergusson calculates that in about 1902 an Agar Dinka called Mattiang went to settle near the Gell river. There he found the root, which a 'jur' (non-Dinka) of Tonj told him to call 'Mattiang Goh', since Goh was his father's name. Fergusson says that the root protects its owner against theft.

influence over those whom he thinks to have wronged him, particularly to enforce the payment of cattle-debts. Its mode of operation is said to be as follows. A man has enemies, or he has a grudge against others for keeping from him what is rightfully his own. He does not feel strong enough to obtain his rights without the assistance of a Power which will work for him individually. Perhaps invocation of Divinity has been of no avail. He therefore buys *mathiang gok*, a purchase which will normally involve a trip to another part of the country, or into the land of the non-Dinka peoples to the south. People may suspect what this trip is for; they will not be quite sure, as a Dinka does not usually publicly admit to the possession of *mathiang gok* and it is not lightly spoken about. This may be partly because the Government has imposed heavy penalties on those who are found with it, though I doubt if it is these alone which surround the transaction with secrecy. The Dinka themselves tolerate, but do not really approve, dealings which involve the manipulation of amoral medicines for purely individual ends. Members of any particular group of Dinka are convinced that *mathiang gok* is a foreign importation, some say from the Agar Dinka, who say it comes from the non-Dinka ('Jur' Beli and Sofi) to the south, and some even say it comes from the Nuer, who also know it, but trace it to the Dinka.

The man returns and hides the bundle of roots somewhere in his cattle-byre. From time to time he speaks to it and tells it his desires, and will also make it small offerings. It, in its turn, will demand sacrifices, which may be covertly carried out, or which may be secretly included by the man in the intention of other sacrifices made to Powers which are not in the same way publicly disapproved. In return for these attentions, *mathiang gok* will go out after a man who owes its owner cattle. The Dinka say that it will come to such a man when he is walking alone, and will speak to him and threaten to injure him or his family unless the debt is paid. It may go further, and actually kill an enemy of its owner by causing swellings, most commonly in the throat and head or in the belly. A man intimidated by *mathiang gok* will often pay his debts, though a man who feels himself to have been wrongly injured by the *mathiang gok* of another will perhaps retort with physical violence if he is sure of the source of his suffering.

I have found that Dinka are never prepared to admit that they are *quite* sure that a man possesses or is using *mathiang gok* until a further stage is reached, that is until a man, having by recourse to *mathiang gok* obtained what he desires, is many years later taken seriously ill himself. He may then either announce himself that he has in the past bought *mathiang gok* to which he has for long failed to pay appropriate attentions, or a diviner will attribute his sickness or death openly to this cause. Then the possession of *mathiang gok* by the man is openly admitted, and sacrifice is made to the Power to try to divert its wrath from the neglectful owner. By this time, of course, the original disputes and enmities for which the *mathiang gok* was obtained are probably no longer live issues, though the Dinka are less sympathetic towards its owner and victim than they are to those who suffer through the unsought intervention of a higher Power, which they have not themselves attempted to harness to their own individual advantage.

Anyone may be a *ran* (*lo*) *wal*, one who possesses medicines. More specifically, however, a *ran wal*, 'medicine-man', is one who is suspected of trafficking in medicines, and though he may not himself admit to possessing them knows their qualities and knows where to get them. A medicine-man is the lowest form of specialist in control and knowledge of Powers, just as medicine-bundles are informed with the lowest, if yet dangerous and fearful, Powers. A *ran wal* is usually, I think, in any part of Dinkaland, a visitor, perhaps an itinerant Nuer or Dinka. Such people may purvey roots and charms as no permanent member of a Dinka village could, for by selling medicines or admitting to their possession within his own community a man would also be suspected of causing the sicknesses of his neighbours. The line between *ran wal* and *apeth*, the possessor of the evil eye, is often not very clearly drawn; both injure others for their own advantage, whatever their justification may be thought to be.

Though 'medicines' like *mathiang gok* are thought to inhere sufficiently in particular bundles of roots to make it possible to transfer them with the roots, and to regard them as residing in the roots, they are yet not totally bound to their material homes. Their influence or virtue—their Power—emanates from them, and its action is upon the mind and hearts of men as well as upon their physical health. So even these lower Powers transcend any material form with which they are associated. There is no question, for example, of simple 'contagious magic' in the use of fetish bundles. They 'speak' to men—or as we might say, to men's consciences, for we cannot fail to notice how like the workings of our 'conscience' is the action attributed to them; and when they speak to men, they are not necessarily visually imaged. I have heard it said that *mathiang gok* may speak, when conjured by a diviner, from the walls of a cattle-byre, and that it has on occasions appeared to people in the form of a small brown dog. When functioning as a Power it does not seem to appear to others in the form of a bundle of roots, though this is known by all to be its physical basis and vehicle, as far as transmission from hand to hand is concerned. The active principle even of this lowly Power is capable of being detached, in thought, from any specific material form in which it may be supposed at times to inhere, and this is true of the relation between any Power and its emblem. It is never, among the Dinka, simply material things in themselves which are of central religious importance, but something formless, immaterial, invisible, associated with them.

Much higher in esteem than men who possess *only* such fetish-bundles are people called *tyet* (pl. *tiit*), a class of specialists that comprises individuals of widely differing reputations for occult knowledge and powers. I begin with a brief description of one of the least of them, one of those who may also be called *acoor*. Acoor is related to the word *car*, meaning to divine, and is also I think connected with the word *coor*, blind. Blind people may often be thought to have special insight. It would be unlikely that any *tyet* with a high reputation would be spoken of as *acoor*, though an *acoor* would also be referred to as *tyet* by those who thought highly of him. Diviners of lower and higher reputation stand in a relationship similar to that between minor fortune-tellers and well-known clairvoyants in our own society.

When we were all a long way from home, my companions who were worried about what might be happening to their families announced that they wished to consult an itinerant *tyet*, diviner, who had arrived in the village. The man had had some schooling. He was asking 10 piastres (about 2s.) to tell fortunes. His mode of procedure was first to set a ring—the gift, he said, of a missionary—in the dust in front of him. We sat

around him, and after a few moments of apparently deep concentration he began to trace tracks in the dust between himself
and the ring. As though reading these tracks as a hunter follows
spoor, he would pause and consider for a while now and then,
and then put forward tentative statements about matters which
he could easily have picked up in the course of a few hours of
ordinary village gossip. For his clients, he referred to their kinsmen's minor illnesses that would pass, cattle-cases that would
eventually be settled, and other generalities such as he might
rightly suppose any Dinka away from his home to be troubled
about. It was clear that he was following up leads given to him
by the conspicuous heightening of interest shown by the audience where he was on the right lines, and he would hazard
guesses, again in generalized and tentative form, until the manner of his audience convinced him that he should continue in
a particular direction. When he divined for me, I deliberately
misled him by showing interest in suggestions which could not
possibly be true—such as, for example, that my father had had
four wives, and that I was worried about half-sisters, who did
not exist, and he reassured me about these matters. The Dinka,
who then knew what was happening, lost faith in his statements
about them, saying that after all there were many fraudulent
tiit, diviners, or people who 'are not real *tiit*'; but of course the
experience of one false diviner, far from calling into doubt the
abilities of all, reminded them of many others who really had
the insight which this man claimed.

The following text from the Twij Dinka illustrates something
of the thought of the Dinka in this matter, and the ambivalent
attitudes they may adopt towards diviners:

A young man was very ill, and his father called in a diviner who
lied and said that Divinity (*nhialic*) wanted a very big fat ox. And the
father of the man said 'Good', and fetched an ox from the herd and
killed it. But the young man was still on the point of death.

And a lion used to come to the homestead and watch the man
from a hiding-place near by, so that some day when he found him
alone he could eat him. And the father of the sick man had walked
and walked until he was tired out [because he was searching for
more beasts to sacrifice from the herds of his relatives and friends].
And everything was finished [in sacrifices]. And that lion knew what
was injuring the man.

One day a man went into the woods to get honey. He lit a fire under a tree (to smoke out the bees) and climbed the tree to cut more wood. The lion heard the axe and made for the foot of the tree. The man heard him coming and put out his fire and sat in the tree.

Two lions met at the foot of the tree, and greeted each other and asked about each other's affairs. The lion called Mangar Dit said 'I ate two men—one was thin but the other was fat.' And the other lion said, 'They have sent for you from your home, for your father and mother say "If you see Mangar Dit, and he has eaten a man, tell him that his sister has menstruated, and will he please bring the man's puddings[1] for her to eat." '

Mangar Dit said: 'Good. I have found a sick man in the village here, but I can't get hold of him because his people sleep by him day and night. And I will tell you that the Power which injures him is not a big Power at all, it is merely a little one.' And the other lion asked 'What sort of a Power is it?' And the first said 'It is a tiny Power which is in the pool in the village. If they bring a small *mangok* ox and kill it in the pool the man will get better at once.' Then the lions picked up their spears and went off to the cattle-camp. And that man in the tree heard all they said.

So the man went off to the home of the sick young man, and said, 'You people of the sick man, give me a little *mangok* ox and I will see what I can do.' The father of the sick man brought a little ox, and the ox was taken along to the pool with the sick man. And the ox was prayed over; and the sick man was possessed. Then they killed the ox.

And the sick man arose at once and ate the meat of the sacrificed ox. The next morning he went to the cattle-camp, and people were astonished by his recovery.

And that man who had climbed the tree had no Power in his body (was not a diviner); they wanted to reward him with a cow in calf, but the man refused and said, 'Just reward me with a single goat.'

Minor practitioners of divination may use mussel-shells, like the Nuer, or scatter grain and interpret its fall, or, more commonly, draw in the sand as a *mise-en-scène* for their display of insight. Their reputation naturally varies according to their luck in hitting upon something which their clients are prepared to recognize as true and perceptive; but their standing is never unambiguously respectable for, as in the above story, they can be thought to defraud while still being called *tiit*,[2] diviners.

---

[1] In Dinka *abyar*, an euphemism for the anus, frequently a topic of jocular impropriety.

[2] The word *tyet* is sometimes confused by non-Dinka with the word *atet*, which

A higher type of diviner is one who is thought to have an important Power, a free-divinity, in his body. This may come about in several ways. He may have become sick, and been told by another diviner that he has been possessed by a Power of such and such a name. This Power then becomes his divinity— it becomes related to him, that is, and he sacrifices to it. When he recovers from the illness he may come to regard himself as inspired by this divinity, and gain a reputation for diagnosis of other people's illnesses and misfortunes by displaying an insight which he attributes to his divinity. Many people whose illnesses are attributed to particular divinities are content merely to offer sacrifice to them and return to their normal way of living; but a few (and, from those I have seen, I should say a few who are nervously very highly organized) become practising diviners. They continue to hoe and tend their cattle like other Dinka, but are called in to diagnose illnesses and causes of misfortune. The divinity may pass from a diviner to any, or none, of his children. Once the divinity has seized a man, he may learn more of the technique of divining from an established diviner

The least regarded of these are also consulted about suspected witchcraft, and they may extract from the patient's body bits of wood, or sand, which have been shot into the body by witches, *apeth*. Such people again may also be suspected of being also prone to bewitch people. More highly regarded are those whom the Dinka sometimes assimilate to the yet higher category of inspired person, later described, by calling them also *ran nhialic*, a 'person of Divinity', or *aciek*, prophet or 'creator'. The categories shade into each other, but a famous 'person of Divinity' and prophet would be demeaned by being called only *tyet*, a mere diviner.

All Dinka give consistent accounts of the way in which established diviners operate. The diviner is invited to the home of a sick man, whose kinsmen sit around him. They place on the ground spears and money as an initial payment, and an earnest of their intention to give a larger present, perhaps even a calf, if the seance is successful. The people of the sick man will then ask the diviner the name of the divinity through whom he

means simply 'someone who has a special skill or facility'. It is applied to bone-setters and masseurs, and more widely to anyone clever with his hands. Some diviners also have these skills, but many who are not diviners also have them.

divines, and he will tell them. The free-divinities earlier mentioned—GARANG, DENG, MACARDIT or COLWIC—are the commonest and most widely recognized in Rek country. In Western
Twij country there are also several others—ATEM, AIWEL YATH,
and BIAR YATH. It is interesting to note that possession by
divinities is thought both by Western Twij and Rek Dinka to be
more common among the Twij than among the Rek, and that
some divinities known in Rek-land are said to have entered
from the land of the Twij, to the north and east, in the direction
of Kordofan. This was a point of contact in the nineteenth
century with the great Arab prophet, the Mahdi, a matter the
significance of which we later discuss.

When the diviner has announced the name of the divinity
through which he divines, the people ask him if he wants them
to sing to it. It is considered usual for the diviner to ask that
they should, and they then sing hymns, in some of which his
particular divinity may be mentioned. After a period of singing
the diviner begins to shake himself and to appear to feel pains
in his neck and his back. He then begins to quiver and tremble
and make curious squeaking noises (these I have heard from
possessed people) and to breathe heavily. It is then thought that
the divinity has begun (as the Dinka say) to 'rise', or to 'wake
up' (*pac*) in his body, or to 'warm' his body. He is then pro-
gressively 'seized' by the divinity, which speaks in an unknown
tongue through his mouth. He translates the sounds, usually
twittering and groaning sounds, into partly intelligible Dinka.
He thus announces, guided by his divinity, the grounds of the
trouble which he has been asked to treat. The commonest and
expected diagnoses are that the sick man or his father or mother
or grandfather committed some hidden sin, or disposed lightly
of a cow dedicated to a divinity. In one case I heard of, but did
not see treated, a diviner called in to cure the paralysis of a girl
of marriageable age attributed the illness to an act of her
grandfather, who had cut off the arm of an enemy to take his
ivory armlet, and had thereby offended the ghost (*atiep*) of
the dead man. In this case the ghost required satisfaction in
the form of an expiatory sacrifice. I had seen the girl before the
sacrifice, and supposed that she was suffering from sleeping-
sickness. She could not stand and appeared to be permanently
dazed. A few weeks after the sacrifice this girl who had appeared

to be incurable was walking about cheerfully with the help of a stick. I mention this to suggest that cures are sometimes conspicuously effected, though the Dinka are prepared to find that their sacrifice may be ineffective. They then, simply resign themselves to the refusal of Divinity to help in a particular case, or suppose that the real grounds of the trouble have not been diagnosed by the diviner.

The diviner's usual suggestion for treatment is that a sacrifice, or dedication of a beast for later sacrifice, should be made. He may kill the beast himself, or he may leave it to the senior man of the homestead or someone asked by him to officiate. A master of the fishing-spear may be asked to carry out a diviner's instruction on behalf of the sufferer, adding his own prayers, to Divinity and the clan-divinity of his clan, to those of the diviner and the people. They pray to Divinity and to the clan-divinities of those descent-groups most concerned in the case, and to such free-divinities or other Powers as are indicated by the diviner. These activities are left for fuller description and illustration later.

As I have said, diviners vary very much in reputation. There are minor personalities, of no great importance, whom many may suspect of practising fraud, or witchcraft, or even sorcery. In the middle ranks are respectable and reputable men whom the Dinka always compare to Arab or European doctors. Sometimes those who know a little Arabic try to distinguish between the lower class of diviners, who shade into practitioners with magic roots, by referring to the latter as *kujur*, a general Sudani, and, I think, originally Nuba term, which might be translated roughly as 'magician', and to the former as *zara*,[1] diviners or soothsayers. At the higher level of reputation, the *tyet* shades into a figure ideally of a quite different type, the *ran nhialic*, man of Divinity, or *aciek*, 'creator', which we here call the 'prophet'.[2]

Prophets of outstanding reputation are not, and have not been, numerous in Dinkaland. In the area I knew best there had been only two whose names were widely known. One, Cyer Dit, may be still alive at the time of writing. The other, Arianhdit, died in about 1948 after a long period of exile, following a patrol carried out against him by the Government

---

[1] This probably refers to the Arabic *zar*, spirits which possess people.
[2] Following Professor Evans-Pritchard's usage in his writings on the Nuer.

in 1922. I failed to reach Arianhdit before he died, and Cyer Dit showed no disposition to receive me, so I thought it better not to force my company upon him. Both men, however, represent an ideal type of religious leader, a type in which the Dinka include also the prophets of other peoples, in particular the outstanding Nuer prophet Ngundeng (Deng Kur) and also, where they have heard of him, the inspired Arab who, as the Mahdi, led his people against the British.

It is said of the great Dinka 'men of divinity' that they unite two 'things'—two principles—in their bodies. They are overtly inspired, more than others of their clans, by their clan-divinities, and it is said that the really great prophets are always also hereditary masters of the fishing-spear, or members of spear-master clans, whose clan-divinities are in any case thought to be more powerful than those of other clans. The special strength of their clan-divinities in them is one of the principles of their effectiveness. The other is that they are in addition vehicles, and representatives on earth, of Divinity. Unlike ordinary diviners, therefore, they necessarily have a place in the priestly organization of Dinkaland, but by special inspiration they are able to show powers which are denied to ordinary masters of the fishing-spear. Their genius is thought to show itself less in the states of possession which the ordinary diviner induces in himself than in the direct insight they have into the truth of situations, and their ability to help or injure others by a mere word or gesture. They are universally acknowledged by the Dinka as true prophets, while many diviners may be thought, by some who have consulted them, to be capable of falsehood or error. Further, the Dinka think of them as being essentially men of peace, who, nevertheless, may be forced by external circumstances into uniting their numerous followers against a common enemy.

Professor and Mrs. Seligman had the advantage, among the Aliab Dinka, of meeting a man who appears to have been of this type, and I quote their account before giving the scattered details which I was able to gather about the Western Dinka prophets whom I never met. They write:

The spirit possessing Wal, an Aliab of importance (he was considered a bañ, probably in this instance signifying a village chief) living in the village of Bang, is not an ancestor but Deng. In 1910

Wal exercised enormous influence, not limited to his fellow tribes-men, for although his spirit only came to him in 1907, Bari and Nuer alike consulted him and paid the strictest attention to his commands. When we visited Wal in 1910 he was a man of about fifty, differing in no obvious external character from his fellows, though deference was shown him in that however dense the crowd around him he was never jostled. We reached Bang early in the morning before the sun was high, but although Wal received us outside his hut he immediately began to make difficulties about talking to us there, saying that he had not been in the sun for years, indeed, it was said that since possession by his spirit he had not left his hut during the hours of sunshine. However, he accepted the loan of a sunshade, which he held over himself until our conversation was finished, when he retired into his hut. Before talking to him we were asked to walk three times round his hut, this being a practice which he insists that all coming to see him shall observe. On being given some tobacco he smelt it and then drew lines with it in the sandy soil on which he sat. Some Kiro men said that if another stone like Madwich[1] were to fall from the sky it would be called Deng, because the spirit of Deng had come to Wal in the village of Bang. Wal was most anxious to make clear his adhesion to the Government, and said that his spirit was 'red' (as Europeans are) and came from Khartoum, which all the black tribes regard as the home of the white man. He was certainly opposed to bloodshed, and had lately condemned the participators in an insignificant brawl, in which but little blood flowed, to an elaborate ceremony of atonement, the essential part of which was that two goats were killed, the flesh of one being eaten while the other was cast into the bush. Wal asserted that this was not an old custom but a new form of sacrifice dictated by his spirit, and this was accepted by those with whom we dis-cussed the matter. It is, however, obvious that the ceremony con-forms more or less closely to a well-known Dinka pattern.

Wal's reputation came to him quickly, for it was noticed that if he quarrelled with a man, that man fell sick, while if the friends of the sick man sang in honour of Wal, the invalid recovered. When Agot, chief of Palek, visited Wal the latter asked him why his people were fighting with bows and spears; Agot knew nothing about this and had not expected a quarrel, but on returning home

[1] A meteorite revered by some of the Dinka visited by Professor and Mrs. Seligman: 'This stone, which is now at Pariak village, fell before the birth of our informant but after the birth of his elder brother. When it fell "everyone", including his parents but not his elder brother, became *muol*; even the dogs became *muol*. This word is applied to the possession of a *tiet* (medicine-man) by a spirit.' C. G. and B. Z. Seligman, op. cit., 1932, p. 150. *Muol* means 'mad' or 'hysterical'.

found that his people had been fighting as Wal had said. Wal is also said to have prophesied the coming of a comet before its appearance.[1]

This description corresponds very closely to what other Dinka say about prophets. It appears here that Wal's divinity was clearly recognized as the free-divinity DENG, the free-divinity most closely associated with Divinity in its totality as I later describe. The divinities possessing the Western Dinka prophets Arianhdit and Cyer Dit are not so straightforwardly identified. Most Dinka are content to regard these men as possessed simply by Divinity (nhialic), but by Divinity known under a special and different name in relation to each of them. What I gathered about these two men is as follows.

The prophet Arianhdit (Great Ariath) was a man whose personal name was Bol Yol, a Dinka of the spear-master clan of Pariath, and of a lineage of that clan which was important in his tribe among the then turbulent Abiem Dinka. The clan-divinities of the clan are divinity DENG (which it will be remembered is also a free-divinity) in a special form as DENG PIOL, 'DENG clouds', and secondarily and less importantly the clan-divinity Hippopotamus. DENG as a clan-divinity is one of several which give those who possess them a special relationship with rain and qualify them to pray effectively for it.

Some time towards the end of the 1914–18 war, it seems, Bol Yol announced that he was possessed by Divinity, and to Divinity as it possessed him he gave the name Arianhdit.[2] He himself became known by the name of the source of his possession, and became himself Arianhdit. He was also regarded as specially inspired by his clan-divinity DENG PIOL, and in the whole compound idea of Divinity, free-divinities and clan-divinities which the Dinka have in mind, it would seem that the name Arianhdit was the name of Divinity as specially present in the body of Bol Yol, and also of the clan-divinity DENG PIOL as specially active in him.[3]

There can be no doubt that Arianhdit was a 'charismatic' personality, and even government officials, who had feared that

---

[1] C. G. and B. Z. Seligman, op. cit., 1932, pp. 188–9.

[2] Ariath is a man's personal name, in this case the name of the founder of the clan. I do not know if it has any other meaning.

[3] Any man may be possessed at times by his clan-divinity; here it is more than this which is implied.

he might become the centre of an insurrection, could not deny him a certain respect. It is said that his power was manifest, not in hysterical possession as with a minor diviner, but simply in the truth of his words. If he looked at a man, or even thought of him, and silently broke a blade of grass, that man would surely die, while if he thought of a man who was sick, that man would be well. So great was his reputation for this power that it seems that for a time he was able to exercise some influence in composing political differences as far east as Meshra-el-Rek, and even to persuade those who had raided cattle to return them to their owners. His writ thus ran far away outside any area over which an ordinary master of the fishing-spear could hope to have any influence. He sent emissaries as far east as the Agar, and Dinka and Luo from remoter parts of the country visited him, some settling around his homestead.

The comparatively newly established Government understood at first that Arianhdit had no quarrel with them, and in his peacemaking his achievements were in principle such as the Government desired. The Dinka to this day maintain that Arianhdit wanted only peace, both between tribes and with the Government, but that he was misunderstood because some Dinka carried lies to the Government, while some hot-headed war-leaders acted contrary to his advice in defying the Government. Whatever may be the true story, Arianhdit and his people did eventually defy the Government, which sent a patrol to deal with the situation. Arianhdit, it is said, prophesied that the bullets of the Government would be as harmless as water; and when the first volley was fired into the air as a warning, it was supposed that the prophecy was fulfilled. Consequently, Arianhdit's followers after the first fusillade looked round and saw that nobody was injured, and were encouraged to charge the patrol, which defended itself, and there was some loss of life. Arianhdit was captured and for long exiled. During his exile the period of modern administration began. Many years afterwards, when Arianhdit was allowed to return to his country, he again began to collect around him numbers of followers, but by this time he was old and the Government well entrenched.

In spite of this failure, Arianhdit's name is held in the highest respect by Western Dinka today. They refer to a prophecy which he is said to have made, that soon the Dinka and the Government would work together side by side and live in one community, and they pointed to the later political developments under the Anglo-Egyptian Government,[1] and now perhaps point to modern political development, as the fulfilment of this. Arianhdit prophesied disaster for those who would not live at peace with their neighbours. The following hymn referring to the disturbed state of the Sudan in the late nineteenth century is sometimes said to be about the words of Arianhdit:

It is spoilt [the earth] as it was in the past
It is spoilt as it was in the past
[It is] As the master (*beny*) who came from above said and we did not hear
It is spoilt as it was in the past. . . .

So, under the name of Arianhdit, Divinity is thought to have come to earth—to have fallen (*lony*) to earth—into the person of the man Bol Yol.

The prophet Cyer Dit is a Western Twij Dinka of the Payath clan, which is related to the important Rek clan of spearmasters, Pagong. He has been cautious not to come into conflict with the Government, to the extent even of avoiding any government centre and letting it be known that he prefers not to receive anyone who might possibly be construed to be its representative. Similarly, and wisely, government officials treated him with a distant respect, and did not insist upon making direct contact with him. It was for this reason that it seemed inappropriate for me to try further to visit him when he showed a disinclination to receive me. His reputation is not so great as that of Arianhdit, but again his name is known and influence accepted beyond the frontiers of his tribal group. In one instance (which may not be unique) the brother of a master of the fishing-spear of one of the tribes of the central Rek Dinka made the difficult journey of some 75 miles to give him a bull in return for his prayers for rain for that central Rek area.

The divinity Cyer (or, perhaps more accurately, Divinity under the name of Cyer Dit) has descended into the bodies of various members of the descent-group of the present prophet Cyer Dit. It first appeared in his grandfather, Deng, who then

---

[1] Particularly the beginnings of a scheme for local government.

became known as Cyer Dit. It then descended on the eldest son of Deng's senior wife, and finally upon the present Cyer Dit, who is said to be the youngest son of Deng's fifth wife. Before the divinity descended the present Cyer Dit was called Jiel, but, as with Arianhdit, when the divinity descended he, as its human vehicle, became known by its name.

'Cyer' means a falling star, or a comet, always regarded as a direct manifestation or mode of Divinity. Cyer Dit is not an old man, and the divinity descended on him while he was quite a young man, when, it is said, he fell sick for a time. He announced that he was the mouthpiece of Divinity under the name of Cyer Dit, and, like other prophets, he demonstrated that this was so by the truth of his statements and the power of his curse. He is now said to have many wives and children. They approach him freely, but others, including his half-brothers and brothers, stay at a distance from where he sits in the cattle-camp, greeting him and speaking with him respectfully without approaching or touching him. The situation recalls the care taken not to jostle the Aliab prophet in the quotation from Professor and Mrs. Seligman above. He has also peculiarities of diet, which Dinka expect of prophets. He is said to take none of the staple foods—quantities of milk, porridge, or meat—but to exist on a few curds. It is said that he is nevertheless fat and strong, because Divinity fills him.

Many gifts of beasts are taken to him in his cattle-camp, in supplication for favours, and it is said that he keeps these gifts there, not killing or sacrificing them, but simply looking at them from time to time. He then remembers the supplications of their donors, and directs his attention, or intention, to their satisfaction. Thus by merely thinking of a man, he is able to help him. Any master of the fishing-spear is thought to have something of this ability, but Cyer Dit, as a prophet also, has it superabundantly. Similarly, it is enough for him to think of rain for some part of the country to make it come; for since Divinity under the name of Cyer Dit is strongly immanent in him, his intentions have the force of divine intentions. The following hymn in his honour suggests what respect is paid to him:

> My father Cyer Deng hold the country
> —A master like the sun and the moon—

My father child of the women hold the country[1]
—A master like the sun and moon—
My father son of Jiel hold the country[2]
—A master like the sun and moon—
My father the son of Jiel gave us the land
My father the great man gave us the land
Mangar Jiel[3] gave us the land
Great master, support the land, don't let the land be spoilt.

Dinka feeling about the power of such a prophet may be further seen in a song supposedly composed by one who has been disregarded:

A man scorns me—
We shall be like the Nile cabbage [which floats away on the stream]
And like a deserted home.

2

We have now seen the ways in which Powers (except for the clan-divinities, which are the subject of the next chapter) manifest themselves and are recognized in the behaviour of men. The lowest Powers are those bound up with magic roots and fetish-bundles, voluntarily acquired by those who are prepared to pay for them and give them the attentions they demand. At this level, and in the minor diviners, the Dinka themselves recognize that they may be duped by frauds. Higher than these fetishes are free-divinities, which manifest themselves in possessing many different persons, some of whom become diviners, or minor prophets, in their name. Highest of all in esteem are the very few manifestations of Divinity, each with its own unique name, which inform the bodies of prophets of the highest reputation. These last are steadily divinely inspired, at every moment in the course of their daily lives, while the ordinary diviner, whatever his success in diagnosing illness, is inspired only from time to time when the divinity rises in him.

Divinity under the name of Cyer, or Arianhdit, seems to

[1] The *wen dyor*, 'children of the women', are a group of related clans closely connected with Longar, the first master of the fishing-spear. This line refers to Cyer's clan, Payath.

[2] Jiel, the personal name of Cyer, is also the name of the founder of his clan.

[3] *Mangar* is an ox-name.

inspire only one individual at a time, and to be known only in him. The free-divinities now to be described are those which may be present in many individuals at the same time. They have associations of forms and colours which give each of them a sort of individuality not entirely defined by their presence in any particular person they possess. I describe one by one the free-divinities best known to the Western Dinka, MACARDIT, GARANG, ABUK, and finally DENG.

MACARDIT (*The Great Black One*)

MACARDIT *ee nhialic*, 'MACARDIT is Divinity', say the Dinka if asked what MACARDIT is, and they say the same of the other free-divinities here discussed. But also they will say, 'MACARDIT is bad', 'MACARDIT kills people', 'MACARDIT does not treat people with respect (kindness)', and 'MACARDIT is stupid'. These are statements which would not be made about Divinity, or about any of the other free-divinities.

The Dinka statement that 'MACARDIT is Divinity' cannot, therefore, be reversed. No Dinka says '*nhialic ee MACARDIT*', 'Divinity is MACARDIT'. Divinity is asked, in hymns and prayers, to help men and also sometimes to leave them in peace; MACARDIT is not I think invoked for help. This divinity can at the best be propitiated and kept away, as the following hymn asks:

> Great black one, if you are given a cow, you will hide yourself
> My black father, if you are given a cow, then you will hide yourself
> COLWIC,[1] if you are given a cow, then you will hide yourself.

MACARDIT is the final explanation of sufferings and misfortunes which cannot be traced to other causes more consonant with Dinka notions of Divinity as just. This divinity thus resolves a contradiction, between the Dinkas' experience of creative and constructive forces in human life, and that of the apparently pointless suffering which is part of the lot of men. MACARDIT presides over the ending of good things, the inevitable and sometimes brutal curtailment of human life and fertility. A Dinka said that MACARDIT was *jaak eben*, all the (harmful) Powers, and MACARDIT is addressed sometimes in the singular, as *yin*, and sometimes in the plural, as *wek*.

---

[1] This name is referred to on p. 83.

Sacrifices are made to this malign divinity as they are to Divinity and to other divinities which have benign aspects. There are differences, however, between the sacrifices for and attentions given to MACARDIT, and those for any of the others. The flesh of sacrifices to all other divinities is treated with respect (*aye thek*), a respect which involves primarily that it should be boiled and not roasted, for to bring it into contact with fire is disrespectful. The flesh of a sacrifice to MACARDIT is not thus respected and is usually roasted. Again, sacrifices for Divinity, other free-divinities, and the clan-divinities are usually made in the centre of the homestead of a man's senior wife, and the colours appropriate for oxen sacrificed are those well marked with white or, in some cases, red-brown, which are auspicious colours. The oxen appropriate for sacrifice to MACARDIT are black, the inauspicious colour, and sacrifice is properly made in the home of a junior wife, and at the edge of the cultivation away from the huts—that is in the direction of the forest, pointing away from the home, the centre of domestic life. Some Dinka say that the proper person to make the sacrifice to MACARDIT is the middle son of the junior wife. Eldest and youngest sons, the *kai* and the *kuun*, are in some respects equivalent among the Dinka, and both are more closely associated than the others with the clan-divinity of the father, which presides over fertility in humans and cattle. *Kuun ee jok*, 'the youngest son is (a) Power', one may hear Dinka say. To eldest and youngest is attributed a spiritual strength denied the middle sons, and they are ideally supposed to identify their interests with each other. They are also materially more fortunate than their brothers, for the eldest son inherits the control of the family herd from his father, while the youngest son inherits from his mother her homestead and the cattle which have accrued to her name through the marriages of her daughters. Both are thus provided for and are comparatively independent. The middle sons, dependent first on their father and then on their eldest brother, are considered less fortunate than the eldest or the youngest, and are thus appropriate makers of sacrifices for the malign divinity.

Again, when she bears her last child the junior wife of a man represents the end of her husband's procreative activity; and the appropriate place of sacrifice to MACARDIT is said to be in her home, and not in the home of the senior wife who is associated with the beginning of the husband's own family and lineage. Sometimes a special cultivation is dedicated to MACARDIT in the junior wife's home, and there one finds a peg or post of MACARDIT and a small shrine of ashes from the junior wife's cooking-fire. The junior wife makes periodical libations of beer, milk, and butter to propitiate MACARDIT at this shrine, so that her child-bearing days may not be cut short. The shrine is set apart from the homestead, where shrines to other divinities are found, and is thus dissociated from the home itself. It is said also that beasts may be sacrificed to MACARDIT in the forest, an idea which illustrates further the imaginative connexion between this harmful and anti-human divinity and the wilds.

MACARDIT is particularly associated with women. While men at sacrifices may become possessed by their clan-divinity or one of the other divinities, women are prone to possession by MACARDIT, for the principal danger from MACARDIT is that it ends fertility and promotes sterility. An ox may therefore be sacrificed to MACARDIT at a wedding, or some time later, if the bride fails in a reasonable time to bear a child.

Most Dinka say that the divinity COLWIC and MACARDIT are the same, and among the Rek Dinka who have had little contact with the Nuer one rarely hears the word COLWIC.[1] COLWIC among the Nuer is the spirit of a man killed by lightning,[2] and it seems to me that where its associations with this are known among the Dinka, they are known through acquaintance with the Nuer. For the rest, this Nuer power has been assimilated to their own MACARDIT, in a way very characteristic of religious syncretism among Nilotic peoples.

GARANG

The free-divinity GARANG has different symbolic colours and associations, and presents rather different problems of

---

[1] The names are given as equivalent in P. A. Nebel, op. cit., 1936. The word *colwic* does not seem to me to be a native Dinka word. In Nuer it could mean 'black head', since *wic* means 'head' in Nuer, but this is not so in Dinka. A text collected by Fr. Nebel and quoted in P. W. Schmidt, op. cit., 1949, p. 161, speaks of *colwic* in a manner entirely consistent with the Nuer conception of it, as meaning the divinity of those whose agnatic kin have been killed by lightning. I suspect that it is most clearly given this meaning among those Dinka who have had most contact with the Nuer, especially the Western Twic.

[2] Fully described in E. E. Evans-Pritchard, 'The Nuer Colwic', *Man*, 1949.

interpretation. Garang is the name given to the first man in the myth of the separation of earth and sky, and Garang is today a very common man's name. The free-divinity GARANG, however, is not this man, or is not simply he. GARANG is a Power of the sky which enters the bodies of some men by falling on them from above, and thereafter becomes their divinity. Such men are known as 'men of Garang', and are fairly common in Western Dinka country. Their fingers are frequently covered with rings and their wrists with bracelets, gifts made by mothers to such GARANG men for curing their children. They often also wear the leopard-skin, which is regarded as their distinctive costume.

GARANG is particularly associated with men; women, I believe, are never possessed by it. It tends to be inherited by the sons of those who are possessed or troubled by it, and to become a cult-divinity of particular families, ranking with their clan-divinities. MACARDIT, on the other hand, is the concern of everyone, like Divinity.

The Rek and Malwal Dinka say that GARANG has come into their land since the time of their grandfathers, and that it is spreading eastwards even now. It is certainly better known among the Western than among the Eastern Rek, and it seems to be little considered if at all among the Agar Dinka. It is generally thought that GARANG (and, some say, the other free-divinities also) have spread into Dinkaland from some point of diffusion in the region of the Western Twic Dinka, and the Eastern Rek know it primarily as a divinity of the Twic. No shrines seem to be made to GARANG in south-eastern Rek country, and there, though it has been heard of, it is said that it does not commonly possess people. In north-western Rek country, nearer the Twic, shrines to GARANG are very common. They are simply slight mounds of earth and ashes, 3 ft. or so in diameter, surrounded by low fences of thorn-branches from the heglig tree (*thou, Balanites aegyptiaca*) which is specially associated with GARANG, and with the horns and other indications of previous sacrifices sometimes seen on them. Some of the north-western Rek said that GARANG was now 'becoming everyone's divinity'.

Among the Western Twic themselves GARANG is associated with a snake, which is there its emblem. I never saw or identified this snake, but its colours, which are the significant feature, are red and white, and it is said to be about a yard long and rather thick. The proper name of this snake also is *garang*, and it is the clan-divinity of the Twic clan Pajook, for whom it operates like any other clan-divinity. Unlike most other clan-divinities it is thought to have influence beyond the confines of its own particular descent-group and has affected large numbers of individuals and families in other parts of the country.

GARANG is addressed, in prayers and hymns, as 'father' or as 'red father' (*wa malual*), for the colours associated with this power are reds and browns and tawny colours, particularly when these colours are found in association with white. So besides the snake *garang*, the emblems of GARANG are the giraffe and the ox colour-configuration *malek*, which is giraffe-coloured, and the heglig tree, the fruit of which is a brownish-yellow in colour. More generally GARANG is associated with red-brown, and red and white combinations wherever they occur in cattle sheep and goats, and in the red wood of the mahogany tree, and in the red ashes of dung from cattle which have eaten *apac*, one of the best pasture grasses of the Dinka.

I do not think it is possible to find with certainty any rationale for these colour associations; for the Dinka there is an imaginative connexion between the colours red, or red and white, and tawny and the sun, and between GARANG and the sun. A red and white bull, with a red-brown body and a flash of white on the belly, is called *makol*, and *akol* is the Dinka word for 'sun'. The clan Panyier of the Abiem Dinka has as clan-divinity the snake *garang*, and members of this clan may be called upon to sacrifice for rain when the sun is injuring people at the end of the dry season. It was said that a senior member of this clan, or any prophet of GARANG, might take a goat and raise it above his head, asking Divinity for rain, before cutting the animal's throat. Men of GARANG are also called in to treat sickness, particularly fevers, which they cure by spitting in blessing upon the feet and hands of the sufferer, and massaging away the fever with their hands, which they move upwards over the body of the sick man until the fever is driven out. GARANG may also be held responsible for small temporary indispositions. When I was travelling with carriers, one man suddenly started to vomit and was therefore sent home. He appeared the next day attributing his condition, which in my opinion was mild sunstroke, to GARANG.

GARANG possesses members of warrior and spear-master clans alike. The Dinka do not take all or most men of GARANG very seriously, and in their attitude towards them there is often an element of the humouring of eccentrics. Some men of GARANG, however, gain a higher reputation than others by demonstrating greater success in curing sickness, and because of the potency attributed to ashes taken from the dung-fires in the centre of their byres, the 'ashes of GARANG', upon which important oaths are sworn. All ashes, and even dust, placed upon the tongue or infused in water and drunk, may be used in oath-taking, but ashes of GARANG are resorted to in important matters. A man who lies in a testimony taken on such ashes expects death or serious misfortune; and since all Dinka seem to feel an accumulative guilt for false oaths they have sworn in the past, they from time to time free themselves from the consequences of perjury by taking a wether, the *nyong arop*, 'wether of the ashes', and having rubbed ashes upon it, wash them away with water. Minor men of GARANG are said to acquire ashes for oath-taking from the hearths of those who are better established; but always a man becomes a man of GARANG by being seized and made sick by that Power, and on recovery announcing that the Power has become his divinity, through which he may divine as I have described above.

The free-divinity GARANG and the free-divinity DENG are related to each other as kin of one degree or another, but the Western Dinka do not represent this relationship consistently. In hymns, which we may perhaps take as embodying the more 'orthodox' tradition, GARANG is sometimes referred to as 'the son of DENG' (*wen deng*). The following hymn, which is widely known through the country of the Western Dinka, mentions this relationship, and also displays some features of Dinka thought about the free-divinities generally:

> GARANG, son of DENG, has fallen from above
> If people assemble in the byre, it is life,
> KUR, and ABUK, and AYI NYANG[1]
> Great one, my father, I have accepted your word

[1] The first two of these are names of free-divinities later discussed. AYI NYANG was also said to be a divinity (*yath*), but my informants knew nothing more about it.

Come, diffuse, and bring coolness
The great bull, the creator [prophet] has fallen from above[1]
GARANG, son of DENG.

Another version of the same hymn is:

The shining master has fallen to the byre
GARANG, son of DENG.
First give unto me, divinity of my father;
My father comes from the place of creation
Fills the byre with life
KUR and ABUK AYAK[2]

Great one, my father, you have fulfilled your promise
You have diffused, you have brought coolness
The children of the prophet [creator] will rise early [to pray]
First give unto me, divinity of my father
The great shining master has fallen to the byre.

The expression translated as 'the shining master' is in Dinka
beny lo giliu. *Lo giliu* means 'radiant', and is said also to apply
to 'a man whose heart Divinity has pierced' (*ran ci nhialic gut
puou*) or 'a man without sin' (*ran cin guop adumuom*). The words
which are translated as 'diffused' are *rot tok*, which means 'to
rise' as smoke or a scent rises and diffuses, and here refers to the
way in which the life-giving spirit diffuses among and restores
the people. The request for coolness (which represents also
peace and ease) does not contradict the association with the
sun: for a Power which, for the Dinka, can produce one effect
controls its opposite.

Another short song about GARANG, composed by a prophet
of GARANG at some time as a protest against the behaviour of
people at a ceremony, is as follows:

Great GARANG is not at the feast
And all the people are stuffing themselves with food.

It was explained that this was a complaint on the part of
the prophet that the people were chattering and amusing

---

[1] When the Dinka are asked to interpret this line, it is clear that it does not
refer univocally either to Divinity as creator, or to the free-divinity GARANG. Both
are assimilated to each other, and also to the prophet of GARANG, and the hymn
honours all three. Similarly the 'shining master' of the next hymn refers primarily
to GARANG, but also to his human prophet.

[2] AYAK is regarded as the mother of ABUK, but otherwise could not be defined
by my informants.

themselves instead of concentrating on singing a hymn, a common situation at sacrifices. Another hymn, in which the colour-associations of GARANG are clearly presented, is

Pray the red and white[1]
Life is prayed for from the red one
Life is prayed for, pray the red and white
We will appease the great one (GARANG)
We of the family of Nyiwol[2]
Your bull will be tethered at its peg throughout the heat of the day[3]
And will you deceive me and not give me life
And come and follow me with evil
My father GARANG, and ABUK DENG
And refuse life to the ants (people)?

A Christian Dinka commenting on this hymn said that ABUK DENG was the mother of GARANG, and that GARANG interceded with his mother.

A war-song, collected among the Apuk Jurwir Dinka, of south-eastern Rek country, mentions again the trio of free-divinities GARANG, ABUK, and DENG. The similarities of allusion between this and the hymns already quoted which were collected several hundred miles away suggests the wide territorial range of this association:

Great bull with testicles has been killed[4]
It is Divinity

---

[1] In Dinka *nyalek*, which is a red (brown) and white heifer. Here it was said to mean GARANG.

[2] This name is an interesting indication of the Twic connexions of the GARANG cult. The Dinka regard this as an old hymn. The version given here was collected in one of the Awan tribes of the north-western Rek Dinka, and there Nyiwol was said simply to be the father of the original composer of the hymn. In fact, Nyiwol was the great-grandfather of an old chief of the Western Twic Dinka, who made a reputation as a prophet and founded a powerful lineage.

[3] The ox or bull will not be released to graze with the rest of the herd, but will be tethered to await sacrifice.

[4] The word here translated as 'killed' is, in Dinka, *gur*, and not the usual word *nok*. It was explained as the trampling or crushing to death of the victim which occurs at some Dinka ceremonies later described. This trampling seems to be associated with the sound of distant thunder, with its promise of rain. Fr. Nebel, op. cit., 1936, does not give a sacrificial meaning of the word *gur*. Capt. J. M. Stubbs, 'Notes on the Beliefs and Customs of the Malwal Dinka', *S.N. & R.*, vol. xvii, 1934, describes the killing of a beast for the clan-divinity, and quotes a text which includes the words *mior yath eguri*, which he translates as 'the bull of the yat is being sat on'. *Gur* does not mean 'to sit' in ordinary usage. Fr. Kiggen, op. cit., 1948, gives the following as the meaning of that word in Nuer: '*Guur*; -*a*: animal sacrifice

The dark clouds and the morning rain blow up
My mother ABUK, Divinity my father, help me
My father GARANG, help me Divinity my father
If we sleep abroad,[1] the white cow of my father
Will bring us cows
Avoid the spear, my age-set Mayom, avoid the spear
An affair of the great spear (a great fight)
O my club!
The spear-haft in the man's back quivers
DENG KUR is a powerful divinity.
If we sleep abroad, it brings cows
White cow of my father, I did not start the fight
The bulls meet head to head!
Cow which gave peace to my father
Cow bringing cows
Make peace as the Kongor tribe did with the Agar
Last year's fighting is ended
Last year's fighting thus is ended.

Divinity and the free-divinities GARANG, ABUK, and DENG (in a special figure later described) are thus all associated in songs, though Dinka are not consistent in their accounts of the relationships between them, and indeed in their service of Divinity and divinities the Dinka characteristically tend to associate them loosely together as here shown. MACARDIT alone stands apart in thought from the rest, in its unrelieved malignity.

ABUK

ABUK is figured as the archetypal woman and mother, and presides over the occupations of women. This is the only well-known divinity of the Western Dinka who is represented as female, and compared with the others she is of minor importance. Sometimes one hears mention of another female divinity, AYAK, but of her little more than the name is known. The divinity ABUK is sometimes said to be the same as the first

to the Dinka god. *Guur yang kuoth jaangini*—an offering of a cow to the God of the Dinkas. . . . They put grass in its nostrils and in its behind and in its mouth, the four open places, then it will be killed and skinned.' Professor Evans-Pritchard has seen among the Nuer such a method of killing a beast as an offering to the Python divinity. The act appears to imitate the suffocation of its prey by the python.

[1] 'Sleep abroad' refers to the custom of warriors on a cattle-raid. The 'white cow' was said to be a white cow of Divinity which belonged to the free-divinity DENG or DENG KUR (see p. 95).

woman, Abuk; she is also variously said to be the mother of the divinity DENG, or the wife of the divinity GARANG and the mother of DENG, or the wife of DENG and the mother of GARANG. Again the variety of these opinions suggests that no exact relationship is of great importance—what is important is that she is the female pole of various relationships.

Songs are sung by women to ABUK in connexion with the harvest. She is asked to bring plentiful grain so that the women (who are notoriously fond of beer and in any case are the brewers) shall be made happy with beer, sesame, and other fruits of the earth, as in the hymn quoted on p. 50 above. I have not found shrines to ABUK, nor cattle dedicated to her, and she does not seem to possess people or bring sickness as do the other free-divinities. Among the Western Twic Dinka (as among the Nuer and now the Anuak) ABUK is specially associated with rivers, and her emblem there is a small grey watersnake; but I have not found these associations so clearly present among the Rek Dinka, nor the association of ABUK with the pied-crow which is found among the Nuer.

DENG

The divinity DENG presents more difficult problems of description and analysis than the others do; for the figures and emblems of DENG, and also a kind of historical depth in the Dinkas' knowledge of it, present us with a more complex picture than in the case of the other free-divinities.

It has generally been held that the Dinka regard themselves as the children of DENG or DENGDIT, great DENG.[1] There are

---

[1] See, for example, H. C. Jackson, 'The Nuer of Upper Nile Province', *S.N. & R.*, vol. vi, no. 1, 1923. There the Nuer and Shilluk view of the Dinkas' ancestry is discussed. Professor and Mrs. Seligman found the same confusions or uncertainties as I myself found, and wrote: 'Another spiritual agency, Deng or Dengdit—literally "Great Rain"—has commonly been regarded as identical with Nhialic, as in our earlier publications, but this is certainly inaccurate so far as the White Nile Dinka are concerned and the same probably holds for the Bahr-el-Ghazal tribes. Our present opinion is that Dengdit is to be regarded as a spirit subsidiary to Nhialic, sometimes thought of as an emanation from or even in a sense as an offspring of Nhialic, analogous to the spirit Lerpio . . . but of greater power and commanding far wider belief. We may add that whatever may ultimately prove to be the precise connection between Dengdit and Nhialic it will certainly be close.' They add a legend in which Dengdit is obviously fused in thought with Divinity as described in our first chapter, sending the bird *atoc* to sever the connexion between heaven and earth, and then report: 'but among the Niel Dinka, he appears

certainly some clans among the Rek and Abiem Dinka—the
related spear-master clans of Payi and Parek, for example—
which regard themselves as ultimately descended from a Deng
(which is a common man's name now among the Dinka). I
have not found, however, that even members of these clans are
clear about the relationship of their ancestor Deng with the
divinity DENG, or with DENGDIT,[1] and the rest of these Western
Dinka do not, in my experience, say that the Dinka are all the
children of an ancestor, Deng. It may be that, in a metaphorical
sense, Dinka would say they were all the children of DENG, for
all Dinka know the free-divinity DENG, and DENG is the free-
divinity most closely identified with Divinity as a whole. We
meet here the typical lack of precise definition of the Dinka
when they speak of divinities. As GARANG, which is the name
of the first man, is sometimes associated with the first man and
sometimes said to be quite different, so DENG may in some sense
be associated with anyone called Deng, and the Dinka connect
or do not connect usages of the same name in different contexts
according to their individual lights, and to what they consider
appropriate at any given moment. Statements about the divinities, as represented in hymns, are imaginative and creative, not
dogmatic or doctrinal. There is no formal orthodoxy, and any
imaginative association which does not contradict the general
configuration of associations for particular divinities in the
mind of any Dinka can be accepted as an insight into the
nature of the divine.

DENG has many emblems and manifestations as compared
with the other free-divinities. It is the divinity most closely associated with the rain, with thunder, and with lightning: *deng*
is the Dinka word for rain, and Archdeacon Shaw in his hymns
from the Bor Dinka[2] has translated *DENG wa* (lit. DENG my
father) as 'Father Rain'; but despite the close association of
DENG with the rain I am not convinced that DENG the divinity

as a less remote being, who at one time ruled his tribe in human guise, and so
approximates to the super-human ancestors . . .'. C. G. and B. Z. Seligman, op.
cit., 1932, p. 179. Fr. Nebel, op. cit., 1936, distinguishes between *deng*, meaning
'rain' or 'thunder-shower', and Déng, Déngdit, 'ancestor and protector of the
Dinkas'.

[1] Capt. J. M. Stubbs, op. cit., 1934, found in his experience of the Abiem Dinka
that they clearly distinguished between Deng as the ancestor of certain clans, and
Deng or Dengdit as a free-divinity (to use the term we have chosen).

[2] Archdeacon Shaw, op. cit., 1915.

and *deng* the rain are thus totally identified.[1] It is true that rain is a manifestation of Divinity and that DENG as a divinity is closely associated with Divinity as a whole and therefore with the rain which is also so associated. Yet the Dinka expression for 'the rain is falling' is *deng a tweny*, while DENG the divinity, like other divinities, is said to *lony*, to fall from on high, perhaps with the sense of being released from on high. This verb would not normally be used of the rain.

Dinka nevertheless consciously connect rain, particularly the first rain, with human procreation and with Divinity: a man said to me, 'This rain which falls, is it not Divinity? When it falls, the grass revives and cattle thrive and the earth becomes cool. And a man sleeps with his wife again and dreams of his child.' Others pointed out that only men who were heartless or who had many cattle would sleep with their wives at the height of the dry season, when they were famished and tired by the heat. The coming of the first rains in Dinkaland is the end of a time of great discomfort and difficulty for many, and it is thought that sickness is at its worst before the rains come. It is true, at least, that with the rains the periodic attacks of cerebrospinal meningitis (along with smallpox the most feared of epidemics) abate. The coming of the rain thus brings and promises new life in the fullest sense of the expression, and ends a period during which, in the past even more than now when famine relief exists, many could expect to die.

With the first rains come violent thunderstorms and dark thunder-clouds; and the divinity DENG, in the very nature of the climatic conditions of the early wet season, is associated with the thunder and lightning which sometimes destroy, as well as with the life-giving rain. *Thiec deng*, the club of the rain, or *thiec DENG*, the club of DENG (for I am not sure which is intended, and it may be both), is a metaphorical name for the lightning which strikes people down. This is thought of as a direct intervention of Divinity in human affairs, and in thunderstorms it is customary to sit quietly and respectfully, for people are in the immediate presence of Divinity. Those killed by lightning are described sometimes as 'whom Divinity has seen'

[1] Though Fr. Nebel distinguishes Dengdit, as ancestor of the Dinka, from *deng*, rain, by different tones, he does not in his dictionary give DENG in the sense of the free-divinity here discussed.

or 'whom DENG has seen', or Divinity is said to have struck them on the head. They are not mourned. The Dinka will not even try to save the contents of a building fired by lightning, nor to put out the fire, for this would be to interfere with Divinity's or DENG's direct expression of will. There are no specially constructed shrines to DENG in Western Dinka country, as far as I could find out,[1] though here and there a large tree blasted by lightning is treated as a shrine for a few years, and the horns of sacrifices are found in its branches or at its foot. I was present when such a tree was cut down for firewood. 'It is long ago', the Dinka said. Of the divinities of the Western Dinka, only GARANG and MACARDIT have their own erected shrines. DENG and the clan-divinities are associated in sacrifice with Divinity and the ancestors, and all are comprehended in the same intention when sacrifice is offered at a single shrine in the homestead.

The colour of the sacrificial beast ideally appropriate for DENG is pied, with bold markings, or boldly spotted in black and white. The beast should therefore be either the *majok* configuration (which has a white body with black at the head and shoulder and on the rump) or the *marial* (which has a bold white belly-flash on a black body) or the *makwac* (spotted black and white). The fittingness of these colours is explicitly related to their representation of thundery skies. The whiteness on the darkness calls to the Dinka mind the patterns of a cloudy sky, or the flash of lightning across the dark night sky.

Unlike other free-divinities, but like Divinity itself as I later discuss, DENG does not exist only in a single mode, and the Dinka themselves cannot state clearly the relationship between DENG unqualified and the various figures of DENG, which are represented by qualifying the name DENG with different suffixes. Fr. Nebel has reported,[2] as I always found, that Dinka will say in general that DENGDIT (great DENG) is 'Divinity itself'. Yet he quotes two hymns which I reproduce below, of which he says: 'These two songs are addressed by the Twic-Denka to their snake-totem Deng, and by the Rek Dinka to their ancestor

[1] C. G. and B. Z. Seligman, op. cit., 1932, p. 180, speak of shrines to DENG among the Cic and Agar Dinka. They also give a drawing of a major DENG shrine in the form of a cattle-byre and huts, the Luak Deng or 'byre of DENG' now in Nuerland. A note on this shrine by Dr. P. P. Howell is appended to this chapter.

[2] As quoted by P. W. Schmidt, op. cit., 1949, p. 158.

DENG.[1] It is clear, from them and from other hymns, that representations or figures of DENG have in common at least that what is said of, or addressed to, one, may be appropriate for another. The hymns quoted by Fr. Schmidt might be translated as follows:[2]

> DENG my father, DENG of surpassing greatness.
> My father DENG, a great person through the ages.[3]
>
> Great DENG refuses (to listen), Great DENG refuses (to help)
> If not honoured, he is offended, indifferent,
> My father DENG, do not forsake me,
> My father DENG, do not abandon me to the Powers [of sickness].[4]

DENG is sometimes spoken of in particular localities as DENG *da*, 'our DENG', sometimes with the implication that others have a different DENG. This is consistent with the association of DENG in any figure with rain, for the first rains are patchy and local, and members of any community are interested in *their* rain, the rain which may fall on their village on a particular day and pass by a neighbouring village which needs it. DENG also is called DENG *nhialic*, 'DENG in the above' or 'DENG Divinity', and DENG *madier* which means, I think, 'DENG Governor or Director', the Dinka here having borrowed the Arab word (*mudir*) for their conception of the Governor as head of everything.

In one or another figure DENG also appears as the clan-divinity of certain clans, and then carries with it the ability successfully to pray for rain. I have said that the prophet Arianhdit's clan-divinity was DENG *piol* ('DENG (in the figure of) clouds'; another similar figure is DENG *nhial*, 'DENG (in the figure of) the above', and more common is DENG *yath*, 'DENG divinity', in the sense of clan-divinity, the emblems of which, in different parts of Western Dinka country, are a small green snake and a larger red and white snake. These are all figures or refractions,

---

[1] 'Diese beiden Gesange richten die Twiy-Denka an ihr Schlangentotem Deng und die Rek Dinka an ihren Ahnherrn Deng.'
[2] Op. cit., 1949, p. 147.
[3] Deng Vater, Deng der Höhe,
Vater Deng, Größer der alten Zeit.
[4] Dengdit erhört nicht, Dengdit verweigert.
Wenn nicht geehrt, ist er beleidigt,
Vater Deng, verlaß mich nicht!
Vater Deng, überlaß mich nicht dem Bösen!

as they have been called,[1] of DENG, the free-divinity presiding over rain and associated phenomena of the above. DENG thus bears a generalized relationship to all Dinka (as indeed do the sky and the rain) but is known by a number of distinct titles in accordance with distinctions between different groups.

Of special interest, since we can trace this title historically to its source, is DENG *kur*, *kur* being an ox-name derived from the *makur* configuration, which has a white body with black markings round the eyes. The Western Dinka understand this figure of DENG to be that which entered the body of some Eastern Rek prophet some two generations ago. It is said of DENG *kur* (here both the divinity and the prophet, for the prophet and his divinity are not in such situations distinguished in thought) that he 'was Divinity', and appeared to a man by putting two fingers through the roof of his byre and raising him up when he was sick. He is also said to have fallen from the sky with a white cow or bull. These fragmentary notions are all I could find among the Western Dinka, and it is of particular interest to be able to trace them to their source, for to do so shows how knowledge of the manifestations of Divinity and divinities spreads by hearsay. We know that Dengkur, historically, was the Nuer prophet Ngungdeng, father of Gwek who rallied the Nuer against the British, and in whom the divinity DENG was manifested. Dengkur built a great pyramid in Lou Nuer country (far from the Dinka of whom I write here, and quite beyond the horizon of their knowledge) in honour of DENG. There can be little doubt that the DENG *kur* of the Western Dinka refers to this Dengkur, for in some Dinka songs the name DENG *kur* is used interchangeably with the name DENG *nuer*, DENG of the Nuer.[2] If indeed, as seems likely, DENG first made himself known as a divinity to the Dinka, it would seem in this case as though, having manifested himself also among the Nuer, he had become known in that special manifestation among the Dinka again, and at a great distance from his Nuer manifestation.

There seems to be no theoretical limit to such special figures or refractions of DENG; and though I have described those which

---

[1] This matter is fully discussed in E. E. Evans-Pritchard, 'The Nuer Conception of Spirit in its Relation to the Social Order', *American Anthropologist*, vol. lv. 2, 1955.

[2] In fact Ngungdeng seems, like so many Nuer, to have been partly Dinka by origin.

are prominent among the Western Dinka, there are others in other parts of Dinka country which are associated with particular clans as their clan-divinities. Among the Bor Dinka, for example, we find DENG *panuet*, again said to 'be' Divinity, but *panuet* comes from the name of an ancestor, Anuet, who was possessed by DENG, and who handed on 'his' DENG to his descendants. DENG *panuet*, therefore, is DENG as he appears in relation to the descent-group of Anuet. Mr. Chatterton, a Sudan Political Officer with much experience of the Dinka and Nuer, recorded in an official file that among the Rueng Dinka *every* clan called DENG by a different name, and some difficulty once arose because when a chief was appointed by the Government, those over whom he was placed in authority claimed that he called upon DENG by a different name from that which they used. This situation could not arise among the Western Dinka, for DENG, in specific forms with distinct names, is the clan-divinity of a few clans only, and the main cults of other clans are directed towards their own clan-divinities, which are not figures of DENG. Yet many, and perhaps most, Dinka families keep a cow dedicated to DENG—the *weng atiem DENG*, cow of the 'ghost' or 'shade' of DENG—which they should not part with, and the milk from which (as from cattle dedicated to clan-divinities) should not be drunk by strangers.

The Western Dinka cannot give an account of Divinity and the free-divinities, in their relationships and in their differences, more consistent and expository than that represented above in my description of what they say. It may be that other Dinka have a more clearly formulated notion of the relationships between Divinity and others of the free-divinities, especially DENG. Certainly, other writers have made such suggestions.[1]

But to attempt to produce an account, however lucid and ingenious, of a kind of Dinka 'creed' and pantheon, would be to start by concealing what, as I see it, is the clue to our understanding of the facts—that is, that Dinka religion begins with *natural* and social experience of particular kinds. This correspondence

[1] The published material on this subject is thoroughly analysed in P. W. Schmidt, op. cit., 1949, *passim*. The authors whom he has consulted, however, vary very much in knowledge and reliability, and in their desire to schematize. A very interesting discussion of the divinities of the Bor Dinka is to be found in R. T. Johnston, 'The Religious and Spiritual Beliefs of the Bor Dinka', *S.N. & R.*, vol. xvii, 1934.

between the Powers and experience is perhaps most clearly apparent in relation to the clan-divinities.[1]

APPENDIX TO CHAPTER II

By DR. P. P. HOWELL

[I am most grateful for Dr. Howell's observations upon the important shrine which I was unable to visit. Dr. Howell has written without reference to the main part of my own study, and thus provides an independent view of some of the problems of Dinka belief so far discussed. He has also provided the three hymns which I reproduce in his translation and with his notes.]

(i) *Some Observations on Luak Deng*

Dr. Lienhardt has asked me to contribute a short note on Luak Deng, an exceptionally elaborate shrine of some significance among those Dinka tribes now living east of the Nile. I do so with some diffidence because although I had an opportunity of visiting the shrine on three separate occasions and came to know its keeper, Rak Yaak, pretty well, I was at the time engaged in a study of the Nuer unconnected with the origin and religious significance of Luak Deng. I had hoped to extend my inquiries and to produce a more comprehensive account of the Dinka tribes of the area, particularly the Rut and Thoi, but in the event was never able to do so. The Rut Dinka of this area are bilingual and my inquiries were made largely in Nuer. Reference should also be made to the mound or 'pyramid' of Aiwel Longar on which I have already written.[2] This latter religious centre, now virtually abandoned, is often associated with Luak Deng in Dinka folklore, though I believe this to have evolved as a later explanation of the existence of two entirely separate culture-heroes who probably originated in the early mythology of two quite distinct sets of Dinka people. In the short account of Luak Deng given below I have made no attempt to interpret the significance of the shrine in relation to Dinka religion in general. The value of this description can only lie in the fact that few people have visited Luak Deng and little or nothing has hitherto been published on the subject.

[1] We are not, of course, in a position to decide whether intrinsically the experience of the Dinka which we seek to understand is in our categories 'natural' or 'supernatural'. I say only that we can best understand Dinka religion by grasping its basis in a 'natural' experience accessible to ourselves.

[2] P. P. Howell, ' "Pyramids" in the Upper Nile Region', *Man*, 1948, pp. 52, 53.

Luak Deng, or Luak Kwoth, the 'cattle-byre of God' as the Nuer call it, is situated near Cuai in the northern part of the country now occupied by the Bar primary segment of the Gaawar Nuer. The whole of this area was once occupied by Dinka tribes but they were driven out, divided, and widely scattered by incoming hordes of Nuer about four, or at most five, generations ago. Round the shrine and within a few miles of it there remains a small Dinka community of some three hundred souls who, unlike so many Dinka lineages in that part of Nuerland, have retained their identity and have not been wholly absorbed into the tribal structure of the Nuer. These people are of Rut Dinka origin and retain close links with the main body of that tribe, though separated from them by more than fifty miles.

Briefly the history of this area (which must one day be the subject of a separate and more detailed study) was one of a series of invasions by groups of Nuer from their original homeland west of the Nile, first into the Zeraf island,[1] and then in an easterly direction across the Duk ridge and towards the Pibor River. The picture in the early years of the nineteenth century shows the Zeraf island occupied by the Ngok Dinka in the north and the Luac Dinka in the south, with the Rut Dinka east of the Zeraf River in the country later occupied by the Gaawar Nuer, and the Thoi Dinka north and east of them. East again the Padang Dinka extended from what is now Lou Nuer country northwards across the Sobat River, with a small Dinka tribe or section known as the Ric on the middle part of the Duk Ridge, and the Nyarraweng to the south. By the end of that century the whole of the Zeraf island had been occupied by the Lou Nuer, who drove the Ngok and Luac Dinka northwards towards the Sobat but were later themselves evicted by the Thiang, Lak, and Gaawar Nuer tribes; the greater proportion of Rut Dinka country had been occupied by the Gaawar Nuer; the Thoi Dinka, once a more numerous people, had been reduced to small pockets now living east of the Rut; and the Padang and Dwor Dinka had been driven northwards across the Sobat. Only the Nyarraweng Dinka had been able to escape large-scale incursions into their territory, and one can conjecture with some certainty that their present boundary with the Gaawar Nuer would have been pushed much farther south had not Nuer expansion in that direction been checked by the establishment of the Anglo-Egyptian Administration at the turn of the century.

This series of invasions left the Dinka peoples of the area scattered, confused, and probably much reduced in numbers, and without an exhaustive investigation of their genealogies, which they themselves

---

[1] The area bounded by the Bahr el Jebel, the Bahr el Zeraf, and the White Nile.

have in many cases forgotten, it is not easy to reconstruct the relationship of the various groups of Dinka who must have formerly lived in
much closer association than they do now. As will be seen, this makes
it difficult to assess the true significance of Luak Deng in the past,
though there seems little doubt that it was of considerable importance
in the tribal structure of the area. Similar shrines, though none built
on so large a scale, are to be found in other Dinka areas east of the
Nile, but such evidence as is available suggests that Luak Deng was
of particular importance to the Rut, Thoi, Nyarraweng, Padang,
Dwor, and Ric, and some lineages of the Twij, known as the
'descendants of the sons of Marbek', and in certain respects was a
symbol of their association.[1] Certainly those Dinka tribes speak with
nostalgic longing of the days when the Nuer had not come. In those
days the sons of Marbek maintained the shrine by collective effort,
each tribe, or more likely particular lineages within each tribe,
having specific functions to perform. Such emotions are reflected in
many traditional songs and Luak Deng is often referred to, often
expressing a sense of guilt that the *luak* has been neglected. Most of
these Dinka tribes still send representatives to the shrine on special
occasions and assist in rebuilding it when the need arises, though
many do not honour their obligations today. Some Dinka of the area
bury their dead facing in the direction of Luak Deng.

Luak Deng consists of not one but three cattle-byres and four
dwelling-huts. The largest and most important is that of the culture-
hero Deng Garang,[2] and is now only a replica of the original,
although the foundations of what is held to be the ancient byre are
still carefully preserved. Besides this are the byres of Garang, Deng's
father, and Pajok, his maternal uncle. Behind the cattle-byres are
the dwelling-huts of Deng's female relatives: of Abuk, his mother;
Arek, his wife; Kerciek, the mother of Pajok; and Nyancar, Pajok's
wife. The relationship of the spiritual owner of these dwellings is
therefore:

[1] 'The sons of Marbek.' Marbek is often alleged to be a descendant of Aiwel
Longar. The genealogical relationship given is:

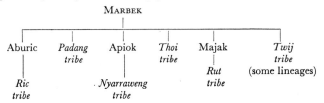

[2] Deng Garang is often referred to by bull or honorific names, e.g. Rial,
Monycaam ('the left-handed one'), Nyiel, Kerjok, Madhol.

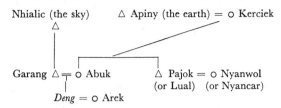

It will be seen from this that the Deng is the issue of a union of Garang, son of Nhialic, the sky, and Abuk, daughter of Apiny, the earth. The arrangement of the homestead is that of a Dinka domestic group in which the notable feature is the common residence of both paternal and maternal kin. This suggests the nature of the religious concept of which the shrine is an expression and a material symbol. In front of the huts of Abuk and Arek are two sacred trees on which are hung offerings of cattle-horns, meat, iron bangles, and tobacco. Near the entrance of Garang's byre is a thick well-polished cattle-peg to which animals of sacrifice are tethered. In front is the mound of cattle-ashes found in most Nilotic homes and known in Nuer as *gol wic*, and at the side is the *riek*, or ancestral pole. While the cattle-byres are open to inspection, the huts of Abuk and Arek are blocked with matting and are carefully guarded against intruders; only the priests of Deng may enter.

On the three occasions on which I visited Luak Deng, Rak Yaak, the 'High Priest' of the shrine, would not allow me to enter these huts. Mr. H. G. Wedderburn-Maxwell, a former District Commissioner of the area, told me that he had once been allowed to look inside and had seen many old rifles of ancient pattern, spears, bangles, and decaying ivory. The whole area is surrounded by huge trees, and there is a large pool of water south of the shrine. Beyond is the dancing-ground, which is used both for religious ceremonies and normal social dances.

The first Englishmen to visit Luak Deng were El Miralai G. E. Matthews Bey and Mr. W. C. P. Struvé, who in 1907 marched through Gaawar Nuer country by way of Luak Deng to Awoi to visit Deng Likea, the Nuer 'prophet' and war-leader, often referred to as the prophet Diu.[1] They describe the shrine as follows:

> Luang Deng is the Mecca of the Dinkas and Nuers and contains a shrine of their deity Deng Dit, a palisade standing on higher ground near a picturesque pool of water surrounded by *Ardeiba* and *Suba* trees. The keeper of the shrine is Deng Agweir, who was curiously reticent on the origin of the sundry bones and immature

[1] See E. E. Evans-Pritchard, *The Nuer*, Oxford, 1940, p. 186, and P. P. Howell, *A Manual of Nuer Law*, Oxford, 1954, p. 31.

tusks that embellished the trees and portals of the huts of this mysterious deity.[1]

Deng Agweir died in the late thirties. He was succeeded by his brother's son, Rak Yaak. The genealogy of those Rut Dinka who are traditionally guardians of the shrine throws no light on their origin and it is clear that they do not consider themselves direct descendants of the mythical owner of the shrine, Deng Garang.

There are two sacred drums attached to the shrine, though these are not the originals, which were hidden in the bush and never recovered during the first onrush of the Gaawar Nuer. Both are long cylindrical drums of typical Nilotic pattern, fitted with ox-hide caps joined by thongs. Each has its 'calf', a much smaller replica of the same pattern. The present drums are known as Bor Deng and You Garang respectively, the first name in each case referring to the colour of the ox sacrificed at their dedication. Bor Deng was made in Nyarraweng Dinka country in 1928, but was captured in the Nuer raid on Duk Faiwel before it could be delivered. It was subsequently recaptured by Mr. Wedderburn-Maxwell in the course of military operations against the Nuer and later returned to its true owners.

Both Nuer and Dinka traditions show that although the priests of Deng fled northwards into Thoi country during the first invasion of Nuer, the shrine was never desecrated, although the buildings fell into disrepair. Luak Deng is now treated with great respect by the Nuer, who have by long association now come to treat it almost as their own. No man can safely approach it without making some small offering, usually by throwing tobacco in the direction of the shrine.

The shrine is frequented by individuals suffering from domestic troubles, infant mortality, and sickness, and sacrifices are frequently made. The method of sacrifice is quite different from normal Dinka practice since the animal is not speared but is expertly cast, its throat being cut with a special spear kept for the purpose.[2]

Collective ceremonies are also performed. In most years, at any rate when the rains are late in breaking, rain-making ceremonies are held. Animals are sacrificed, and the rainstone of Deng, *pam* Deng, is brought out and rubbed with the intestinal fluids, and water is poured upon it. Although other rainstones are said to have existed in the past among the Thoi and Rut Dinka, I know of no other used by Dinka today. The stone is of granite, possibly from the Zeraf hills, the only source of stone within hundreds of miles. The mud

---

[1] Unpublished government records.
[2] This is the normal Western Dinka practice (G. L.).

fire-screens (Nuer *buor*) which are built outside the huts of Abuk and
Arek are also of exceptional interest since they are of abnormally
large size, though similar in pattern to those found in all Dinka
homesteads and regarded as a symbol of the domestic home.

Deng Garang, whose spirit is present in the shrine, is frequently
mentioned in Dinka mythology, and although the details of his
wanderings are quoted by Dinka with a wide variation of detail, it
is significant that he is almost always in one way or another associated with another Dinka culture-hero, Aiwel Longar.[1] The story
told by the present occupants of the shrine is as follows. Deng Garang
originally came from the north, but travelled far south into Twij
Dinka country, accompanied by Aiwel Longar. Luak Deng, or
rather the high ground on which the shrine is now built, was originally occupied by the ancestor of the Thoi Dinka, a man of exceptional spiritual powers known as Mutjok, who was eventually ousted
by Deng. The story relates how Mutjok had a fine herd of red
cattle. On his arrival Deng noted these cattle being driven into the
byre at night. Next morning, to the astonishment of Mutjok and his
followers, the cattle had changed colour. Mutjok did not at first
suspect Deng, but being friendly towards him told him that his sons,
together with his own children, might suck at one of the cows. Two
of Deng's sons took the right teats and two of Mutjok's the left,
but though milk poured in streams into the mouths of Deng's
children, the teats sucked by the sons of Mutjok remained dry.
These displays of magical power caused Mutjok to recognize Deng
Garang as his spiritual superior and to abdicate from his position as
paramount spiritual leader of the area.

Little mention is made of Aiwel Longar in this particular story,
though the Rut say that he accompanied Deng Garang at the time.
Together they built the cattle-byre with the help of the Dinka tribes
of the area. A surprising feature of this story is that the byre was
originally built without doors. Important tribal leaders were in turn
summoned by Aiwel and bidden to say where the door should be,
but all failed the test until at last a man named Gargar gave the
right answer. Gargar was appointed by Aiwel as his successor, and
assistant to Deng. Aiwel then moved westwards across the Zeraf
River to Jumbiel, where he built the Pwom Aiwel, the pyramid of
Aiwel, which exists to this day.

Stories about Aiwel Longar are legion and his association with
Deng Garang in Dinka mythology is not restricted to that I have
quoted above. As already suggested, a comparative study of such
mythology among all Dinka tribes east of the Nile might well reveal

---

[1] This is not so, in my experience, among the Western Dinka (G. L.).

that the cult of Deng and the cult of Aiwel originated among two distinct sets of Dinka peoples who have in the course of history migrated from different areas and merged, either in the course of conquest or friendly association. This would account for the fairly widespread association of these two mythical figures.

(ii) *Three Hymns collected by Dr. P. P. Howell*

[These hymns are known to the Rut, Thoi, and Luac Dinka, of whom those Dinka chiefly described in my own account know little or nothing. Some of the proper names necessarily remain obscure.]

(i) We bend our knees to GARANG and Kerjok
DENG of the byre (*luak*: byre or shrine) help me
Father it is you who will let me go through your legs[1]
You will give us the ashes called Muonylek[2]

(ii) BUK (ABUK), mother of DENG
Leave your home in the sky and come to work in our homes
Make our country to become clean like the original home of
    DENG,
Come make our country as one; the country of Akwol
Is not as one, either by night or by day
The child called Deng, his face has become sad
The children of Akwol have bewildered their chief's mind.

(iii) Oh we are going to DENG
At our ancient byre (shrine)
Let us reach up to the poles of the byre
In our original home. I have put sandals on my feet[3]
Nyiel is going to his byre[4]

[1] To go through the legs of a person: ritual in which sick persons crawl through the legs of a magician, leaving the sickness behind.

[2] Muonylek (connected with the ox-colour *malek*) probably refers to sacred ashes.

[3] i.e. as for a long journey.

[4] Nyiel, as well as being a personal name, is the python, though whether it has that meaning here is not clear (note by G. L.).

III

DIVINE UNITY AND MULTIPLICITY.
(ii) CLAN-DIVINITIES

I

IT will be remembered that the divinities—free-divinities and clan-divinities—belong to a wider class of Powers, and are described by the Dinka as 'Powers which are related to human beings' (*yath ee jong e ruai ke koc*). From the Dinka point of view the free-divinities described in the last chapter *force* this relationship upon persons individually, irrespective of their tribe or descent-group. They then correspond to experiences (which I later try to analyse) which are potentially common to all Dinka as individuals, and even to the Nuer neighbours of the Dinka also, while Divinity understood as a unity corresponds to experiences common to all men. Some Dinka assert that the free-divinities are comparatively recent introductions, and they are certainly prepared for revelations of new free-divinities which may enter Dinkaland at particular times and places, and from there perhaps spread to other areas. In a hymn, Dinka sing:

Let us pray to the master, the original master, the master of the
  centre of the camp,
Our masters [now] are not masters of time long past,
Let us pray to the master, the original master.

and I was told that the interpretation of this was that the Dinka turned to an original master of the fishing-spear, and away from the diviners inspired by MACARDIT, GARANG, and other free-divinities. 'Master', *beny*, is a title for any religious leader, and now for any government official. More particularly, it is used for masters of the fishing-spear, representatives of the long-established priestly clans of Dinkaland. It is asserted by many Dinka that long ago (*watheer*) they knew only Divinity, and DENG who was 'Divinity itself', and the clan-divinities. Of these clan-divinities, the most powerful, because the most effective when called upon for help, were those of the masters of the fishing-spear, and it was these masters, and not masters of free-divinities, who mediated between Divinity and their tribes and subtribes.

This view which many now hold finds some support in the earliest account of the Dinka by a Dinka in English, the work of a man captured as a child by slave-raiders and eventually brought by a missionary to England where he became an evangelist and married, I believe, a widow in Scunthorpe. This man, Hatashil Masha (really Macar) Kathish, wrote two books[1] in praise of his people, and with the intention of showing the original purity of their religion and morals. He reports:

The religious rites before going to war, were very significant of their belief in an unknown God. The Chief as Priest would rub the knees of all the warriors with milk and butter, asking God to fill their bones with marrow, and ease their joints, and give them a brave heart to do credit to themselves before their enemies. The Chief (who was called Beyn 'the all-sufficient') then anointed himself, sprinkled dust on his head, and sat in the burning sun all day fasting and praying for the success of his army. This service was a duty which required no remuneration. *Prayer for success or protection was not allowed to be performed by such persons as ventriloquists or those who suffer from indigestion, or necromancers.* [My italics.] The Dinka people, as a nation had a wonderful faith in the Supreme Being's power to help and deliver in all times of trouble, in answer to their Chief's prayers.[2]

It would seem here that by 'ventriloquists, or those who suffer from indigestion, or necromancers', diviners are indicated, and the text suggests that originally these did not have the religious reputation which some of them now have. As some Dinka now say, there were originally only Divinity and the masters of the fishing-spear and their clan-divinities. Inspiration and strength and protection came from clan-divinities, and in describing them, we begin to explore the relations of Divinity with a

[1] Hatashil Masha Kathish, *Jehovah Nissi, A Life Story* and *The Ethiopia Valley*. From internal evidence it would seem that the author was a boy in Dinkaland some time after the middle of the nineteenth century. In a preface to the latter work he writes that he is 'better known as Salim Wilson, the black evangelist of the North'. Despite a tendency to idealize his people before their contact with foreigners, Kathish refers to some features of Dinka life which have not changed up to the present day.
[2] *The Ethiopia Valley*, p. 50.

permanent Dinka social order, and with their experience of that permanent order.

In a later chapter the reader will find many examples of the way in which Divinity and clan-divinities are invoked before a sacrifice. The following is part of such an invocation made by a master of the fishing-spear of the important clan of spear-masters Pagong, 'the House (clan) of the Hedgehog':

So be it. You of my ancestor ('great father') Luol, and you of my ancestor Ayok, son of Luol, and you, (clan) divinity of my father, I tell you what I have to say. And you, flesh (*ring*) of Pagong, I call you in my prayers, and you *awar* grass of Pagong, I call you in my prayers, and you great hedgehog of Pagong, I call you in my prayers. I call you, because you support us, and if we call upon you then you will hear us because we are your children, and if a man calls upon the divinity of his father, he must get something from it because he is its child. You, divinity of my father, you will help. And now evil has overtaken us.

Here, Flesh (*ring*), *Awar* (a grass), and Hedgehog are all clan-divinities of the spear-master clan Pagong, which takes its name from one of them, the hedgehog (*gong*). They are what the Dinka call 'divinities of the father' (*yeeth wun*), usually addressed in the singular as *yanh wa*, 'divinity of my father', and it is by this, their direct and original association through the father with all the paternal ancestors, that the Dinka distinguish what we have called clan-divinities from free-divinities. If a Dinka is asked what his divinity is, he may, if he has been personally affected by one of the free-divinities, mention its name; but if he is asked what the divinity of his clan is, or the divinity of his father, or of his ancestors, he will give the name of his clan-divinity, that which he inherited from his paternal ancestors and which he thinks of as linking him with all of them. The clan-divinity, 'that of the father', follows (*bwoth cok*) those who have inherited it, supporting and protecting them. They rely upon it to help them when they are travelling and lonely. They may call upon it for help in misfortune or danger, and if they neglect sacrifices to it, they expect it to bring sickness.

Most, but not all, clan-divinities are manifest in, or inform, material species, in which species they may receive special attentions from their clansmen; but clan-divinities are something more than the material emblems which symbolize them.

The emblems are of secondary significance, as may be shown by an example. The clan Padiangbar, 'the house of Adiangbar', founded by Akol Adiangbar, has as one of its divinities Giraffe; its members, therefore, have a special relationship with all giraffes, and will not spear them. Its members will say 'Giraffe is our (clan) divinity' (*mir ee yanhda*), but they would not say '*giraffes* are our *divinities*'. Of any particular giraffe, a man of this clan would say, 'I do not kill it, it is our divinity'. The emblems are many, therefore, though the divinity manifest in them, or represented by them, is one.[1] As mentioned earlier, this distinction is made in this account by the use of the capital letter for the clan-divinity, as 'Giraffe', and of the small letter for any particular instance or emblem of it, as 'giraffes'.

In some parts of Dinkaland giraffes have not been seen for many years, and there are members of this clan with Giraffe as divinity who have never seen a giraffe. This is also the case with some members of clans with the clan-divinity Elephant, in country where elephants have not been seen for many years. I asked men of the Padiangbar clan who had never seen a giraffe how Giraffe could help them, when it was no longer found in their part of the Dinkaland, and what indeed would happen if all giraffes were exterminated, so that (as we put it here) the emblems of the Giraffe divinity ceased altogether to exist. They replied that it would make no difference at all. Giraffe had helped their ancestors and it would continue to help them, their children, and that even if all giraffes were dead there would still be the *atiem mir*, the 'ghost' or 'shade' of giraffe which would support them as strongly as ever. So by use of the word *atiep*, a shade, Dinka are able to make the distinction between the 'spirit', or divinity, Giraffe, and any particular giraffe or giraffes, though naturally they do not normally find it necessary to do so.

Though most clans have divinities with emblems which still exist among them as material species, it is thus not necessary that they should. An old man of the clan Pareng, for example, which has the *reng* colour-configuration in cattle as one of its

[1] To this extent the Dinka clan-divinities resemble 'totems' as defined by Sir J. G. Frazer, *Totemism and Exogamy*, 1910, pp. 3–4. Since not all the clan-divinities have emblems which are material species, I have thought it better not to use the word 'totem' in this account.

divinities and the members of which will not keep a beast of this configuration, told me that another clan-divinity, *Arec*, was 'a tiny little thing in the river *which men never saw*'. In studying clan-divinities, then, we have to deal with something more and other than the veneration of natural or artificial species and objects in their physical form.

The clan-divinities even of the Western Dinka alone are too numerous to list at all completely, but the following paragraphs give some account of their variety. I begin with some of the more important spear-master clans, which have, in addition to the clan-divinities mentioned below, the common divinity of spear-master clans called *Ring*. This literally is 'flesh', and because of its importance is separately discussed later in the present chapter.

The spear-master clan Pagong has the divinities Hedgehog and *Awar* grass, as we have already mentioned. Most lineages of this clan also claim a Power of the river, named *Malek, Malengdit,* or *Maleng yath,* as a divinity. Malek is the name of the river-Power which impregnated the mother of the first master of the fishing-spear, Aiwel Longar, according to Western Dinka stories. It is also the Power to which smallpox is attributed, and hence, in a sense later discussed, Smallpox is a divinity of this clan. Some lineages of Pagong also incorporate among their divinities the Fresh-water Oyster (*jual*), and other species with strong riverain associations, because the genitor of the clan-founder was a river-Power. The clan Paghol, 'the House of Thigh-bone', has the Thigh-bone as its divinity. Members of this clan will not break the thigh-bones of beasts, and, more widely, respect the thigh and upper leg of men and beasts, though when they acquired their divinity, in circumstances later described,[1] it was the thigh-bone of an ox only which was given to them for veneration. Some lineages of Paghol also have *Malek* as clan-divinity, and members of the clan generally express regard for this Power, though not all at once mention it as their clan-divinity. Parum, 'the House of Arum', Pabuol, 'the house of Abuol', and Padior, Pakwin and Palau, which are related lineages, are collectively called *wen dyor*, which is 'the sons of the women'. In Western Dinkaland, there are somewhat vague and confused traditions which derive this group of clans

[1] Chap. V.

from women of the household of Jiel, the husband of the mother of the first master of the fishing-spear.[1] The divinities of these *wen dyor* are *Rual*-tree (the 'sausage-tree', *Kigelia ethiopica*), Winnowing-tray (*atac*, or *atany dyor*, 'the winnowing-tray of the women'), and among some at least a red snake known as *aiwel yath*. I have not seen this snake, which is said to be a type of cobra (*pyen*). Pajiek, 'the House of Ajiek', who was its founding ancestor, has the divinity *Wec*-grass (*Sporobolus pyramidalis?*). Objects made of this grass, which is used primarily for brooms and rings for carrying pots on the head, are also accorded special treatment, and even the act of sweeping, which calls to mind the grass from which brushes are made, is sometimes spoken of as a divinity of this clan. Payi, 'the House of Ayi', so named after its founding ancestor, has Sycamore-tree (*kwel*, a giant *Ficus*) for clan-divinity. Some lineages also express attachment to *Malek* or *Maleng yath*, as in the case of Pagong and Paghol mentioned above. Pangwet and Pariath, both named after their founding ancestors, venerate DENG in the figure of light clouds, DENG *piol*. In addition Pangwet has the divinity Cattle-tick (*acak*), and some lineages at least have the Catfish (*cur*). This fish is related to rain, since there is a story of how it went into the sky to bring rain. *Cur*, the catfish, is the Dinka name for the constellation Scorpio. Pariath has the Elephant, in addition to DENG in the figure of clouds. Patek has the clan-divinity Crocodile, and some lineages also say that Fire is their divinity. This list is sufficiently representative of the clan-divinities of spearmaster clans.

The warrior clans, called collectively *kic*, do not have the important divinity Flesh. They vary considerably in size and area of distribution, from Padiangbar which is perhaps the largest and is found all over Western Dinkaland, to small lineages which are confined to very limited areas. Padiangbar, named after its founding ancestor, along with a related clan Paceiny, has the divinities Heglig-tree (*thou*) and, in places, Giraffe. Pajieng, 'the House of Ajang', has Black Cobra (*pyen col*). Pakeou, called after its founding ancestor, has Gourd (*kuot*). Padolmuot and Paguor both have the divinity Lion, and Padolmuot in addition speaks of Ant-hill (*rel*) as clan-divinity. Lions often hide in the bushes which cover large ant-hills.

[1] As described in Chap. V.

Smaller clans are Pareouken, with its divinity Cattle-egret, Pa-kwacdiem, with Hippopotamus, Pamanjur (Fire and Water), Pagor (Deleib Palm), Patuic (a species of moth), Paluoth (Mud-fish (*luth*)), Paluac (a type of grain, Pestle, and Deleib Palm from which mortars for grinding are made), Panior (Pelican and Viper), Pagak (Deleib Palm and Viper), and Pawan (Monitor Lizard).

In addition to the clan-divinities mentioned above, the following have been listed as clan-divinities in various parts of Dinkaland: Tamarind tree (*Tamarindus indicus*) and several other trees, *Apac* grass (*Echinocloa stagnina*), Vulture, Head (that is, the heads of animals), Heart (the hearts of beasts), a species of grain-eating bird, Termite, Jackal, Stone, a species of lizard, Needle, Saddle-billed Stork, Crested Crane, Slow-worm, the river Nile (*kir*), the Forest (*roor*), the planet Venus, and Comets (*cyer*), and various figures of DENG already mentioned, some with snake and some with cloud emblems. Among the Bor Dinka the following are prominent clan-divinities: Fire in association with Flesh, Spears (two particular ancient spears), GARANG with a snake emblem which is also found among the Rek and Western Twic Dinka, and grasses and snakes of various kinds.

The Dinka have no theory about the principle upon which some species are included among clan-divinities, and some omitted. There is no reason, in their thought, why anything might not be the divinity of some clan. When I asked what I myself should invoke as my clan-divinity, it was half-jokingly suggested that I should invoke Typewriter, Paper, and Lorry, for were these not the things which always helped my people and which were passed on to Europeans by their ancestors? So, clan-divinities are explicitly regarded by the Dinka as represent-ing, for their clansmen, qualities and strength which a man derives from his agnatic descent. More widely, for each indivi-dual they represent what is derived from heredity, for a man should pay special attention to the divinities of his mother's people. Some go further and profess respect for the divinities of all those, male or female, from whom they can trace descent, though in fact few remember the clan-divinities of those of their maternal kin in the female line more distant than their maternal grandmothers. As in Dinka descent-group structure agnatic descent is remembered in clear outline and non-agnatic descent is gradually forgotten, so the clan-divinities are remembered as centrally important, and divinities acquired matrilineally fade in significance. They are not representative of any abiding social groups.[1]

In the examples given, there are indications of a significant feature of Dinka thought in relation to divinities in general. In some cases the emblems of a divinity or divinities form little groups of associated images, as it were, around a central theme. The imagery of the divinities of the Pajieng clan is an illustration of this. It may be said of this clan, by those who are not members of it and when no members are present, that its clan-divinity is Excrement. Pajieng, as recounted later in this chapter, acquired the black cobra as its clan-divinity; this is a deadly snake, and the Dinka regard its swift bite as inevitably fatal. The black cobra, as I have elsewhere described,[2] is for this and other reasons specially associated with night-witches, who are thought to use its blood and venom to injure their victims. The darkness of the cobra and its unexpected and deadly attack connect it with the secret nocturnal operations of the most powerful witches the Dinka can imagine; and as the cobra sheds and leaves its skin (*roc kuac*) and disappears, to appear anew and claim further victims, so witches are thought to renew themselves and return to cause further injury. One of the signs which lead a man to suspect witchcraft is to find human excrement in his homestead when he wakes in the morning. To excrete in the homestead, as an anti-social act of particular unpleasantness, is thought to be a witch's habit. Hence the total constellation of imagery around the black cobra includes human excrement, and thus the notion that Excrement may be the divinity of the clan which respects this creature.

In this case the set of associations of the black cobra is not accepted by its own clansmen, and they would regard the suggestion that they respected human excrement as disgusting and untrue; but it illustrates the process of associative thought

[1] In some instances, where whole lineages are defined by their descent from a woman, a subsidiary clan-divinity is regarded as coming from that ancestress; but it is rare for the Dinka to know the name of the clan from which such a founding ancestress came, and by no means usual for her clan-divinity to be known.

[2] In 'Some Notions of Witchcraft among the Dinka', *Africa*, vol. xxi, no. 4, Oct. 1951.

by which divinities and emblems of certain clans may form
little groups. The association is obvious in the case of Pajiek,
for example, who respect brushes, head carrying-rings, and
more widely the whole action of sweeping, because brushes and
carrying-rings are often made of the *wec* grass which is their
clan-divinity. Less immediately obvious to those unfamiliar
with the Dinkas' world is the association of Lion and Ant-hill
as divinities of a single clan; but it is comprehensible when one
knows that in Dinkaland the lion takes shelter in the tangled
bushes of large over-grown ant-hills, and it is in such places
that it is most likely to be surrounded and killed. Those who
wish to avoid lions in Dinkaland are thus wise also to avoid
large ant-hills. Again, it is natural that Paluac should venerate
the *deleib* palm and a species of grain in association with the
pestle, for the connexion between the grain and the pestle is
obvious, and for the Dinka, the association of the pestle with
the *deleib* tree from the trunk of which the mortar is often made,
is equally clear. The association of the divinities Giraffe and
Heglig Tree for some subclans of Padiangbar, and the further
association of these with the free-divinity GARANG, has underlying it the associations of red and tawny colours with which all
are connected. The constellation of associated images around
the theme of the river, which explains some of the consociated
divinities of the clan Pagong, is considered in a later chapter.[1]
Fire and Water, in another clan, go together because water
extinguishes fire, and respect for the clan-divinity involves
among other precautions that of not bringing its emblems
into contact with fire. Such connecting threads cannot be
demonstrated in many cases, and often the divinities of a clan
may be consociated by chance, it is supposed, or by some significant marriage in the past, the children of which have been
unusually influenced by the divinity of their mother's agnates.
I draw attention, however, to ostensible connexions, in the
belief that a deeper knowledge of the Dinka than I was able to
acquire might reveal latent associations of the type we have
mentioned, even where it would not occur to the Dinka to
make them explicit to themselves.[2] Since interconnexions and

---

[1] Chap. V, *passim*.

[2] For example, the river-Power MALEK, which impregnated the mother of the
founding ancestor of Pagong and is also the grounds of smallpox; Hedgehog, and

PLATE IV

a. Libation

b. Shading the goat

PLATE V

a. Invocation

b. Sacrifice

imaginative associations at a profound level may be so taken for granted by those who make them that it would be impossible to conceive that everyone might not take them for granted in the same way, we must sometimes look behind the explicit 'collective representations' to discover the implicit principles upon which they may be understood.

Though some clans take their names from their divinities, many take them from their founding ancestors. Pagong, for example, is 'The House of Hedgehog', but Pajiek is 'The House of Ajiek'. Hence, one does not *necessarily* know which clan a man belongs to by knowing the name of his clan-divinity, nor the name of his clan-divinity by knowing the name of his clan. I have never heard Dinka inquire spontaneously into the divinities of strangers, though they inquire into their clan-affiliations and their homelands.

A clan-divinity thus does not face outwards to other clans, so to speak, appearing as a label or sign by which outsiders may know with whom they have to deal, but relates inwards to the clansmen. By knowing from genealogical evidence that they are agnatically related, they know also that they are united in relation to a common divinity, which for them symbolizes their relationship. A traveller, able to gain a wider experience of Dinkaland than any Dinka, finds clans of different name now widely scattered over the country yet retaining common traditions and divinities, and many clans even in the same area share divinities without being genealogically linked. To have a clan-divinity in common is no bar to intermarriage, for exogamic prohibitions are ultimately calculated by the counting of actual degrees of relationship genealogically. A clan-divinity common to two people thus does not necessarily signify clan-relationship, though clan-relationship necessarily implies a common divinity. The knowledge and experience of relationship, that is, comes first.

Even in Western Dinka country there are undoubtedly many

Awar grass, are all divinities of Pagong. The ox-colour *malek* is red or tawny and white, and is associated with markings on the lek fish (*Heterotis niloticus?*). The pustules of smallpox are *malek* in colour, and their 'weeping' associates them with water, and hence the river. The *awar* grass is a grass of river-banks, and produces bristly, compact tufts when burnt. These tufts resemble the bristles of the hedgehog, which is addressed in hymns as *wa maiyual*, 'my hairy (bearded) father'. Masters of the fishing-spear are sometimes said to grow beards more readily than others.

small clans which I never encountered, and it is difficult, therefore, entirely to exclude the possibility that anything might be
the clan-divinity of some clan. It may be worth mentioning,
however, that varied though the list of clan-divinities is, there
are many things and creatures which are very striking and
which yet do not seem to be common clan-divinities. The most
obvious of these are the leopard[1] and the buffalo, both of which
are frequently referred to in songs and hold great imaginative
interest for the Dinka. It may be noted that these beasts, unlike
the lion which usually does not attack unless it is first attacked,
will pursue and injure men as no other animal of Dinka country
does. They are therefore beasts which must sometimes be injured by Dinka in self-defence, while the principal rule of
behaviour towards the emblems of the clan-divinities is that
their clansmen should avoid injuring them, particularly shedding their blood. Crocodiles also attack people, but those who
have Crocodile as their clan-divinity are supposed to be able to
control its attacks both upon themselves and upon others, and
crocodiles will certainly sometimes avoid men, whilst it is supposed that the leopard and the buffalo are more aggressive.
Again, few of the many varieties of antelope[2] which abound
in Dinkaland seem to be clan-divinities. Dinka are not keen
hunters, but they all hunt a little when the grasses are fired at
the beginning of the dry season, and antelope of various kinds
are then the staple game. There are many species of lizard
which are not clan-divinities, and none of the batrachians seem
to be represented. Among the birds, again, there are many
varieties which are not represented, including some which are
again of imaginative importance and figure in many songs and
metaphors. Few fish, considering the varieties which exist and
which are important for the Dinka, are represented. Insects,
grasses, and plants are minutely represented in proportion to
their numerous kinds.

Respect for the clan-divinity requires that its emblem should
not be killed or injured, and in principle that it should not be
eaten. But of the clan-divinities we have listed, few are of any
dietetic importance, and where they are the respect paid to

[1] This is in my experience of the Rek Dinka and those to the west of them.
Leopard is the divinity of one Agar Dinka clan.
[2] One Agar Dinka clan has the bushbuck.

them may yet permit them to be eaten. Crocodiles, for example, may neither be killed nor eaten by the clan which has Crocodile as its divinity, but crocodiles are nowhere an important article of Dinka diet. The fruit of the heglig tree is a rather important subsidiary item of food at certain seasons; but the respect paid to heglig trees by those who have Heglig as a clan-divinity does not preclude the eating of its fruits. The prohibition is against cutting it down and burning its wood. Giraffe-meat is relished by the Dinka, and a giraffe may provide food for many men at a time of hunger. Members of the clan with Giraffe as their divinity have argued (perhaps casuistically) that they are permitted to eat giraffe-meat, but are prohibited from spearing giraffe and shedding their blood. Catfish are popular fish, and may neither be killed nor eaten by those who have Catfish as their divinity; but there are many other sorts of fish which are preferred, and the prohibition involves again little real hardship. Where artificial species are divinities (Head Carrying-Ring, and Pestle, and Gourd prepared as a container for food) their emblems may be used in the ordinary way by those whose divinities they are, but they must not be deliberately broken or burnt or cast away where someone else might break or burn them. Very many objects in common use in the home, and particularly important pieces of equipment for cattle-herding, are absent from the lists.

Look at it how we will, then, it is impossible to see the species selected as clan-divinities as clearly connected collectively according to any principle whatsoever, except that of their being clan-divinities and of their being non-human; and indeed, if Dinka stories of how clans acquired their divinities are considered, it seems that the Dinka themselves often think of them as acquired by chance—a chance association, though an important one, between the founding ancestor of a clan and the species, which then becomes the clan-divinity of all his descendants. In general there would seem to be a negative correlation between the species which have a reputation for being specially powerful clan-divinities—for not all divinities are thought to have the same power—and the natural resources of Dinkaland most important for material and economic well-being.[1] In Western Dinkaland such necessary things as Fire

[1] The divinity Flesh later discussed may again be a significant exception.

and Water are not thought to be very powerful clan-divinities, while on the other hand, species of little or no utilitarian importance, such as the hedgehog, the sausage-tree, and the giant *ficus* (though these latter give welcome shade), rank very high as the emblems of powerful divinities. It seems clear that we cannot understand the meaning of the clan-divinities by concentrating on their nature, or rather the nature of their material emblems, in themselves. They are not selected as divinities because they are practically important. They derive their importance from their associations with the agnatic descent-groups of the clansmen who revere them, and their reputation for comparative strength or weakness from the religious reputation of the clans with which they are linked.

Stories tell how clans first received their divinities and account for the prohibitions against injuring them. Some spear-master clans were given their divinities by the first master of the fishing-spear Longar (Aiwel), as is recounted in the myths of Chapter V. The divinity Flesh in particular comes from him. The warrior clans are not thought to have received their divinities from him. I have heard it suggested, by members of important clans of spear-masters, that some of the minor warrior clans have really no clan-divinity at all—that they have in fact invented the divinities which they now lay claim to.

When Dinka are asked generally where their clan-divinities came from, they usually say simply that they were given to their clan-ancestor by Divinity in the beginning, to help and protect them. The stories of how the particular divinities were acquired by particular clans are subsidiary to the idea that Divinity intended that each clan should have its divinity or divinities, and so disposed matters, either directly or indirectly. Some Dinka in fact do not know any more circumstantial story of how their clan-divinity came to them. Others know elaborate stories, and I give as an example here one of the most elaborate, that which tells how the clan Pajieng, a large and important warrior clan distributed through much of Rek country, received its divinity, Black Cobra. This story was collected in the Awan (Awan Pajok, or Awan Kon Pioth)[1] tribe of the North-Eastern Rek, where Pajieng is the foremost warrior clan. It derives some of its detail from local relationships between clans within that

---

[1] There are several tribes called Awan.

tribe, in a typical manner later illustrated at some length in accounts of the myths of the origin of spear-master clans. The story is as follows:

A black cobra bit a cow belonging to Ajang, the ancestor of the Pajieng clan. He speared it with a spear belonging to Akol Adiangbar, the founder of the Padiangbar clan, and the cobra escaped down a hole in an ant-hill with the spear still in its body. Ajang went and told Akol Adiangbar what had happened, and offered to compensate him for the loss of his spear. His offer was refused, and Akol insisted that he would be satisfied with nothing less than the return of his own spear. Ajang therefore went and tunnelled into the ant-hill, and reached the land of the cobras, a land like Dinkaland but inhabited by cobras.

Here it was said that the cobras were in the form of men and women, but they were 'really' cobras and could change their form into that of cobras. When the Dinka speak of changes from human to animal form—as, for example, when they hold that some men are really lions and can change into lions—they suppose that the outward form changes, but the essential nature remains the same. A person human in outward appearance may therefore be *in his nature* an animal of some kind. It is of some importance for an understanding of Dinka thought about the animal emblems of some of their clans, to recognize that they do not always draw a sharp dividing line between the human and the animal as we draw it. When, as later in this story, a man marries a snake and they have children, it is not suggested that he sleeps with it in its animal form, but that it has a human form while really belonging also to an animal world.

In the land of the cobras, Ajang found the cow which the cobra had bitten, and the cobra itself displaying the wound made by his spear. The cobras asked him what he wanted, and he asked for the spear. He put himself at their mercy, and told them that they might kill him, or keep him there, or return the spear, but he would not return without it. He told them that they might keep the cow as compensation for the injury he had done the cobra. The cobras returned his spear, and told him also to take one of their daughters to be his wife. They offered him a choice of wives—the *byar* (a red cobra?), the *kwalek*, a snake which is said to break into several pieces when it strikes, each piece having poisonous fangs (a mamba?), and the black cobra. He first thought of choosing the *byar* because it was so beautifully red,[1] but the cobras advised him to choose the black cobra, and to take her home as his wife and keep her until she had borne two children, when she should return to them.

When Ajang arrived home with the spear and his cobra wife, he found that Akol Adiangbar's son had died, and that Akol had buried his son in his, Ajang's, sleeping-hide. Ajang demanded its return, refusing a substitute, and Akol in a rage dug it up, put his spear through it, and flung it into the river.

Therefore, it is explained, there is even now bad blood between Pajieng and Padiangbar, and they cannot live happily together as neighbours.

The cobra-wife bore Ajang two children, who, at a dance, bewitched some of the children of Akol Adiangbar, and so they still hate each other. Pajieng, the children of Ajang, are thus all related (*ruai*) to the black cobra, and they do not harm it and it does not harm them.

The clan Pajieng is not everywhere in Western Dinkaland on bad terms with Padiangbar. In some versions of the story of the acquisition of Cobra as clan-divinity, Padiangbar is not involved. Captain Stubbs has recorded a version of this story collected among the Malwal Dinka,[2] in which it is a quarrel with Ayi, founder of Payi, which indirectly results in the marriage of Ajang to a cobra.

Most stories—except those myths of the beginnings of spearmaster clans which appear in a later chapter—are much simpler than this. The clan Pangwet has Cattle-tick as one of its divinities because its founding ancestor is said to have been born with a lump like a tick on his head. Giraffe is one of the divinities of Padiangbar because a giraffe once rescued the founding ancestor of the clan from a flood by carrying him on its neck. It refused any payment for this act, but said that in future the children of the giraffe and the children of Padiangbar should help and not injure each other. Crocodile is the divinity

---

[1] The Dinka admire copper-coloured girls, or those whose blackness shows a reddish tinge. They are less common, of course, than others amongst the Dinka, who are mostly intensely dark in pigmentation.

[2] J. M. Stubbs, op. cit., 1934, pp. 250–1. In this version the quarrel arises over a black cow, which in the end is given to Ayi ('Ayei') by Ajang. His clan then will never keep a black cow in its herds. It may be noted, as characteristic of the Dinkas' consistency in colour imagery, that the cow, like the cobra, is black and not of some other colour.

of Patek because its founding ancestor was born as a twin with a crocodile. The crocodile was returned to the river and 'severed from' human beings with the sacrifice of a goat. Therefore children of Crocodile and children of Patek do not injure each other. It is sometimes said that Lion and Hippopotamus were acquired as divinities similarly, through twin births with men, and Professor and Mrs. Seligman[1] speak of twin-birth stories as 'usual' among the Dinka farther east. The head carrying-ring of grass, which is one of the divinities of Pajiek, is sometimes said to have rolled ahead of the ancestor of the clan when he was lost, and guided him home.[2]

Most Dinka show less interest in the stories of how clans acquired their divinities than in the myths of the origin of the masters of the fishing-spear. I sometimes got the impression that the stories were being made up by some Dinka as they went along, by connecting remembered fragmentary details into a narrative. The stories are not frequently referred to, nor are their details equally well known to all adult members of a clan. They provide an historical reason, if one be needed, for the behaviour of men towards the emblems of their divinities, but they do not provide a complete explanation of that behaviour. If a Dinka is asked why he will not injure the emblems of his divinity, he will be more likely to reply that if he were to do so he would suffer by it than to give these historical explanations.

Clans usually have more than one divinity, though one or two in each clan are of primary importance. Different subclans of the same clan often have different secondary divinities,

---

[1] C. G. and B. Z. Seligman, op. cit., 1932, p. 149. An interesting variant of the straightforward 'twin-birth' story is also reported there (p. 146). This relates to a Niel Dinka clan which has Hyaena as clan-divinity. Professor and Mrs. Seligman write: 'A woman was sleeping when a hyaena stepped over her. Some people wanted to kill the hyaena, but others restrained them, seeing some purpose in the animal's behaviour. The woman eventually gave birth to a boy who limped like a hyaena. . . .' Resemblances of this kind play a considerable part in confirming, for the Dinka, the intimacy of the relationship between certain divinities and their human clansmen. Thus it is thought that children whose arms or legs are bent are thus affected by the Crocodile divinity if they respect crocodiles, and children with large heads are directly affected by Hippopotamus, and so on.

[2] Fr. P. A. Nebel, op. cit., 1948, includes this detail in a lengthy text about the origin of the Parek clan of the Malwal Dinka. There can be no doubt that common traditions relate widely separated Dinka clans which never normally come into contact with each other. Fr. Nebel also includes several other interesting texts about the origins of various clans.

though they have the same clan-name and the same original founding ancestor. The Dinka do not expect all subclans of a clan, which may now be widely separated, to have exactly the same range of divinities; for the divinity is 'that of the father', and when ancestors more recent than the founding ancestor of a whole clan have been for a long time separated in different parts of the country, their descendants, as groups, are differentiated in a way which is reflected in their different range of divinities. The divinities of members of a clan thus may differ as the range of those who are recognized as particular agnatic ancestors differ, while they are the same in so far as the same founding ancestor is recognized for any clan throughout Western Dinkaland. Here we see that primary clan-divinities have a close connexion with the Dinkas' experience of the widest groups they recognize, in any area, as having the same agnatic descent. We can illustrate the nature of that connexion, and also perhaps justify our use of the word 'experience', by considering how the divinity and its emblems are treated and addressed.

In invocations, as we have seen, a clan-divinity is addressed by its clansmen[1] as 'you of my father', and 'you of my ancestors'. It is further addressed and spoken of as *wadit*, 'my "great" father', which means 'my grandfather' or 'my ancestor'. The emblems of the divinity—giraffes, for example, where a clan has the divinity Giraffe—are usually referred to by clansmen as *wen e wa*, 'son of my father', as distinct from 'son of my mother', and hence as 'half-brother' in a classificatory sense. All clansmen regard themselves in this way as 'half-brothers'. In invocations the clan-divinities are usually addressed by their proper names, as 'Fig-tree' or 'Hedgehog' followed by the word *wa*, which has the sense of 'my father' or 'of my father'. Examples of this are seen in many of the invocations given in Chapter VI. Also, as will there be seen, and as appears in the brief invocation quoted earlier in this chapter (p. 106), the clan-divinity may be invoked as 'that [thing] of' certain specific named ancestors who have been of particular importance in any lineage the members of which are invoking it.

---

[1] Fr. P. A. Nebel, op. cit., 1948, p. 122, includes the following statement in Dinka: 'We believe that God gave its totem to every clan, to protect it like a father and we shall honour it as a father.'

Emblems of a clan-divinity are thought to show special preference for the homesteads of their human clansmen, and in some
cases are thought to manifest themselves in the clansmen themselves. So it is said that members of a clan with the divinity
Cattle-tick are sometimes born with tick-like lumps on their
heads, as was their founding ancestor; those clans which have
Rual, Sausage-tree, as their divinity may have children born to
them with fleshy lumps resembling the fruits of that tree growing on their fingers.[1] These signs give pleasure to the parents of
such children, for, as a Dinka said, it is 'as though their divinity
has shown itself' (*ciet yahnden ci rot nyooth*). Also the emblems
of tree, plant, and grass divinities are thought to spring up of
their own accord in the homesteads of their clansmen. In fact,
one often finds a homestead of Payi with a giant ficus, a homestead of Parum or Padior with a sausage-tree, a homestead of
Padiangbar with a heglig, or a homestead of Pajiek in which
a tuft of the *wec* grass is growing. Once a widow of a man of
Padiangbar to whom I was speaking under a *heglig* tree in her
homestead stroked the tree with a caressing gesture and said
'this is my husband'. Padiangbar has Heglig as a clan-divinity.

The Dinka deny that they themselves have anything to do
with planting these emblems; indeed, they think it significant
that they should have come *of themselves* to be near their human
clansmen, whose faith in their divinities they certainly strengthen by doing so. Since the emblem of the clan-divinity is not
injured it is of course more likely to survive in the homestead
of its clansmen if by chance it starts to grow there. Crocodiles
also are thought to come to live in the rivers near people who
have Crocodile as their divinity, and snakes come to the homes
of those who have Snake divinities. Again, there often seems
to be a certain basis for this belief, in that in places where
snakes are particularly numerous, there are sometimes concen-
trations of members of clans with Snake divinities, and where
crocodiles are numerous, there are members of the clan with
Crocodile as divinity. It is said that snakes, when they come to
live in the huts of their human clansmen, are given bowls of
milk and sometimes anointed with butter, and that they will
not injure those who are their kinsmen. No Dinka, however,
will readily kill a snake, though those who do not have poisonous

---

[1] More fully referred to on p. 123 below.

Snake divinities do not encourage them to live at close quarters with them.

I have never seen snake-emblems anointed with butter or fed with milk, and in my experience those who have dangerous creatures as emblems of their divinities—snakes, crocodiles, and lions—usually treat them with as much circumspection as other Dinka, though they have the faith that they will not be injured by them, and often that they can exercise some control over their dealings with other people. If a man should be injured by the emblem of his divinity—and it is known that this sometimes happens—the injury is readily put down either to some fault on his part, or to the fact that this particular emblem was not really a clansman, or had broken kinship. All Dinka are required to be careful and gentle with the emblems of their clan-divinities and the special avoidance of dangerous emblems by their clansmen may result in the latter's being less readily injured by them than are others, who are less careful with them and notice them less. The Dinka perform no ceremonies for the multiplication of the emblems of their divinities, and on the whole seem to take little interest in whether or not they are numerous.

Although Dinka speak of themselves as the 'children' of their clan-divinities, they do not suppose themselves to be physically descended from them. Even in the case of those divinities acquired by twin-births, the human clansmen stem from a collateral, human line of descent, separated from that of the creature born as a twin with their ancestor.[1] The crocodile born with the clan-founder, for example, is put back into the river, there to propagate its kind. It does not itself give birth to human beings, and, of course, many of the clan-divinities I have mentioned have emblems which could not be thought to give birth at all. But though the clan-divinity is not itself an ancestor, it is fully merged in idea and linguistic usage with all agnatic ancestors, and with the whole of Dinka experience of ancestry and agnatic heredity.

---

[1] Though in a note on the Pabut of the Agar Dinka in a government file in Rumbek, and apparently written by a Dinka, the following statement occurs (I quote *verbatim*): 'To prove this relationship of Pabut and the crocodile, it is obvious that certain people of Pabut can bore pure crocodile, which is then put in the water where it became real crocodile.'

The following is a text written by a young Dinka, then a schoolboy, William Deng. It displays some of the essential features of Dinka thought about clan-divinities as seen by a Dinka himself, and introduces some important terms which I later explain. William writes as a member of the spear-master clan Parum, which has the divinity *Rual*, the striking *Kigelia ethiopica* with its sausage-like fruit hanging on long strings. These fruits are used in various children's games, and as ready-made headrests and stools. He writes:

The tree called *rual* is a very great divinity for three descent-groups (*dhieth*): Parum, Pakwin and Pabuol. Parum is very great throughout Rek country, followed by Pabuol. Pakwin is great in the land of the Malwal Giernyang.

The three descent groups came out from the three children of one wife; Akwin, and Rum, and their sister called Abuol. Parum are the children of Rum, Pakwin are the children of Akwin, and Pabuol are the children of Abuol their sister.

These three descent groups keep cattle dedicated (*mac*) to *Rual* at the central hearth (*gol nhom*). The rope with which the cow of *Rual* is tethered is decorated with rings, and the milk of this cow is not drunk by any other man, any mere stranger. If it is a man from one of these three descent-groups, he will drink. These descent groups do not marry between themselves, for if they do so, they are injured by [the disease brought by] incest. They have other divinities which they respect (*thek*), but I write only of *Rual*.

A man who is related to *Rual* will not cut down the fruit of the *rual* tree; if he does so, he will become blind. Tiny children are strongly forbidden to play with the fruits of the *rual* tree. The mother of a child of *Rual* also very much respects the *rual* tree because of her child, but not because she is related to *Rual*.

It is only the husband [man] who is related to Rual, and if a girl of another descent-group marries, then those from whom she marries are not people of the same divinity. But her brother and mother, those who have received the cows, will not treat the *rual* tree lightly either. Its wood is not to be used for firewood or burnt, and its fruits are not to be cut off [by them], for if they do so, then the son of their sister [who has married a man of *Rual*] will be blinded. And they do not drink the milk of the cow dedicated to *Rual*.

If a *rual* tree is in the homestead of a man related to it, it is not cut with an axe. They respect the foot of the tree, and they sprinkle it with beer when beer is made. When the milk of the cow of *Rual* is brought to the home from the near-by camp, part of it is first put in a bowl decorated with rings, so that it is first to be taken to the foot of the tree and poured there before the rest of the milk is drunk.

Children are called after *Rual*, a girl being called Arual, a boy Rual.

A bull is kept, uncastrated, at the central cattle-hearth, and when it is grown it is killed at the forked shrine (*ghoro*) in the home of the eldest son; if the father is still alive, it is killed [*for Rual*] in his home; and it will be a 'green' [*mangok*—greenish-grey] bull, like the rual *tree* itself.

If a child is born with growths like the fruit of the sausage-tree on its fingers, the parents are delighted because they think it is as though their divinity had revealed itself. These growths stay on the child's hands for about fourteen days. This really happens and I have seen it. I myself was born with these fleshy things hanging from the small finger, but they disappeared after two weeks. I was told by my mother and I have seen it happen even now. Hymns are sung when the bull of *Rual* is killed.

People of Parum say that they found grain first in the fork of the *rual* tree. It was a bird called *alal* [the hammer-headed stork] which brought it out of the fork of the tree. . . . Parum, now, are the masters of grain (*bany rap*). If the birds eat the grain, a man of Parum is called to protect it. This may not be true throughout the Dinka tribe but it is true in some places, especially where I live. Parum and Pakwin are spear-master clans; Pabuol is not[1] because it is descended from a woman.

The important thing is that things connected with the *rual* tree should not be put on the fire.

Most of the text is self-explanatory, but there are in it several references to religious observances towards the clan and other divinities, which require further comment. I begin with the notion of respect, *thek*, which is the attitude any Dinka must adopt towards his clan-divinity, and which is expressed in his behaviour towards its emblem, where that emblem is of a nature which permits it. A man can respect the emblem of a tree-divinity, for example, by not burning its wood or cutting it down; he cannot physically do anything with clouds, the emblems of DENG-clouds, though if this is his divinity, he yet speaks of respecting it.

Thek, respect, is a word which in Dinka has two strands of meaning, related to each other in that language, but which, in

---

[1] In fact in some parts of the country members of Pabuol do regard their clan as a spear-master clan.

English, we are forced to tease apart. Only one of these strands is conveyed by the word 'respect'. An ill-mannered or aggressive child, without decorum in the presence of those senior to him in age and status, is said to have no respect (*acin athek*). A man who behaves with respect is courteous to his elders and superiors. He will join an assembly of senior men or strangers in a markedly quiet and self-effacing way, gently snapping his fingers to indicate where he wishes to pass, and taking care not to jostle anyone as he takes his place. When approaching a homestead such a man will pause before entering its central court-yard and clap his hands to announce his presence and ask permission to enter. Teasing, joking, and horseplay, which are not inappropriate between those who regard themselves as familiar equals and perhaps in some sense rivals, are improper between those who practise *thek*.

At the least, then, this type of respectful behaviour covers what we should call 'good manners'. It involves particularly a firm control of personal self-assertiveness, and to a greater or lesser degree a conspicuous self-effacement which demonstrates that aggressive intentions are absent.

It is from the element of demonstrated unaggressiveness in respectful behaviour that the word *thek* derives its second range of meanings, which may be summed up as 'avoidance'. In this sense a man is required to *thek* his wife's mother, and to a smaller extent her father. 'Respect' here requires that he must not be seen by his wife's mother, and especially must not be seen naked by her,[1] for some time before and after the marriage. He must avoid approaching her homestead, and make a detour if he should see her approaching in the distance on the path which he is taking. He may not eat in her homestead, or with his wife's father, and is required from time to time to send them gifts.

In the sense of 'avoidance', *thek* may be used where no respectfulness in our sense is present. The Dinka may thus say that they *thek* certain kinds of food eaten by the Bahr-al-Ghazal Luo—voles, for example—but this is not 'respect' in any English sense, for such foods are much despised. A man will also *thek*,

---

[1] Though a bridegroom during the marriage ceremonies wears a leopard-skin which covers his genitals, the Dinka emphasize that it is primarily the buttocks which must be covered before in-laws.

avoid, a woman in her periods,[1] so that the word is also a euphemism for menstruation; but the relationship does not here
demand either the scrupulous avoidance prescribed for the
relationship with the wife's mother, nor the display of kindliness,
gentleness, and solicitude which according to the Dinka should
characterize the relationship between a man and his mother's
brother.

It is difficult to discover to what extent the Dinka regard the
various senses of a word as related to each other. During inquiries into the meanings of the term, I started a discussion
among a group of Dinka. One of them stated that there were
three different kinds of *thek*—respect for seniority and polite
behaviour generally, the avoidance of menstruating women
and of the mother-in-law, and the special treatment of the clan-
divinity and its emblem. He suggested that these meanings
were unrelated.[2] Other Dinka denied this, and one of them gave
a revealing example, saying: 'When your brother has married
a wife, and you go to visit them, and the wife cooks food for you
and brings it, kneeling to offer it to you, is that not *thek*? And is
it not because you are related with each other? And is it not the
same thing as offerings and sacrifices to the clan-divinity—
because you are related?'

Thek is thus a compound of behaviour which shows unaggressiveness and deference to its object, and of behaviour
which shows esteem for it. The 'respect' which it denotes is
also connected with a formal shyness which the Dinka call
ryoc (a verb which also has the senses of 'to fear', or 'to be
shamefaced' in the original sense),[3] and which indicates a
measure of withdrawal and reticence in those who are said to
feel it. As the most extreme expression of unaggressiveness and
self-effacement which can be made is a deliberate shrinking
from contact, so the extreme expression of formal *thek* is formal
avoidance. Displays of respectful esteem vary from the small

---

[1] Menstruating girls 'respect' milk and the cattle, and it is probably basically
because they are not allowed to come near the cattle that men respect or avoid
them. In practice, what is involved is that a menstruating girl wears a skirt and
often a bracelet of red or blue and red beads. This warns the young men not to
touch her when a group of youths and girls are playing together. Dinka say that to
touch a menstruating girl weakens the spear-arm.

[2] Though in being able to understand that they might be related, he in a sense
relates them.

[3] As the virtue, that is, of being 'shamefast', bashful or modest.

courtesies of social intercourse we have mentioned, to the conspicuous mutual kindness, affection, and generosity which are supposed ideally to characterize the relationship between a man and his maternal uncle. When two young men are observed to walk together hand in hand and treat each other with special gentleness and complaisance, one often finds that they are in the classificatory relationship of mother's brother and his sister's son.

The 'respect' in such relationships is related to the gift-giving which accompanies them. The notion of *thek*, respect, is frequently present between those who give and receive prestations, and the more important the prestations, the more clearly marked the 'respect' between the partners to them. Thus the father and the mother of a girl receive, apart from small gifts, her bride-wealth, and her husband receives in exchange the girl. The girl 'respects' her husband and his male kin, in the sense of showing them great politeness, and the husband respects, to the point of formal avoidance, her mother. He respects her mother more strictly than her father partly on account of the sexual difference, but partly also because it is the mother of his bride to whom he primarily owes her birth and upbringing.[1] A man's maternal uncle is also expected to exchange gifts with his nephew, the son of his sister; but in addition he has usually married with the cattle given in exchange for his sister. Hence the most important of the gift-exchanges of the Dinka are associated with the notion of 'respect' between those who are party to them. This combination of formal respect with a kind of gratitude and idea of gift-giving is also present in the relationship between the Dinka and their clan-divinities, in ways I later consider.

Though the relationship of *thek* is not always highly conscious and formalized, as it is in the relations of a man with his wife's mother, with his mother's brother, and with the clan-divinity, these provide the very type of *thek* relationship which is something more than mere politeness; and it is of some interest to inquire whether these three major formal respect-relationships

---

[1] As is suggested in the text about the clan-divinity Rual (p. 123 above) the Dinka think of the bride-wealth as given primarily to a girl's mother and her full brothers, though in fact if the father is alive it is he who has ultimate control over it, and it is he primarily who negotiates for it.

(different though the details of required behaviour are in each case) have anything in common.

To be touched by the blood of the emblem of one's clan-divinity is one of the greatest misfortunes that can happen. I have known a man of a clan respecting Crocodile refuse to travel along a path where part of a dead crocodile had been carried some time previously, and to kill a man's emblem in a river prevents him from entering the water until he assumes that every trace of its blood has been carried away. It is supposed that the blood of the emblem of a clan-divinity causes, in the clansman who comes in contact with it, a skin-disease akin to leprosy called *akeeth*,[1] and perhaps also barrenness and blindness.

Akeeth is also incest. It means both incestuous intercourse and the skin disease which is supposed to be its automatic sign and retribution. Incest is thought to result in barrenness, unless ritual action is taken to overcome this, and this barrenness is visited upon the guilty by their clan-divinity. Incest is a most serious offence against that divinity. Thus, as far as expected retribution is concerned, avoidance of the blood of the emblem of the clan-divinity is parallel to the avoidance of sexual congress between those who cannot legitimately marry and produce children (which, for the Dinka, is the central purpose of marriage).

There is a third major cause of the skin-disease *akeeth*. That is to be touched by the blood of a maternal uncle who, in this context, is the figure chosen to represent the maternal kin (excluding the mother) in general. *Panerda*, 'the home of my maternal uncle', includes in a wide sense the whole agnatic group of the mother. We see then that two principal relationships of formal respect—with the mother's brother, and the emblem of the clan-divinity—involve avoidance of the blood of that which is respected. I never heard Dinka speak of the consequences of being touched by the blood of the mother-in-law, but since she is avoided, and, unlike the maternal uncle, is not likely to be engaged in the same pursuits as her son-in-law, the situation probably does not arise.

The respect which the bridegroom is required to show to the bride's immediate family, and which is at its most formal in the

---

[1] Related to the word for rust, *keeth*.

avoidance practised between him and his prospective mother-in-law, is paralleled in the next generation by the respect between a man and his maternal uncle. The two situations are related. Since by the time a child is born of the marriage those who were originally affines begin to develop a real kin-relationship, it is to be expected that the respect between a man and his mother's brother should involve greater kindliness than that between the same man's father and the father's affines. The maternal uncle is regarded as the guardian of his sister, and in Dinka thought it is to his maternal uncle that a boy is grateful for the provision of his mother. The Dinka remark frequently that the maternal uncle also has married with his nephew's father's cattle. Hence, in the Dinka way of thinking, when two families have a marriage between them, each has provided the means for the continuation of the other. Each is in this respect the source of the life and growth of the other.

Again, as I have pointed out, it is particularly to his wife's mother that a man is thought to owe a debt of gratitude for the upbringing of her daughter, and in fact the training of a daughter as a wife is the responsibility of her mother. The daughter, on her marriage, produces children for her husband's lineage, and hence from the husband's point of view his wife's mother is a primary source of the continuation of his own agnatic line. A feature which the maternal uncle—and mother-in-law—relationships have in common, then, is that they involve the notion that the partners have a most important debt between them. One owes to the other the means by which its generation is assured.

Children and cattle multiplying and prospering from generation to generation are the ultimate value of Dinka life and the only assurance of a kind of immortality. In each marriage this guarantee of continuing life is obtained only through the provision of a woman by an unrelated family. In the ways we have suggested, the maternal uncle and the wife's mother personify for proximate generations the source from which new members come into a family and a lineage, the external means of its continued existence. Both these persons are the object of respectful behaviour.

If, as we suggest, 'respect' goes with this gratitude for life, we may see why 'respect' is not expected between coeval clansmen and women, for by the rules of exogamy they must not provide each other with children.[1] Yet the continuing generation and regeneration of the clan are a testimony to a source of life and fertility within the agnatic line. This source of life, unlike the different women who provide for its continuance from family to family, is constant throughout the clan over its generations. For the Dinka it is such a constant generative power which the divinity represents for its clansmen. As Divinity ultimately produces all children, so it is the clan-divinity which produces the children of its clan, through the women married into the clan.

The respect for the clan-divinity may thus be related to the other chief situations in which formal respect is required. The clan-divinity is respected as the source of life of the clan. As such, it is thought of as being both external to the clansmen, and also within them. It is 'in them', as the Dinka say, but also 'in the giraffe' (or whatever the emblem may be) and 'in the sky'.

And it is not to go far from the Dinkas' own way of thought to say that a generative power in each clan is represented by its clan-divinity,[2] and that respect for the clan-divinity is related to this representation. Hence, husbands respect the clan-divinities of their wives, who will bear their children, and wives respect those of their husbands on account of the children they bear to them. Similarly, when cattle are handed over in marriage, those who receive them respect the clan-divinities of those from whom they are received, though of course the range of remoter kin to whom such cattle are distributed do not do so. The cattle are thought to carry with them something of the clan-divinity of those to whom they have belonged, and are a sign that a girl has been handed over to produce children for it. Cattle specially dedicated to the clan-divinity may therefore, in extreme cases, be more safely handed over in marriage than

[1] It must again be emphasized, however, that it is not possession of a common clan-divinity which makes intercourse incestuous. It is human relationship, genealogically counted or, in some cases, strongly suspected. Consequently it is rather that the knowledge or suspicion of incest evokes in the guilty parties the notion of the anger of the clan-divinity, than that the notion of the clan-divinity evokes the notion of the guilt of incest.

[2] It is relevant here to point out that beasts reserved for sacrifice to the clan-divinity are uncastrated, and that their organs of generation play an important part in the sacrifice as we later describe (Chap. VII, pp. 269–70). Further, a Dinka told me that if he dreamed of his clan-divinity, he would have a nocturnal emission.

disposed of in any other way for, as I have heard Dinka explain in addressing such cattle, they are being given for a girl who will produce children for the clan-divinity.

I have mentioned that the restrictions which the obligation to *thek* the emblems of clan-divinities impose are not very irksome, and it cannot be observed that the Dinka have any desire to use those emblems in ways which are prohibited. Undoubtedly, the related prohibition against incestuous congress is felt to be more restricting than the respect for clan-divinities, particularly since it can be used by parents to discourage marriages of which they do not approve. Hence, though close incest and injury to the emblem of the clan-divinity are sins of the same order, and in some respects have the same consequences, it seems true to say, on the evidence available to me, that incest represents a temptation which injury to the emblem of the divinity does not, and it might well be argued in a different type of analysis that the strength of the prohibition on the latter derives from the strength of the prohibition on the former.[1] For those interested to pursue such a line of thought, it may be mentioned that the clan-divinity of masters of the fishing-spear, Flesh, is the only divinity which is ritually eaten by those who respect it,[2] in circumstances of great solemnity. This fact, considered in relation to some features of the myths accounting for the first master of the fishing-spear, in one of which his quasi-incestuous conduct is explicitly mentioned, supports a familiar conclusion of psychological analysis which, however, it is beyond our power or intention to discuss further.

Respect for the emblem of a clan-divinity is in the main seen only in small details of behaviour. Those who respect *wec* grass, for example, may be seen to place head carrying-rings made of this grass slightly out of the way, so that they reduce the likelihood that someone unrelated to the grass will burn or destroy it. Those who respect particular animals try to avoid seeing them killed or cooked, and in one or two cases I have seen, show real distress if by chance they come across such treatment. Those who respect trees of various sorts refuse to cut them down and

---

[1] That is, if it be assumed that the strength of the prohibition upon injuring the emblem of the divinity argues a strong emotional attitude towards it which cannot be explained by the temptation it presents in itself.

[2] As described on pp. 143–4.

try to avoid any homestead in which they are being burnt or damaged. It is said also that such animal emblems as lions are sometimes given offerings of food. Professor and Mrs. Seligman report several examples of such behaviour.[1] Respect for a clan-divinity is in general more systematically shown by the sacrifices made to it, and the offerings of parts of these sacrifices at shrines to it, and I think it would be true to say that these are a more important part of the cult of clan-divinities than the respect shown to their emblems, which have the status of 'clansmen' when regarded as individual creatures, and as 'fathers' and 'ancestors' only when regarded as representatives of the species and thus of the divinity itself.

Though I have never seen any very elaborately developed kinship-behaviour in the relationship between men and the emblems of their clan-divinities, there can be no doubt that it sometimes occurs; and I am indebted to Professor Evans-Pritchard for the following example, copied by him from a Sudan Intelligence Report. It is the more striking in that it appears to have been witnessed by the European author of the report:

The appearance of a seven feet long crocodile in the Dinka village of Aweil (Northern District, Bahr-al-Ghazal) gave occasion for a practical demonstration of totemistic belief. The animal was taken charge of by a man of the crocodile totem, and spent the night in his hut, where it was supplied with a meal of two goats. It showed no fear and made no attempt to attack human beings. In the morning it was escorted by its host back to the swamp, killing and eating a cat on the way. An analogous case occurred some years ago in the same district, when a man clearly demonstrated his ability to call birds.[2]

It may be imagined that many Dinka have at some time had some experience of such appropriate behaviour by the emblems of their clan-divinities, if of a less dramatic nature; and it is clear that it would confirm their faith in the non-material object of their belief, the clan-divinity itself, manifest in its clansmen and its emblems.

Relationship with the clan-divinity is regulated and maintained by the dedication and sacrifice of beasts to it. The Dinka

[1] C. G. and B. Z. Seligman, op. cit., 1932, pp. 144, 145.
[2] Sudan Intelligence Report, Feb. 1930.

word for dedication is *mac*, which is the ordinary word for tethering a beast to a peg, or imprisoning someone, or reserving something to be released only in special circumstances. When cattle are prayed over by heads of families, and thus dedicated to the clan-divinity, they are kept for special use. Their milk is to be drunk only by clansmen, and they can be parted with only as marriage-cattle for a member of the clan. Even then it may be thought that to part with them will bring future misfortune. The Dinka say that such cattle are *mac*, reserved for such and such a divinity; or, members of a clan may say, they *mac* their clan-divinity, in such an expression as *Pagong aa mac gong, ee yahnden*, 'Pagong "keep" Hedgehog, it is their divinity.' Similarly, when an individual dedicates a beast to a free-divinity which has affected him and become for him personally a divinity, he is said to *mac* that divinity. The word is difficult to translate by a single term in English;[1] but in its use we find the idea that the dedication and reservation of beasts to particular divinities also expresses, even compels, the attachment of those divinities to the people who dedicate beasts to them. The beast dedicated to the divinity is very closely associated with the divinity itself, of which the beast becomes representative. So ideally the colour of beasts appropriate for dedication to a divinity is sometimes a colour of the material emblem of that divinity—the beast of *Rual*, as we have seen, should be as near as can be to the colour of the fruit of the sausage-tree, and the beast of the spear-masters' divinity, Flesh, should be 'red' (brown), like flesh.

Dedicated beasts are intended only for future sacrifice to the divinities to which they are dedicated. It is so strongly believed that to part with such dedicated animals will bring sickness and misfortune that it is not considered equitable for a creditor to seize a dedicated beast from his debtor, no matter how pressing his needs. He would be held responsible for subsequent sickness or death in the debtor's family if he did so, and public opinion would certainly be against him. When cattle fines are imposed in modern courts, the Dinka think that execution of the

[1] Fr. P. A. Nebel, op. cit., 1936, gives the following translations: '*Mac*, v. to tie, fasten, to put in prison; *mac (nhialic, yath)*; to worship: *kek a mac mir, ee yahnden*; *mac kedang (tene ran) ku akolda abi war*, to give a pledge.' The last two sentences, literally translated, mean: 'They *mac* Giraffe, it is their clan-divinity', and 'to *mac* something (to or with a person) and another day will redeem (it)'.

judgement should be delayed rather than that a dedicated beast should be seized by the Government, and one may sometimes see a man with the tethering-cord and peg of such a beast, trying to persuade someone in authority that it should be returned to him. The tethering cord and peg are evidence of his original ownership, just as a tethering cord may be attached to a forked-branch shrine[1] as a testimony to a past sacrifice.

Other expressions for the relationship of clansmen with their clan-divinities are that they 'meet' or 'are together' in them. One term for this conjunction is *rom*, perhaps best simply translated as 'to meet together' or 'to have in common'.[2] Those agnatic kin who are obliged to help each other in the blood-feud (*ter*) say *ter aramku*, 'we are joined in the blood-feud' or 'we have the blood-feud in common'. The Dinka state, for example, that members of a clan 'are joined with Giraffe, it is their divinity' (*kek rom kek miir, ee yahnden*); and they are thus saying that members of a clan respecting Giraffe are joined with it as agnatic kin are joined with each other. It is sometimes said that clansmen will demand compensation from those who kill the emblem of their clan-divinity, and it was once suggested to me that I should be required to pay compensation if I shot a crocodile in an area where many members of Patek, a clan respecting Crocodile, were settled. Professor and Mrs. Seligman report that '. . . when a clan is particularly strong in a given locality, its members tend to forget that their totem is but one among many, so that they may show annoyance if other folk do not treat it with respect'.[3]

When two clans have a divinity in common, but are not related to each other, they are not both 'joined' in the divinity in this sense. They merely 'come together in it' (*mat thin*). So also in the prosecution of a blood-feud, many people come together to help the central agnatic groups involved, but only those central groups will say *ter aramku*, 'we have the blood-feud in common'. The difference between *rom* and *mat* in both cases is the difference between inescapable, obligatory conjunction and mere association.

[1] The *ghoro* described in Chap. VII, pp. 257–60.

[2] Fr. P. A. Nebel, op. cit., 1936, gives: '*Ram*, p.t. *rom*, to meet, to do or have in common; . . . *og a ram* (greeting on the road); *rom thok*, to join in conversation; . . . *ram akeuic*, to abut . . . *koc ram nhim*, capricious.'

[3] C. G. and B. Z. Seligman, op. cit., 1932, p. 149.

I have intended to suggest so far that much of what the
Dinka say about their clan-divinities connects the notion of
those divinities very closely with their lived experience of the
relations between agnatic kin, and of the values of agnatic
kinship. The clan-divinity is the very type of agnatic ancestor;
the emblems are the very type of clansman. Real human clansmen are in fact differentiated from each other by generation,
or by personality, or by family and lineage. The emblems of
the clan-divinities, perhaps by virtue of their being non-human,
can be thought to form a single undifferentiated group. Each
giraffe, for example, is seen by human beings as equivalent to
every other giraffe, in space or in time, and is to be treated in
the same way by all members of a clan respecting Giraffe. In
purely human social relationships this ideal of the equivalence
of human clansmen is not fully realized, for they are individuals,
and members of families and lineages, and are conspicuously
differentiated from each other in these ways. The clan (like the
total Dinka world discussed in an earlier chapter) is a divided
unity; but in relation to the clan-divinity and its emblem the
Dinka transcend the divisions and oppositions between clansmen. As clansmen, not simply as men, they are undifferentiated
classificatory half-brothers of an animal or species standing in
the same relationship to all, and children of a common ancestor.
Hence all the clan 'ancestors' become one ancestor in the clan-
divinity, and all the clansmen become equally 'half-brothers',
socially equivalent to each other, in relation to the emblems of
the divinity. Actual agnatic ancestors give place to each other,
changing and dividing the structure of the clan; actual clansmen must be more or less distant from each other, in genealogical space and time. But the clan-divinity and its emblems for
the Dinka transcend that space and time, and the differentiations of human clansmen which it produces.

2

If clan-divinities represent, as we have said, the ideal and
permanent values of agnation for the Dinka,[1] we should expect
that the spear-master clans, having collectively different gifts

---

[1] It may be mentioned that in the very few days I spent among the Cic Dinka, it
appeared that a word, *mel*, could be used to mean both 'clan-divinity' and 'agnatic
relationship'.

and qualities from the others, would also collectively recognize a clan-divinity which none of the other clans has. This is *ring*, Flesh.

Ring is the ordinary word for meat or flesh, but it is best translated 'Flesh' because in Dinkaland it comes from a creature whose death one has usually witnessed, and the twitching of the flesh after a sacrificial beast is skinned makes it appear still to have a life of its own. This 'life' in the flesh is observed by the Dinka.

Those who have *ring* as their divinity are related to Flesh, and in the myths of the first master of the fishing-spear given in a later chapter, it will be seen that he divides the raw flesh that comes from his sacrificial cattle among the founders of spear-master clans; that the founder of one clan tries by subterfuge to acquire a larger share, a reflection of the claim of his descendant of the present day that his clan is more strongly inspired by the divinity Flesh than others are; and that, in a myth of the Bor Dinka, this divinity Flesh is said to be the same as the divinity Fire, which the first master of the fishing-spear left behind in a gourd for his descendants when he disappeared. In the country of the Western Dinka, where that myth is not known, there is still some connexion between Flesh and the red light of a fire. The divinity Flesh manifests itself in a red light, as is suggested in the hymn beginning:

The Flesh kindles like fire

quoted later (p. 227). It is clear that such a conception is not easily to be translated into English by any single term.

I begin with an account of how any observer at a Dinka ceremony may hear the word *ring*, Flesh, used, and in a sense see it in action, before he comes to know the full and complicated range of its associations. The sacrifice I describe was for the recovery of a sick master of the fishing-spear, and the gist of the invocations there made is given in Chapter VI. Here I describe only those parts relevant for an understanding of this Flesh divinity of spear-master clans. On the usual pattern of a Dinka sacrifice, masters of the fishing-spear—in this case members of the powerful clans Pagong and Payi—were invoking, in this case over a tawny (*mayan*) bull-calf. As the invocations proceeded, the legs of some of the masters of the fishing-spear began to tremble, a trembling which came from the quivering of the upper leg and thigh. This, it was said, was the divinity Flesh, which was beginning to awaken (*pac*) in their bodies. The divinity Flesh is specially manifested in this quivering of the legs and thighs, which sometimes spreads further to the whole body. When masters of the fishing-spear speak of Flesh, they often touch these parts of the body, and the right shoulder, as places in which the divinity Flesh particularly manifests itself, though it is closely associated with the whole body.

The masters of the fishing-spear continued to invoke with the mounting force of Flesh in them; they did not become 'hysterically' possessed, as do those who are possessed by free-divinities. Two young men, members of these spear-master clans though not themselves masters of the fishing-spear, then also began to show signs of the 'awakening' of Flesh in them. They were much less controlled, and their arms and legs were soon trembling violently. One was sitting, one standing, and both gazed blankly before them with their eyes open and turned slightly upwards. It was possible to go up to them and stare closely into their faces without either's registering that he saw anything.

Nobody at this stage paid much attention to them; it was said that when thus possessed by Flesh in the homestead, they were safe, and that if the condition persisted for too long the women would put an end to it by venerating the divinity Flesh in their bodies, giving those possessed by it their bangles, and kissing their hands. Later, women did kiss the hands of these possessed men, but bangles were not offered.

As the invocations increased in speed and intensity an older man became overpowered by the divinity Flesh, and staggered about among the invoking masters of the fishing-spear, slapping and leaning on the bull-calf and jostling people. His behaviour was that of a man who is very giddy. At this stage visiting masters of the fishing-spear were in turn pouring libations of milk from a ring-decorated gourd over the peg to which the calf was tethered. Each made his libation, kissing his own hands before and after handling the gourd of the Flesh, the gourd reserved for libations to this divinity. When one master of the fishing-spear returned from this act of veneration, he told me that his own Flesh was 'waking up', though he behaved with self-control for the rest of the ceremony.

The mounting or awakening of the divinity Flesh in the body seems to be a well-known sensation to all adult male members of spear-master clans. Females do not have it. A Christian Dinka of the Pakwin clan told me that he dared not draw near when a beast was being sacrificed to his clan-divinity, as the awakening of the Flesh in him brought on a sensation of faintness, which might result in his falling unconscious. His further account of what *ring*, Flesh, was, is of interest, coming as it does from a sophisticated man. Flesh, he said, was the divinity of all masters of the fishing-spear, standing ahead (*tueng*) of all other clan-divinities. In the past, he said, there were not all the divinities—free-divinities and clan-divinities— which there now are in Dinkaland. There were only two great 'things' (principles, one might say in English)—Divinity (*nhialic*) and Flesh. It was these which had supported the Dinka in the earliest times. 'Flesh is one word', he said. The Dinka expression 'one word' (*wet tok*) means the word which is superior to many words, the decisive word, beyond argument and addition, and hence the true word. So a man of few words (whom all Dinka profess to admire) is a man whom people hear and obey, while a 'man of many words' is thought to be wavering, ineffective, and unreliable. Many words conceal the truth while 'one word' proclaims it. So, in the words of this Dinka:

Flesh is one word. Our ancestors knew about it, but none knew everything about it. Some say they have seen it. It is a single word, it is of the furthest past, what has always been.

Other Dinka too have remarked that Flesh is a matter of few words, which they either know little about or do not wish freely to talk about, for they tend to discuss it in subdued tones not noticeable when they talk of Divinity and other divinities.

The veneration of the divinity Flesh in the bodies of those who manifest it is, from an observer's point of view, the most solemn religious act of the Dinka. At one ceremony the women of the homestead of the officiating master of the fishing-spear came in turn and kissed (*cim*) his hands, his forehead, and his feet, kneeling before him before performing the last of these, in an attitude of deep humility not often seen among them. The only other situation in which I have seen a man's hands kissed was one in which an old woman wished to show great respect and gratitude to a benefactor.

The divinity Flesh is said to make the tongues of masters of the fishing-spear 'really cold' (*lirthwat*). A 'cold tongue' among the Dinka has something of the significance of a 'cooling' tongue, a tongue which speaks words of good counsel which pacify those to whom they are addressed. It represents, that is, calm and incisive speech, without anger or aggressiveness, detached and succinctly effective. Dinka often ask in prayer that their bodies may be cool, that the comforting cool breezes may come to them, for coolness stands for peace and calm, health, contentment, and equanimity, and the absence of passion and conflict. In hymns also the divinities are sometimes said to have 'brought coolness' to the people and the earth, and I have mentioned how it is said that with the coming of the coolness of spring, a man will again sleep with his wife and dream of his child that is to be born.

Morally, then, to have a cool mouth and a cool heart[1] is the opposite of having 'many words' and a 'hot heart' (*twic puou*). The latter show themselves in hot temper, unreasonableness, violence, disorder and aggression, and deception; the former are associated with peacefulness, order, harmony, and truth. A man whose tongue and heart are cool is a fit person to adjust the differences between those who quarrel, to see the rights and wrongs of both parties and to reconcile them. This is the character of the ideal master of the fishing-spear, and all masters of the fishing-spear aspire to exercise that influence which a cool tongue and a cool heart are supposed to give a man.

The divinity Flesh is perhaps most importantly supposed to ensure that a man who speaks by virtue of it speaks absolutely truthfully. The very truth, *wet yic alanden*, is by definition spoken when a man speaks inspired by Flesh. Dinka say that if a master of the fishing-spear speaks in his office and is shown later to have lied, then *ring*, Flesh, could not have been in him and inspiring him when he spoke. The word *yic*, which is translated as 'truth', has in fact a somewhat wider range of meanings than our word now has. It implies uprightness, 'righteousness', and justice. The truth which a man inspired by Flesh speaks may be also a prophetic or proleptic truth, giving his people the very substance of what he states in prayers and invocations.

[1] It may be remembered that the great spear which is an important clan-divinity among the Bor Dinka is called *Lir piou*, 'Cool-heart'.

He penetrates to what really and truly *is*, and thus can define truth. It is this gift which leads Dinka to say of masters of the fishing-spear with high reputations that 'they are able' (*a leou*), which is perhaps better translated as 'they prevail', for they know what really underlies the deceptive appearances which mislead others who are not so inspired, and their knowledge ensures effectiveness in their dealings with reality. This knowledge is figured as an illumination, and the divinity Flesh gives it.

It will be remembered that in one of the myths of the separation of Divinity and Man, Man asks for a chink of light so that he may see.[1] Light is what men want. On the simplest level of experience, to do something by day in that country is an entirely different matter from doing it by night, and the presence or absence of the moon becomes an important factor in deciding upon such things as cattle-movements. To move in the dark is dangerous, for there are snakes, scorpions, pot-holes, thorns, and fallen branches which cannot be seen, and also wild animals, witches, and other evil influences, sensed rather than conceptualized by the Dinka. But dreams, some of which are thought to give knowledge of facts which could not otherwise be known by the dreamer, occur at night, and in dreams Divinity may communicate with men.

Some masters of the fishing-spear were once sitting in my hut after tea, and the evening had drawn on. They were discussing a topic which interests them and which they sometimes try to explain to Europeans—the difference between masters of the fishing-spear and 'medicine men' or minor magicians and diviners, all of whom governments at times tended to class together and proscribe as 'kujurs' or wizards. A hurricane lamp, newly trimmed, was burning very clearly and brightly on the table, and around it were strewn the cups and saucers left over from tea. One of the men there, the son of a sister of a well-known master of the fishing-spear, remarked:

See, our masters of the fishing-spear are like that lamp. Look now it gives a bright light, and we see each other and we see what is here on the table. If the lamp goes dim, we shall not see each other so well and we shall not see what is on the table. If it goes out, we

[1] Also it will be remembered that injury to the clan-divinity in some cases causes blindness.

shall not see each other at all, nor the things on the table, nor anything. Divinity made our masters of the fishing-spear thus to be the lamps of the Dinka.

He added:

Masters of the fishing-spear are like that, and Divinity is like that (lamp). See, here is a broken cup set apart. It is not like the whole cups, but it is there in the light apart. So it is at death.

He had in mind another topic we had discussed—the putting in the grave of ageing masters of the fishing-spear before their physical deaths, a ceremony now officially forbidden. The references to the dimming of the lamp were allusions to the ageing and weakening of a master of the fishing-spear.

This is perhaps an unusually articulate and explicit statement about the 'illumination' provided by masters of the fishing-spear, but it is not only the eccentric product of an unusually vivid imagination, for there are similes in hymns in which masters of the fishing-spear and prophets are likened to sources of illumination. I have already quoted (p. 79):

> My father Cyer Deng hold the country
> —A master like the sun and moon—

Other examples are the 'shining master' of the hymn on p. 87 and

> My father Longar is like a comet
> Encircles the earth like a rainbow . . .

and, collected by Fr. Nebel,

> Divinity my father, you are prayed to
> You will wax like the moon. . . .

In the hymn to Flesh, earlier quoted, the reference to Flesh as 'lighting up like fire' is not a reference to heat, but to light. On a dark night, when a fire is blown, one sees for a moment in the flame the contents of the homestead which are otherwise hidden in darkness, and for the Dinka, except for the moon, the fire is the only source of light at night.

There is yet further reason to regard the divinity Flesh, with its associations of truth-telling, knowledge, and proleptic vision, as associated also with illumination at night, when those who do not possess it cannot 'see'. One of the principal functions of a master of the fishing-spear is to pray at night (*long col wokou*) for the protection of cattle and men in the camp at this dangerous period, and many people from different parts of Dinkaland have the belief that the divinity Flesh shows itself to masters of the fishing-spear in the form of a light at night. One master of the fishing-spear said:

> Flesh comes to me in the middle of the night, when I am lying in my hut and the hut is dark. Flesh shines like a lamp for me, like a fire. I can see my wife and everything in the hut as if there were a lamp there. Others do not see the light like this, it is only those who have the divinity Flesh who see it lighting up the hut at night.

Another said that this light appeared near his head, on his left side. Finally the association of Flesh with firelight is explicit in a myth of the Bor Dinka briefly mentioned above and more fully given in Chapter V.

The appropriate colour for beasts sacrificed to Flesh is red (from our point of view light reddish brown, *malwal*), and this is explicitly because this colour resembles, as far as a cattle-colour can, the colour of flesh and blood. In a hymn collected by Fr. Nebel both the colour associations and the gift of clairvoyance which Flesh gives are mentioned:

I give to divinity Flesh my red bull
If I am forsaken [by it], I shall give no more
Flesh of my father, if you are clairvoyant (*tiet*)
You will spy out (*car*) the man who hates, and him who loves. . . .[1]

Also among the Western Twij Dinka, one emblem of Flesh is a small and harmless red snake, and Rek Dinka have told me that Flesh will sometimes manifest itself to masters of the fishing-spear (in a dream?) as a tiny new-born child of a light red colour, lighter than any Dinka child is even at birth. To dream of a small red snake, or a red new-born child, is counted as a good omen. One man told me that Flesh manifested itself in a dream as a red baby coming out of the river, a clear association of ideas of the divinity Flesh with the origin of the first master of the fishing-spear in the river, and that recurrent theme of Dinka thought, the impregnation of a barren woman

---

[1] Flesh and Fire are further connected with knowledge and protection in the Bor Dinka hymn quoted in Chap. V, p. 188.

by a Power of the river.[1] I can only report this association between Flesh and the notion of birth, and that those who have Flesh as divinity are also thought to be powerful in sacrificing for the cure of barrenness.

The divinity Flesh has as its emblems real flesh and blood, primarily in the bodies of men, the masters of the fishing-spear. There is a ceremony for 'feeding' the Flesh in their bodies, though I have never seen it. It is said that at certain sacrifices to the divinity Flesh, which unlike other sacrifices take place at night, masters of the fishing-spear take small pieces of raw flesh from the victim and eat them with great solemnity before day breaks.[2] A master of the fishing-spear of the clan Paghol, which has the primacy in the Apuk Patuan tribe of the Rek, said that he would very respectfully take three small pieces of raw flesh from the thigh of an ox sacrificed for Flesh,[3] and would eat them to feed (augment) the Flesh. When asked why he should eat *three* pieces, he simply said that for a man it was three —when a man died was not the first ceremony performed after three days, while for a woman it was performed after four? Masters of the fishing-spear of the *dhindyor* group of clans, reputedly tracing descent ultimately from women or from a woman, said that *four* pieces were eaten. Many others say that it is not any particular number of pieces which are eaten, but several small pieces taken from all parts of the body.

Whatever may be the significance of these details in themselves, they are observances connected exclusively with masters of the fishing-spear, and they set them apart from others in sharing a mystery which others do not share. It is said that the 'red' beasts sacrificed for the divinity Flesh are to be consumed

[1] The matter is more fully discussed in Chap. V, *passim*. Professor C. G. Seligman commented on the associated themes of birth and the river among the Dinka of Khor Atar: 'Long ago, men and women of the "river-people" would sometimes come out of the river and marry and settle down in neighbouring villages. The description of the coming to land of one of the "river-people" is curiously like the birth of a child. . . .' *Report on Totemism and Religion of the Dinka of the White Nile*, privately circulated, and partially incorporated into the article 'Dinka' by the same author in Hastings, *Encyclopaedia of Religion and Ethics*, 1911.

[2] Cf. W. Robertson Smith, *Lectures on the Religion of the Semites*, note to p. 221 of the 1907 edition: '. . . certain Saracen sacrifices, nearly akin to the Passover, which were even eaten raw, and had to be entirely consumed before the sun rose. In this case the idea was that the efficacy of the sacrifice lay in the living flesh and blood of the victim. Everything of the nature of putrefaction was therefore to be avoided. . . .'

[3] Thigh and Thigh-bone is the principal divinity of this clan.

utterly by the elders of their community in a byre at night, after the sacrifice. This is the only case of a solemn eating of the clan-divinity. The sacrificial procedure is different from that of ordinary sacrifices to Divinity and divinities, when the beast is often killed in the morning and the flesh eventually distributed to be taken home by those attending the sacrifice. Flesh, however, is often invoked at sacrifices not made specifically for it.

Flesh is acknowledged by members of spear-master and warrior clans alike to be the most powerful of all clan-divinities, and although I have not seen what are described as its most striking manifestations at sacrifices, I mention what the Dinka believe about them. It is said that when the divinity Flesh is really strong in a master of the fishing-spear, not only may *he* be overcome by it to such an extent that he will fall heavily to the ground, but that the victim itself will sink to its knees under the force of the invocation, and would, in effect, have its 'life' (*wei*) released for the people before it was physically killed. It is believed that where the divinity Flesh is really 'running' (*kat epei*) in a praying master of the fishing-spear the horns of the victim will droop and fall forward. A man told me that his father had seen it happen. Such reports undoubtedly enhance for the Dinka what is certainly before their eyes at many quite ordinary sacrifices—the fact that the invoking masters of the fishing-spear, and others, often make a transition to what appears as a state of *partial* dissociation, and that the victim, tethered for a long period during the rhythmical invocations and often in the sun, often becomes sleepy, quiet, and dazed, as I have sometimes seen.

The respect and even awe, as it would appear from descriptions, with which masters of the fishing-spear eat their small pieces of raw flesh, and which the women certainly show when venerating the Flesh in the bodies of men, is an extreme form of the *thek* already described as 'respect' for the emblems of other clan-divinities. The masters of the fishing-spear are said to be 'afraid' or 'shy' (*guop ryoc*) when they eat it. It seemed to me that in relation to Flesh, the Dinka who have this divinity really did inwardly experience the sensations which they represent exteriorly and formally by attitudes of avoidance and respect in their dealings with other clan-divinities and their emblems. *Ring* is Flesh, and Blood also, for the Dinka say 'flesh and blood are one'; and the sight of blood flowing is said to weaken the Flesh divinity in the body of a master of the fishing-spear, so that he tries to avoid seeing the flow of human blood. This is one of the reasons why masters of the fishing-spear are supposed not to take part in actual fighting, but to stay at home and pray for victory. It is consistent, of course, with what has been said of the treatment of the emblems of other clan-divinities, that those who have Flesh (and blood) should not see flesh and blood injured. A master of the fishing-spear who took me to see the head-scarification of some girls—a very bloody operation—suddenly said that he was feeling faint, and must go and wait elsewhere: 'It is Flesh in my body, it hates to see blood.' Such an idea is congruent also with the position of masters of the fishing-spear as mediators and peacemakers.

There is one possible exception to the statement that only spear-master clans have Flesh as a divinity; it is sometimes claimed by members of the clan Padiangbar, a warrior clan. Where the Padiangbar clan is represented in any force, it is my experience that its members regard themselves as having a spiritual equality with masters of the fishing-spear. They base their claims upon a tradition that members of the clan Padiangbar in any community had the first right to repeat the prayers and invocations of masters of the fishing-spear. (When masters of the fishing-spear invoke, each phrase is repeated by some of those present, usually their classificatory sisters' sons.) They regard themselves then as traditional 'prayer-repeaters' (*gam lung*) to masters of the fishing-spear, and they argue that if they are to repeat such prayers then their own tongues also must be 'cool' and truthful. They also must have a special spiritual strength, for it is thought that powerful prayers can injure those who in themselves are not strong enough to repeat them. Some members of Padiangbar even claim to have sacred spears, but most do not, and it is generally agreed by others that if any have sacred spears they did not receive them legitimately but must at some time have counterfeited them.[1]

---

[1] This raises an interesting point about which I should like fuller information. I have found in some parts of Dinkaland that members of an outstandingly influential lineage of a warrior clan sometimes like to suggest that they have the right to hold sacred spears. Members of other clans deny this privately, or suggest that the spears must have been acquired in some unorthodox way and are without traditional validity. In other words, there seems some reason to suppose that marked

A man of Padiangbar of the Awan Pajok tribe of the Rek Dinka said that Padiangbar had the divinity Flesh as a result of an incident which occurred in the life of its founder, Akol Adiangbar. Whilst Akol Adiangbar was spreading dung to dry, eight small pieces of raw flesh fell from the sky on to his thigh. (This story thus again associates Flesh particularly with the thigh and upper leg.) Ayi, the founder of the important spear-master clan Payi, which is the spear-master clan with tribal primacy in Awan Pajok, told Akol Adiangbar to eat the flesh, some raw and some cooked. After he had done so, he and his children afterwards were able to repeat the powerful invocations of the masters of the fishing-spear of Payi, effectively and without harm to themselves. Further, the masters of the fishing-spear of Payi were not able to prevail in invocation if they turned against the people of Padiangbar.

Ring, Flesh, the divinity of all spear-masters, is thus incarnate in them, and it is intrinsically part of them. They are not 'separated' from it as men are separated from other clan-divinities, and are thus themselves partly divine, like their prototype later described. It is a divinity carried in the flesh and blood, passed from generation to generation of masters of the fishing-spear, the perfect type of agnatic inheritance and physical regeneration. As a Dinka said: 'Flesh is in a man's body, and it was in his father's body and the bodies of his ancestors from great Longar, the first master of the fishing-spear, and from Divinity, who gave it in the beginning. It is in their bodies and it is in their spears.' It is the principal inspiration of masters of the fishing-spear, the grounds of their ability ideally to 'light the way', to pronounce and define truth, to prevail in prayers, and to reconcile conflicting groups and interests.

We have now considered Divinity and all the major divinities known to the Western Dinka, describing them for the most part within a Dinka frame of reference. The major problems which they present for analysis are the subject of the next chapter.

social pre-eminence of a lineage of a warrior clan results in its members approximating themselves to spear-master clans in religious endowment as well as political influence.

IV

DIVINITY AND EXPERIENCE

To the Dinka the Powers are known by personal encounters, as living agents influencing their lives for good or evil. Europeans may perhaps concede an objective reality of this order to the Dinka Divinity, where it most resembles the 'God' of the universal religions; but no European actually encounters DENG, GARANG, or the other Powers as the Dinka claim to do. For analysis, then, the Powers (and logically all equally, including Divinity) must be regarded as representations of realities more accessible to a universal rational knowledge than they need to be in the Dinka view of them; and our final and interpretative task is to ask, if the Dinka Powers be representations, what it is that they represent. I have described them for the most part as the Dinka themselves understand them; but in this chapter I try to give a different account of them, not now as ultra-human 'beings' which might form the subject-matter of a Dinka theology, but as representations (or as I here prefer to call them, 'images') evoked by certain configurations of experience contingent upon the Dinkas' reaction to their particular physical and social environment, of which a foreigner can also have direct knowledge.

It is true that the Powers may be as much part of the Dinkas' total experience—as much phenomena—for them, as are the physical and social realities to which we later refer them; but the Dinka themselves are quite able to discuss the latter without at once introducing Powers as their grounds. Thus, one can discuss the prospects for the harvest without necessarily introducing the free-divinity ABUK, to whom good harvests are attributed, and one can discuss thunder, lightning, and rain up to a point as purely 'natural' phenomena, without talking of DENG or Divinity. To take a slighter example, a Dinka may complain of a cold or a headache without reference to Powers as the grounds of these minor discomforts. Should the cold turn to high fever, or the headache become persistent and agonizing, his thoughts will turn to the possible activity of Powers.

Thus even for the Dinka themselves, a Power is not an immediate *datum* of experience of the same order as the physical facts or events with which it is associated. To refer to the activity of a Power is to offer an interpretation, and not merely a description, of experience; and in this chapter I consider some features of the type of interpretation offered in relation to the experience which is interpreted.

The clue to this problem lies, it seems to me, in a Dinka statement which is itself problematical—the statement that a Power is 'in men' and also (in many examples) 'in the sky'. So the free-divinity DENG may on occasions be 'in' men, but it is also 'in' the sky and in the phenomena of the sky. It is clear that for the Dinka, men, whether or not possessed by DENG, are not permanently 'in the sky', while the rain, lightning, and thunder, regarded as physical phenomena only, are not 'in' men. In this example the free-divinity DENG provides a link between moral and physical experience, integrating experience of the human and the ultra-human in the world.

Traditional teaching affirms the existence of Powers and endows them with some of their specific characteristics; but their effective relationship with men at particular times, in the direct encounters which make them so much more vividly present to the Dinka than they can be to ourselves, are matters to be discovered or revealed. Some indication has already been given of the way in which the Dinka try to make such discoveries by divining and questioning. In divination an attempt is made to specify a Power as the grounds of a particular human condition. Until its name is known it remains as it were latent and undefined within the affective condition of the suffering individual, and action cannot be taken to remove it or propitiate it until it has been identified.

The process of treating a sick man whose sickness is attributed to a Power is thus to isolate for the sufferer and his kin a particular Power which can be regarded as a subject of activity within him, from the self which is its object. Hence, when a man is strongly possessed, it is held that 'it is no use speaking to *him*', as a human person, for what is acting is not the man but the Power. It is the process of making manifest what I have called an 'image', corresponding to the affective state of the sufferer as cause to effect, which I now discuss.

It raises first a difficult question of differences between Dinka and European self-knowledge which I can discuss only inadequately. The Dinka have no conception which at all closely corresponds to our popular modern conception of the 'mind', as mediating and, as it were, storing up the experiences of the self.[1] There is for them no such interior entity to appear, on reflection, to stand between the experiencing self at any given moment and what is or has been an exterior influence upon the self. So it seems that what we should call in some cases the 'memories' of experiences, and regard therefore as in some way intrinsic and interior to the remembering person and modified in their effect upon him by that interiority, appear to the Dinka as exteriorly acting upon him, as were the sources from which they derived. Hence it would be impossible to suggest to Dinka that a powerful dream was 'only' a dream, and might for that reason be dismissed as relatively unimportant in the light of day, or that a state of possession was grounded 'merely' in the psychology of the person possessed. They do not make the kind of distinction between the psyche and the world which would make such interpretations significant for them.

A man who has lived for a time in a place very foreign to him may think that that place (we should say, its 'influence') follows him (*bwoth cok*), as divinities are said to 'follow' those with whom they have formed a relationship. A man who had been imprisoned in Khartoum called one of his children 'Khartoum' in memory of the place, but also to turn aside any possible harmful influence of that place upon him in later life. The act is an act of exorcism, but the exorcism of what, for us, would be memories of experiences. Thus also do the Dinka call children after Powers, and after the dead, who to the Dinka way of thought are less likely to return to trouble the living if their place and constant presence are thus explicitly acknowledged. In such namings, the Power which has once affected a man or one of his close kin, kin themselves who are dead, or the places which have formed a man's personality, are regarded as potent still to affect him as they once certainly affected him, directly, and from without.

That the experiences of the past, whether of people, places, or events, may have permanent and profound influences upon

[1] And still less of conscious and unconscious elements, of course.

the personality is of course a commonplace of European thought also; but there they tend to be regarded as proximately and most importantly derived from the mind or imagination of the remembering self, on which their traces are thought to remain. Our view of the passage of time influences the value we attach to past events far more than is the case for the Dinka, whose points of reference are not years counted serially, but the events themselves.[1] In the example of the man who called his child 'Khartoum' it is Khartoum which is regarded as an agent, the subject which acts, and not as with us the remembering mind which recalls the place. The man is the object acted upon. Even in the usual expressions of the Dinka for the action of features of their world upon them, we often find a reversal of European expressions which assume the human self, or mind, as subject in relation to what happens to it; in English, for example, it is often said that a man 'catches a disease', but in Dinka the disease, or Power, always 'seizes the man'.

One example of this apparent 'extrapolation' of memories has been mentioned earlier (Chap. II, pp. 65–68) in a description of the fetish MATHIANG GOK. This fetish, according to Dinka accounts, works analogously to what, for Europeans, would be the prompting of a guilty conscience. The European emphasis there is upon an integrally interior subject of activity, the conscience. For the Dinka, MATHIANG GOK is a presence acting upon the self from without, and employed by someone to do so. The image (as we have called it) of the experience of guilty indebtedness (to take the usual situation in which MATHIANG GOK is thought to operate) is extrapolated from the experiencing self. It comes (as memories often do) unwilled by the debtor, and is interpreted as a Power directed by the creditor. Though I do not describe Dinka beliefs about witchcraft in this book, it is similarly possible to interpret them as imaging, in another person, states of a person's own conscience. An envious man, for example, not recognizing the envy in

[1] In the early days of European-type court-procedure among the Dinka, it was found very difficult to persuade them to see that the period which had elapsed since an event was at all significant in the attempt to settle a dispute. Even now, a Dinka may think it unreasonable and unjust that a cattle-debt or an injury of many years' standing should be less serious as a subject of litigation than an event of the immediate past.

himself, transfers to another his experience of it, and sees its image in him, 'the witch'.

Another example of this imaging of experience is seen in the relationships which Dinka think themselves to have formed with objects, or more usually illness, which have affected them individually, and which are akin to 'individual totemism' or 'nagualism'.[1] The clan-divinities are such items passed on as species from the founder of a clan to his descendants as a group. When a man has formed an individual relationship, he will *thek*, respect, the emblem of the thing which has affected him, and count it among his divinities. Here again he seems to see in that which has affected him the self-determining subject of activity, and himself the object of it. People do not choose their divinities, they are chosen *by* them.

It is perhaps significant that in ordinary English usage we have no word to indicate an opposite of 'actions' in relation to the human self.[2] If the word 'passions', *passiones*, were still normally current as the opposite of 'actions', it would be possible to say that the Dinka Powers were the images of human *passiones* seen as the active sources of those *passiones*. The practice of divination illustrates the way in which a division in experience, with the discovery of an image which is the active counterpart of human *passiones*, is regarded as a necessary preliminary to human action. A diviner is a man in whom the division is permanently present; a Power, or Powers, are always latent within him, but he has the ability to dissociate them in himself at will, letting them manifest themselves in him. While thus dissociated, the diviner *is* a Power, for which his body is host. It is therefore often impossible in hymns to the Powers to distinguish between the diviner and the Power as subjects to which activity is attributed, and to which the address is being

[1] This applies to others as well as the Dinka. Dr. A. N. Tucker told me of a Shilluk who said that his 'totem' was a razor-blade, with which presumably he had at some time cut himself. Mgr. Mlakic records that a milleme coin which had been lodged in a child's ear became the subject of a totemic relationship among the Nuer. An illustration of the wider contentions about the relation of Powers to other experience with which we here deal is given by Dr. J. H. M. Beattie, who tells me that among the Banyoro, people may be possessed by the 'spirits' of such things as motor-buses, and of *Abapolandi*, Polish expatriates encamped in Bunyoro during the war of 1939–45.

[2] This point is made, for example, by R. G. Collingwood, *An Autobiography*, Penguin edition 1944, p. 86, note.

made. Further, as will be seen in examples of invocations later given, it is often impossible to distinguish the beast from the Power to which it is being sacrificed, for it becomes as a whole representative of the Power in the sacrificial situation. It represents at once the activity of the Power and the passivity of the Power's human victim. The fitness of cattle for such a role in imaging experience has already been suggested in the account given of the way in which Dinka deliberately image experience, for poetic purposes, in them.

If a diviner is called in to diagnose the grounds of possession or sickness, it is because the patient has not himself been able to dissociate an image as the active subject of his experience from its affective accompaniments—because, from the Dinka point of view, the Power has not spoken and made itself known through the mouth of the man whom it is presumed to have attacked. The diviner's activity is here significant for an interpretation of the Powers; for it is his professional task to dissociate the grounds of the suffering from the sufferer, either by himself going into a trance-like state or by inducing such a state in the sufferer or his kin, or both. The diviner, that is, vicariously makes a division in the experience of suffering and suggests or discovers its image, where the patient is not able to do so.

The diviner is expected also to discover a reason for the action of the Power, in some human sin of omission or commission, and to recommend a course of action. This reason may be something the patient has half forgotten—one among the many things which are, as we should say, 'on his conscience', and which begin to become significant for him when he thinks himself in danger. The parting with the beast of DENG in the case of possession we have described is such a reason, and other common reasons are the neglect of Powers known to have been at one time in the family, or acts of cruelty or injustice committed by the sick man or one of his kin. In the last case, where a man has been wronged, it is usually supposed that it is either that man's clan-divinity, or Divinity itself—the image, as we earlier suggested, of the experience of truth and justice among other things—which visits the wrong upon the wrong-doer. When such reasons have been made public, acts of reparation and propitiation become possible; the patient is led to focus

upon one among possibly many latent elements in his experience or the experience of his kin which give rise equally to bodily
sickness and uneasy conscience. Confession, by which the
wrongful acts of the self are made present to it and to the community, is therefore often part of the Dinka way of dealing with
sickness. When the affective condition is imaged in a Power,
both its grounds and the reason for it become manifest not only
to him but to those who care for him, and his experience is
represented in a form in which it can be publicly understood
and shared.

The theme of separation of an image, the active counterpart
of the passive element in human experience, from the self is
carried further in the symbolic action taken by the Dinka to
deal with suffering once its grounds are recognized. As will
appear more fully in later descriptions of sacrifice and invocation, the Power is said to be 'cut off' or 'separated' from the
man, and his suffering and guilt placed 'upon the back' of the
sacrificial victim, to which the man's *passio* is thus transferred,
to be carried away in its death. The recognition of a formal
separation, within the person of the sufferer, between the self
and the Power, is thus followed by the positive *enactment*, in
dedication and sacrifice, of a material division also. The 'inner'
division of experience is sacramentally and externally confirmed.

It is not suggested, of course, that the Dinka apprehend their
beliefs in this way; yet in their own language we find a parallel
to our use of the word 'image', and one which illustrates partly
what I have intended to convey by that use. The Dinka word
which would normally be translated as 'ghost' is *atyep*, which
means a shadow and a reflection. Questions about 'ghosts'
which imply that they are in any way 'materialized', and independently of particular human encounters with them have
an existence such as that we sometimes unthinkingly attribute
to ghosts, are quite meaningless to the Dinka. Ghosts are to be
understood as reflections of a kind of experience, not as a class
of 'beings'. It would be wrong to suggest that in the offerings of
food and tobacco which men make to the ghosts of the dead they
assumed that the ghosts 'physically' consumed these offerings.
The offerings are to the 'hearts' (the seat of affective life) of the
dead. Our own thought tends far more than that of the Dinka

to 'materialize' the ghosts, by representing them in the categories of external physical space. Among the Dinka ghosts appear
to their kin in dreams, and I have never heard of an encounter
with a ghost as occurring in the 'external' 'objective' physical
world, as sometimes imagined by us when we use 'ghost' and
'spectre' interchangeably. Such encounters are undoubtedly
encounters within the self, as is a dream (in Dinka, to dream is
rot nyoth, literally 'to show to oneself').

The ghosts are asked not to return to their kin, for their
appearance usually portends evil; if they return it is because
their kin have failed to remember them sufficiently, or have
failed in some way to carry out injunctions which the dead
made in life. The worst kind of visitation from the dead is
acyen, when a dead person who has died with bitterness towards
someone whom he thinks to have wronged him haunts that
man until he kills him with a swift and incurable sickness.
Ghosts thus reflect, for those they visit, the relations which the
latter have had with them in life and still have with them in the
conscience and the memory. The Dinka do not have a theory
of the nature of ghostly existence in itself, any more than they
have theories of the Powers in themselves. Ghosts are 'shadows'
or 'reflections'—words surely not far removed in implication
from our 'images'—of the dead, as the living involuntarily still
experience disordered relationships with them from the time
when they were alive.

It is not dangerous for the living deliberately to call their
dead to mind; indeed it is a pious duty to make offerings of
beer, milk, and tobacco to them from time to time, and to
recall their names when Divinity or the clan-divinities are invoked for aid at sacrifices. Those who themselves voluntarily
remember their dead in this way, who are conscious of taking
the initiative in relation to them, do so that the dead in return
may passively receive their attentions, and leave them in peace.
Their disturbing appearance is to those whose consciences are
yet disturbed, and who, being themselves insufficiently active
in carrying out the obligations of the living to the dead, permit
the dead themselves to take the active part. Similarly, in human
relations with the Powers, it is commonly thought to be neglect
of voluntary human action to propitiate them which results in
direct and dangerous passive experience of them, an experience

from which a man can begin to be free only when human action is taken on his behalf.

I have mentioned also in a previous chapter (Chap. III, p. 107) that the word *atyep* is used not only of ordinary shadows and reflections, and of ghosts, but also on occasions of the Powers themselves. A man whose source of possession is not known may equally be said to have an *atyep* in him, as to have Divinity or the creator in him. To speak of a cow dedicated to DENG as *weng atyem DENG*, the cow of the 'shadow' (of) DENG, is the same as to speak of it simply as 'the cow of DENG'. Such images all partake of the same kind of reality, a mental reality which has no extension in space or time, and can therefore be conceived as indivisible into parts. If a Power manifests itself in one place it is not therefore the less conceivable elsewhere; the concept of extension is as inappropriate for a Power as it would be for a thought. Similarly, what of the dead remains in the experience of the living consists of the ghost, and what is called the *dong piny*, which literally means 'that which remains on (or in) the ground'. Yet it would be untrue to say that the Dinka think that the dead 'dissolve' into two kinds of components, the *atyep* or ghost and the *dong piny*, the 'what is in the ground'. The distinction between *atyep*, ghost, and *dong piny* is not a distinction of substances in the dead, but a distinction between two experiences of them—the experience of them as in some way still present to the memory as in life and without any single physical location, and the experience of them as dead in the grave. The *atyep*, therefore, may disturb its living kin wherever they may be, though its activity is more readily regarded as purposive and reasonable if it appears to a man in his home, where he can act to satisfy it. Like the Powers, however, it may 'follow' him abroad for—as we see the situation—it exists in him. The *dong piny* may of course be 'called to mind' anywhere, in that a man may voluntarily think about them; but they are thought to act directly only near the grave. The experience they reflect or image, as their name 'that which remains in the ground' implies, is the encounter with the bodily remains in their particular place of burial.

It is thus not a simple matter to divide the Dinka believer, for analytic purposes, from what he believes in, and to describe the latter then in isolation from him as the 'object' of his belief.

The Dinka themselves imply this when they speak of the Powers as being 'in men's bodies', but also 'in the sky' or in other particular places. Their world is not for them an object of study, but an active subject; hence the world (*piny*) as a whole is often invoked for aid along with other Powers.

If the Powers image different ranges of experience, we should not expect the several accounts of them given by the Dinka to agree in details, nor their assertions about them severally, when pieced together by us, to have the connectedness and logical consistency of reflective thought. Dinka experience naturally differs from group to group and person to person. It has appeared from the preceding chapters that the Dinka Divinity is spoken of as both single and manifold. All the sky-Powers are said to 'be' Divinity; yet Divinity is not any one of them, nor are all of them merely subnumerations of Divinity. They are also quite distinct from each other, though considered together in relation to men they have a reality of the same kind. The Dinka assert with a uniformity which makes the assertion almost a dogma that 'Divinity is one'. They cannot conceive of Divinity as a plurality and, did they know what it meant, would deeply resent being described as 'polytheistic'. What account can we now give ourselves of these Powers, both the same as and other than Divinity, which are not merely alternative names for it—for their attributes are not identical with those of Divinity—nor are they thought of as distinct, subordinate existences of the order of Divinity?

Our answer is that Divinity as a unity, and Divinity as a multiplicity, are not the products of logical or mystical elaboration of a revealed truth as are our own theological considerations of similar apprehensions. Divinity is manifold as human experience is manifold and of a manifold world. Divinity is one as the self's manifold experience is united and brought into relationship in the experiencing self. The Powers are distinct from each other, and from Divinity, as the experiences they image are distinct from each other and from the total experience of the world and the self.

Divinity, then, corresponds to experience common to all men, and to the Dinkas' recognition that a single human nature and condition embraces all. Divinity is thus everywhere, and everywhere the same. The different names by which different peoples know it are matters only of different languages. So in Divinity the Dinka image their experience of the ways in which human beings everywhere resemble each other, and in a sense form a single community with one original ancestor created by one Creator. Divinity therefore transcends the individual and social differentiations the Dinka know, as they recognize them in some ways to be transcended in a fundamental unity of human nature. This theme is frequently stressed in Dinka invocations and hymns:

... and you, Divinity, I call you in my invocation because you help everyone and you are great towards [in relation to] all people, and all people are your children ...

and

> Divinity, no other man is hated
> Divinity, my father, creator, no other man is hated ...

and in a hymn quoted from Fr. Nebel:

> God, Father, no man hates another in the whole world.[1]

When, therefore, a prophet like Arianhdit shows that he is able to make peace between normally exclusive and hostile communities, to persuade them to observe between them the peaceful conventions which they had previously observed only internally, and to unite people of different origins in a single community, he proves that he is a 'man of Divinity'.[2] It is not enough for a man to claim to be a 'man of Divinity' and expect such a reputation to follow from his claim; the conviction that a man is genuinely divinely inspired follows upon actual experience of his ability, which in turn strengthens his hand and makes future success more likely. The man is recognized as a powerful 'man of Divinity' because he creates for people the experience of peace between men and of the uniting of forces which are normally opposed to each other, of which Divinity is understood to be the grounds. Without providing that experience a

[1] In P. W. Schmidt, *Der Ursprung der Gottesidee*, 1949, vol. viii, p. 145.

[2] Hence the Dinka often say figuratively *hakuma ee nhialic*, 'the Government is Divinity', not as an attempt at flattery nor a mark of affection, but because it achieves what they could not themselves achieve. But if the Government is in this context assimilated to Divinity, no Dinka would say that Divinity was the Government.

man would not be regarded as truly a 'man of Divinity', whatever his claims to revelations. It is safe to say also that were a
man to show ability to unite people and bring peace between
them—were the force of his personality such—the Dinka would
attribute contact with 'divinity' to him even though he were to
make no claim to it.

Divinity, then, images here the lived experience of community
and concord, and as imaging the widest community the Dinka
can conceive, also represents truth, justice, honesty, uprightness, and such-like conditions of order and peace in human
relations. Where these are considered absent, Divinity is also
said to be absent from human affairs. And experience of living
is here clearly the basis from which comes such theoretical or
purely cognitive apprehension of Divinity and the Powers as
the Dinka have, for moral and social disorder are more immediately known than Divinity, whose existence does not need to
be posited before their results are felt. When their results are
felt, in sickness, discord, malice, and so on, to understand them
as reflecting the absence of a Divinity is also to recognize them
in a way which makes action to restore Divinity, to restore order
and health, possible. It is thus that their notion of Divinity may
be seen to arise in the experience of order in relation to disorder,
life in relation to death, and in other experiential opposites
which we have mentioned in an earlier chapter. Divinity is
thus comprehended in and through natural experience, and not
merely as a theoretical force producing the order of the world
from without.

Connected with the conceptualization, as Divinity, of the
basis of community, and of the widest community they can
conceive, is the attribution to Divinity of a universal fatherhood. We have already discussed some of the detailed ways in
which relations with Divinity and with the father are represented by a single model; but although from one point of view
all human beings are equivalent in relation to him collectively
as his children, it will be remembered that the eldest and
youngest sons among the Dinka, who are favoured by the rules
of inheritance and often actually favoured by the father, are
also regarded as the special favourites of the Powers. The eldest
and the youngest, the *kai* and the *kuun*, are *jok*, 'are [of the kind
of being of] Powers'. The usage is consciously metaphorical;

but we see that what is known to be their special fortune in relation to the family is reflected in the understanding as a specially close association with Divinity.

Finally, there is the attribution of creativity to Divinity; and here we must consider more generally the way in which the Dinka image in the Powers the diversities and polarities of experience. Divinity and MACARDIT concern every Western Dinka, and the two stand in apposition to each other as we have seen. They are not thought, however, to oppose each other as two warring 'beings' or 'principles'. MACARDIT is also Divinity, though Divinity is not MACARDIT. Since Divinity ultimately is the grounds of everything that is in man and nature, Divinity is the grounds of sterility, barrenness, and pointless or apparently pointless death as he is the grounds of creativity, fertility, and prosperity. There is no theoretical problem for the Dinka of reconciling an infinitely good Divinity with the presence of these evils in the world, on a logical or moral plane, because Divinity represents the grounds of what actually happens. Yet the particular affective experience of fertility and prosperity, and of a just, kind, and reasonable order in the events of men's lives, is distinct from that of sterility, barrenness, and sudden inexplicable death. Similarly, the moral order of the homestead and community is explicitly contrasted with the amoral life of wild beasts in the unordered life of the forest.[1] One of the worst insults which can be offered to human beings among the Dinka is to liken them to game. Darkness with its unseen and sudden dangers is similarly in opposition to daylight. All these contrasted experiences are reflected in the apposition of Divinity and MACARDIT. They are not conceived as 'beings' actively pitted against each other, as experiences in themselves cannot actively oppose each other. The difference between them is not intrinsically in them but in the human experiences they image.

Similarly, the free-Divinities DENG, ABUK, and GARANG correspond to fields of experience which are special aspects of the total to which Divinity corresponds. We have indicated what these fields are in general—that imaged by DENG includes

[1] This polarity has frequently been noted among primitive peoples; but it is interesting to note that among the Anuak, who are ethnically related to the Dinka, and among whom the same·contrast is found, Divinity is associated rather with wild nature than with human society. Anuak religion is consistently very different from that here described.

the phenomena of the sky associated with rain, that imaged by ABUK is the life of the gardens and the crops, and that imaged by GARANG, the 'shining master' of the hymn on p. 87, includes the heat of the sun and certain heated conditions of the human body. The configuration of experience which these three, separately and together, image is very complex, and I do not claim to have been able fully to explore it. It is clear, however, that if we consider only the complete connotations in Dinka life of sun, rain, and vegetation, the fact that the three images are regarded as in some way related as husband, wife, and son has a significance beyond that merely of their being understood on the pattern of the human family. GARANG's and DENG's father–son relationship with ABUK as wife and mother is consistent with the association of sun and rain and earth necessary for the herds and the crops.[1]

The Dinka do not of course break down the imaginative complexes we have discussed in this way into related but separate constituent parts. Did they do so, in fact, we should not expect to find them imaging them in the Powers, and part of our difficulty in interpreting the Powers lies in the fact that the experiences they image are not correlated by the Dinka in alternative ways. As I have said, they include what we should distinguish as physical and moral experience in an organic unity. Thus, for example, rain–coolness–pastures–cattle–milk–procreation–abundance–life–light and also rain–clouds–thunder–lightning–sudden death, not in that or any sort of successive order, are all represented by DENG. In addition, there is the association of DENG with ABUK, as son or husband, and the association of ABUK with the vegetation and particularly the crops. Again, taking only one of the elements of the experience imaged by DENG and ABUK in relationship, the rain-associations of DENG suggest equally the lush pastures which the Dinka want for their cattle, and the rich harvests from which their women will prepare porridge and beer. The cattle are the affair of men—of husbands and sons—and DENG is a male divinity, and a husband or a son. The gardens, though partly worked by

---

[1] In a hymn collected by Fr. Nebel, and quoted in P. W. Schmidt, op. cit., 1949, p. 143, there appears the line: 'Sonnen-regen (*DENG-akol*) wird uns erhalten Leben auch', to which Fr. Schmidt adds the footnote: 'Der leichte Regen ist der keimenden Saat sehr zuträglich.'

men, belong primarily to the women, who in any case do the work of turning their produce into food. ABUK similarly is a female divinity and presides over women's affairs, and she and DENG are called upon together, often as mother and son, to bring the Dinka the fertility and prosperity—the 'life'—which the joint labours of men and women among the cattle and the crops in suitable conditions of rain and sun will bring. GARANG, associated with the sun among other things, is part of this family of three. By the association often made between GARANG the Power and Garang the first man, between ABUK and Abuk the first woman, and between DENG and Deng, their son or ABUK's husband, the whole configuration of experiences they image together is further enriched by the inclusion in it of an original fatherhood, motherhood, and sonship. In our earlier description we could only proceed by considering the 'imagery' of the Powers *seriatim*; but it is in the representation of extremely complex configurations of moral and physical experience, the elements in which are not distinct from each other but are embedded, as it were, in extensive metaphors, that the Powers have their force. It has taken several paragraphs of description to re-create only a part of the total experiential connotation of the word GARANG, for example, which the mere word GARANG immediately represents for Dinka. We have to take into account not only the experience of the natural environment imaged in the Powers, but also the Dinkas' particular relationship with it, the way in which it is intimately linked with the moral life, the hopes and fears of men.

DENG, for example, is not merely a 'personification' of rain, lightning, &c.—rain and lightning endowed fancifully or through ignorance with human personal qualities. The name DENG re-creates for the Dinka the whole syndrome of experiences of these natural phenomena as they touch directly upon human life. Rain and its associated phenomena, for people like the Dinka whose subsistence economy makes them directly dependent upon the grass and the crops, do in fact mean life and abundance, just as their absence, or their presence at the wrong time or place, can mean death and misery. When DENG is 'in' a man's body, to use the Dinka expression, that man becomes as it were a meeting-place for the human and ultra-human influences in their lives. To use our European type of distinction between Nature and Mind, it is rather that some men on occasion incorporate in themselves the ultra-human forces of Nature, than that they endow Nature with qualities which they recognize in themselves and in human kind. When the Dinka ask, as in a hymn,

DENG, Governor, support his life . . .

the term DENG represents an integration of political and moral experience with experience of nature in a single image. Through the colour-symbolism we have already mentioned, this image also includes the black-and-white configurations in cattle, which again impress themselves upon the minds of the Dinka as does the lightning in dark, lowering skies which signifies the activities of DENG.

Such associations of the Powers as we have mentioned still do not exhaust their 'meaning'; for as experience, though it be fundamentally experience of the same basic situations of Dinka life, varies from place to place, time to time, and in a smaller measure from individual to individual, so there are local and individual variations in the Powers known and the ways in which they are represented. First, since divinities are manifest in human prophets and diviners who claim to speak for them, the particular characteristics of these prophets, as men, modify the Dinkas' representation of the Powers themselves. Hence we find the numerous refractions of DENG, for example, to be distinct from each other as those in whom they have been recognized are different persons, alike in the fundamental experience they image. Also, even as representing only rain or meteorites or thunder and lightning, DENG is likely to fall anywhere, but does in fact fall in particular places at particular times. As rain, or thunder and lightning, or a meteorite, which fall in one place, are not, and yet are, the same as those which fall elsewhere at some other time, so DENG is one and many.

There is further the imaging in the Powers of what must be presumed to be external influences of whole groups of people, but for which unfortunately, for the Dinka, there is little independent historical evidence. We hear that Powers have come into particular parts of Dinka country, or have spread from one part to another. GARANG and DENG are thus at one and the same time an original father and son, two Powers with the general experiential associations we have mentioned, and also known in some parts of Dinkaland as the clan-divinities of particular clans. We cannot now know the historical factors involved in this supposed appearance or reappearance of Powers in particular places and at particular times, nor in the relationship between DENG and GARANG known to be the divinities of particular clans, and DENG and GARANG as free divinities potentially affecting all people. It is interesting to note though that a traveller forms the impression that the Dinka whose countries are nearest to foreign influence are those among whom the Powers are regarded as most strongly operating. Western Twij Dinka country is singled out by the Rek as a source of diffusion of knowledge of the free-divinities. It is generally held that GARANG in particular entered Western Dinkaland from there. GARANG is also well known among the Bor and Twij Dinka of the east bank of the Nile, and there can be no doubt that the Western Twij Dinka came originally from there.[1] DENG seems to be particularly strong among the Ngok and Rueng, and to judge by the earlier literature, among the northern groups of Dinka.

It is these parts of Dinkaland which have been for longest in intimate contact with the northern Sudan and, I suggest, it is possible that among them not only has the experience of a strong influence coming from without been assimilated to the experience imaged in the free-divinities but in the case of GARANG, at least, some of the associations of that Power are particularly appropriate also to the Dinka experience of the Arabs to the north. The north is known as a hot land, from which, however, the cool winds come; and GARANG, as in the hymn we have quoted (p. 87), though associated with sun and heat, is asked to bring coolness. The Arabs themselves are to the Dinka red or yellow-brown men from a land of sand. These are the colours of GARANG; but further, the cattle-Arabs to the north of the Ngok and Twij Dinkas have a particular reputation as great hunters of the giraffe, the game with which GARANG is also specially associated. It is possible then that these free-divinities (which according to many Dinka have always existed,

---

[1] Western Twij who have not visited the east bank of the Nile not only speak a dialect resembling that of the east bank, but also have traditions which agree in detail with some of those of the east bank Twij.

and are associated with original human figures)¹ have come to
be regarded as 'seizing' men the more powerfully as powerful
external influences have impinged more forcibly upon them. It
is quite clearly held by the Dinka that minor fetishes and earth
Powers have entered their country from the little non-Dinka
tribes to the south of them, people who to the Dinka appear to
have an unpleasant interest in magical roots and herbs found
in their country. The fetishes which have come from them are
unpleasant and despicable and, compared with the sky-Powers,
of minor importance, like the influence of the peoples from
whom they come.

Whatever may be the historical factors involved in knowledge
and spread of the Powers, the absence of dogma and definition
about them permits great imaginative freedom of associations
of ideas and images. It was not necessarily, it seems to me,
flattery or caution which prompted the diviner to whom Professor and Mrs. Seligman spoke (Chap. II, p. 75) to say 'that
his spirit was "red" (as Europeans are) and came from Khartoum', even though it was also a refraction of DENG. The Power
includes in its imagery the experience of human influence also.
News of the Northern Sudanese prophet, the Mahdi, reached
Dinkaland too, and in some places, though known only by
name, the Mahdi (in Dinka, *Maadi*) is assimilated in thought
to the prophets of the Powers. This may be seen in two versions
of the same hymn, the one collected in the Awan (Pajok or
Kon Pioth) tribe of the north-west of Dinka territory, nearer
to the centre of Mahdist influence, and the other collected in
central Rek territory, farther from northern influence. The
north-western version is as follows:

> It is *Maadi*,² the son of DENG
> To whom we ants pray on earth, our DENG,
> We invoke the clan-divinity along with DENG.
> The ant-men have been miserable for eight years.
> What hurt us in the past
> What the creator [prophet] from above spoke of

¹ It may be that, viewed in one way, DENG and GARANG have always existed,
since despite their association with an original human family they are non-mortal
by nature, but that as 'seizing' people, they are spoken of as of more recent origin
just as the powerful external influences of which we speak are thought of as of
comparatively recent incursions into Dinkaland.
² *Madi* is also a Nuer spirit.

It is *Maadi* son of DENG we ants pray to below, our DENG
We invoke the clan-divinity and Longar.

The old man who sang this hymn said in reply to a question
that *Maadi* was a great prophet they had heard of in the north:
'We have heard that Divinity appeared in the north.' The
details to which the 'eight years' and 'what hurt us in the past'
referred were not known, but this reference to a prophecy of
suffering is found in other hymns and is connected vaguely by
the Dinka with the times of the troubles at the end of the nineteenth century, 'when the earth was spoilt'. Apart from the
introduction of the Mahdi, the hymn contains a typical set of
Dinka religious images. The version of the hymn found in
central Rek country differed in two details. There the first line
was given as:

It is *maric*, son of DENG . . .

and the third line as

We invoke the clan-divinity *gong* (Hedgehog). . . .

This reading gives the hymn an entirely and consistently Dinka
range of reference. *Maric* is 'thunder', and is therefore fittingly
referred to in a poetic image as 'son of DENG'. Hedgehog, the
clan-divinity of Pagong, is appropriately linked with Longar,
the founder of that clan. It would seem, then, as though the
substitution of *Maadi* for *maric* here was the incorporation of
the news of a new manifestation of Divinity in the north into
an older hymn. A full understanding of the free-divinities in
general might thus require a more detailed knowledge of the
historical factors than is now available.

The clan-divinities are easily seen as representative of a
particular limited field of Dinka experience, that of agnatic
kinship, as we have pointed out. They reflect experience of the
abiding descent-group structure of Dinka society. If Divinity
represents among other things the situation of human beings as
the children of a common father, the clan-divinities are the
counterparts of the particular and distinct patrilineal descent-
groups and reflect experience and knowledge of them and the
value attached to them. By this I do not mean that they are
merely the devices by which social groups, considered as enti-
ties, are represented, to focus loyalty and affection, on the

familiar analogy with national flags or heraldic emblems. We have seen that the clan-divinities do not primarily face outwards, so to speak, from the clans to which they belong, providing a mark by which others may know them. The name of the clan is enough for that, and Dinka often know the names of clans other than their own without also knowing what their divinities are. The clan-divinities have their meaning in relation to the nature of clanship as members of their clans know it, as membership of agnatic descent-groups which transcend their individual members, and yet of which each individual membership is representative. They provide the clearest example of the structure of experience represented by the Powers.

The separation of peoples into different original groups, the break-up of an original community into opposed factions, is often assumed in the stories of how clans acquired their divinities. In the story of the way in which Pajieng, for example, acquired the black cobra (pp. 117–18), the event which brought this about was a situation in which the relations between its founder and the founder of Padiangbar were conducted with such unreasonableness and inequitable insistence on exact reciprocity that they could not live together in friendship. A similar situation appears in the story of how the clan Pareng acquired the *reng* marking in cattle as one of its divinities. A child of Pareng was accused of stealing and swallowing the beads of a member of another family while he was bathing. The family whose member had lost the beads insisted upon having the Pareng child cut open to retrieve the beads, which were later found in the dung of a *reng* cow which had in fact swallowed them. Pareng then left the village of its unreasonable neighbours, and thereafter 'respected'—here with the main sense of 'avoided'—the *reng* configuration.[1]

Even where the division of peoples is not represented as integrally bound up with the acquisition of the clan-divinities, it is assumed as a condition for that acquisition. In historical sequence, then, the distinctions of human clanship are always represented as preceding the knowledge of clan-divinities.

---

[1] Versions of this story are found among the Nuer and other Nilotes. Stories in which the same principle is illustrated—the principle that unreasonable insistence upon exact reciprocity involves the separation of communities—have a wider distribution in Africa. See, for example, I. G. Cunnison, *History on the Luapula*, Rhodes–Livingstone Papers No. 21, 1951, p. 11.

Clanship, as we have earlier emphasized, does not proceed from the presence of the clan-divinity; the presence of the clan-divinity proceeds from the fact of clanship. Similarly, it will be remembered that while those who are forbidden to marry by the rules of clan exogamy naturally have the same divinity, to have the same divinity is not in itself a bar to intermarriage.

We have considered the ways in which the clan-divinities are addressed and spoken of, and the respectful regard for their emblems where these are species which can be touched and handled. All these forms emphasize the relationship between clansmen and their divinities, in their emblems, as one of conjunction and disjunction at the same time. In the case of twin-birth relationships between men and their divinities (in the emblems) it is explicitly said that the animal emblem is 'separated' from its human clansmen, and placed in its own element —the river, in the case of the crocodile for example. In that separation the humans and their divinities' emblems respect each other. The theme of division in unity is found again in the reference to the clan-divinity usually as 'grandfather' (not 'father') and its emblems as 'half-brother' (not 'brother'), for the essential element of Dinka clanship is that it is the relationship between children of a common ancestor (or 'grandfather') whose lines of agnatic descent are different. The Dinka clan member is united with and divided from his clansmen[1] as clansmen as a whole are united with and divided from the clan-divinity and its emblems. The clan-divinity thus images the widest experience of agnatic relationship which a Dinka has. It helps its clansmen, as clansmen have the obligation to help each other; they 'are together' in the divinity as they 'are together' (theoretically) in the blood-feud and in the obligation to help each other in the payment of compensation for homicide. That obligation, of course, can only be effective within a certain territorial range, but the Dinka always insist that in principle it binds clansmen wherever they may be.

Normally, the senior lineage of any group of collateral lineages within a tribe is thought to be more effective in invocation of the clan-divinity than others are, and by Dinka customs of

---

[1] Full-brothers are also clansmen, of course, but no Dinka would refer to his full-brother as his clansman, any more than one would refer to a brother as a relative.

inheritance it is normally the eldest son who is chosen to succeed the father and who represents the father to his brothers. The senior son, or the senior lineage, thus not only *in*vokes the divinity more effectively, but also *e*vokes more fully sentiments of agnatic solidarity. The reputed strength of the invocations of a man or a lineage, therefore, on the whole corresponds to their social importance within the clan or family. Within a tribe, the whole subtribe with which the senior lineage of the clan of spear-masters with tribal primacy is found is called the *wun yath*, the subtribe of the divinity. In this way the strength of the clan-divinity is regarded as greater in those whose importance for the structure of the clan is greater.

It is to be expected, therefore, that the divinities of the clans of spear-masters should be regarded as more powerful than those of the secular clans, and should sometimes be said to be the only original clan-divinities. Members of spear-master clans particularly maintain that in the past they were more influential politically than they are today, when the warrior clans have multiplied—as, incidentally, according to this account, have the numbers of clan-divinities. A master of the fishing-spear said that warrior clans 'did not sacrifice for divinities, but only for the ghosts of the dead'; and the fact that the propitiation of ghosts of the dead is a family cult implies here the suggestion that at one time the warrior clans were scarcely to be regarded as clans at all, but as disunited families with no sense of a wider agnatic relationship. In fact also the spear-master clans can on the whole produce clearer and longer genealogies than the rest. Members of warrior clans, asserting their own importance also, deny that they have acquired their clan-divinities more recently than the clans of spear-masters, saying that they too have their clan-divinities which help *them*.[1] They admit, however, that their divinities are not on the whole as strong (*kec*, literally 'biting' or 'hot' or 'bitter') as those of the spear-masters, and that the divinities of the spear-masters when called upon by masters of the fishing-spear will help whole tribes and subtribes, whilst the divinities of warrior clans help only members of those clans. Similarly, the master of the fishing-spear is regarded as belonging to and supporting everyone in his community: 'no

[1] It may be also that the modern administrative system has given more scope to outstanding men from warrior clans.

man has a master of the fishing-spear all of his own' as the Dinka say.

Finally, as the spear-master clans as a whole are known to be superior to the warrior clans in influence and endowment within the whole social system of the Dinka, so their homogeneity and superiority in relation to the warrior clans are imaged in the common and supreme clan-divinity they all possess—*ring*, Flesh. As will be seen in the myths of the spear-master clans with which the second part of this book starts, these clans are regarded as deriving their superiority from a common original experience from which the warrior clans were excluded, and they accordingly share a common divinity in addition to the different divinities which correspond to their different lines of agnatic descent.

In this chapter I have tried to describe the contexts of experience within which Dinka assertions about the Powers may be understood and harmonized, as they cannot be understood by us if they are regarded as referring to theoretical 'beings' whose existence is posited, as it were, before the human experience to which they correspond. As images, the Powers contract whole fields of direct experience and represent their fundamental nature each by a single term. The Dinka sometimes indicate that originally the free-divinities did not affect them so powerfully as now; that they knew only the power of the clan-divinities, and more particularly of the clan-divinities of the spear-master clans, and Divinity itself which those clans represented to their political communities. We do not know whether this is historically true; but it is significant that, according to the Dinka, the effects of free-divinities on individuals have been the more widely and deeply felt as their own political autonomy has been undermined. 'Everyone now wants to be a master', say the masters of the fishing-spear; and in general the rise of the free-divinities, potentially equally affecting all Dinka as individuals and families, corresponds to their recognition of increasing individualism in their life and intimations of changes in the basic structure of their society. So also do assertions that witchcraft and the use of fetishes have increased and are increasing. On the other hand, the reaction to loss of political autonomy also makes possible wider political combinations than were previously possible, and the influence of prophets is undoubtedly made possible by a response on the part of many Dinka, traditionally divided from each other, to a common influence or set of influences. The great prophets, those who are also masters of the fishing-spear, are thought to have a place also in the original system of religious and political institutions before these were modified by external forces. In this they correspond to the balance of change and permanence in their life which the Dinka encounter in experiences of foreign influence and control.

I have suggested that the Powers may be understood as images corresponding to complex and various combinations of Dinka experience which are contingent upon their particular social and physical environment. For the Dinka they are the grounds of those experiences; in our analysis we have shown them to be grounded in them, for to a European the experiences are more readily understood than the Powers, and the existence of the latter cannot be posited as a condition of the former. Without these Powers or images or an alternative to them there would be for the Dinka no differentiation between experience of the self and of the world which acts upon it. Suffering, for example, could be merely 'lived' or endured. With the imaging of the grounds of suffering in a particular Power, the Dinka can grasp its nature intellectually in a way which satisfies them, and thus to some extent transcend and dominate it in this act of knowledge. With this knowledge, this separation of a subject and an object in experience, there arises for them also the possibility of creating a form of experience they desire, and of freeing themselves symbolically from what they must otherwise passively endure. The symbolic action by which this is accomplished is described in later chapters.

PART TWO

V

THE MYTHS OF THE SPEAR-MASTERS

I

THE pre-eminence of the clans of spear-masters, their hereditary priesthood, is established by myths which the Dinka recount in some detail, and with much interest. They represent the beginning of a systematic correspondence between religious conceptions and traditional political experience. The myths as known in different parts of Dinkaland have fundamental features in common, though also differences between them correspond to differences in political realities between parts of Dinkaland. I first give examples of the myths, and of the way in which they are linked with political history up to the present time.

The following version was collected among the Apuk (*Patuan*) tribe of the central Rek Dinka:

Long ago, lions used to hold dances, and a man called Jiel[1] attended a lions' dance. A lion asked him for his bracelet (or ring), and when it was refused, the lion cut off his thumb in order to pull off the bracelet:[2] As a result of this, Jiel died, leaving an old wife with a daughter but no son. In bitter distress, she went to weep by

---

[1] There may be some connexion between this name and the Bor Dinka word *pajiel*, meaning 'one who is [left] by himself'.

[2] Lions which change into men and back are a common subject of Dinka story. The lion symbolizes a fierce enemy. The introduction of lions here thus suggests that Jiel was among enemies. Some who have told me this myth have placed its incidents in the last century, saying that his thumb was cut off by a *turuk*, which might be any lighter-skinned foreigner. In view of the fact that some of the Shilluk are traditionally supposed to have passed through the Bahr-al-Ghazal region, it is interesting to note that in D. Westermann, *The Shilluk People, their Language and Folklore*, 1912, the story of the cutting off of the bracelet is given as part of a story of the migrations of the Shilluk under their first king, Nyikang. There the incident occurs when Garo, the son of the Sun, is defeated by Dak the son of Nyikang.

the bank of the river. A Power of the river, MALENGDIT,[1] came to her and asked her why she wept, and when she said that it was because her husband was dead and she had no son, the Power called her to him in the river. He told her to lift her skirt, and to draw the waves [or the foam] towards her with her hand so that they might enter her. He then gave her a spear [which, carried by a woman, is a sign that she has borne a male child] and a fish to sustain her, and told her to go swiftly home, for she had conceived a son whom she would soon bear.[2]

The woman went home and bore a male child whom she called Aiwel.[3] The child was born with its teeth complete. [Dinka regard this as an augury of religious power.] One day, while Aiwel was still a tiny baby, his mother left him sleeping in the hut and went out for a while. On her return, she found that a gourd of milk which she had left in the hut had been drunk, and she punished her daughter for taking it, though the girl denied that she had done so. When this happened again, the mother pretended to leave Aiwel alone in the hut with a gourd of milk, but hid herself where she could watch him, and saw him get up and drink the milk. She told him then that she had seen him, and he warned her that if she told anyone she would die. Eventually she did tell someone else, and 'she died by Aiwel's word'.

This last detail is not found in all versions, but it illustrates that Aiwel already had in childhood the power for which important masters of the fishing-spear are renowned, that of speaking what is (becomes) true, and to do this even in childhood. To kill the mother, which any ordinary Dinka would regard as particularly wicked, is accepted in this child of the Power without criticism.

[1] This is also the Power to which smallpox is attributed.

[2] Fr. P. A. Nebel, *Dinka Dictionary with Grammar*, 1948, gives another version of this situation as told of the Parek clan of the Aweil District Dinka. Here the child, also the child of the wave 'which goes and returns', is called Awutiak, which means 'Wave', and the following song celebrates his birth:

Arek the Great followed the River-Lord up to the Kir (Bahr-al-Arab)
The river where the Arabs are, which borders on death,
Which builds a dam and closes a door,
To be not found on this side of the Arab country.
She followed the Lord into his home.
The Wave is my mother's husband,
Arek the Great followed the Lord up to the Kir . . . .

[3] Ibrahim Eff. Bedri, 'Notes on Dinka Religious Beliefs in their Hereditary Chiefs and Rainmakers', *S.N. & R.*, 1939, says that among the Northern Dinka this name means a ground-nut left over at the harvest, which sprouts by itself in the following year, but this meaning was not known to the Rek whom I questioned.

Aiwel then left his mother's people and went to live with his father, the Power, in the river, and grew up there. When he was a grown man, he came back from the river with an ox which had in it every known colour, but was predominantly *mangok*, the colour of rain clouds.[1] This was the ox by the name of which he was to be known henceforth: 'Longar'.

Aiwel Longar then lived in the village tending the cattle which had belonged to Jiel. At this time, there was a drought in the land and all the people had to take their cattle for long distances to find a little water and grass for them. While the cattle of the village were thus thin and dying those of Aiwel Longar were fat and sleek, and some of the young men of the village therefore decided to spy upon him to see where he watered and pastured them. They found that he took his cattle outside the village, and there would pull up tufts of the *awar* grass[2] from beneath which springs of water flowed for his herd to drink. Longar knew that they had spied on him and when they returned to the village and told the people they died.

Longar then called together the elders of the village and said that they should all leave their land, for cattle and men were dying, and would die, there. He offered to take them to the fabulous pastures of Lual Aghony,[3] where there was endless grass and water and no death. The elders refused to be led there by Longar, but set off alone.

Aiwel Longar then left the people; and Divinity placed mountains and rivers between him and them. (It appears here that after all they were trying to follow him, but this is not explained.) And across one river which the people had to cross, Divinity made a dike like a fence (the reed dike which the Dinka now make for catching fish, and which shows them where to dart the spear by the motion of the reeds as fish touch them). As the people tried to pass this fence of reeds to cross to the other side, Longar stood above them on the opposite bank of the river, and as soon as he saw the reeds moved as men touched them, he darted his fishing-spear at them and struck them in the head, thus killing them as they crossed.

This is the event in the myth which seems, as the Dinka tell it, to concentrate the whole significance of the first part; and when they reach this point they almost always raise the arm,

---

[1] The fact that the ox was marked with all known cattle-colours has probably the effect of suggesting untold wealth in cattle. The ox is made to stand for all the herds of the Dinka.

[2] For the significance of this particular grass (*Vetiveria nigritana*) to the Western Dinka, see Introduction, (i), p. 7.

[3] The 'promised land' of the Dinka. A Dinka commented to me: 'But I don't think now that it really exists, or surely the Government would have found it.'

as though holding a fishing-spear, and make the rapid and vigorous darting movement by which they spear fish, especially the large catfish as they move at certain seasons in the shallow floods of the pastureland. This version of the myth then continues:

> The people were thus being finished altogether, and a man named [in this account] Agothyathik called the people together to make a plan to save them from the fishing-spear of Longar. His plan was that his friend should take the sacrum of an ox which he had fastened to a long pole, and should move through the water before him, holding out the sacral bone so that it would move the reeds. They carried out this plan, and Longar's fishing-spear, darted at the sacrum which he mistook for a human head, was held fast there. Meanwhile, Agothyathik left the water and seized Longar from behind and held him. There they remained for a long time locked together until Longar was tired with wrestling.

This is a second point of heightened interest in the telling of the myth. The seizing and wrestling are often mimed by those telling it, and Longar is sometimes represented as a Protean figure who changes his form into that of various beasts in order to escape from his captor, who still holds him firmly and eventually overcomes him. This version continues:

> Aiwel Longar now told Agothyathik that it was enough, and that he should call his people to cross the river in safety and sit around him and Agothyathik. Some came when they were called, but others were afraid and did not come then. To those who came, Aiwel Longar gave fishing-spears to pray with, and to some he also gave a type of spear called the *tong alal*.[1] With the spears, Aiwel gave to these men the power to invoke effectively with them (*lam*), and the power of his spittle to bless and of his tongue to curse, and the divinity Flesh, which was his originally. He also gave them [or some of them] other clan-divinities; and he took a bull of the colour of the sky and removed from it the thigh-bone while it still lived and gave it to Agothyathik, telling him that this would be the clan-divinity of Agothyathik and of his children, and that they must never damage or break a thigh-bone.

Those who were given these things by Longar were the founders of the clans which are now clans of spear-masters. Those who did not come at first when they were called founded the warrior clans,

---

[1] A *tong* is normally a war-spear, while the fishing-spear is *bith*.

the *kic*, who are now the 'people of the war-spear' while the spear-masters are the 'people of the fishing-spear'.

When Aiwel Longar had given out his powers with the spears, he told Agothyathik and the other masters of the fishing-spear to look after the country, saying that he himself would leave it to them to do so and not intervene, except where they found some trouble too serious for them to deal with alone, and he would then help them. [As a Dinka put it, Longar would be 'like the Governor-General, and they would be like Provincial Governors'.]

Most of this particular version represents what was known and thought of the myth by a senior member of the Padolmuot clan, who was himself the sororal nephew of an important master of the fishing-spear of the Pagong clan, the clan founded by Longar. The tribe to which it refers is the Apuk Patuan tribe,[1] in which the clan of spear-masters with tribal primacy is Paghol, the clan descended from Agothyathik himself. Within the tribe, however, the Pagong clan is regarded as very important and influential, and in some ways superior to Paghol. The largest subtribe is under the influence, not of Paghol, but of Pagong. In that tribe there is an undercurrent of rivalry and even hostility between Paghol, and Pagong with their classificatory sisters' sons Padolmuot. This comes out partly in another version of the same myth from the same tribe, this time as it was told by Chief Gir Kiro, who has for long been the official chief of the tribe and is himself a man of Paghol. The Paghol subclan in the Apuk tribe is composed of four main lineages and the founders of three of these are mentioned in the narrative. I have retained most of the actual expressions of Chief Gir, as they give a lively impression of the spirit in which the myth is recalled; and I have included details which illustrate the blending of the past and the present, and of myth and traditional history. They may be of value to any Dinka who some day tries to reconstruct the history of his people, for there are few men of Chief Gir Kiro's age and experience whose memories remain so clear.

Great Longar of the clan Pagong was deceiving people in order to kill them. People were waiting in the river. My ancestor Agothyathik spoke with the people there. Longar said that people must cross the

---

[1] The political structure of this tribe is more fully discussed in my essay on the political system of the Western Dinka, op. cit., 1958, pp. 121–5.

river and dive under the water. There were reeds in that river called the Kir.[1] As people dived, Longar struck them in the head with his fishing-spear, and people tried to run back but Longar said 'Come, dive'. And Agothyathik thought and said 'All you people, Longar's word is a deception, I will make a plan' [literally, 'I will work my own word.']

The story from here to the capture of Longar is not appreciably different from that already given. Chief Gir named the helper of Agothyathik as Awiceou, of which small lineage there are representatives near his mother's home.

Then Longar lifted up Agothyathik before the crowd, and said 'You Agothyathik, you will carry the spear in war in this country.' And he spat on an *alal* spear and a war-spear and gave them to Agoth, and sang
'Who is brave as Thik [Agothyathik] who avoids the *alal* spear of Longar?'
Longar had a bangle on his wrist which had cut deeply into his flesh and when he cut off his thumb to remove the bangle, he died —or perhaps he went into the grave alive.
Agoth married and Akol Kwec was born. He fought with those foreigners who build mounds to live on, who lived at Angac, near Bor. Akol Kwec died there and his sons by his three wives were Ring, Jok and Anau. Jok had a full brother, and Anau had a full brother, but Ring was the only son of his mother. Ring was a child of a woman of the Luac tribe, who were his maternal uncles.

This passage refers to political realities of the present day. Akol Kwec is the founder of the main lineage of the Apuk subclan of Paghol to which the narrator himself belongs. He is here represented as the *father* of three sons, who are the founding ancestors of the other three main lineages of the subclan of Paghol in Apuk. Other genealogies, however, show Akol Kwec as the *brother* of Anau and Jok. The history here reflects a claim to personal dominance which the narrator and his father achieved. The account continues:

Anau, the eldest son, said 'You, Ring, you will be the fighting chief and you Jok, you will follow Ring. The cattle-camp [tribe] will be divided, and your camp, Jok, will be called 'Amakir', after the river, and your camp, Ring, will be called 'Aluala', and my

[1] The Bahr-al-Arab and the Bahr-el-Jebel are equally 'Kir'; here the Bahr-el-Jebel is intended.

PLATE VI

Spearmaster's shrine and spears

camp will be called 'Abaga' [after a small bird]. And you Ring, if your camp [section] fights against Amakir, I will put you together again [I will reconcile you], and I shall stay to do Divinity's work [literally, 'his word'] on earth. Divinity exists.[1] And I shall be like your maternal uncle, if a man is angry with another I will make peace between them. And you shall not fight against me.

Here the reference is to the original three subtribes from which the present tribe of Apuk Patuan is thought to have developed, Amakir, Aluala, and Abaga. Abaga now is very tiny, and is administratively incorporated in another subtribe. It remains, however, the subtribe containing the senior main lineage of the subclan of Paghol in Apuk, which has there tribal primacy, and it is therefore called 'the subtribe of the (clan) divinity' (*wun yath*).

Then they fought with a red-skinned people called Lwel,[2] and chased them out of the country of the Cic Dinka, opposite Bor. They came to another land called Padang, and another place called Angac, and they were fighting their way through all the time. So they came on westward, leaving the Agar and the Cic Dinka behind them. The father of all the Agar was called Arol, and the girl Amou, who bore the Rek, was Arol's sister.

This is not common knowledge to the Dinka. The narrator, with greater experience and the characteristically wider political vision of important members of spear-master clans, has linked up tribal groupings in a way which little concerns ordinary Dinka.

On the way, they met the Luac, who killed Duyak, the brother of Jok. Ring was heart-broken, because the Luac were his maternal uncles and had killed his half-brother. Jok said that it would be impossible to avenge his brother Duyak, because that might mean that Ring himself would be killed in the feud with his maternal uncles. Jok said that they should just go on their way.

But Ring behaved craftily, and said to Jok 'You go and lead the cattle out, and I will stay and catch up with you in three days'. So Ring stayed, and Jok moved on; and when he had gone, Ring took a lot of old cattle and cut them in pieces, so that the vultures would

---

[1] A pious exclamation.

[2] The Lwel are a legendary people of the Bahr-al-Ghazal, thought to have been Lwoo-speaking. Sometimes in the north of Western Dinkaland a light-skinned Dinka, with finer bones than most Dinka and a delicate appearance, is pointed out as being of Lwel ancestry. The name is probably from *lual*, 'red-brown'.

come in large numbers to feast off them. The Luac saw the vultures, and thinking that an elephant had died, they went to the place. Ring and the young men of his camp were hiding in the woods, and they fell on the Luac and killed them, thus avenging Duyak.

This passage represents a typical Dinka conflict of loyalties, to which we later refer, between the agnatic and the maternal sides. It also represents the resolution of this conflict in favour of agnatic loyalty, since Ring avenges his half-brother even against his maternal uncle's people. The trick by which the Luac are led to the place where they are killed is suggested by the Dinka custom of watching the sky for scavenging birds which indicate where a large beast has died.

Ring took a dog which was accompanying the Luac, and which was the dog of his maternal uncle. He stuck a needle into its neck, and it ran home, where his maternal grandfather pulled out Ring's needle, and knew that Ring had killed his people. He told his people to remain at home, and went himself to see Ring who was making a feast. Ring blamed the killing upon Jok's people who had left, but a man of Padolmuot[1] sang a song revealing that Ring had killed the Luac. Ring, who was making a rope while his people danced, got up and struck the man of Padolmuot, knocking him to the ground where he lay dying. Padolmuot took their spears to avenge their man, but the dying man stopped them, saying: 'Do not start blood-vengeance, it is better that you accept compensation. Ring is a master of the fishing-spear, and our spears will break if we try to take vengeance.' So Ring's people paid compensation.

Ring's maternal grandfather said, 'We will break relationship; your chieftainship ['mastership'] will be alone.' Ring and his people set out to follow Jok. They came to Panyang on the borders with the Luac, and there they divided and some became the tribes of Apuk Jurwir, and Thoiny, and Muok. The country became too small for them. They went to Apuk Patuan. Jok and Anau were there, but Ring wanted to follow the Luo and fight with them, and he followed them as far as Dok Kuac in the country of the Awan Riau tribe. Then he went on following the Luo as far as Malwal country and as far as the Akwang Ayat tribe. He told the Malwal that they should stay there on the river Lol, and he would return to Jok and Anau. And he left some people there.[2]

---

[1] This reflects a hostility between this clan and the clan of the narrator in the tribe at the present day. It also represents the narrator's clan as spiritually too powerful to be challenged.

[2] Hence, according to the narrator, there is a branch of his clan there.

When he returned, he found that Jok had found the great dry-season pasture at Panhom, and Ring said that Jok should 'have the country' for the time being. Ring bore Koriom, Jok became big and took the land.[1] Then Koriom's people became strong, and then Dac, the son of Ring's junior wife, became important in the land and then Mathiang Dit, the son of Jok, became important and seized the country.

And then the Dongolawi came. And my grandfather Thik made peace with all the other Dinka, and fought with the Nuer and the Arabs. And then he made peace between them all.[2] And Thik was followed by Kiro his son, and then some other people were made chiefs and there was much fighting. Then Gir (the narrator) came and made peace with the people of Yol Mayar (the Ajuong tribe) and the Awan Riau tribe, and it was agreed that Apuk should share their good dry-season pastures with the Agwok tribe. And the present Government[3] came and the Dinka were afraid of it but then they came to know it. So it is (*yenakan*).

This history has involved a digression from the main themes of myths of the spear-masters, but it shows clearly how, from the point of view of one very able man, the past and present are related; and we shall have reason to emphasize this relationship in explaining other versions of the myth which follow.

The following version is that known in the Kuac tribe of the Rek Dinka. There the clan of spear-masters with primacy throughout the whole tribe is Pajiek, the clan of Ajiek, who, as will be seen, becomes there the hero of the struggle with Longar. This version was largely given by an old man of the spear-master clan Padheou, the clan of Adheou, which accounts for the prominence with which Adheou figures in it.

Long ago, people were all in the river, and the first to come out of the river was called Longar. He was the eldest son, the eldest son of Divinity. As the rest of the people tried to follow him through the reeds to the bank, to get out of the river, he stood on the bank with a fishing-spear and speared them in the head. And there was a man called Ajiek in the river. He was the middle son. Ajiek said, 'Everyone will be finished by Longar, but I have thought of something to do.'

[1] The subtribes in which the Pajok main lineage has primacy are large and flourishing.

[2] This wide-range peace-making is a sign of a claim to wide political influence, as we have pointed out.

[3] That is the Anglo-Egyptian Government.

The trick by which Longar is seized is then described as in the other versions.

Longar called the people, and called upon them all in turn to repeat his invocations (*gam lung de*); as soon as they did so, they died.[1] And there was a man called Adheou, the youngest son created in the river, who said he would try to repeat the invocations of Longar. Ajiek tried to dissuade him, telling him that he would surely die, but Adheou began to repeat the invocations and he did not die. Longar was baffled, and thought of another trial. He transfixed Adheou's foot to the ground with a fishing-spear, and took the ribs and flesh of a slaughtered bull and hung them around Adheou's neck and head. With Adheou thus held, he prayed that Adheou might die.

So they stayed for many days, until the flesh covering Adheou putrefied, and he still lived. When after seven days of Longar's invocations made by day and night he saw that Adheou still lived, he freed him from the place where the spear held him and removed the putrefying meat from his head and chest, and said: 'Adheou, I am tired after my invocation: if I begin to fall asleep, then you must wake me up.'[2] That night, Adheou let Longar sleep heavily. And Longar had brought eight oxen which he was going to slaughter. While he slept, Adheou killed them all, and took small scraps of flesh from all over their carcasses, and hid them under the chyme [*wei*, which seems to be the same word as that for life or breath]. Longar awoke and saw that the oxen had disappeared. He asked Adheou where they were, and Adheou replied: 'Master (*beny*), I have killed them.' Longar said: 'Have you mixed up all the flesh?' and Adheou said that he had not done so, though he had hidden small scraps of it all. Longar said: 'Adheou, nothing will ever kill you, you are a clever one.' The people came and Longar told Adheou to divide the flesh of his oxen among them, giving each a small piece. Adheou divided the flesh thus, though he kept his own heap hidden away, and Longar did not know that there was so much flesh left over for Adheou.

---

[1] At sacrifices, masters of the fishing-spear invoke as we later describe, and others, especially their classificatory sisters' sons, repeat their invocations. The point here is that, as in the story of Padiangbar on pp. 145–6, those who repeat the invocations must themselves have a special strength if they are not to be injured by the repetition of them.

[2] The Dinka say that a really powerful master of the fishing-spear will not sleep at night, which is a time of danger for his people, but will remain awake to pray. One may compare the reported wakefulness, though for different reasons, of the king of the Shilluk (see C. G. and B. Z. Seligman, op. cit., 1932, p. 90). The point of the Dinka story here is to suggest that Longar was in this weaker than the founding ancestor of the clan of the narrator.

Ajiek then came, and stood on the fringes of the gathering, and sang the following song:

The Kuac tribe, among all people
Think of the word of Longar[1]
My father was abandoned by DENG
He was left without [the breath of] life
My father prayed to DENG and his mother ABUK
The sons of a man of Kuac are called to pray [to][2] their master [Longar].

Longar said: 'Who is that, and what is it that he sings?' and when he heard that it was Ajiek, he called him to him. Ajiek came with a white calf which he had brought for sacrifice at the shrine of Longar, and a gourd of milk for libation. Longar told the people to sit around him, and said, 'So, Ajiek, you think of the word of Longar?'[3] Ajiek said that he did, and so Longar called for the hind leg of a sacrificed ox and gave it to Ajiek.[4]

That night, Adheou took his scraps of flesh from beneath the chyme where he had hidden them, and took them to Longar, saying: 'My father, here are some things.' Longar said: 'Adheou, you have exhausted me. You shall be the foremost of the people to whom I have given my flesh, and even though I invoke against you myself, I shall not prevail.' The people stayed thus. The land was good and well-ordered. It was so. It was great Longar; he divided [shared out] the fishing-spears, and he shared out the flesh.[5]

In this version the point of insisting that Adheou received many scraps of flesh was to indicate the effectiveness and strength which the teller attributed to the invocations of members of his own clan, Padheou. Adheou had taken them, he said, 'so that the divinity would be great in him' (*bi yath dit ye guop*).

To illustrate the differences of emphasis which can be made even among members of a single tribe by informants of different

---

[1] 'The word' here has the force of 'everything Longar stands for'.

[2] The text has *rok*, a word which might be translated as 'to honour with hymns'.

[3] The story might be supposed to reflect some historical acceptance of a new cult, as suggested by Ibrahim Eff. Dedri, 'More Notes on the Padang Dinka', *S.N. & R.*, vol. xxix, 1948, p. 44, and Dr. P. P. Howell, pp. 102–3 above.

[4] The hind leg appears here as in the version given by members of the clan Paghol (p. 174); but since the thigh is not a clan-divinity of Pajiek as it is of Paghol, it is here said to be given to Ajiek because he was an honoured guest. The right hind leg is the portion of the maternal uncles of the sacrificing lineage.

[5] From which the divinity Flesh (Chap. III, pp. 135–46) derives.

clans, as well as to show which details remain constant, I give the myth now as it was told by a member of the Pajiek clan, of the same tribe:

Great Longar when people were created was the first created, and he commanded people to go, to cross the river, to take everything they had across the river.

The story from here to the seizing of Longar is then much as in the other versions. The differences are that in this story Longar cries out to the people who are trying to cross: 'Run away, run away, I am a Power (*jok*) which kills people', and that the plan by which Ajiek deceives Longar with the ox's sacrum is said to have been suggested by his wife. I asked whether Longar was really a man, or really a Power, and was told:

Longar was like a Power (*jok*) and he was like a man. It was he who was the first of all to be created. He had just come from Divinity's hand. He was at the head (source) of all life. He wanted to try everything, to test everything.

The myth was then continued:

Longar tried and tried to escape from Ajiek, and pulled himself away and ran into his hut. Ajiek led his cattle-herders across the river. Then the people of Longar began to die because of the people he had killed, whose ghosts (*atip*) returned to kill them. He called one of his men, and said: 'Go to Ajiek, and say "Why should my people die, when your people live?" ' Ajiek heard this and called the young men and girls of his camp and took them and the cattle away and hid them in the forest, leaving only a few old people at home. Then he took mud and made many graves in the village, so that, if Longar came, he could say that his people also were dying. But a tale-bearer told Longar what Ajiek had done.

Longar then began to beat his drum, and cried: 'I call everyone to come to my feast (sacrifice).' All gathered together there for seven days but the people of Ajiek did not attend. He stayed with his people in the woods during Longar's feast. And Ajiek made up a song there, and filled all the pots of his people with butter, and called for all the newly-born calves, and for great gourds of milk, and with these and his people he set out for Longar's feast. Longar had said: 'If Ajiek's people come to the feast we will kill them all.' But when they arrived Ajiek sang his song in praise of Longar, so that Longar would be well disposed towards him [literally, 'so that

Longar's heart would be sweet towards him']. Ajiek sang this song:

Release the white cow[1]
And all the camp watches
The gourd, the gourd, the gourd of great Kuac
Is filled to the brim [with milk]
Nurse the young calves in your arms!
Ajiek's cows of last year
Increase and multiply
The Kuac tribe among (above) all people
Think of the word of Longar
Divinity refused life[2]
My father prayed [to] DENG and ABUK daughter of AYAK[3]
The feast of the man of Kuac comes late
Yet will still call upon [pray] the master [Longar]
Kuac among all people
Think of the word of Longar.

Longar remained silent in his hut, while Ajiek walked round and round outside it, with the calves, the pots of butter and the gourds of milk, and singing the song of praise.

Longar said: 'I know that this is the voice of Ajiek. Make way for him to come to me, you people.' So Ajiek went to Longar and put his gifts on the ground before him and approached him on his knees with the greatest respect.[4] Longar said to him 'Ajiek, I have seen everyone else at my feast, but you I have not seen.' Ajiek said: 'My father, if I stayed away, it was because I was thinking about your word in my heart and in my head. And here, I bring you your cattle which I took only to pasture them.' And Ajiek gave the calves to Longar.

Longar brought out an ox the colour of the sky (*mangok*) and put it there before the people. He took a fishing-spear and gave Ajiek the head and the shaft separately, saying: 'Here is a spear-shaft, and here the spear-head. If there is nothing evil in your heart [that is 'if you are virtuous' but in a wider sense than that now implies in English] you will be able to throw the shaft into the socket in the head, which you will stick into the hearth over there.' Ajiek took

---

[1] Explained as 'in order to propitiate Longar'. The word is that used for releasing the cattle with which marriage negotiations may be started or completed, and thus implies gifts.

[2] Explained as 'Divinity refused life when he allowed Longar to kill people'.

[3] This and the previous line again may suggest some historical change of cult.

[4] This is the way in which men approach a cattle-peg upon which they are to make libations to the divinity Flesh, and the way in which young men enter a company of their seniors and women approach men with formal respect.

the shaft and the head, and darted with the shaft once, twice, and then the third time threw the shaft into the socket of the spear-head.

Longar killed his sky-coloured ox, and sent Ajiek into the woods to get some grass, the *wec* grass [*Sporobolus pyramidalis*?].[1] Longar squeezed the flesh of his ox in his hands until it became a pulp, without bones, and he took the grass which Ajiek had brought and squeezed that into it too, so that when he had finished it was all like mud. Then Longar spat on it, and gave it to Ajiek saying: 'Flesh and *wec* grass shall be your divinities, and those of your children. And Ajiek, I shall never quarrel with you. If you quarrel with me and revile me, you will die, and if I quarrel with you or insult you, then I shall die. Our words together are finished.' So they made peace between them.

In their details these myths include parts of a local historical tradition which cannot now be completely disentangled from the dominant and more ancient themes. The version in which Adheou figures prominently is probably connected with historical struggles between the Kuac people, personified in their spear-masters Pajiek, and the neighbouring Wau Dinka, among whom the Pagong clan has the primacy. There are vague and confused traditions of a conflict between the Wau and the Kuac, in which a man called Wol Agit of the Padheou clan plays a part. It seems that he was originally opposed to the Pagong of Wau, and at some time took his people over to join the Kuac and their Pajiek spear-masters. Eventually peace was made between them all as the myth records. These historical traditions, when they are investigated in themselves apart from the myths in which they are partially embedded, are far less certainly ordered than they are as parts of the myth, which of course gives them a deeper significance by associating them with the origin of spear-masters.

If we ignore the apparently historical incident, however, we see that what appears in all the versions given is original opposition between leaders of the Dinka, in which some wrest strength from an original master of the fishing-spear, who is at the same time a human being and a Power, and receive a mandate from him. The man who causes him to share his powers is one who acts intelligently to outwit and oppose him, and finally propitiates

---

[1] An alternative story to that on p. 119 above of the way in which *wec* grass became a clan-divinity.

him. The themes of human initiative, and propitiation, appear similarly in the effective regulation of human relations with the free-divinities. The men who in these myths eventually save their people from the human Power, Longar, are those who act, with force and intelligence but, finally, with respect.

Versions of this myth are known throughout Western Dinka-land, though not everywhere or by all in such circumstantial detail as in those so far given. Before turning to consider what these versions imply or state in relation to the position of spear-master clans today, I record versions from other parts of Dinkaland, one from the Western Twij Dinka, one from the Nyarreweng Dinka of the east bank of the Nile, and one from the Bor Gok Dinka also of the east bank. The myth of Aiwel is also found among the northern groups of Dinka. It is not recorded among the Nuer, whose priests, the leopard-skin chiefs, are in any case politically less significant, and significant in different ways.[1]

The Nyarreweng and the Twij Dinka have been in closer contact with the Nuer than those whose versions of the myth have so far been given, and their versions thus indicate to some extent how far the myth is preserved among Dinka even when they are most in contact with foreign peoples for whom it is not centrally important, if it is known at all. Further, versions of the myth from widely separated parts of Dinkaland throw into relief those features which transcend locality and local historical tradition. The myth of migration told by Chief Benjamin Lang Juk, a valued friend of mine, and the chief of those of the Western Twij Dinka who are nearest to the Bul Nuer, is very different from those so far given, though those also are known to him, as he has had many opportunities to meet the Rek. His version is as follows:

Ajing Noi[2] was a great fighter and was always killing people. This made his father Noi very tired of him, and his father therefore sent him to Cikom, a man who killed people, to fetch tobacco. Ajing

---

[1] There are, however, some similarities between this Dinka myth and the myth of Kir, the founder of the Jikany tribe of the Nuer. Some traditions of the Nuer relevant for comparison are included in H. C. Jackson, 'The Nuer of Upper Nile Province', *S.N. & R.*, vol. vi, 1923, though the information there may have come from Nuer much influenced by the Dinka.

[2] Ajing Noi is the founding ancestor of the clan of spear-masters with primacy in the Nyang tribe of the Western Twij Dinka, from which the narrator comes.

went to see Cikom, but found that he was away from home. He spoke to Cikom's wife, who said that she was sorry he had come, as her husband would kill him. She asked him if he had quarrelled with his father, but he denied that he had done so. The wife told him that it would be better for him to leave before her husband came back, but that in any case her husband would certainly follow him to try to kill him. The wife told Ajing that when he left, he would come to a river, and there he would meet her husband, who would tell him to dive into the river and then strike him in the nape of the neck with a fishing-spear. In order to avoid being killed in this way, she told him, he must take the sacrum of an ox, which she gave him, and push it out towards Cikom as he stood there with his fishing-spear poised to strike.

Ajing went off with the sacrum, and at the river met Cikom, who asked him why he had come. Ajing said: 'I have come for tobacco for my father.' Cikom said: 'There is no tobacco here, but if you want to go back to your father, come here to me and I will make sacrifice so that you may return in peace, and I will bless you.'

Ajing entered the river to cross to Cikom, but he pushed the sacrum first, as Cikom's wife had instructed him, and Cikom speared it. Ajing came out unhurt. Cikom was surprised, and said to Ajing: 'I am sorry that you have been in trouble with your father, but now you have been helped by Divinity', and he told Ajing that he ought to go to another land and not stay with his father any more.

Cikom went home, and Ajing went to the cattle-camp of his father, and called the young men together, and told them that he was going to leave his father. He said that those who so wished must decide then and there to accompany him. Those who did so were the ancestors of those clans now found in Twij Nyang. When Ajing left his father, the people were on the east bank of the Nile, and when they came to the river at Shambe they prayed that the river might part to make a way for them, and it did so. Ajing's father, having heard that they had left, followed them. On the way he found a squirrel, and killed it, and took its bowels with him. He came to the river and found that there was no way to cross, and that Ajing and his people were on the other side. He called out to his son: 'If you take my people away, don't take them to a dry land, take them to a place where they will hear the fish-eagle cry.' And he added: 'Your people will increase like the bowels of this squirrel which I draw out, and will then be reduced like the bowels of this squirrel which I squeeze in my hand.'[1]

---

[1] The significance of this is not known, The emphasis upon leading people to a riverain country 'where they will hear the fish-eagle cry' is to be noted in relation to our later discussion of the significance of these myths.

The middle of this story tells of the journey of Ajing and his people through the land of the Cic, where at a dance Ajing saw a very beautiful girl, and arranged to meet her later at night in her hut. She would show him where she was by placing her hands out of the entrance to her hut. Ajing's people saw that she wore a very beautiful bracelet, and cut off her hand to get the bracelet. There was a fight with the Cic for this reason, and the Twij left the country taking many of the Cic cattle with them. They then met a people who built mounds,[1] called the Ber Ajou, and stole their cattle, and went on until they reached the country near Meshra-el-Req. The story continues:

Ajing had two sisters with him, and when they all reached the river near Meshra, they found it very deep and the cattle were drowning as they tried to cross. Ajing took one of his sisters and killed her in the river to open the way. The other sister, Akuac, was so bitter at the death of her sister that she went off alone and founded the Kuac tribe.[2]

Among the Kuac tribe of the Rek Dinka, Akuac is known as a Twij girl who married Ajiek, but I was not able to find that this alliance was politically significant at the present day though there were connexions between the Twij and the Kuac early in the century. It is not referred to among the Kuac in the myth of Ajiek.

In this Twij myth, despite very fundamental differences from the others, some similarities in theme are apparent. There is the conflict with the frightening figure who tries to spear the founder of the clan in the head, and the outwitting of that figure, which is followed by the receipt of his blessing. There is the constant theme of river-crossing, and, in quite a different context from that in which it appears in the other myths, the severing of a hand to remove bracelets. Further, Ajing is helped by a woman, the wife of Cikom, to outwit her husband. We leave some of these details for comment after versions of the myth from the east bank Dinka have been given.

It was on the east bank of the Nile that some of the incidents in the myth and history so far recorded are said to have taken

---

[1] Cf. the detail of Chief Gir Kiro's story, p. 176 above. The Ber are the Murle, but I cannot identify the Ber Ajou. Various mounds of some previous inhabitants in Dinkaland have still not been properly investigated archaeologically.

[2] The tribe from which came the myth of Ajiek (pp. 179–84).

place. The following versions, from the Bor Gok and Nyarre-weng Dinka, further reveal a basis of typological similarity between different versions under the variations of local historical tradition.[1]

The following version comes from the Bor Gok Dinka:

Aiwel came out of the river, and sat on the bank. He was the first to come out, with his Power (*jok*), fire (*mac*) which is the same as *ring* (Flesh).[2] He sat on the river bank at a place called Gutacol, and sang the following song:

> On my landing-place at Gutacol
> I can do everything
> And all the people hate [me]
> Flesh (*ring*) of my father is like the flanks of an army
> It protects me on all sides, scattering [enemies]
> Flesh of my father is drawn out of the river
> Scattering enemies on all sides
> What comes unseen from behind, it drives away
> What strikes me in the eye, it drives away
> It is driven away, my red father [Flesh]
> Flesh of my father scatters them.

In another song, the Flesh divinity of Aiwel is said to have been 'brought by the wind from behind [the east]'; I do not understand this reference, though 'the east' is the direction of new life, associated with the rising sun.

After singing thus, Aiwel began to cut off people's calves, so they died.[3] Divinity disliked this behaviour of Aiwel, and he took the fishing-spear of the moon and transfixed Aiwel through the head and through the whole body so that he was pinned to the ground. Earth and sky were joined by this fishing-spear, and Aiwel was unable to get off it by moving up or down.[4] Aiwel spoke to his children and told them that nothing would ever be able to overcome or injure them.

[1] An exhaustive examination of the total distribution and variations of this myth, which I was unable to make, would make a valuable ethnographic study; but it is not easy to relate the versions at once to their tribal setting and to the personal position of the narrator without a prolonged stay in each area.

[2] The word *jok* for the clan-divinity is more commonly used among the Bor Dinka than the word *yath*, though that word is also known.

[3] This act, not otherwise explained, appears to be a sign of the mad freakishness of Aiwel. The Dinka believe that a deep cut in the muscle of the calf is fatal.

[4] A clear statement of the Dinkas' idea of the master of the fishing-spear as an intermediary between the above and the below, parallel to earlier statements that he was 'like a Power and like a man'.

Here local details are included. The story ends as follows:

And where Aiwel was, the earth was darkened. It became the colour of storm-clouds, and Aiwel disappeared. People were afraid that they might be treated as Aiwel had been treated. Nobody knew where he disappeared to, whether up, or down, or back to the river. The people found *mac* (Fire/Flesh) in a gourd where Aiwel had been transfixed, and those who found it took it and it became their clan-divinity. All the people were afraid of giving offence to those who had Flesh and Fire as clan-divinity. In the past, Flesh used to glow like Fire and it is the same as Fire.

The following is a version found among the Nyarreweng Dinka:

Aiwel's father was 'one by himself' (*pajiel*). His mother was called Acieng, and she conceived him in the river. Divinity made some people and he made Aiwel in the river. He came from the river and said: 'I will be master (*beny*)'. He sent some men to the country of the Sun, to bring food. The Sun's wife told them that her husband would burn them up if they did not take care, and told them to go into a hut, there to shade themselves from the rays of the Sun. Two men went into the hut, but one stayed outside. When the Sun came out of the river, he burnt up the man who had stayed outside, but then showed his power by reviving the man who had been burnt by sprinkling him with water. He called the two men from the hut and gave them a small pot of porridge which, he said, would never be finished no matter how much of it was eaten. He told them to take it back to Aiwel.

Aiwel complained that the porridge was not enough, though however much they ate of it it was not finished. The Sun told them: 'Do not try to finish this food and play with it [treat it lightly] or I shall kill you.'

Aiwel was tired of the food and he threw it into the river. He put a fence of reeds in the river, and he called people, and when they tried to cross the river to reach him he speared them in the head with a fishing-spear. Aiwel's daughter had a lover among the people who were trying to cross the river. She told her lover: 'Take a *kwoc* [the circlet of grass used by women for carrying their round-bottomed pots on the head] and place a stone in it and hold it before you in the reeds. My father will think that it is a man and when he strikes it it will bend the point of his spear.' The man did this, and the spear was bent on the stone, and the man came out of the river and seized Aiwel. He then called the other people to cross.

Aiwel was released. He asked his captor who it was who had taught him the trick. The man said: 'I thought of it myself.' Aiwel said: 'No, that is impossible. You have learnt it from my daughter Atong.' He took Atong and killed her and told her lover [husband] to bury her, saying: 'If some day evil befalls you, you will call upon the help of my daughter, saying "Atong daughter of Aiwel, help us".' And he gave the man the spear with which he had killed his daughter Atong.

A man from Bor abducted one of Aiwel's daughters. Aiwel followed, and on the way there was a great drought, and his followers complained of thirst. Aiwel pulled up sods of the *awar* grass and water flowed from beneath them, and his followers drank.

Aiwel then left his followers behind, and turned himself into a small child and went to the cattle-camp of the Bor where his daughter was. He then grew up very quickly, and his hair grew very long because he was a master of the fishing-spear. He had long hair, like a ghost.[1] Rain fell very heavily, and the people of Bor used him to sweep away mud from the cattle-camp, and gave him bad milk to drink.[2]

There follow a number of incidents which have local historical significance, and account for the distribution and relationships of some spear-master lineages of the Bor Dinka at the present day. They belong rather to a study of Dinka political structure than to an account of their religion, and I therefore omit them, but a detail of one of these incidents is relevant to the analysis of the role of women in the myths made later. It tells how Aiwel, when displeased, held up the rain, and then released it by killing the husband and child of one of his daughters, whose heads he pierced with a stick and roasted.[3] He then told his widowed daughter to go and seek another husband 'in the river'—in other words, to find a husband like himself and the Power which begot him.

Aiwel established some masters of the fishing-spear in Bor, and then returned home. The story concludes:

When he arrived home, he said: 'I will not stay in the open for the Sun will kill me for throwing away his food into the river.' So by day

---

[1] Allowing hair to grow is one of the signs of mourning.

[2] Aiwel is also maltreated as a child in the version of the myth known among the Northern Dinka. What is emphasized (as in his appearance from the river) is that he is not by descent a member of the community in which he first lives, and comes ultimately from outside human society.

[3] A detail reminiscent of the story of Dak, the son of Nyikang the Shilluk king, who roasted the children of the crocodile, the people of his mother (D. Westermann, op. cit., 1912, p. 155).

he stayed in his hut, and came out only at night. The Sun spoke to the Moon, and gave the Moon a fishing-spear, saying: 'He hides in the daytime so that I cannot injure him. You spear him in the head with this fishing-spear when he comes out at night.' The Moon did so, and Aiwel was held fast to the ground, unable to move. His camp came and gathered about him and built a hut around him, and he was buried inside it. The site is at Puom, where there are many *akoc* [*Cordia rothii*, referred to *passim*] growing over it. To his children Aiwel left the ability to invoke with the fishing-spear, and gave their clan-divinities.

Finally, here in abbreviated form is an account of a version found among the northern Dinka of Upper Nile Province and published by Ibrahim Eff. Bedri.[1] This version is also said to be current among the Twij Dinka of Bor District, who may be historically related to the Northern Dinka. Ibraham Eff. Bedri records the impregnation of a barren woman in the river and the birth and early development of Aiwel much as it appears in the Rek Dinka version. Here, however, when his mother died she told Aiwel that she had also a married daughter, whom Aiwel sought out. His half-sister, however, refused to acknowledge him, and said he was a sorcerer. Aiwel worked in the cattle-standings, and was regarded as an orphan and badly treated. Aiwel was then adopted, and in the home of his foster-father during a drought he produced water for his cattle as recorded in a version given earlier:

... He led the way and the cattle fed on fine green grass which sprouted and grew in his tracks. To water them he heaped a little earth in a cone and with the palm of his hand tapped the top. There gushed out a spring of very clear water and the cattle drank.

His foster-father persuaded him to manifest his powers and help the people:

... He agreed and set to work to drive the evil out of the country. He ordered grain seeds, even if very little, and cow butter, to be brought to him. He offered the usual sacrifice and then mixed the grain with butter and gave the mixture to the people to sow. He told them it would grow and yield in a few days and, hungry as they were, they should on no account eat any but bring him the whole yield. Heavy rain also fell the same day. ... He repeated the process

[1] Op. cit., 1939, pp. 125–9.

seven times and the people had good harvests seven times in one season.

Aiwel was then acknowledged as leader and saviour, and given many wives. His foster-father asked only that he and his descendants should be recognized as the owners of the land.

There here follow several incidents which clearly relate to the disposition of spear-master lineages at the present day, and an account of the behaviour of Aiwel towards his sister and his sons, which is quoted at length later in connexion with the position of women in the myth. It is to be noted that in this northern version the account of Aiwel's spearing others in the head as they try to cross a river does not occur. This does not necessarily mean that it is not known there; but in any case, its place is taken by an account of how Aiwel pretended to spear his own sons in the head which, as will later be seen, somewhat confirms our own view of the significance of the theme as it appears in different form.

The examples given suffice to illustrate how a few central and fully mythical incidents are re-created in local terms which place them in the context of the little social world each Dinka knows today, with its particular relationships of descent-groups and personalities. The Dinka themselves are not surprised that the account of the events connected with the origin of masters of the fishing-spear varies from place to place; they are accustomed to variations between what is known by different men even in small local communities, and accept the fact that any member of a spear-master clan will be inclined to stress the place of his own first ancestor in the story.

Leaving aside the local and personal details which the versions incorporate, there still remain aspects of the myth which are comparable, each in isolation, with details of Nuer, Shilluk, and Anuak myths at least,[1] and which probably are more widely distributed. But the pattern which these features form in the Dinka myth—like the particular configurations of associations of the Dinka Powers—seems to represent an experience common to all Dinka, and as characteristic of them as a whole as their single language in its several dialects.

---

[1] The essential feature for comparison is the riverain origin of the royal clan of the Shilluk and the noble clan of the Anuak.

One central element in this pattern is the representation of the prototype of masters of the fishing-spear as a person of unusual powers emerging from the river, and in other ways closely associated with it. We first turn our attention to the significance of this relationship between Aiwel Longar and the river, referring more particularly to this association as it appears among the Western Dinka, where the most detailed versions of the myth were collected.

Dinka masters of the fishing-spear, whose origin is explained by the myth, have the sacred fishing-spear as their symbol of office as their name itself suggests. The fishing-spear is not of greater practical value than the fighting-spear for the Dinka. In the past, indeed, the fighting-spear must have been even more essential than it is today. Though the practical value of fishing-spears is undoubtedly great at some seasons, the Dinka have other means of catching fish in quantity—nets, baskets, and traps—and in any case the older sacred fishing-spears are not of the most effective, barbed, type (*binh mec*) now most usually used for fishing, but are unbarbed, and rather unwieldy. It cannot, therefore, be maintained that the religious value attached to fishing-spears derives from the great importance of fish and fishing to the Dinka. The sacred spears of the Dinka are fishing-spears because their prototypical master of the fishing-spear was a river-man, and his use of that type of spear is consistent with his other associations with the river.

These include also, in the myth as it is generally told, the association of Aiwel with the *awar* grass (*Vetiveria nigritana*) which is the characteristic grass of most of the river-bank pastures of Western Dinkaland, and is of importance for grazing in the crucial period at the end of the dry season and in the dry period (*yak*) which often follows the early rains.[1] Some Dinka mention that the mother of Aiwel rested under the 'sausage-tree' (*Kigelia ethiopica*), which is particularly striking in the vicinity of riverain pastures, and which is the principal clan-divinity of the *wen dyor* group of clans, with their special association with Aiwel Longar.[2] It is also sometimes said that Aiwel's mother, after her impregnation in the river, was given a fish to sustain her

---

[1] The long roots of this grass do in fact permit it to reach down to moisture in the drought.

[2] See Chap. III, pp. 108–9.

on the way home. For the burial ceremonies of masters of the fishing-spear, of whom Aiwel Longar is the prototype, the wood of the *akoc* tree (*Cordia rothii*) is required, and this tree is specially associated with water.

The myths refer to the riverain pastures, in Dinka *toc*, a word which at once evokes the image, not of grass only, but of grass well watered by rivers when the rest of the land is arid, and where both herds and men may survive that harsh dry season. In some versions Aiwel offers to take the people to pastures which cannot—like their real dry-season pastures—fail them, fabulous pastures which represent for the Dinka a life of ease and plenty, without the anxieties and suffering which their real environment involves. Here, then, Aiwel Longar offers the fulfilment of everything which the Dinka hope of the river.

Aiwel Longar's own clan, Pagong, has a general association with whole ranges of riverain phenomena, as we have already mentioned (Chap. III, p. 112, n. 2) and as may be seen in a set of texts later reproduced.[1] Another strong evocation of the river and activities connected with the river in some versions of the myth is that Aiwel spears men like fish as they attempt to cross the river which he controls. Only when he has been outwitted, and in some measure mastered, does he hand on to others his powers and his blessing.

The significance of the prototype of masters of the fishing-spear, and hence of the masters of the fishing-spear today, is thus closely linked with the significance of rivers; and it is in trying to understand what configurations of experience 'the river' produces for the Dinka that we can begin to interpret the myths.

It is not necessary to add much to the brief account of Dinka oecology already given to emphasize that, for the Dinka, the river is not simply a constant physical feature of the landscape. Its seasonal movements, and the small irregularities of its seasonal movements from year to year, control men's lives; and the relation between human beings on the one side, and on the other, the correlated conditions of land, river, and weather at any particular place and time, is one which may ensure prosperity or bring disaster. They are not merely external physical

[1] Chap. VI, pp. 224–6.

conditions which men may ignore or modify. They enter directly into moral experience as conditions of life and death.

It is during the dry season, however, that the river impinges most exactingly upon men's lives. As the rivers fall, the cattle must be moved to those places where the roots of the grasses can still reach moisture,[1] and when at the height of the dry season the rivers have fallen to their lowest point, men look anxiously for the first rains which will revive the dry, cropped pastures. With the first rains rivers begin to rise again and the fish return to them from the permanent swamps.

There are several features of the myth of the first master of the fishing-spear which make it clear that its main setting is the dry season. The Dinka do not need to state this, for the images and associations of the myth directly evoke the experiential situation which we have to describe piece by piece. In some of the versions we have given there are the cattle dying of thirst and pastures exhausted, the rejected offer of unlimited grazing, the *awar* grass which survives drought better than others, the ox of Longar which is the colour of a sky promising rain, the fishing-dike or fence of reeds, and the fishing-spear used at those seasons when the river is rising or falling—that is, at periods of crucial change in the Dinka oecological cycle. It is at those times that the fish either move along the rivers to the swamps to breed, or return from the draining pastures to the deeper channels. In either case the Dinka know that the fish they intercept have been moving in order to live, as the season requires, and that those which escape their spears and dams survive.

For the Western Dinka as for the fish, the movement towards the swamps in the dry season is a condition of life. For most this movement involves 'crossing the river', so that 'to cross the river' in many contexts is equivalent to 'to find fresh pastures'. To find fresh pastures when they are required is, quite simply, to survive, and in this sense 'not to cross the river' is a euphemism for 'to die'.[2] The original Dinka of the myth in 'crossing the river' are thus seeking life, and the abundance and prosperity with which life intensive is associated.

---

[1] This is in fact where the variation between high- and low-water levels is not more than a certain distance, and where the banks of the rivers are less steep than they are in many places in which the Dinka have their permanent settlements.

[2] An example of this usage is given in the invocation on p. 227.

In reaching the dry-season pastures also it is often necessary to cross the river with the herds when the river is high, and here the crossing is associated with dangerous effort, the risk of crocodiles and other perils, and with the danger of cattle plague in the pastures, as well as with the reward for taking this necessary risk in the new pastures of the other side. So in the myth, when Aiwel Longar prevented people from crossing the river, he was denying them life, which was in his power to give; and the image of them as fish trying to evade the spear, and as men wanting to cross the river, both refer to an effort, and sometimes a risk, to be taken in order to take advantage of the conditions for life which the river provides.

For the river is itself an obstacle to the very seasonal movement which it itself makes necessary, and which, once obstacles are overcome, is rewarded by new life in better pastures. This is part of the content of the experience imaged in the figure of Aiwel. He offers to lead people to fine pastures, but turns upon them as they cross the river with which, by the circumstance of his birth, he is identified. He kills them or threatens them with death. Then, when he is finally mastered, he makes available the blessing and the 'life' which is in him. He thus both kills and gives life, as in a simple physical sense the river does; for the flooding of the rivers and the dwindling of the rivers, if excessive, both limit the pastures, and the flooding in many areas can also ruin the grain. There is perhaps some reflection of this last danger in the Bor Gok myth, where Aiwel destroys the grain which the Sun has sent him and his people by throwing it into the river.[1]

So far, then, the myth of Aiwel Longar might be described as a 'nature myth', though such a description would give only an impoverished understanding of the situation it represents for the Dinka. For them, the natural conditions to which attention has been drawn are directly apprehended as a source of life, and the mythical representation of those aspects of the river which particularly affect life is something deeper than a 'personification' of natural phenomena. To interpret the myth by simply identifying Aiwel Longar with 'the river' would be greatly to understate the significance of the whole, in which those features

[1] It may be significant too that here grain, even an inexhaustible supply, is rejected, since the bias of Dinka interest is strongly towards pastoralism.

of Dinka experience which we have so far examined are related to others to which I now turn.

Aiwel Longar is generally held, even where the versions of the myth given do not explicitly state it, to have the status of the 'eldest son' in the framework of this myth, or (again in this framework) to be the 'first created'. In this capacity he tries to kill those who follow him either out of the river or across the river, towards life, as we have seen. I have already commented on the positions of sons, particularly the eldest son (pp. 45–46 and pp. 82–83). It remains to add, however, that the eldest son is regarded as 'the opener of the way' for the rest. The Dinka suggest by their manner of speaking that a woman's children are all potentially there within her, awaiting, as it were, the time when they will emerge. If the first child is not successfully delivered and cannot be removed (as I was told not infrequently happens) then the child and the mother and the potential lineage of the father from that wife all die. Hence the importance of the eldest *son* as the 'opener of the way' for the rest of his brothers and sisters (for the eldest child, if a daughter, would not equally continue her father's lineage).

Life for the rest of the children, whose existence is already anticipated in thought, then depends upon the successful birth of the eldest, and since among the Dinka the eldest child is ideally a son, the eldest son is potentially both an obstacle to and a means towards emergence into life for the rest. We recall here the values attaching to the position of the eldest son—his position as both representing the other children to the father and the father to the other children, his assimilation to the clan-divinity in thought, and the element of opposition in his relations with the father and in the relations of his brothers, except for the youngest, to him. The opposition between Aiwel and his 'younger brothers' who follow him, his superior power, his ability to deprive those who follow him of life, and the greater power of his curse, along with the necessity of his help and support, thus all image a structure of relationships present in every Dinka family. Like eldest sons in relation to their fathers and brothers, the masters of the fishing-spear today represent human beings to Divinity, the common father, and Divinity to human beings, his children. People say equally of the eldest son, of the masters of the fishing-spear, and of their prototype Aiwel Longar, that *aa leou*, 'they are able'; it means less that they are able to do any particular thing than that they are able to prevail and achieve what they set out to do, for themselves or others.[1] The first of the Dinka masters of the fishing-spear, like 'the river' and 'the eldest son', is thus at once an obstacle, and a means, to life intensive for the rest.

The role of women in the various versions of this myth is here of some interest; for around women and cattle, closely interconnected as they are, centre Dinka ambitions and fears connected with life and death, with prosperity, abundance, and fertility, and with barrenness and sterility and misfortune. Even in the myth of the original separation of heaven and earth, these two themes are associated with the first woman; for it must be remembered that the pounding or planting of more grain than is absolutely necessary to sustain life indicates for the Dinka a plenty they all desire. That is why the attitude of the Dinka to the situation of that myth is ambivalent. The bid for plenty in the act of a woman is followed by the separation of Divinity and Man, and the introduction of death and hunger into the world. In the Agar version of that myth also (Chap. I, pp. 34–35) the first man receives the axe, with which he separates Divinity and Man with all the good and evil consequences of that separation, as a result of performing a service for Divinity's wife who suggests that he should be rewarded.[2] It is perhaps further significant that it is through a woman that Man is separated from Divinity in the origin myth; for Divinity images among other experiences that of a universal and undivided community, while Dinka refer to the part played by women in setting up factions leading to the separation of peoples, and in dividing the lineage. At the same time it is

[1] Cf. Jacob's address to Reuben, Genesis xlix. 3: 'Reuben, thou art my firstborn, my might and the beginning of my strength, the excellency of dignity and the excellency of power. . . .' In the Book of Genesis too there are several situations indicating an ambiguity between the values attached to eldest and youngest sons, such as is found not only among the Dinka, but also among the Shilluk, whose king has the praise-names 'first-born of God' and 'last-born of God'. See W. Hofmayr, *Die Schilluk*, 1925, p. 150.

[2] It is to be noted that actions performed in some versions of the myth by the first master of the fishing-spear in relation to other men are in other versions attributed to Divinity in relation to the first master of the fishing-spear. Masters of the fishing-spear are sometimes called *bany nhial*, 'masters of the above', and are representatives of Divinity on earth, as indeed the river, both in its appearance and its movements, reflects the condition of the sky.

through their fertility that communities increase and flourish, and that new members are born to ensure the survival of the lineage.

The mother of Aiwel, where she appears in myth, is either barren, or has no male child. She goes to the river in the same unfortunate situation, and with the same distress, as that in which women among the Dinka today go to seek the help of masters of the fishing-spear and diviners to make them fruitful. The Power of the river, the father of Aiwel, is thus miraculously life-giving in the fullest sense the Dinka know, in impregnating a despairing old woman who wants a child. Aiwel himself too, in his vigour as a child, his rapid maturity, the prosperity of his herd when others are dying, and perhaps even in the Protean changes of form which he is able to assume when wrestling with his adversary in some versions, undoubtedly is a figure filled with vitality as strong as any the Dinka can imagine.[1] Yet though full of life, he is a source of death to people until he has been overcome in one way or another.

It is clear, and explicit in most versions, that the trick by which Aiwel is overcome, and through which, therefore, the life associated with him is seized by others, is suggested by a woman, or a woman is instrumental in bringing it about. The exact relationship of that woman to Aiwel—whether his daughter or his wife —at this level makes little difference; only where (as in the Nyarreweng version of the myth and in some of the historical details I have omitted) the political relationships through women of present clans of spear-masters with others is significant, is the relationship significant in myth. For our present discussion it is important only that women, and for the most part women standing in some relationship to Aiwel Longar, are the means by which his killing power is counteracted, and his 'life' becomes available to others. His mother, where she appears, first discovers his powers. Then the sacrum of the ox (*pic*) which deflects the fishing-spear of Aiwel is for the Dinka a female possession; it is a piece of cooking-equipment most often seen in the hands of women, who twirl this bone on the end of a stick as a porridge-stirrer (*pic*). It is women also who suggest the trick by which the spear is deflected and men seize the prototype of masters of the fishing-spear. In those versions in which the instrument by which the spear is deflected is a

---

[1] Cf. the statement on p. 41 above: 'He was at the head of life.'

circlet of grass for carrying pots, the emphasis again is on a female possession. Men, even when it is necessary for them to carry, prefer not to carry on the head if they can avoid it. Finally, in the Bor Gok version of the myth, where (in the version I have given) there is no mention of Aiwel's mother, and where his power is transmitted in the gourd of Fire/Flesh which he leaves behind him after he himself has been transfixed by a fishing-spear, it is particularly made clear that it was the Moon which transfixed him. For the Dinka the moon is female; for obvious reasons she is connected in thought with women and wives.[1]

The part played by women in making available Aiwel's life-giving powers to men reflects their importance as a means to the life which the Dinka wish for—abundance and fertility in human beings and in cattle. It reflects also and at the same time an aspect of the relations between spear-master clans and others at the present day, for the Dinka think it good to marry into and from such clans. In their idiom they 'climb up the roots of the masters'. To have a master of the fishing-spear as a brother-in-law, and as the maternal uncle of one's children, is to make specially available for them the benefits of the invocations which he has the power effectively to make. The way, then, to harness for oneself the life-giving powers of the masters of the fishing-spear is through a woman who will relate one to them. Again, looked at from the point of view of the spear-master clan, the woman in one way is not a means to an advantageous alliance, but passes from her father and brothers into the control of her husband and his family, by whom her loyalties are commanded. Similarly, in the myths, from the point of view of the first master of the fishing-spear the woman is betraying his secret to others, while from the point of view of the others she is a means to life for them. So a woman, by leaving her father's home, is a source of new life for her husband's family. The female element in the myth is thus doing what women in marriage must always do—transferring, or becoming a means of transferring, the vitality of her agnatic kin to the lineage for which she will bear children.

Particularly interesting in this connexion is the conclusion of the version of the myth collected by Ibrahim Eff. Bedri among

[1] Women count their periods by the moon.

the Northern Dinka. I have earlier (pp. 191–2) given the sense of the first part of this version; here it is desirable to quote in full Eff. Bedri's account of the later part. In this version, it may be remembered, Aiwel settles down as a leader of the community, with many wives, after being rejected by his sister and her husband and performing various miracles in the home of a foster-father. The version continues:

Now Aiwel Dit remembered the ill-treatment he received in Gal's country [Gal is his brother-in-law] and desire for revenge haunted him. So he ordered his warriors to raid that country, to kill Gal and his warriors, and to bring him his sister alive. This was successfully done. On her arrival he gave her one of his huts to live in and showed her all brotherly love.

One day she complained that pumpkins were stolen from her cultivation and Aiwel Dit, as all her sons were killed during the raid, ordered the villagers to give her a girl as compensation. She received the girl and adopted her as a daughter and consequently Aiwel recognised her as a niece and loved her so much that, in many instances, he preferred her to his children.

His wives were jealous of this preference, and when she attained the age of puberty, they conspired against her. They brewed marissa in quantities and persuaded Aiwel Dit, in the wife's hut where he was spending the night, to drink such a lot that he got dead drunk. They did the same with the girl in another hut. They then put that wife's armlet (*afiok*) on the girl's arm, and carried and laid her in the same bed with Aiwel Dit, and they spied. In the night he awoke but, being under the influence of drink and with the assurance of the *afiok*, without any suspicion he lay with her and fell asleep again. The girl did not awake. The women outside expressed their satisfaction and carried the girl back to her hut. The wife regained her *afiok* and crept into the hut to sleep beside her husband.

When Aiwel Dit heard that his niece was pregnant he became very angry and changed his manners towards her and her mother. The girl gave birth to a male child who was named Goj, and as his father was not known, his grandmother's name was given him for surname, Goj Ashwai. The child grew up in Aiwel Dit's kraal with his sons.

Aiwel Dit became old and wanted to select his successor. He took his sacred spear and, at night in the kraal, pretended to spear in turn each of his sleeping sons in the head. Goj Ashwai alone was awake and remonstrated with him saying 'Why do you want to kill me father?' He did this for several nights and Goj Ashwai always repeated the same words. Aiwel Dit was struck by these words and became suspicious. He collected his wives who under pressure confessed their deed. 'Cursed women', he said, 'as you have done so, this will be your reward. Goj Ashwai will be my successor, to him I hand my sacred spear and his descendants will be more powerful than those of your sons.'

The remainder of this account makes it clear that part of the significance of this myth lies in the explanation which it gives of the history and relationships of certain spear-master lineages in the tribes of the Northern Dinka at the present day. As before, we do not attempt to display this in its details here, where the political significance of these myths is taken for granted. There are, however, other elements in Ibrahim Eff. Bedri's report which may be seen to relate to superficially different details in other versions so far considered. Those to which I draw attention are the killing, by Aiwel, of his sister's husband and his people; the deception practised upon Aiwel by women of his family, in this case his wives; the consequent transmission of his spear and primacy to a line not fully his own (for it is specifically stated that Aiwel recognized the girl upon whom he begot his successor as his niece); and the threat to spear his sons in the head, by which he discovers that the son of his 'niece' alone knows his intentions and remains awake, thus showing himself fit to be his major successor.

The killing of the sister's husband may be seen to occupy, in the structure of the myth, a place similar to that of the killing of the daughter's husband and child in the version of the myth on p. 190. In that version the widowed daughter was told to 'seek a husband in the river'—to bear children, that is, to a river Power like Aiwel's father and like himself. In this version it is Aiwel himself who begets his successor upon his niece who, to all intents and purposes, is a girl of his own family. In both, then, the first master of the fishing-spear is represented as killing his male affines, and remains the unique male of the extended family group, demonstrating, voluntarily or involuntarily, that his gifts can be handed on only by him or (in the version in which his daughter is told to seek a husband in the river) by the Power which begot him. The implication would seem to be that the male children of the women of his own family cannot be allowed to rival him unless he himself, or a

Power like himself, has begotten them. Again, as in the other version of the myth a woman's trick results in the deflection of Aiwel's spear and the subsequent dissemination of his powers to descent-groups not fully his own socially, so here a woman's trick has the same effect, though the trick is on the face of it of quite a different nature from those we have so far considered. Finally, though there is no mention of a river-crossing as the scene of the spearing in the head which occurs in other accounts, the effect of Aiwel's threat to spear his own sons in the head is the same as the effect of the spearing of his followers at the river-crossing. It is by finding the man who knows what Aiwel is doing that he finds his successor. In the accounts of the spearing in the head at the river-crossing, and in this account, Aiwel's motives are equally unconsidered. The point of both is to reveal as his successor the person who can in some way outwit or circumvent Aiwel in his display of hostility, able to inherit from him his power to prevail against the difficulties of life. We have seen how far this situation corresponds to the Dinkas' experience of the river from which Aiwel came, in the course of their ordinary oecological cycle. The mastering of Aiwel is the mastering of his power over the river; and the mastering of the river, in its detailed effects upon Dinka life, is part of what their present masters of the fishing-spear are required to attempt by symbolic action later described. For them, that control is a means to life.

There is a further element in this pattern. Women lead to the mastery of Aiwel; and women in Dinka life have a particularly close association with rivers which in part, as we have seen, Aiwel may be said to represent. The river is the place to which women regularly go, and go alone without question, to fetch water. The paths to the river, or near the river bank itself, are especially known as places where adultery or other illicit intercourse may take place. It is natural, in the myth, for a distressed woman to wander alone to the river; that is what she would be likely to do in Dinkaland today. Women have to spend many hours at the river, fetching water and preparing grain for beer. A man will not fetch water if he can help it, and if there is a woman present, even though he be at the river's edge, he will ask her to offer water to him rather than help himself. The bringing of water by women is of such importance that I have been told that Dinka living near the Nuer have adopted the Nuer pattern of head cicatrization 'because the Nuer girls laugh at the Dinka marks and will not bring water'. In this way the women have special associations with the river.

There are other features of Dinka custom also which imply that rivers and water generally have an influence on and are influenced by women who are pregnant or who have just borne children. They should ring a bell when crossing water,[1] in order to ward off Powers which might injure their children, and there are prohibitions upon eating certain varieties of fish. These varieties differ from one part of Dinkaland to another, but the attention paid to products of the river in the dietetic prohibitions of pregnant and newly-delivered women is common to all. When a child is born, its mother receives from a master of the fishing-spear a sacred fishing-spear, which she points in all directions to ward off harm from the child. That women are held to have an influence on the river may be seen clearly in the Western Twij story above (p. 187), where a woman is actually sacrificed to part the river so that men may cross, and in the Nyarreweng version, where Aiwel kills his daughter for showing her lover how to overcome him, but where the lover is told that in trouble he may call upon her to help him. These incidents are particularly striking in view of the horror with which the Dinka normally regard the idea of human sacrifice. Finally, a detail of evidence collected quite independently of that from which the foregoing argument has been developed points to a profound connexion in Dinka thought between women and the river. Fr. Nebel records that when in danger of drowning, the Dinka will offer a short ejaculatory prayer to the female free-divinity, and patroness of women's activities, ABUK; they will cry, he says, 'O water of my great mother ABUK.'[2] I did not hear of this, nor did I find among the Dinka the explicit association between ABUK and rivers which occurs among the Nuer,[3] though the emblem of ABUK in some places is a water-snake.

[1] Reminiscent of the theme of the danger of crossing already mentioned.
[2] Quoted by P. W. Schmidt, op. cit., 1949, p. 142.
[3] In a comparative study of Nilotic religion and mythology, the ABUK of the Dinka and Nuer would have to be considered in relation to the mother of the first Shilluk king, spiritual mother of the whole of Shillukland, who was the daughter of the crocodile and presides over the phenomena of the river.

The association to which we point, then, is between the river as a source of life for the Dinka, women as sources of life, and the prototype of masters of the fishing-spear as a dispenser of 'life'. As Aiwel Longar in the myth can initially withhold life, and kill people, so the river can endanger life as we have described, and so also can women, by default and barrenness, withhold the life which the Dinka eagerly hope for from them. These themes are interwoven with others in the myths of the first master of the fishing-spear, and I shall later describe in more detail the reference they have to the ideal functions of masters of the fishing-spear at the present day.

Basically, then, the myth is a representation of the polarity of life and death in the Dinka world. Aiwel's mother, in her barrenness, is a figure of sterility and death, but she overcomes these through her relations with a river-Power and bears the first master of the fishing-spear. The close juxtaposition of the theme of her miraculous pregnancy with the theme of death in the hymn already quoted:[1]

Arek the Great followed the River-Lord up to the river Kir
The river where the Arabs are, which borders on death
Which builds a dam and closes a door . . .

is thus not the product of a merely fortuitous association, but is deeply rooted in the central experience of the Dinka which the myths of Aiwel Longar represent. There Aiwel's mother, like the fish which pass the dam or dike, moves through barrenness to produce life. In religious action, as we shall see, the Dinka think themselves able to achieve such a transformation of their state at the present day.

The analysis of the myths so far made may be summarized as follows. Like the Powers earlier described, Aiwel Longar, the first master of the fishing-spear, images or represents in a single term a particular range of Dinka experience. In this case the image connects the strength of certain men, the masters of the fishing-spear, with the influence of the river upon Dinka life. Aiwel, 'like a Power and like a man', makes a bridge between human and ultra-human forces and influences. He transcends, that is, the polarity of the Dinka world which, according to their story, started in the initial separation of Divinity and Man, the

---

[1] p. 172, note.

sky and the earth. That is why masters of the fishing-spear of the present day are represented as transcending death, as described in a later chapter. In accounting for local political and social realities in different parts of Dinkaland, the versions of this central myth also relate these to a deeper experience of the natural conditions of life and death in Dinkaland. Its significance for an understanding of the position and functions of masters of the fishing-spear at the present day may now be exhibited more fully.

2

The present functions of the masters of the fishing-spear are summed up in the expression *aa muk weikua*, 'they carry (support) our life'. *Muk weikua*, 'carrier of life', 'holder of life', may sometimes be heard used as a very respectful form of address to a generous person. The supreme gift which the Dinka ask, from Divinity, from Powers, from prophets and masters of the fishing-spear, and even from anyone who makes them a gift,[1] is life. Individually inspired prophets, from whom this life is available also, are few, and their powers are not transmitted according to fixed principles which would ensure their constant services in all communities from generation to generation. It is with the masters of the fishing-spear that the means to 'life' becomes available to all, and we have seen how the theme of life is represented in association with their prototype in myth.

'Life', *wei*, is the same word in Dinka as that for breath.[2] If the Dinka are asked whether insects which are not observed to breathe have this 'life', they will say that they have it, since they are alive and animated; but as the word is usually heard, it refers primarily to the life of higher animals and human beings. *Wei* is something which living creatures have and which is the source of their animation, and more, the source of their vigorous animation. Life is therefore in creatures to a larger or smaller degree. It is convenient, in translation, to use the expression 'the breath of life' or equally consonantly with Dinka ideas, 'vitality', for this conception.

A dead body has no vitality, and a dying body has little

---

[1] A polite expression used when a gift is accepted is *ghan apir*, 'I live'.
[2] As also of course in Hebrew, Arabic, and Greek, and more widely.

vitality, and when all signs of external animation have completely ceased the *wei* has gone, and that which was living (*pir*)
is now dead. To be dead is to be inert, without vitality, and it is
because the *wei* goes at death that the word is sometimes translated as 'soul' or 'spirit'. It will serve its purpose for those conceptions in the defined contexts in which it is used,[1] but *wei* in
Dinka is not, as 'soul' and 'spirit' tend to be in popular English,
a kind of dematerialized replica of the personality. Consequently
we cannot speak in Dinka of 'the souls of the dead', but only of
their ghosts, or of the 'life' which has left them.

'Life' is thus something which can be augmented or decreased,
and a large and vigorous beast or man has more of it than a
small and weak one. The bull which, as I have pointed out, is
the very figure of vitality, fertility, and strength has much *wei*.
When it is killed this vitality leaves its body, but it does not
merely disappear. I have heard Dinka say when a beast has had
its throat cut but still kicks, twitches, and trembles, that 'it has
died (*aci thou*), but its life is still running (*kat*)', and it is important for an understanding of what the Dinka suppose to occur at
their sacrifices to recognize that when a beast moves vigorously
in its death agonies its life is not being 'lost'. Released from the
particular confines of its body, its vitality is made available to
others.

Every living person has *wei* in proportion to the power of
resistance shown against death and sickness, so a grown man or
woman has more life than a small baby, and a bull has more
life than a man. The masters of the fishing-spear are thought to
have in them more life than is necessary to sustain them only,
and thereby sustain the lives of their people and their cattle.
This force in them can also be dangerous, and masters of the
fishing-spear whose reputations for efficacy are outstanding are
treated by others with something of the self-effacing gentleness
of the attitude of *thek*, respect. An extreme exaggeration of this
attitude is seen in the story that the King of England is secured
as a dangerous bull might be secured at the head with ropes,[2]
and so that he cannot turn his head to glance upon his people

---

[1] That is in teaching English and Christian theology.

[2] The Dinka term for a king, or a really outstanding leader like the prophet
Arianhdit, is *muor ngak nhom*. *Muor* is 'bull' and *nhom* is head. I am not sure of the
meaning of *ngak*.

who sit behind him lest his power kill them. The prophet Cyer Dit is said to sit at a distance from his people for whom it is dangerous to come too near, as I have mentioned. Like Divinity and the Powers, those who have close associations with them have the dual nature of life-givers and death-dealers.

It is because the master of the fishing-spear's life is bound up with the vitality of his people that he must not be supposed to die as other men die, for this would be the diminution of the vitality of all, and it will be seen in another chapter that in the ceremonies for the deaths of masters of the fishing-spear the militant vigour of the young men assembled for the ceremony is actually augmented by their attendance. The tribe or the sub-tribe in which the ceremony is held is in fact made aware of itself as a living unity in opposition to outsiders.

In theory[1] certain parts of the sacrificial victim are the per-quisites of the masters of the fishing-spear present. One of these is the *tak*, the spleen, which some Dinka expressly associate with the verb *tak* or *nhom tak*, to think and remember.[2] I was told that when their wives were pregnant men would often want the spleen of a beast to give to them, so that their children would remember well all the things of the past, which means that they should be wise. Other parts which can be claimed by a master of the fishing-spear are the heart, the liver, the kidneys, and certain glands (*abeng*). It was said that his right to these parts was based upon the fact that they were the seats of life, *wei*, and that they were the particular parts of the body in which life was located because, if any of these parts of a man were seriously injured, he could not hope to survive. Further, it is said that in taking these the master of the fishing-spear puts them together so that these centres of life shall be united for the people for whom he prays. In addition, he takes the pizzle of a sacrificial bull, the organ of generation, as we later describe (Chap. VII, p. 270).

As the Dinka know well, there are in fact many small and unimportant masters of the fishing-spear, and only a few attain really outstanding reputations. The Dinka know that many do

---

[1] I say 'in theory' because there is no way of knowing whether it invariably occurs in fact. The Dinka, like most people, are capable of asserting a principle which they do not exactly follow even at the moment of asserting it.

[2] Though Fr. P. A. Nebel, op. cit., 1936, gives different tones for the two words, and it is possible that this is a piece of *ad hoc* etymology.

not *kec*, which is a technical term for effectiveness in prayer and invocation, and means to 'bite' or 'be strong' as hot and bitter things are 'biting', a sensation at once painful and pleasant. The little cucumber *kuoljok* (*Cucumis prophetarum*) used for protection against sickness and rubbed on the chest, head, and back of a sick man is associated with the Powers, by the *jok* (*jok*-Power) part of its name, and is noted for its acute 'bite'. Yet the failure of some masters of the fishing-spear to attain the ideal does not affect the standing of masters of the fishing-spear in general. The prototype of them all in the myths shows them all as ideally effective, and also in many small ways the Dinka think they see the marks of that effectiveness in them. Minor misfortunes which occur to those who are known to have offended them, or know themselves to have offended them, are attributed to their power working even involuntarily. There are also stories which attribute miraculous powers to the recent ancestors of masters of the fishing-spear living today. In a way these men of only one or two generations past whose powers are still remembered strongly reinforce the conviction carried by the more distant mythical situations from which ultimately it derives. Everyone knows, for example, the name of some master of the fishing-spear whose cattle and crops flourished like those of Aiwel, when those of others near by were languishing. In Dinkaland people who live in the same neighbourhood may have very different fortunes in the early rains, which are extremely local; and it is upon rainfall at particular places and limited times that the Dinka harvest there depends. Files of the Sudan Government report cases in which even European officials claim to have been present when a master of the fishing-spear has prayed for rain, and rain has fallen within a small radius almost at once. This may well happen in early spring, and when it does so it supports the reputation first of the master of the fishing-spear who has prayed, but also of all masters of the fishing-spear for what they may potentially achieve. Sons of masters of the fishing-spear will tell how rain has fallen on their fathers' gardens when neighbouring gardens have been dry. When any master of the fishing-spear invokes, darting his spear as we later illustrate, he is functioning like his mythical prototype, and is by definition able to prevail, or to 'hit his thing in the head' as the Dinka say, as in one version of the myth Ajiek threw the shaft of the fishing-spear into the socket in the blade. The masters of the fishing-spear are not only priests mediating and representing 'life' to their people; they are also political leaders, and seen by the Western Dinka as having been their leaders in the migrations which they suppose themselves to have made in order to reach their present lands. Such historical traditions as we have already included in the account of the myths show this political leadership, and we have to bear in mind that, in assuring life for their people, they must also assure success against enemies of life. Some of the qualities and gifts which enable them to do this have already been described in the account of their divinity Flesh, and others will have been amply apparent in the myths just considered.

It should be made clear, though, that Aiwel Longar is throughout an essentially mysterious figure to the Dinka themselves, and they do not pretend to understand the motives of some of his actions. If asked why he initially killed his people, they have no answer, except that it was in him to do so, and as much part of his nature as his subsequent kindness to them. Indeed, to ask the question is, to the Dinka, as pointless as if one were to ask why the sky or the river were sometimes sources of benefit and sometimes of suffering, and the answer given is likely to be the same—*acie nhialic?*, 'is it not Divinity?' So from this point of view Aiwel is as motiveless as nature itself. The cutting off of people's calves in one version of the myth, which no Dinka could explain, is an example of the mysterious caprice which may mark the actions of a Dinka holy man. Sometimes, when asked why Aiwel behaved as he did, the Dinka will reply, not unindulgently, 'ah, he was bad'. Bad, *rac*, can also have the meaning of 'extreme', suggesting the pre-eminent possession of a quality, as when one hears *adheng arac*, 'extremely handsome', or *amit arac*, 'extremely tasty'.

So the first master of the fishing-spear, and the successor who overcomes him, and ideally those who have now succeeded them, may be experts at trickery and cunning, given to strange freaks of behaviour, capricious and unpredictable; and so, we would observe, do the forces of nature seem to those whose lives are a constant struggle against them. As leaders, then, the masters of the fishing-spear must have cunning, resolution, and ruthlessness, as well as the qualities which seem to us, perhaps, more 'priestly'.[1] Political and religious leadership are combined, and require in the person who combines them the qualities necessary for both.

The functions of masters of the fishing-spear mentioned by all Dinka are their prayer, invocation, and sacrifice for the cure of the sick and the vitality and prosperity of their people, their driving away of lions and other dangers of the forest and of the river, their mediation between enemies and settlement of feuds, and finally and most important, in the past at least, their invocations for victory in war and raiding. I could not see the masters of the fishing-spear of a tribe perform their functions in war, but these in Dinka eyes are more important than the rain-making functions for which they are best known in the literature on the Dinka.[2] Effective prayer for rain is not limited to masters of the fishing-spear, and anyone who has the Power DENG as his divinity, or has one of a certain number of clan-divinities, is thought to be able to bring rain. In war, however, the invocations and sometimes 'magical' acts of masters of the fishing-spear (the gouging out of eyes and breaking of legs of beasts symbolizing the enemy, or the symbolical tying up of an enemy in grass) are thought to be as essential for success as the courage and physical combat of the 'people of the war-spear'.

There is no contradiction between the function of the master of the fishing-spear as a guide in war and as a mediator and peace-maker. They are functions of different situations, which have in common the assurance of the welfare of the tribe and subtribe. The masters of the fishing-spear do represent an inclusiveness in the Dinka political system, in that anybody who succeeds in attaching himself to one of them makes himself sure of help through his prayers and invocations. Individual strangers, therefore, may seek out masters of the fishing-spear if they want protection, and 'praise their heads' with gifts or songs. As in the myth the masters of the fishing-spear are placed above and before others, so they are theoretically above and outside their conflicts, and can mediate between them. On the other hand, the master of the fishing-spear represents the

---

[1] There is plenty of evidence for the attribution of such qualities to 'culture-heroes' in many parts of the world, of course.

[2] This aspect is stressed in C. G. and B. Z. Seligman, op. cit., 1932. I differ from the view not on point of fact, but of emphasis.

exclusiveness of any political community attached to him, and masters of the fishing-spear with the primacy in tribes and subtribes are necessarily opposed to each other as their communities are opposed to each other in the total political structure.

It is common knowledge among Dinka that masters of the fishing-spear are rivals, and their rivalry is usually represented as a rivalry for religious reputation. Also, since the master of the fishing-spear represents the exclusiveness of the community for which he functions, hostilities between communities are represented as hostilities between masters of the fishing-spear. Within a tribe the masters of the fishing-spear with whom the largest sections, the sub-tribes, are politically associated may be members of a single subclan with primacy throughout the whole tribe. Their oppositions are thus the oppositions between different lineages or subclans within the framework of a single clan. The subtribe associated with the senior lineage is known, and has the role of peace-maker. There is no such inclusive organization linking different tribes.[1] So, although spear-master clans are of one category in relation to warrior clans, they form no 'freemasonry' among themselves, but are identified with and embedded within the communities for which they function, acting as mediators and peace-makers within, and representing their communities in opposition to others of the same order.

Even within a single subclan, however, and between father and son, rivalries about which master of the fishing-spear has the greater effectiveness in invocation—about which is the more 'biting'—are known to occur. It is said, for example, that when Mabyor Akot, a very renowned Western Dinka master of the fishing-spear of the last generation, was still a boy, he claimed that he would be more 'biting' than his father, who insisted upon a trial of strength between them. (It is unusual for a boy to behave in this way, as a man does not usually function with the fishing-spear until he is fully adult and married.) Mabyor and his father each took a cow into the forest, tethered them there, and invoked protection for them each over his own beast. Each then stuck his fishing-spear into the ground near his cow, and the cows were then left tethered in the forest

---

[1] This is most plainly the case among the Western Dinka; the Eastern and Northern Dinka present a slightly different picture.

all night. The next morning they returned to find that Mabyor's father's cow had been killed by a lion, while that of Mabyor was unhurt. The father then had to concede that his son's invocations were more effective than his own.

Fr. Nebel collected two stories of the rivalries of masters of the fishing-spear which illustrate the interest of the Dinka in this theme. The first[1] tells how two masters of the fishing-spear, called Adol Thiang and Dwardit, decided to have a contest to see which of them was the more effective, and after being at first dissuaded from thus putting their powers lightly to the test, they smelt each other's arm-pits which, according to a note given to the text, is thought to cause immediate death. Both died as a result of this test, and sang underground a song which includes the lines:

. . . we merely played, the company of our kraal will be dispersed,
We omitted on earth to be reconciled.

The other story introduces the theme of the conflict of loyalties, in the children of masters of the fishing-spear whose mothers are also from spear-master clans, which comes from the rivalries of which we have spoken:[2]

A lion changed himself into a man to eat people. When somebody went there, he was eaten. Forty people were so eaten. My ancestor Dengdit got angry that a lion should exterminate his people in the grass-plain, and sent his son called Ajaang and gave him a spear.

His mother's father got also a spear and said: 'Go, son of my daughter, you will kill him with this my spear.' His father Dengdit said: 'It is a lie, it is my spear with which you will kill him.'

His father Dengdit was the owner of a sacred spear; and his grandfather, his mother's father, had also a sacred spear.

The son went with both those spears to the place where the lion was.

After a struggle he eventually kills the lion with his father's spear, and the narrative continues:

When he reached the outskirts of the village where he lived, his mother met him and asked: 'My son, with whose spear did you kill it?' He said: 'I killed it with my father's spear.' The mother said: 'My son, you will say: "I killed it with my grandfather's spear." Your

---

[1] From an early cyclostyled, but I think otherwise unpublished, collection.
[2] Fr. P. A. Nebel, op. cit., 1948, p. 134.

father is rich, and his people shouted so: "He, whose spear will kill it, will take the other's cattle." [1]

Ajaang does so, and when asked by his father if it is true that he killed the lion with the maternal grandfather's spear, he maintains that it is. The father then says:

'As your mother has prompted you, you shall lie down at the dung-fire, and I will lie down at the other side. If it was your grand-father's spear with which you killed it, you will rise up in the morning from the dung-fire, but if it was my spear with which you killed it, and you have been prompted by your mother and agreed, you will not rise up from the dung-fire tomorrow.'

And Ajaang consented and lay down there. In the morning he was found dead.

His father's only comment on the death of his son is:

'Let him be gone; he was persuaded by his mother and consented to her deceit.'

Such conflicts of loyalty undoubtedly occur when both the mother's and the father's kin are members of spear-master clans. It is understandable, therefore, that when the mother's kin are spear-masters and the father's kin are not, the tendency will be for the child to turn to the mother's brother, who has the greater prestige and power to help. Hence for a whole tribe or subtribe, the spear-master descent-groups with which these groups are politically identified have their influence recognized in being called *naar wut*, the maternal uncles of the camp. Their daughters have in general borne into the lineages of the others grouped around the spear-masters, the 'life' which in quite different contexts it is also the function of spear-masters to give. In one story a master of the fishing-spear is said to have decided to invoke over the beast of his sister's son, in order to show the power of his clan-divinity. The indication here, as in the other stories we have given, is that his claim to effectiveness is also a claim to influence beyond his clan. Underlying the story, and underlying other incidents in versions of the myth, is the desire and practice of the spear-master clans to conserve their powers and to draw towards them those with whom they enter into

[1] In the Dinka text this is *ke ngek anyeei gol e ngek*, which means 'one will take away the *gol* of the other'. This implies both the cattle of the cattle-hearth (*gol*) and also its people. *Gol* is both a herding-group and a descent-group.

relations. Such is their political function, and in the myths and in life its exercise is brought into close relation with their wider religious powers in providing the symbolic control of experience later described.

The rivalries of masters of the fishing-spear, in which one can appear greater than another, are thought by the Dinka to lead in time to changes in the leadership of political groups, for a conspicuously effective and successful master of the fishing-spear will attract followers from a weaker one who may be their traditional leader. In the Western Twij myth quoted, for example, a son takes away part of the following of his own father; and in the story of Ajaang earlier it is said that the master of the fishing-spear with whose spear the lion has been killed will take away the people of the other. Consequently, in Dinka 'political theory', changes in political alignments occur in consequence of the rising or falling reputations of spear-master descent-groups and the leaders they produce.

To test this theory it would be necessary to have more information about Dinka history than is now available, but there are indications that it may have some basis. When one finds that people who once shared the same wet-season cattle-camps have divided in very recent times and are now moving separately at that season, one also may find that members of two different subclans of spear-masters have been in the camp, and that those who are more recent arrivals have split off from the camp taking with them others who were followers of the putative founding lineage. In a tribe the presence of two spear-master subclans of approximately equal reputation is accompanied by rivalries and, according to the Dinka, these may eventually split the tribe into two in a way which cannot occur where one spear-master clan has the undisputed primacy. The latter is the case, for example, with the Kuac tribe of the Rek, and with the Awan (Pajok) tribe. In the Akanyjok tribe of the Abiem, however, two clans of spear-masters divide the tribe between them, and the unity of the tribe as a whole is conceived in relation to a very prominent warrior subclan, but this was the only case I found in which the subclan identified with a tribe as a whole was not a subclan of spear-masters. There is evidence also to suggest that the changing fortunes of lineages of spear-masters within the subtribes of a tribe may result from time to time in changes in social distance between those sub-tribes. I have elsewhere given an example of this in the Apuk (Patuan) tribe of the Rek.[1] A way in which the Dinka represent the change is in the changes of leadership of age-sets. Masters of the fishing-spear cut the age-sets of their subtribes, and it is the ambition of all masters of the fishing-spear who have cut a subtribal age-set to keep it open as long as possible, so that their names may be associated with large sets whose fame will be handed down. On the other hand, junior ranks of an age-set often want to have a new age-set started, so that according to their custom, they may become the senior members of a junior age-set, rather than the junior members of a senior set. Where there are rival masters of the fishing-spear in a subtribe, one may succeed in attracting the younger men of an age-set opened by the other, and making them into his own age-set. This is part of an account of Dinka political structure rather than of their religion and, like the political position of masters of the fishing-spear, is not treated in detail in this account.

The actual lineages of spear-masters with which groups are politically identified may thus change over periods of years, but the system itself remains the same. Though one lineage of spear-masters may supersede another—if what the Dinka suggest is true—it performs the same functions, and its ability to perform them is validated in the same myth. Also the forces making for conservatism are strong, in that considerable importance is attached to the master of the fishing-spear's hereditary ties with his tribe or subtribe. The myth of the origin of spear-masters establishes a covenant between Divinity and men which derives its strength from its continuity through successive generations.

Among the Western Dinka the clan of Aiwel Longar himself, Pagong, and its ancillary clans composing the *wendyor* group, is represented in many, perhaps all, tribes. In some it provides the subclan with primacy throughout the whole tribal territory. In all, however, it is accorded a religious status higher, in an ill-defined way, than the rest, as Aiwel Longar himself was the first among spear-masters. In my experience also, members of Longar's clan have a wider knowledge of their distribution

---

[1] In the essay on Western Dinka political structure, G. Lienhardt, op. cit., 1958, pp. 124–5.

beyond the limits of any particular tribe than have other Rek clans. The comment of the Dinka who said that Longar remained 'like a Governor-General' while the others were like Provincial Governors was indicating this sense of a wider responsibility and reign, outside the tribe, of the descendants of Longar. It is held by some Dinka also that in the past, when tribes were autonomous and war on a large scale possible, only the masters of the fishing-spear of Pagong and its ancillary clans, or an outstanding prophet, could make effective peace between tribe and tribe. The descendants of Longar disposed widely throughout the country seem to represent the potentiality of an inter-tribal polity, for which their specially close association with Divinity, imaging that wider community as we have seen, would fit them. In some of the versions of the myth of the masters of the fishing-spear Aiwel Longar is represented as standing above the masters of the fishing-spear to whom he gives his powers, and in some versions it is explicitly stated that when problems—disputes—cannot be settled by other masters of the fishing-spear, they are to go to him. Dinka have told me that Pagong, unlike other clans of spear-masters, is found everywhere, and seem therefore to sense that it has a wider distribution than any other clan. In the absence today of the situations in which Aiwel Longar's clan would have been required to act as peace-maker, I can only report that it is believed to have had this function, and that there are indications that it did so.

Among the Dinka of the east bank of the Nile, Longar's clan is not called Pagong, but its primacy *inter pares* is more strongly marked. It is represented by many lineages all descended from Aiwel Longar, which in numbers and influence far exceed lineages of other spear-master clans in that region. In the Bor and Nyarreweng versions of the myth, the passing on of Aiwel Longar's powers does not occur in the same way as in the Rek versions. Most of the masters of the fishing-spear of the Nyarreweng are regarded as being descended from Aiwel himself, and the genealogical structure of his clan there is co-ordinate with the territorial structure of the Nyarreweng. It seems from Bedri's account of the Northern Dinka also that their masters of the fishing-spear are all descendants of Aiwel, and the myth as known there tells how various lineages descended from Aiwel were established in their primacy in different parts of the land.[1] It is not so among the Western Dinka, though members of Aiwel's clan are in no doubt about their primacy among other clans, and are proud of their descent, as the following quotation from a hymn sung by them suggests:

It was great Longar, first created by the creator,
And Jiel of the *awar* grass, first created
Shrines and fishing-spears and the *alal* spear
And prayer and invocation.
Do not cease to pray, do not cease Longar,
The child of the warrior clan cannot head the camp,
You will be married into the camp. . . .
The warrior clans cannot head the camp,
You will be married into the camp. . . .
The warrior clans cannot head the camp
If masters of the fishing-spear and Divinity do not help the land.
Yet the creator will listen, he who created Longar in the past.
If it be war, then we shall ask Pagong, all Pagong,
Pagong of the Awan tribe, Pagong of the Wau tribe.
In the subtribe Biong, do not Pagong lead there?
Great master of the *alal* spear
If Pagong pray, the great one [Divinity] is brought to the country. . . .

Such is the boast of Aiwel Longar's own clan, Pagong; but as the myths indicate, the ability to pray effectively, and the gifts of insight into the underlying truths of situations, are thought to have been widely distributed among other clans, whose members today also have the task of attempting to control human *passiones* by the symbolic acts now to be described.

[1] Ibrahim Bedri, op. cit., 1939.

VI

THE CONTROL OF EXPERIENCE:
INVOCATION AND PRAYER

IT is rare to see a Dinka pray individually. On occasions of difficulty or danger he may address a short petition for help to Divinity or divinities, but much the greater and most important part of religious practice is collective and formal. I have heard Dinka remark upon their difference, in this respect, from the neighbouring Nuer, whose frequent individual prayer seems to be consistent with their less developed priesthood.

An ideal presentation of Dinka sacrificial rites would place before the reader the oral and manual elements in combination, as they occur in life; but it is difficult to contrive such a presentation without loss of clarity in exposition. In this chapter and those which follow I have therefore separated the oral from the manual elements, and begin here with several texts which represent what is actually said at certain Dinka ceremonies. Collection of such texts is made somewhat easier by the measure of formality in Dinka religious practice. Each phrase in an invocation is brief, and is repeated by some of those attending the ceremony, as will appear. In many speeches made at sacrifices, ideas and phrases are repeated again and again, so that eventually it is possible for the listener to concentrate only on new words and expressions, which occur infrequently. It is possible to jot down the gist of what is said on the spot when one is among friends, and finally with their help to re-create the ceremony. The Dinka are not ashamed of their religion or secretive about it, and indeed seem to recall with satisfaction the force and dignity of the invocations made by some of their masters of the fishing-spear. These texts therefore come as much from a Dinka memory of the situation as from my own. Further, masters of the fishing-spear are professional speakers of prayers and invocations, and pride themselves upon their fluency. Those whom one comes to know well are prepared to tell one what they *would* say, in a hypothetical situation, and indeed are not displeased that one should take an interest in their abilities, and set them at their own evaluation.

The following set of texts was collected at a sacrifice for the recovery of a young man called Akol Agany, of the Padiangbar clan. He had been wasting away, apparently from pulmonary tuberculosis, and was coughing painfully. He lay in a platform hut in the homestead of his father's brother, where he had lived since the death of his father, Agany. He had quarrelled in the past with his father's brother, Akol Dit (big Akol), and it will be seen in the course of the texts that Akol Dit now wished his nephew to get well, fearing that their quarrel might have had some part in the development of the sickness.

The people of Akol Dit fetched an ox of the *malith* (a shade of grey) colour at about 10 o'clock in the morning on the day of the sacrifice, and tethered it to one of four cattle-pegs permanently fixed in the centre of the homestead as shrine to the clan-divinity, the ancestors, and Divinity. Invocations were then made over the tethered beast, most importantly by masters of the fishing-spear of the clan Parum, one of the ancillary *wendyor* clans related to Aiwel Longar's own clan, with a high reputation for efficacy in invocation. These Parum spear-masters were the classificatory mother's brothers of Padiangbar, the clan of the sick man, in the subtribe to which they both belonged, and one of them was actually the mother's brother of the sick man.

Women and girls and a few male spectators sat in the shade of the platform huts, the women and girls sitting slightly apart as is their custom on religious occasions. A number of modern fishing-spears, brought by those who were to invoke over the ox, were piled together against a hut until the ox had been tethered and invocations might begin. The first to select his spear was Akol Dit, the sick man's paternal uncle. Emphasizing each phrase with a slight downward thrust of the spear, he spoke as follows:

Repeat this [literally 'seize', *dom*] son of my sister. You of my father
(Chorus: You of my father)
I call upon you because my child is ill
(Chorus: I call upon you because my child is ill)
and I do not want words of sickness
(Chorus: and I do not want words of sickness)

and I do not want words of fever
(Chorus: and I do not want words of fever).[1]

The chorus thus repeats what is said in staccato phrases throughout the invocation. For the rest these indications of the actual sound and rhythm of the proceedings are omitted. The invocation continued:

And you of my father, if you are called, then you will help me and join yourself with my words. And I did not speak [in the past] that my children should become ill; that quarrel is an old matter. And you, *malith* [ox], even though you have not urinated, you urinated on the way when you were being brought here.[2] And you my prayer, and you prayer of the long distant past, prayer of my ancestors, you are spoken now.
Meet together, ee! It is that of my ancestor Guejok,[3] it is not of the tongue only, it is that of Guejok, it is not of the tongue only.

When Akol Dit had finished his invocation, his place as solo spokesman was taken by a master of the fishing-spear of the Parum clan, who spoke as follows:

Repeat, ee! You, Flesh of my father, you will not deceive me with lying words [you will not mislead me] and if you are called upon, you will quickly accept my speech. And you, O earth, if you are called [upon] you will help me also, and you DENG, divinity of my father, you will help me also if you are called. And you of my father, you will help. I have no great speech to make to you, what I have to say is ended and my [clan] half-brother will carry on.

Another, older, master of the fishing-spear of Parum then proceeded:

The promise that you promised,[4] you of my father, where is it? You, trees, hear my words, and you grass hear my words, and you Divinity hear my words and you earth hear my words. Repeat, ee![5] O Divinity, because of sickness, you will help out my tongue. For we have dedicated the *malith* [ox] and invoked over it. And if a man

---

[1] The word used here, *jwai*, can be used for many conditions marked by high temperature in the patient.

[2] The urination of a beast during invocations is taken as a sign that the sacrifice is acceptable to the Powers. Here they establish that the victim has urinated, though not at the ideal moment.

[3] The name of a prominent ancestor.

[4] In Dinka, *thon thoon yin*. I am quite unsure of the translation. It may mean 'the trust placed in you'.

[5] He reminds those present that they are not to allow their attention to wander.

has hated Akol [and his sickness is the result of malice] then that man will find what he deserves.

After some repetition of ideas already introduced, this man was followed by another of the same spear-master clan who said:

Repeat, ee! A person whom I shall spy out I will knot up in grass, and you Akol will get up. And you *malith* we have given you to the Power (*jok*) [that is, to the illness]. And you fetish-bundles, they say that you kill people.[1] Leave off, you are shamed (frightened). You fetish I have separated you, cease! And you MACARDIT they say that you kill people, I have separated you, cease! Thus! [*yenakan*, the expression with which Dinka speeches are punctuated.][2] My words are finished. You of my father, I have called you to help me; and you of my mother, I have called you to help me.

A master of the fishing-spear of the Pagong clan, senior to those who had so far invoked, then spoke:

O you earth, and you divinity of my father, we have refused death this day. And you Divinity, we have refused death this day. You fetish, a man buys you for a cow and you come in order to help him. If a man goes to a distant country (and possesses a fetish) he travels in health, and if a man goes to collect cattle which are owed to him, you walk with him. For if a man finds evil in the path, he will call you, saying: 'Come, let me be in health'. And you *malith* [ox], it is not for nothing that we have tethered you in the midday sun, but because of sickness, to exchange your life for the man, and for the man to stay on earth and for your life to go with the Power [illness]. You Divinity hear my speech, and you clan-divinity hear my speech, and you Power I have separated you from the man. I have spoken thus: 'You leave the man alone, you have been given the ox called *malith*.' Thus! You child of my sister, repeat my words!

I am not a man from another tribe, I am a man of this land in the tribe of Apuk Jurwir here. I am not a bastard coming with its mother, the bastard fathered by some stranger outside. If such a one prays, he calls upon no clan-divinity, because he is a child which comes with his mother alone and he will be unable to do anything in a case of sickness. Divinity is within the man who has him.[3] The

---

[1] One theory about the cause of the young man's sickness was that it was caused by the fetish MATHIANG GOK which his father had once acquired, and which had then been neglected.

[2] This is the characteristic sound punctuating the phrases of all Dinka orations and even conversation. I have omitted many repetitions of it here.

[3] In Dinka, *nhialic ala yic ran la yen.* I am very doubtful about this translation.

earth is spoilt [by this illness]. Flesh of my father, come forth! *Wuu* away the sickness!

Here those present make the sound *wuu* loudly and move their heads and arms in the direction of the non-Dinka tribes to the south, sending the illness there.

The concluding invocation was as follows:

You, Divinity, I do not want words of such sickness, that a man should be ill. O you of my father, do not let me speak a lie! And you Divinity, I have called upon you because Akol Agany had no sister born with him, and you of my father, Akol Agany has been very unfortunate [miserable, poor, unlucky] in Apuk, the tribe of his father.

Why is it, O Divinity, that when one son is left alive alone out of all the children his mother bore, you do not help him, that he may be in health? You Divinity, if you have left Akol Agany behind to beget children, and he now becomes ill, we have refused [to accept] this illness in him.

For Akol Agany has no sister born with him, and no brother born with him, and if Divinity does not help him to bear his children, then the children will become the children of the mother.[1] And you Divinity, you are the great person, father of all people, and if a man has called upon you you will strengthen his arm, that no evil may befall him.

And you Agany senior [the dead father of the sick man] why have you left your child in misery in his father's tribe? In the past, when you were alive, you left Akol as an only child, with no sister and brother, and he himself begot his own brother and sister.[2]

It is you divinities of my father that I call upon to come and help the child Akol Agany, that he may live. He is the child of your daughter, and if you abandon him to death, then all the Powers will mock at you (despise you). And if you let him live, then you have helped the child of your daughter. And you of my father, I did not neglect you (treat you lightly) on the occasion in the past when my father died, it is not so, it is not true that I caused confusion in the descent group of my father.

You my own father, and you my grandfather and you my grandmother and you my mother, I have called upon you that you may help me when I pray about sickness, the sickness of my sister's child.

[1] That is, the agnatic line will gradually die out, and the children will become attached to the families of their maternal uncles.

[2] This means that Akol Agany, since he had no sister to provide him with bridewealth, has no wife of his own and his children are begotten on a wife of his deceased father.

My sister's child shall be well. I did not quarrel with the family of your daughter, I stayed in peace with them, and I meant no malice against my sister's children. If I call upon you, then you will agree [to accept my prayer].

This concluding invocation was made by a master of the fishing-spear of the Parum clan, the maternal uncle of the sick man. He reveals that his conscience is uneasy about some incident which occurred when his father died, and also about quarrels with the family of the sick man. After this invocation the ox was thrown and its throat cut.

Here is another text of a rather different nature. This was collected at a large fishing-camp on the banks of the Tonj river at Wan Alel, where fish abound at a small ironstone outcrop which makes a little cataract in the river, and a large number of people of the Apuk Jurwir tribe had gathered for several days to catch and dry their fish. One evening there was a quarrel between a woman and the little daughter of a master of the fishing-spear of the Pagong clan who controlled the fishing in that part of the river. The woman struck the little girl, and threw her basket of fish into the river. The master of the fishing-spear intervened, and there was an angry altercation. The result of this was that the master of the fishing-spear, in a rage, called upon Divinity and his clan-divinities to send the abundant fish away to the swamps downstream. He went for his fishing-spear and muttered some prayers alone[1] on the river bank, asking that *abiliny* (tiny fish which the women had been catching by the basketful) should return to the *apac* grass of the swamps. One or two people who saw this with me said that sooner or later the master of the fishing-spear would relent, and the women would appease him with presents of fish and perhaps a women's dance in his honour. He would then withdraw his curse (*waak*) and call the fish back to the river. They allowed the prayers to take their course without complaining or even taking much interest.

The next day boys played at fishing, and the women seemed to be having an enjoyable holiday from their task. They held little singing and dancing parties, and sat about gossiping, with no sign of distress at the break in the fishing. They made no effort to fish because (according to them) there would be no

[1] For a master of the fishing-spear thus to pray privately is an indication that trouble is brewing.

fish there. We in fact caught nothing with our net either. The offended master of the fishing-spear chatted, apparently amicably, with the men, without any discussion, as far as could be seen, of the curse of the previous day.

Later in the afternoon it was said that he had relented, and was going to perform a ceremony to bring the fish back to Wan Alel. He and his paternal nephews split several of the little yellow cucumbers (*kuoljok*) which are used for sacramental healing and blessing and placed them in a gourd of water. They then floated the gourd on the river, and drawing it with them by a piece of *apac* grass started from a point a little way upstream and walked slowly downstream invoking so that those on the bank could hear:

1st Invocation, by the master of the fishing-spear

You Ripple (wave)[1] of my father, hear my words. And you ironstone outcrop of my father, hear my voice. And you *Awar* grass of my father I have relented, and I have separated (*dok*) the tribe of my father [from my previous invocations]. And you O fish, do not refuse [our demand] there in the upper reaches of the swamps, but come now, this very night. Come by night, and come by day, so that the tribe of my father shall not mock me (for the weakness of my invocations). If I call upon you, you river of my father, then you let the fish come now at once, and the people will be pleased with me (lit. 'their hearts will be sweet towards me') and with the river of my father also.

2nd Invocation, by one of the nephews

You *Awar* grass of my father, we tell you what we have to say to you, we the children of my father. You Flesh of my father, we quickly call upon you because it is you who are of the most distant past when men were first created there at the earth's end. And you, *ngok* fish,[2] we have separated you [from us]. If we have invoked the river of my father, then I shall not hear it said that a *ngok* fish has pierced a man's foot, or I shall be heart-broken. You river of my father, help people now as in the past my father looked after you. For if my ancestor had feared the Thony tribe[3] in the past, then you

[1] The wave which impregnated the mother of Aiwel Longar, the founder of his clan.
[2] The fish *Synodontis membranaceus*, which is somewhat sluggish, and has sharp serrated spines which frequently injure people who step on it.
[3] A neighbouring tribe disputing with the tribe of the man who is invoking the fishing rights in this part of the river.

had belonged to the Thony tribe today. But my ancestor held to you, and you were that of my ancestor, and it was he who gave you to us, and we call upon you in our prayers. If you are called, then you will assist.

3rd Invocation, by the other nephew

You river of my father, indeed we call upon you because it is said that witches called Pagong bewitch the river here, for they have forbidden the fish to come. And that is a lie; for each man has that of his father.[1] O you Ripple of my father, and you *Awar* grass of my father, if we call upon you you will hear us. And you, O fish, we have called you; do not stay in the swamps, but come, this very night.

The men then came out of the river, and the crowd was asperged with water from the gourd. Several people then entered the river one by one, and drew the water towards them with their hands in the direction from which the fish were expected to come. Later the fishing started again, but the catch was small, a fact which seemed to cause no surprise.

Another sequence of invocations comes from a ceremony for the recovery of a sick old master of the fishing-spear of the Pagong clan.

The background to this sequence is, in brief, that the master of the fishing-spear had twice previously fallen sick, and had now become sick again after an unclaimed fishing-spear had been found in his homestead. The owner of this fishing-spear could not be identified, and it was thought, therefore, that it might have been left by a 'witch'—a person intending to injure the sick man.

In the subtribe to which the old man belonged, the clans Payi and Pagong, both spear-master clans, are much intermarried, and traditionally when invocations are made for the benefit of members of Payi, Pagong has the last word[2] and vice versa. The following invocations have again been abbreviated to avoid undue repetition.

1st Invocation

So it is. You man who have injured the master of the fishing-spear

---

[1] The significance of this is that people have said that, since they have acted to injure people, they are no better than witches, while in their ancestral association with the river they can claim a legitimate power over it.

[2] In Dinka, *aa luk tem*, 'they cut (conclude) the words'.

in his home, if it be that your word is the stronger, then you will live. But you man who have injured the master of the fishing-spear, you shall not [live to] finish this season's grain. If you are a very strong hawk,[1] then we will stop the mouths of our spears[2] and invoke with them no more. But if you are not the stronger, then we shall send the clan-divinity of my father to strike you in the head, wherever you may be.

O you [clan-divinity] of my ancestor Ayok Kerjok, and you of Aken Lual, and you of the Pagong clan, we of this subtribe are distressed because our master of the fishing-spear has become ill, and a person has left behind a fishing-spear in his homestead. If it be a child which brought this spear and forgot it,[3] then we have no quarrel with it. But if it is a man who came to bewitch, then we shall not cross the river together with him this year.

And you *mayan* [bull-calf] provided by the child of his sister to make his maternal uncle well, and to make the whole camp of my father healthy, you *mayan* set out on your journey. Go to the Apuk tribe and to the Kuac tribe and to our tribe Agwok[4] and take away the Powers which spend the dry season with people and spend the wet season with people. Take them all away from us, *mayan*. *Wuuuu* away the illness to those with lower incisors![5]

Here those present all made the loud sound *wuuuu* and turned towards the south. There followed a brief hymn:

> The Flesh kindles like fire
> As the sun comes here

and then a further invocation by another man:

Repeat my words, ee! You Flesh of my father, I call you in my prayer because of the man who came to bewitch and left his fishing-spear behind. Therefore, I call you to hear me. A man became sick because of a witch. And I have thought thus: if it be a child who brought the spear and forgot it, then I have no quarrel with him. But if it be a witch who came to bewitch, then you Flesh of my

---

[1] To speak in metaphor like this is thought to be characteristic of those whose invocations are particularly powerful. The stranger who has left the fishing-spear is the hawk who has pounced upon the sick man.

[2] The darting of the spear is part of the act of speech in the situation of invocation.

[3] The implication is that if the spear has merely been forgotten, it must have been forgotten by a child, since no grown man would be so thoughtless.

[4] These are neighbouring tribes and the ceremony was taking place near a common boundary, where members of the different tribes were at that time at peace.

[5] See later, p. 239.

father show him your strength, that he may see for himself what you can do. I have no long speech to make to you, I shall soon be silent.[1]

If I call upon you, you Flesh of my father, and you Fig-tree of my father [a clan-divinity of Payi, the clan of the man who is speaking], then you will put together your words in my mouth, to work together as one word. You of my ancestor, and you of the Flesh of my father, I have called upon you that you may help. And you, man who have bewitched, I have nothing much to say to you. If you are very much stronger than we are, we of the clans Payi and Pagong, then we will stop the mouths of our spears; but if you are not the stronger, then you will get your deserts in a few days.

There followed another hymn:

> If I am hated, then I hate,
> If I am loved, then I love,
> If a kite swoops upon what is mine
> Then it regrets it, seeing what I am
> It trembles inwardly.[2]
> If a kite swoops upon what is mine, ee
> Its wing breaks.
> When it sees, it fears and trembles.

There followed a further invocation:

Repeat my words. Thus it is. You Head carrying-ring of my father I call you because you are one who wastes the limbs[3] and if I call upon you you will hear my words. And you O Divinity, you are the great person whom all people venerate (*mac*) and you do not repulse (*jol*—rudely dismiss) your people if no one has given you offence. And if a man has done wrong, then yes, you will be heart-broken because of him, and if a man has kept malice in his heart,[4] then you will decide between him and his enemy, because it is you who are the father of all people. And I will mention the witch, because he came to bewitch, and a man was left behind him, sick. O you Divinity, if it be a child who brought the spear, and nothing evil comes with it, then we have no quarrel with the child. But if it be a witch, then may he get his deserts. And though he be a very strong witch, yet will he be overcome by the fishing-spear of my father.

[1] A mark of respect, and also of incisiveness.
[2] In Dinka, *yic nger*, which Fr. Nebel, op. cit., 1936, p. 126, translates as 'to have compassion'. I think more widely it means to weaken and shrink inwardly, so that the source of action is paralysed.
[3] This clan-divinity has the reputation of causing paralysis of the legs.
[4] The Dinka means literally 'if a man has failed to give his heart to another', which was explained as 'if he has concealed his hatred'.

Another invocation

So it is. You, Flesh of my father, we are now no longer as biting in invocation as our fathers were in the past. A witch has bewitched us now, and you Fig-tree of my father and you of the most distant past I call upon you that you may come and look after the people of my father's tribe. Look after them well that no evil may overtake them. It is you Flesh of my father and Fig-tree of my father and Head carrying-ring of my father, if I call upon you then you must listen to my words.

Another invocation

You Wuny, subtribe of my father, I have few words to say to you all, and you Agwok, tribe of my father, I have few words to say to you all. I shall say one small thing. You witch, if you have come to our ceremony, and are here now, then leave at once. And you man who may have had any hand in this [illness] then you must leave our ceremony when you hear that we invoke over a bull because of a witch. And you Flesh of my father, I have little to say. So it is.

As the invocations at such a ceremony proceed, the tempo rises, and by this time the invocations were becoming more incisively and energetically delivered. The bull-calf tethered to its peg in the homestead was drooping its head and looking drowsy. The divinity Flesh was beginning to manifest itself in the quivering of the limbs of some of those who spoke invocations. Another member of the Payi clan continued:

You Flesh of my father I call you in my prayers, and you Fig-tree of my father and you Head carrying-ring of my father and you *Malek* river Power of my father I call you in my prayers. And you fishing-spear the witch brought into the homestead, I call you in my prayers, and you Agwok, tribe of my father [living and dead], I call you in my prayers. Hear my words, they are few. You witch, I have not much to say to you.

You Flesh of my father, you will do your work alone, and you [listing the other clan-divinities] will work alone,[1] and you witch I have little to say to you. If your word be the stronger, then we shall just listen to (endure) you, but if the words of our fishing-spears are the stronger, then you shall hear the word of the Flesh of my father. And you Divinity, you are our father, the father of us all, and if a

---

[1] It was later explained that all the divinities were told to work alone in the sense of working independently of the master of the fishing-spear. The retribution to overtake the witch would thus not be the result of human action, like witchcraft, but of divine action.

man has hated another, then it is you who see him, and if a witch has come to bewitch and left this fishing-spear behind in the homestead, then you Divinity will see [justice done] between us and the witch. So it is.

There followed the invocation already quoted (Chap. III, p. 106), and spoken by a master of the fishing-spear of Pagong. Then came another of the same clan:

You Flesh, divinity of my father, and you *Awar* grass and Hedgehog of my father, I have little to say to you, and you Longar my ancestor, I have little to say to you. And you witch, who went in health but left a sick man behind you, I have little to say to you also. You came at night to bewitch, and no snake bit your foot, and no thorn pierced your foot, and you did not fall into a hole and break your leg; but now *we* have known you, and you shall not avoid the points of our fishing-spears. If our spears miss their mark, then we have insulted you,[1] but if we have not insulted you, then you will not live to eat this year's grain with us.

Fishing-spear of my father, you will strike him in the head!

Here the invocations were reaching their climax, and at the command that the fishing-spear should find its mark in the head of the enemy, like the fishing-spear of Aiwel Longar in the myth, it was darted particularly vigorously and flourished over the tethered calf. Then came the last invocation by a member of the Payi clan, who calls upon the clan-divinities of Payi and Pagong together:

You Earth, you are called by my words, and you Divinity, you are called by my words, because you look after all people, and are greater than anyone and all people are your children. And if evil has befallen them, then you are called to come and join with them in it also. And you are not now called for good, you are called for evil, come help.[2] O you Flesh, divinity of Pagong, if you are called then you will indeed hear me, and you *Awar* grass you will hear. And you Flesh of my father and Fig-tree of my father and Head carrying-ring of my father, you will hear.

O Power (illness) we have separated you from our man, release him; we have given you the bull *mayan*, release him indeed.

[1] The idea is that their invocations will not injure the guiltless.

[2] This means that the sacrifice is not a routine sacrifice for life and health in general, but a sacrifice for the removal of some specific evil, which involves the intention of injuring an enemy.

Here the calf was thrown, and was almost at once hidden under a crowd of people, mostly young men, who slapped it and trampled on it. This, with other actions of the sacrificing group, are described and discussed in the next chapter.

The above invocations were made at public ceremonies; I now give an example of the kind of private prayer which a master of the fishing-spear will offer for someone who asks for relief from a minor ailment. A man with a persistent tropical ulcer asked a master of the fishing-spear to pray for its healing, and his prayer was as follows:

So it is. You of my father, when a man has been speared, and the next day masters of the fishing-spear are called in to speak about it, then the wound will heal. It is you Divinity [who ordain] that that which you gave to us masters of the fishing-spear, if we have not misused it,[1] [enables us] to pray with our mouths and Divinity will help us, and the edges of the wound will come together and it will heal. You of my father, you Flesh of my father, if we have not misused our powers, then you will help us.

The master of the fishing-spear spat on the wound, and took a grass stem and split it apart. He then bound it carefully together again with thread to represent the coming together of the edges of the healthy flesh, and told the patient to carry this stem with him until the ulcer healed. Meanwhile he was to take good care not to graze the ulcer against anything, and to get European medical attention when that was possible. Then, said the master of the fishing-spear, everything would work together towards the healing of the ulcer.

Finally, here are a few invocations which masters of the fishing-spear[2] composed for me to take down, and which, composed without the stimulus of a specific occasion, show the general structure of an invocation and the pattern according to which those made on specific occasions are constructed. The first is an invocation for a sacrifice to Divinity:

You Divinity, we shall kill your ox [bull], and better that you should be pleased with us. You will let us walk in health, and we have made a feast [a ceremony] so that there should be no fever, and that no other illness should seize people, that they may all be well.

[1] In Dinka, *na acuk col kerac*, 'if we have not prayed evil'.

[2] The later ones are composed by Majak Madut, a Rek Dinka master of the fishing-spear whose shrine is shown in Plate VI.

And if my clansman travels, then let him complete his journey without sickness, and let no evil befall him or anybody. And you Divinity do not bring evil upon us, and I shall be pleased. You women clap your hands,[1] and sing and *wuu* away the fever, that nothing may be wrong with us. You tribe of my father, walk in health, nothing shall harm us, and Divinity will be pleased with us, and we will pray to Divinity that there may be no bad thing and sing. . . .

Here he sang a little hymn about Abuk Deng.

Here are further theoretical invocations made, as a sequence, by another master of the fishing-spear, and representing what he would say and what he would expect others present to say:

So it is. You of my father, if we have brought out your ox (bull) and dedicated it to you, then you Flesh of my father, will help us so that we may be well. Nothing must come to injure the tribe of my father. If I have restored them (*kooc*),[2] then they will be healthy this year.

The following invocations were then composed:

So it is. Now that Majak has spoken his prayer, what I say is like what Majak has said. O you Divinity, if we have brought out your ox this year, then in the whole country nothing must injure people. Sickness will depart, and Divinity will come and help us. You, Flesh of my father, people must walk in health. And you, Flesh of my father, and you of Thigh-bone,[3] and you of Agoth,[4] if I call upon you all, then you will join yourselves together and be one.

You of my father, you must look after people this year. Crocodile in the river, I want it thus, that you must not take any man of the tribe of my father; and you, *ngok* fish, you will not pierce the foot of any man of the tribe of my father. And you, hole in the forest, you will not be fallen into[5] so that a man breaks his leg, and you thorns of the forest, you will not pierce a man's foot. And you cattle, you will go off to graze in the dry-season pastures, and you will find no disease there. Cattle and men, all shall return in health, if you let it be so,[6] you of my father. And I have not prayed (for) evil, and I have not made spells[7] to kill anyone. If you let it be so, you of my father,

---

[1] As in Plate III.　　　　　　　　　　　[2] The term is discussed later.

[3] The clan-divinity of his clan, Paghol.

[4] The founding ancestor of his clan.

[5] He characteristically makes the hole, and not the man, responsible.

[6] In Dinka, *na pal yin*, which also has a sense of forgiving.

[7] The word is *theeth*, which means to 'conjure' lions, Powers, &c., with spells.

then you [addressing the sacrificial victim] will fall on the right flank.[1]

Many repetitions of ideas and phrases have here been omitted. Everything which the Dinka desire is stated many times and these repetitions themselves are chorused by the rest of the company. This rhythmical repetition of particular sets of words and ideas, spoken first singly then in unison, gradually has an effect which may be observed by anyone attending a sacrifice and, moreover, comes to be felt by the foreign observer himself. At the beginning of such a ceremony there is usually a lot of chatter and disorder. People come and go, greet each other, discuss their private affairs, change their places, and so on. It is common for those officiating to try to call people to some order. The newly tethered victim also may be restive and uneasy.

As the invocations increase in tempo, however, the little bursts of incisive speech by the invoker and his chorus draw the congregation more and more towards the central action. In theory (though not always in practice) the senior and most important men speak their invocations last, when the others have prepared the congregation for them. As the invocations proceed, the repeaters of the invocations work together more smoothly in rhythmical speech, and a collective concentration upon the main theme and purpose of the gathering becomes apparent.

This concentration of attention on a single action ends when the sacrificial victim is thrown and killed, and there is then a sensible release of a tension which has been slowly mounting throughout the ceremony. People now begin to argue and jostle each other, as they go about their several tasks in preparation for the butchering and distribution of the carcass. It is thus at the moment immediately preceding the physical death of the beast, as the last invocation reaches its climax with more vigorous thrusts of the spear, that those attending the ceremony are most palpably members of a single undifferentiated body, looking towards a single common end. After the victim has been

[1] The Western Dinka usually throw the beast and cut its throat, so that in fact, unless it is very clumsily managed, it can be made to fall on its right flank, which is auspicious. The frequency with which the Western Dinka refer to falling on the right (which also is connected with falling towards the east, the direction of the rising sun and hence of life) might suggest that their older custom was that of spearing the animal, but they do not say so. Dr. P. P. Howell's comments (p. 101) are here of interest.

killed, their individual characters, their private and family differences, and various claims and rights according to their status, become apparent once more.

In the account of the role of cattle, I mentioned the Dinkas' way of figuring the unity and diversity of kin-groups in the unity of the bull or ox and in the customary division of its flesh (p. 23). Similarly in a sacrifice, whilst the victim is still a living whole, all members of a gathering are least differentiated from each other in their common interest in that whole victim. With its death, interest turns towards the customary rights of different participating groups in the division of its flesh, rights which, though clear in principle, permit of some dispute about details of their entitlements. People begin again to see themselves in relation to others, and not only in relation to the victim.

Sacrifice thus includes a re-creation of the basis of local corporate life, in the full sense of those words. The whole victim corresponds to the unitary solidarity of human beings in their common relationship to the divine, while the division of the flesh corresponds to the social differentiation of the persons and groups taking part. And in this connexion it is significant that in certain sacrifices to the divinity Flesh, the central mysteries of the masters of the fishing-spear, the victim is not distributed to the territorial community as at the usual sacrifice. In its death also it is regarded as an undifferentiated whole, to be consumed in its entirety by a single agnatic group, amongst whom it is shared, but not divided.

This brief digression in anticipation of the next chapter is necessary in order to suggest how the form and procedure of the oral rites of the Dinka lead towards a climax of 'aggregation' which immediately precedes the killing of the victim. Only after the ceremony has been in progress for some time do some of the participants begin to become possessed by one or another divinity, according to the ceremony; and it is particularly the speakers of the final invocations who begin to quiver in ways already described.[1] Such behaviour is clearly (in part at least) connected with the suggestive influence of particular words and phrases spoken with increasing rhythmical intensity.[2] In the

---

[1] Chap. III, pp. 136–7.

[2] The effect may be similar to that produced by the singing by which the apparent state of dissociation of a diviner is partly induced.

invocations made at a sacrifice the individual interests and doubts of those taking part are gradually transcended by a collective confidence in the omnipotence of sacred speech, spoken by those who have a right to speak it effectively and endorsed by the whole gathering. During such a ceremony the Dinka express none of the anxious doubts about the effectiveness of human action which in ordinary circumstances they can entertain.

It may be the case (and in my opinion often is) that those who display symptoms of possession in the course of a sacrificial ceremony at first deliberately encourage them, yielding to any involuntary twitch or spasm of the body, and by doing so exaggerating it. The body is then quickly given over to sensations and movements which faith and tradition lead the mind to expect in such circumstances, and to some degree wilfully to anticipate.[1] The fact that in the initial stages states of possession may be self-encouraged, or even counterfeited, is recognized by the Dinka, but unlike us they do not think that this voluntary co-operation of the conscious person in any way invalidates his final state of possession as coming from a source other than himself. Again we see the difference between the underlying passivity of the Dinka in their relation to events, and the active construction which we tend to place upon our own role in shaping them. The Dinka are less interested in the action of the conscious self in bringing about states of dissociation, than in the eventual replacement of the normal human personality in those who have surrendered themselves. Their interest in and explanations of such conditions start where ours often end, that is, at the point where conscious control has clearly largely abdicated. They are interested in 'what came about' rather than 'how it came about'.

When the invocations end, and the victim is finally thrown, those who have been invoking are often supposed to collapse entirely, and certainly they appear nervous and exhausted quite out of proportion to the physical effort they have been required

---

[1] Cf. a detail from a description of the enstoolment of the King Anei Kur of the Shilluk: 'The act of substitution upon the stool symbolizes to the Shilluk the possession of the *reth* by the spirit of Nyikang, and we saw that the *reth* was seized with a trembling fit at the critical moment, and certainly he appeared to be in a dazed condition immediately afterwards. . . .' P. P. Howell and W. P. G. Thomson, 'The Death of a Reth of the Shilluk and the Installation of his Successor', *S.N. & R.*, vol. xxvii, 1946, p. 62.

to make. It is held that they should be in a state of trembling excitement, if their invocations have been really powerful. It seems that eventually all those taking part are living only in a situation which the ceremony has gradually created. The collective expressions of will and desire in the invocations undoubtedly play a large part in the creation of a temporarily autonomous action. I later return to the implications of this.

. I turn now to a commentary on some of the more significant words and expressions connected with the texts already quoted. The Dinka word which has here been translated as 'invoke', 'invocation', is *lam*. The noun form is sometimes *lam-lam*. It must be admitted that the translation is not entirely adequate, and in some respects misleading. *Lam* may be used both transitively and intransitively, and this has led me sometimes to use the verb 'invoke' intransitively, with some violence to English usage. Further, in English we should use 'invoke' transitively with God, or spirits, or whatever it might be which was to be called in, as its object. In Dinka it is precisely *not* the Powers which are the objects of *lam*, though in the total situation of *lam* they are called upon.[1]

Where *lam* is used transitively, its object is a victim, and we may properly say that the Dinka *lam* the bull they intend to sacrifice, and also that masters of the fishing-spear may *lam* their enemies. In this latter sense its meaning comes near to that of a (ritual) curse, though for a solemn curse there is another word, *waak*. In the act of *lam*, men think themselves to be actually *doing* something to the object of their invocation; and they are also calling in various Powers to act upon it on their behalf. It is important to note that it is the spoken invocation, which is said to affect and weaken its object, whether a sacrificial victim or a human enemy. Therefore, to cut the throat of a sacrificial ox is merely the necessary physical conclusion of a sacrificial act of which the most important part has been already accomplished by speech. Without speech, or at least an intention which could be verbalized, there is no sacrifice; and we have seen that attention is more concentrated upon the final invocations than upon the physical death.

---

[1] 'To invoke' in the transitive English usage is in many ways nearer to the Dinka expression *long col*, 'to call upon in prayers'. Fr. Nebel, op. cit., 1936, gives '*Lam*, invoke God or spirits . . . *lam kerac*, to curse . . . '.

Invocation in this sense, and reservation of a particular beast for a particular sacrificial purpose (in Dinka *mac*), are complementary acts. The appropriate action for Dinka who have some reason for propitiating Powers is to reserve a beast and to invoke over it (*bi muor mac, bi lam*). I have already discussed the word *mac* in connexion with the clan-divinities (pp. 133–4). In the simplest sense it means the tethering of a beast to a peg in the homestead so that it may be held there for invocations to be made over it. Thereafter it may either be sacrificed at once, or again reserved in the herd, with special restrictions upon its use for any purpose other than that for which it has been prepared: as an offering to some Power or divinity. If it is thus dedicated, and allowed to live, it is later brought out again and invoked over before sacrifice. A reserved or dedicated victim is produced by the dual action of *mac* and *lam*. By becoming the ox of DENG, for example, it becomes the 'locus' of the activities of that free-divinity within the homestead and the herd. DENG is in a sense confined to it. This is part of the complex of meaning of the statement that 'people *mac* DENG'; people, by reserving a beast for sacrifice to DENG, hope to confine DENG's activities, which might otherwise be dangerously diffused among human beings, to a particular known animal, in which DENG can be both encouraged to inhere locally, and venerated.

Reservation and invocation thus prepare a victim for death in a particular, and fully stated, context of human intention. This is abundantly plain in the texts I have quoted. The victim is required to hear the words spoken to and over it. As the ceremony proceeds, and the tethered beast often tends to become pacified and drowsy, the Dinka say that the *lam* itself is weakening it; and invocation thus makes a passive victim.

As I have said, the ox, and more particularly the bull, are for the Dinka creatures in which vitality is especially abundant, and are in songs the figures by which aggressive vigour is most commonly represented. Here, then, in invocations, a human act of speech made by those qualified to make it, converts this figure of activity and energy into a feeble victim, ideally[1] submissive to the demands which the congregation make upon it. The exaggerated accounts one hears of the power of the *lam* of a really effective master of the fishing-spear, moreover, suggest

---

[1] I say 'ideally' because sometimes a beast remains restive to the end.

that the horns, the weapons of the beast's aggression, wilt before his words.

Invocations are also thought directly to weaken those who, as enemies, are mentioned in them. In the set of invocations for the recovery of a master of the fishing-spear who was thought to have been bewitched, we see that the witch also is to cease to be active, and to die. Throughout the invocations there is an emphasis upon the play of strength against weakness, of action and retraction, between the supposed witch and the masters of the fishing-spear. The figure of speech by which the enemy is there represented is of interest:

If a kite swoops upon what is mine
It regrets it, seeing what I am
It trembles inwardly [the source of its action is paralysed]. . . .

For the birds of prey, with a fittingness which we may also perceive, represent for the Dinka powerful, self-directed activity.[1] The invocations themselves, directed against the victim and also against enemies and dangers, are thus a matter of actively taking control of 'a situation', so that what the participants wish becomes accomplished for them. Their victims, or enemies, are 'made' totally passive. This interpretation is confirmed by the manual rites, in which the victim is often buffetted, and also made the object of a mock demonstration of warlike hostility.

Expressions in the invocations indicate the form which victimization takes: the victim is a prisoner, tethered in the mid-day heat to await its death; it is given to the agents of sickness, to suffer in the place of a man. In invocation also, all kinds of illnesses are often mentioned by name, along with magic roots, and told that they must now be 'without an owner', and must 'meet together on the back of the ox' to travel away with it in its death.

In sacrifice the Dinka exchange (*war*)[2] the life of the victim

---

[1] They thus figure in songs. The following is an example from a song about a man who wishes to take his girl away from her people who oppose their marriage:
Were I a battailleur eagle, I would snatch her up
Were I a chanting goshawk, I would snatch her up
Were I a vulture, I would snatch her up . . . .

[2] Christian Dinka use this term for 'to redeem'. The doctrine of redemption in Christian theology should present less difficulty than some other doctrines, since the notions of a kind of redemption and vicarious suffering are embedded in their own thought.

for the life of the man for whom the sacrifice is made. The Powers take the ox, and the man is spared. We have earlier described the numerous situations in which cattle are substituted for human beings, and here in the central act of sacrifice the ultimate form of this transvaluation is dramatically represented. All the agents of human *passiones* are assembled in the invocations, and 'separated' or 'released' from their human victims. Given the firm Dinka idea that such agents are positive forces, it is clear that they cannot be annihilated. At the best they may wander 'without an owner'; but they are also, in invocation, transposed to an animal victim, and often told also to go to the land of foreigners. They are sent, however, to the lands of the foreigners 'with lower incisor teeth', and not to the land of the Nuer who, like the Dinka, remove the lower incisors, and for whom the Dinka, living a life which presents the same problems, have much fellow-feeling.

While the agents of human suffering are together symbolically detached from human beings in the invocations and sacrifice, conversely the sources of human vigour and success are brought together and asked to meet in the mouths of the masters of the fishing-spear, so that all may work together to achieve the end which the sacrificators desire. This conception of the necessity for joint activity of the strengthening forces, especially Divinity and the clan-divinities, is very important in Dinka religious thought. Since, as we have seen, what they constantly call upon is 'that of the fathers', in invocation they are demanding the help of their whole human inheritance. The fact that, despite the difficulties and dangers of human life, they are themselves living and multiplying, testifies to something in that inheritance which is stronger than the forces of death and sterility which constantly threaten its transmission. In the invocations we see that though 'that of the mother' may also be called upon, the main emphasis is upon agnatic heredity, and upon the intrinsic historical association of some of those invoking with the political community for which they make their invocations. It is these claims to a traditional and legitimate authority that are represented by such expressions as 'and I am not a bastard coming with its mother' (p. 222); 'help my people now as in the past my father looked after you' (p. 225); and 'you my prayer, and you prayer of the long-distant past, prayer of my ancestors, you are spoken now' (p. 221). The reiteration of the word *wa*, 'my father', throughout the invocations identifies the speakers with the authority of the father which every Dinka recognizes in his experience of his own family.

The notion that united action, by all the agents which can strengthen men, is necessary in an effective invocation is parallel, on the plane of human society, to necessity of the co-operation and unity of members of the lineage and of the community taking part in the ceremony. Quarrelling and divisions weaken men's effectiveness in sacramental speech and action, and it is for this reason that past quarrels are denied in some of the texts. Further, members of a lineage of masters of the fishing-spear may emphasize in their invocations that they 'are one, not two', in the sense that they have never divided for purposes of marriage, as some large lineages do.[1] We shall have occasion to refer again to the necessity of collective action in sacrifice; for such action requires co-ordination, and therefore some principle of leadership. In their masters of the fishing-spear the Dinka have a type of leadership which is less marked among the Nuer, whose religious practice is similarly less confined to corporate acts.

In the act of invocation as a whole, men claim to exercise a measure of control over the ills which assail them; but the speeches of which the total act is composed include much supplication, accompanied by statements of the situation in which help is required. These supplicatory and expository speeches are called *long*. When this verb is used transitively, its object is always Divinity, divinities, or Powers, while the complete act to which the speeches contribute is directed, as we have said, at a victim.

Anyone may *long col*, 'call a prayer', making a statement of his predicament and his requests, but masters of the fishing-spear do so with more authority than others. One of their main tasks is to pray thus at night in the cattle-camps, asking protection for their people and their herds and stating their intentions with regard to them, as in the following song:

A master of the fishing-spear called Majok Akot prays at night:

---

[1] It is interesting to note that the Dinka, who have the reputation of being far less systematically united politically than the Nuer, should place such emphasis upon unity and collective action in religious situations.

> Let the cattle move, let the cattle move across the river
> Which becomes dry, which is not to be deep:
> I have released the cattle ⌊by prayer⌋.

One man said that it was now no longer so necessary as in the past for the masters of the fishing-spear to pray for their people in the camps, for the Government had taken over the task of protecting people from their enemies, and from lions.[1]

The supplicatory prayer and speech made when people *long col* does not in itself require a victim. Masters of the fishing-spear may make it privately, and without necessarily flourishing a spear, whereas in *lam*, the total act of invocation, they require a spear, or something to represent a spear, by which the assertions of those taking part may be accompanied by emphatic thrusts of the right arm. The chorus at a ceremony therefore repeats (*gam*) the *long*,[2] the speech; it would make no sense in Dinka to speak of 'repeating the *lam*' for the *lam* is the complete oral and manual rite of which the *long* are constituents. Among the Bor Dinka and perhaps as far west as the Agar, the function of making such speeches is recognized as belonging specially to a particular lineage of each subclan, 'the lineage of the *long*', but I did not come across this among the Western Dinka where most of this material was collected.

The speeches and spoken prayers are accompanied and supported by acts of praise for the Powers from which help is needed; these acts are called in Dinka *rok*, and consist primarily of songs or hymns. Two examples appear in the texts of this chapter, and in earlier chapters most of the hymns recorded are *wak rok nhialic, yath*, &c., songs honouring Divinity or divinities. I include here three more. The first is a song in honour of the clan-divinity Turtle:

> Where has Turtle gone?
> It is sought but not found.

[1] Where a lion is exceptionally dangerous, people may now persuade the Government to send a policeman to help kill it.

[2] In official government-sponsored courts, the speeches of those involved in a case are either repeated phrase by phrase, or the last word of each phrase is repeated by someone appointed to perform this task, also called *gam long*. In effect, this produces an orderly procedure, since any interrupter has to contend with two voices and cannot make himself heard unless the *gam long* takes up the phrases of his speech.

> Sit at the foot of the tamarind tree
> Milk the cows for it [for Turtle]
> ABUK DENG, and Turtle, ee!
> They have left behind the riches of the father.

Here we see the characteristic statement that the divinities are absent, in order to make them present. The cows are to be milked, and the gourds placed at the foot of the tamarind tree, in order that libations may be made to Turtle; and the line

> They have left behind the riches of the father
> (*kek anyieng jiek wun wei*)

is the expression used of those who leave home and do not return to claim their inheritance. Here the reference is to the offerings which the Turtle clan wishes to make to the 'absent' divinities.

The following is a hymn in honour of Lion, here as divinity of the clan Paguor, though others have the same divinity:

Let us kill the white ox, and prepare our shrine (*yik*)
We shall kiss our shrine tomorrow[1]
We shall sharpen the fangs of the white one
White one, son of Acol, if a man hates me let him be pierced by the lion's fangs,
Many [lions] are concealed in the clumps of high grass of the rains.

Here, the assimilation of the white ox, the victim, to the divinity Lion needs comment. 'The white ox' and 'the white one' are represented in the Dinka by the same word, *mabyor*. This is also a common name for lions in folk-tales and, I believe, was the name of a lion-son born as a twin with the founder of the Paguor clan from their common ancestress Acol ('the black one'). In 'sharpening the teeth' of Lion (by preparing a sacrifice) its clansmen are, of course, making it ready to 'bite' on their behalf. In this hymn the common Dinka word for lion, *koor*, does not appear, nor do any of the other terms for lion which, like *koor*, are emotively associated with the fear and hostility lions normally evoke; and in the last line the word 'lions' is my insertion—in Dinka it is only implied.

In the final example I have omitted two lines which I cannot translate:

---

[1] An act of honour and respect described in Chapter VII.

Children of the ants, we have suffered from dryness[1]
Why I am without cattle, why I am without grain—
That is what I ask, ee!
I am a man who boasted of himself
I slaughtered in my greed my *majok* ox[2]
Children of Aghok, my father, the children of the ants are forsaken (?)
[Yet] my father the creator indeed created men
We honour our lord (*banydan yeku rok*) that he may look in upon us
Mayan [a diviner or prophet] honours (*rok*) Divinity
Mayan son of Deng divines
It is GOLONG[3] which devours our cattle.

The verb *rok*, used transitively, may have as its object either
the victim at a sacrifice, or Divinity and Powers, or a master of
the fishing-spear or prophet. Fr. Nebel translates it as 'to propitiate',[4] and there is undoubtedly a strong propitiatory element
in it; but its meaning is not merely that those to whom it is
offered should permit, negatively, the realization of people's
desires. In ordinary English usage 'propitiate' has come to imply
a somewhat more defensive activity than the Dinka suggests,
and 'to *make* propitious' retains more of the meaning of the
Dinka. The object of *rok* is *made* propitious by the honour which
the singing offers it.

In secular situations also the Dinka use choral singing as a
means of honouring a person of importance. European visitors
are often thus approached by choruses of men or women, who
confidently expect to be generously rewarded for the compli-
ment they have paid. This is not *rok* (which, I think, is used only
in religious contexts) but it is the secular analogue of the honour
rendered to the Powers, and is expected to create a favourable
disposition in those to whom it is rendered. In one of the myths
of masters of the fishing-spear (p. 181) there is an example of
the way in which the original master of the fishing-spear is

---

[1] 'Suffered from dryness' is represented in Dinka by the one word *yal*—a holo-
phrasis compared with the English, which suggests the holistic nature of this Dinka
experience.
[2] He connects his past pride and self-complacency with the present decline in
his fortunes.
[3] GOLONG is an injurious Power of the same class as the fetish MATHIANG GOK,
but less widely known among the Western Dinka. It devours the cattle because
many beasts are sacrificed to satisfy its greed. Now Divinity is asked to help.
[4] P. A. Nebel, op. cit., 1936, p. 142: *Rok* (*nhialic, atim ran*); to propitiate, expiate
(God, soul of a deceased).

finally flattered and conciliated by a song composed in his honour.

Functionally, choral singing punctuating the speeches at a sacrifice reinforces their effect of temporarily imposing a single controlled rhythm on those taking part. It differs from the speeches primarily in not being impromptu, so that the chorus in singing does not merely repeat the words of its leader. It complements them. The choral singing noticeably improves as a ceremony proceeds. At first it is often necessary for those officiating to chide their people into concentrating upon the song. Later, people 'lose themselves' more and more in the ceremony, and it is often after a hymn that the first signs of possession are apparent. In secular songs of honour for a visitor, the leader of the chorus has similarly to rally his men in the early stages, for half-hearted and indifferent efforts cannot be expected to bring generous returns. The song, when vigorously sung, does not merely beg for attention, but demands it, and even in secular situations it is so aggressively directed *at* (and not simply sung *for*) the person whom it honours that he cannot but be actively engaged by it.[1] There are thus three main elements in the oral rites of the Dinka: statement, supplication, and honour rendered. These are not serial 'movements' of the sacrificial rites, but are intermingled and combined in them. The statements represent the predicament for which the ceremony is being held, and ultimately claim a measure of human control over it. They involve the assertion of an intrinsic strength and authority in certain human acts of speech. The supplications are admissions of human dependence upon a higher 'nature' in them and their world, and hence of inferiority and weakness. The honouring of Divinity and divinities in the confident hope that they will thereby be rendered actively propitious is an act of freedom and dependence at once; it

---

[1] The significance of hymn-singing can be fully understood only in the context of a complete study of song and dance among the Dinka, which would here be out of place. We may mention, however, that choral song expresses and re-creates shared, corporate, experience, and one of the deprivations which Dinka who live away from home seem to feel most strongly is their difficulty in sharing in foreign songs and dances. A complete study of the social range of different types of song would involve a description of a wide range of Dinka social groupings. Only a man's friends and kin are likely to know his ox-songs, or understand their allusions. Variants of songs honouring clan-divinities are known by clansmen over wide areas, while variants of songs honouring free-divinities are still more widely known.

implies dependence and inferiority, but, in ways we have seen, it also assumes that the human act of honouring higher powers may come near to compelling their active help.

It has in the past been proposed in anthropology that 'magic' and 'religion' should be distinguished from each other by regarding as 'magical' those acts which attempt to compel and control, and as 'religious' those acts which involve propitiation and supplication. Such a distinction probably no longer has much influence or interest, but it may be worth while, in view of what we have described, to note how inadequately it would equip us to begin to understand the structure of Dinka sacrificial rites. For in them, supplication and control are complementary parts of a single act. As we later consider more fully, experience of the freedom and of the contingency of human action is there re-created so as to emphasize finally the possibility of effective human action.

A relationship between human control and human passivity apparent in the main elements of the oral rites is also clearly shown in the myths; and the myths of the separation of Man from Divinity, and of the masters of the fishing-spear, must be taken together as the total *mythos* of Dinka religious practice today.

In the first set of myths, it will be remembered, Man's first freely independent action has as its corollary the introduction of suffering and death into human experience. The myths of the masters of the fishing-spear show a reverse relationship between human action and human suffering, for in them men are being killed by Aiwel Longar until one man forms a plan to counteract that killing power. Then men receive a strength to prevail ultimately over the conditions in which Man's first independent act has placed them all. The myths of the original separation, and of the masters of the fishing-spear, thus complement each other in much the same way as the confessions of dependence and assertions of strength which together form the basis of the oral rites.[1]

Outside strictly religious situations also, it may be observed

---

[1] It is to be noted too that in versions of each myth, women appear in complementary roles. A woman is instrumental in producing the original separation of Man and Divinity, while in myths of the first master of the fishing-spear a woman suggests the means whereby his killing power may be counteracted.

that the relationship between freedom and contingency now seen in the myths and the oral rites has its analogues in Dinka life, especially in the structure of relations within the Dinka family which we have earlier discussed. If one can judge by the frequency with which the theme appears in songs and conversation, the authority of the father irks the young man who begins to look towards his own family and independence. He challenges his father's dispositions towards his marriage, and there may be clashes of will. But in the end the son always has to make a gesture of conciliation, for in traditional Dinka society he remains ultimately dependent upon his father or guardian until his own independent homestead has been established with their help.

More widely, the twin themes of human forcefulness and human weakness are diffused throughout the poetic imagery of the Dinka. Men are mere 'ants' which can be crushed; they are 'like game' to be hunted and scattered; they are neglected children; they are 'like the Nile cabbage' carried willy-nilly in submission to the force of the river, and so on. Constantly the ox-songs return to the theme of frustrations imposed by conditions outside the composer's control. Yet also, and in the same songs, men are bulls and birds of prey, lions and buffaloes, self-reliant and self-directing, shaping circumstances to their will by heroic acts of self-assertion. One popular Dinka story is a set of variations on a theme of tremendous Herculean acts—of taking a live leopard to wear as a dance skin, a cobra as a string of beads, the tail of a living buffalo as a belt, and so on. So also, then, in their fantasies and in the imagery of their songs, the Dinka return to the paradox of human strength and human weakness which we have discussed in relation to the structure of their myths and their oral rites, and which we meet again in considering the manual rites.

I now consider more closely those elements in the oral rites which we have earlier called 'statement', and which are essentially assertions of the scope of human control of experience. It has been noted that the Dinka quite explicitly state that *individual* action in religious contexts is ineffective. It is true that masters of the fishing-spear may invoke without any congregation to assist them, but no important sacrifice can be carried out by a master of the fishing-spear alone. Further, even in the private prayers which they make at night in the camps, the masters of the fishing-spear are not invoking as individuals, but as representatives of their whole community and agnatic group, living and dead. 'If a man calls upon himself and not upon that of his father he can do nothing.' In the field of mystical action individual action is witchcraft or sorcery; the measure of control which men can assert over experience by religious action is closely associated with the strongly corporate nature of their religious intention.

This may, in part, be referred to the interpretation of Divinity and the Powers which we have already outlined (Chap. IV). If the major Powers (whatever other basis in reality they may have) image shared experience of various kinds, the symbolical manipulation of those images in sacrificial rites demands the presence of those who share the common values which gave them meaning. Thus, for example, if the clan-divinities necessarily image the experience of clanship, their evocation must depend upon the presence, in fact or in idea, of those who share that experience. It is thus that individual Dinka who suffer misfortune when away from home think themselves to be in such danger, for they miss the confidence in dealing with their suffering which derives from the corporate act and intention of those who can fully share their experience. Individuals are weak, but social groups are strong, both in the ordinary secular affairs of life and in dealing with the Powers.

The belief that effective control demands a corporate intention in religious action has deeper roots than this, however. We have pointed out that the centrally important gift which masters of the fishing-spear are thought to have had transmitted to them by their ancestors is the gift of insight into truth, and of speaking 'the true word', that is, of representing a situation as it really and absolutely *is*. This 'truth' is something more than the opposite of lying, though that is part of it. The truth ideally spoken by masters of the fishing-spear, and guaranteed by their ancestors, is the truth which is the opposite of error; and in Dinka thought it is this kind of truth which is arrived at and stated by a *communal* intention. Thus in ordinary secular disputes points of difference between the disputants, and many other matters, are represented at length before any gathering which will attend to them. In traditional Dinka 'law' it is said that there always were such gatherings (*luk*) between the 'big people of the settlement' (*koc dit de baai*) who would 'put their words together' (*wet matic*) and arrive at a true assessment of the rights and wrongs of a case. This procedure is followed today in government courts; but now the conclusion to which the gathering comes is partly governed by foreign rules of procedure and the admissibility of evidence, and is formulated as a decision which can be imposed upon the disputants.

Among the Dinka, as among many other primitive peoples, the traditional *luk* of the past was not a 'case' in this sense. The word now denoting a law case, *luk*, has usages which imply quite a different kind of procedure. It is possible to say, using it as a verb, that 'they have cut the *luk*, and yet people have not *luk*'. This means that a decision has been given by a government court, but that the people concerned in it have not been reconciled to that conclusion. To avoid too great a digression we may say that the traditional purpose of *luk* was the presentation of the whole of a situation to the disputants and to the community, so that its rights and wrongs, the true (the same word, in Dinka, as the 'right') and the false, were apparent in such a way as to transcend the individual views of truth held by those in conflict. The word *luk* has thus something of the sense of 'taking counsel together' in order to see the objective truth of a situation, so that those who were in disagreement will, ideally, adjust their separate views to each other in the light of that representation. Men gathered together with that intention are thought to be able, up to a point, to arrive at this kind of truth; in order to do so they often introduce evidence which by European rules would be quite irrelevant, but in Dinka eyes may have an important bearing upon the whole truth of a situation. So, in one case in which a man was being tried for adultery, a witness was allowed to speak for some time upon the adulterer's refusal to give him a little of the sugar which the latter had bought. The sugar had no bearing on the adultery, but both were expressions of the nature of the man, and hence of the total situation upon which the gathering was to base its conclusions.

Men gathered 'in council' are thus permitted, in the thought of the Dinka, a measure of insight into the objective truth of the situations which confront them. It is only as a last resort, when human judgement in this matter fails, that they have recourse to oaths and ordeals, by which the decision is referred directly to the Powers. The Dinka are reluctant to go to these lengths, for they know that the consequences of lying may then be far heavier than the lies which men will tell to bolster their position are worth.

The word for the speeches in a court case, *long*, is the same as that for the speeches at a sacrifice, and if we turn again to some features of the texts, we see that the 'statements' to which we have referred are in fact full delineations of a situation as it really is or (from our point of view) as the Dinka would wish it to be. This may be clearly seen in the statements (p. 221) 'and I did not speak in the past that my children should become ill: that quarrel is an old matter' and (p. 224) 'I did not quarrel with the family of your daughter, I stayed in peace with them and I meant no malice against my sister's children' and (p. 223) 'You of my father, I did not neglect you in the past when my father died, it is not so, it is not *true* that I caused confusion in the descent group of my father.'

It is clear that if in historical fact none of these things had happened, there would be no occasion for stating that they did not happen. Do the Dinka then think that they can deceive the divinities? That interpretation would be naïve in attributing to them any such *naïveté*. The very presence of these denials is a confession of the faults. When a man states that it is not *true* that he did this or that, in this context, he implies something other than the statement that he never did it at all. From our point of view, he states that he does not wish it to be true: he wishes it had not happened, and his intention, publicly expressed, is that it should not be ultimately true. In other words, whatever he may have done or said on specific occasions does not, and is not to, represent his permanent dispositions, and his permanent dispositions and intentions are what constitute the real, existential truth of the situation he depicts. Similarly, in our own way of talking, we should not consider it true to say that a man was of an angry disposition because of one outburst of rage.

What Dinka statements assert in the cases discussed is that the way in which the situation is to be seen, absolutely and objectively, by Divinity and divinities, should not be in the light of past acts or attitudes, but in the light of what the man now states to be his real general intention towards the sick man. The community, in repeating and assenting to his speech, endorses the truth of that statement. He and they together create, in the world of the ceremony, the meaning which they wish to attribute to the incidents referred to in it. By being thus corporately stated and endorsed, what is said is, by definition, proleptically true. So it is with the common statements of righteousness made by those invoking at a ceremony. They assert, not invariably righteous *actions*, but a permanently righteous intention. It is for this reason also that in the situation of the sacrifice, quarrels and hostilities between members and groups within the congregation are denied, and must not appear in their behaviour. Of course the Dinka know that their disagreements are only held in abeyance within the ceremonial situation, and we have suggested how, when the ceremony is at an end, individual differences once more become apparent. By that time, however, the ceremony itself has created the conditions which are thought to be necessary for its effective performance. The community has been re-created in the form in which its members ideally see it, united and single in intention. We shall see in the final chapters how this re-creation of unity—a conscious sense of community—necessarily also involves a recognition of the hostility of a group to other groups of a similar nature, and also a kind of hostility on the part of men to Powers which their symbolic action aims to control.

What is represented, then, in the oral rites, is what the Dinka see as the truth of a situation—an existential truth, if one may so call it, and not the truth of specific facts in space or time. We have pointed to the conviction that human beings are able thus to create their own 'situation as it really is', induced by the affective movements of the oral rites. The texts show also how the content of what is said defines and publicly acknowledges a predicament as the ceremony moves towards the control of the experience of that predicament. Because the ceremony is thought to re-create the truth of the situation which it states, it is of particular importance that care should be taken in the statement so that no conscious error is made. Therefore, the masters of the fishing-spear often ask that they may not speak falsely—not, primarily, about the past, but that their words shall not prove to be lies. In the last set of texts quoted, for example, great care is taken that allowance should be made for the possibility that an innocent child may have left the fishing-spear which may belong to a witch. They do not wish the intrinsic effectiveness of their invocations to injure an innocent person. When people believe that they receive the substance of what they pray for, they must be very careful to be accurate in their statement of what is required. Like prophecies, the ceremony eventually represents as already accomplished what the community, and those who traditionally can speak for them, collectively intend. Thus the masters of the fishing-spear eventually state that they have freed the man from the agent which is troubling him; ideally, he should get up at once and return to normal health and vigour, and this is what sometimes happens in accounts of idealized sacrifices. The 'patient' becomes 'convalescent' in the full etymological sense of those terms. In fact, some delay is expected, and the delay shakes no faith. For the sacrifice is its own end. It has already created a moral reality, to which physical facts are hoped eventually to conform.

We have seen that the main oral rites, those at sacrifices, assert by a combination of assertions of control and admissions of weakness a relationship between freedom and contingency in human life, in which freedom appears eventually as the stronger. Human beings explicitly assert their ability to act upon the conditions which they constantly passively experience. It is of particular importance, in this regard, to recognize that the sacrificial rite is first and foremost an act of victimization. A strong and active beast is rendered weak and passive so that the burden of human *passiones* may be transferred to it. It suffers vicariously for those for whom sacrifice is made, and men, thus symbolically freed from the agents which image their sufferings, and corporately associated with each other and with the agents which image their strength, proclaim themselves the creatures whose deliberate action prevailed over the first master of the fishing-spear and received his gift of 'life'.

VII

THE CONTROL OF EXPERIENCE:
SYMBOLIC ACTION

THE material properties used in Dinka rites are not elaborate, and the places at which sacrifice is made, though varying somewhat in detail, conform to principles which are easily isolated. Only a brief account of them is therefore necessary as a preliminary to a study of the gestures, and manipulation of parts of the physical world to serve a mental and religious intention.

The most important of the *materia sacra* are the spears used in invocation from which, in Western Dinkaland at least, the masters of the fishing-spear derive their title. Sacred spears (as they are usually called by writers, though it will be apparent that the adjective requires some qualification) are of two main kinds. The commonest, in my experience, are unbarbed or unserrated fishing-spears (*bith lal*). There are also occasional leaf-bladed spears (*tong lal*) which are of the general type normally used in hunting and war. The meaning of *lal* as applied to these spears is obscure. When used of fishing-spears (even of those not specially used for religious ceremonies) it normally distinguishes unbarbed spears from those now more commonly used for fishing, the barbed *bith mec*, which are the ordinary trade fishing-spears of today. The heads of *lal* fishing-spears are simply smooth points of iron, circular or rectangular in cross-section, and a foot or so in length. Some such spears, supposed to be older than the rest, and to which special religious value is therefore attributed as later described, have much longer points, and in their short shafts resemble metal pointing-sticks of up to 4 ft. in length. They would clearly be of little use for fishing. The Dinka think the *lal* fishing-spear to be an older variety than the serrated spear they now mostly use, which is a spear requiring greater technique to contrive and is probably a more efficient practical instrument. The meaning of *lal* as applied to certain leaf-bladed spears is less clear, and seems simply to indicate that the spear is associated with religious use and with the prototype of masters of the fishing-spear who, as a hymn already quoted (p. 218) states, is thought first to have introduced it. I was unable to find any significant difference between the form of the *tong lal* and other ordinary leaf-bladed hunting and fighting-spears, except for the fact that sometimes the *tong lal*, like the sacred fishing-spears, may have a larger blade than those used for practical purposes. Some Dinka suggest that the typical form of the *tong lal* is that of a leaf-bladed spear with two pointed flanges stemming from the blade at the end which enters the shaft. It seems from accounts of the Northern Dinka that sacred leaf-bladed spears are more typical of that area than are sacred fishing-spears, and everywhere they are specially associated with clans tracing descent from Aiwel Longar.

The spears I have seen flourished in invocations seem to be of no great age, and are in no way remarkable in appearance. Dinka often decorate the shafts of their spears with coils of copper or aluminium wire, which serve to strengthen and balance them. Some of the spears used in invocation are perhaps rather more richly embellished in this way, and I have seen a few such spears with their shafts almost completely overwound with metal. The comparatively few spears which are thought to be of great age are treated with some reverence, and are not brought out for the common run of ceremonies which we have so far considered. They are kept with their points or blades sheathed in skin, shaft downwards, in their owners' huts, and it is thought that they should be shielded from the sun 'for respect'.[1] It is difficult to persuade their owners to expose them to gratify foreign curiosity, and even the prestige of government officials has with difficulty prevailed over this reluctance. It is said that a goat must be sacrificed before they are brought out. I have seen such spears which have been taken into government custody in the past on the assumption that they have formed a focus for rebellion or a means by which 'wizards' gain influence. Because of this interest known to have been shown in spears by

[1] That which is sacred should not normally be exposed to the full glare of the sun. An example of this appears in our earlier account of the shading of a 'prophet-goat' (Chap. I, p. 51). Cf. also the shading of the master of the fishing-spear and prophet of the Bor Dinka described by C. G. and B. Z. Seligman, in the passage quoted in Chap. II, p. 75.

the Government, I never thought it desirable to show great interest in having one exposed for myself. Those in government custody have obviously been frequently anointed with butter in the past, and are still protected by their skin sheaths, but are not in other ways striking.

It seems likely that the real importance of the older spears was for invoking aid for victory in war, and whilst I was in Dinkaland the occasion for their use did not arise. It is important to note, however, that although the Dinka show respect for the old spears, and venerate them as relics, they are not intrinsically indispensable for the task they perform. The reputed strength of sacred spears derives from their association with generations of ancestors who have invoked with them. It is the invocations which consecrate the spear, rather than the spear which guarantees the invocations.

Consequently, at some sacrifices, new fishing-spears are consecrated by being placed in a semicircle around the carcass of the victim during the ceremony. Also, a sacred spear is thought to be ineffective in the hands of those who are not its legitimate owners. The power inherent in spears is thus really a reflection of the power inherent in the descent-groups which own them, and members of those descent-groups may be thought to invoke effectively, even with a stick. A stick, or a new spear, in their hands represents the effectiveness of all the sacred spears of the past in 'striking what they want in the head'.[1]

For this reason the sacred spears used in invocation are closely linked with the ancestors and clan-divinities of those who use them. It is said that the clan-divinity 'is in the clansmen, and in their spears'. The way in which masters of the fishing-spear, when mentioning their divinity Flesh, touch their right shoulders, suggests the idea of a force rising from the body and flowing along the arm into the spear, which directs it towards a desired end.

The point is further made by a story collected in the Rek Dinka tribes of Thoiny and Apuk Jurwir. At the present day, in

---

[1] Cf. J. M. Stubbs, op. cit., 1934, p. 247: 'The "Bith" or fishing-spear (sometimes called "Lal") plays an important part in the ceremonies performed by the "Bang". Some of these spears are extremely old and have been handed down from father to son. Some "Bangs" are in possession of new spears, which nevertheless are accorded great respect, and on a certain occasion a "Bang" was seen to be performing with five "Biths" which were obviously new.'

Thoiny, a branch of the clan Pangok is reputed to have a very strong spear. This reputation does not refer to any particular physical spear, but to the supposed effectiveness of the invocations of masters of the fishing-spear of Pangok in that tribe. In the neighbouring Apuk Jurwir tribe Pangok count only as ordinary warriors, though they remember their relationship with the spear-masters of Thoiny. This is explained by a story of how, in the past, Pangok were also spear-masters in Apuk Jurwir. One master of the fishing-spear of Pangok in that tribe made invocations for help against the Nuer. Nuer attacks did not abate, however, and therefore this master of the fishing-spear renounced sacred fishing-spears and the divinity Flesh for his descendants, since 'that of his father had not fulfilled its promise' (*kene wun akec wetden tieng*). Thus the power of the spears, like that of the clan-divinities, is a reflection of the effectiveness attributed to their owners; and it is for this reason that in some parts of Dinkaland Pajieng and Padiangbar, though they are warrior clans, may be said to have 'forged' sacred fishing-spears—that is, to have counterfeited the authority of the spear-masters.

It is said that a master of the fishing-spear who is really angry with his people may break the shaft of his fishing-spear before them, and scatter the ashes of his cattle-hearth. This is supposed to bring disaster for the tribe or subtribe which has given offence. The breaking of the spear represents the destruction of the spiritual power which had sustained them, and the scattering of ashes represents the dispersion of the people. Again, it is the will and intention of the master of the fishing-spear which produces the moral effect. Accidental damage to a fishing-spear used in invocation would not produce the same effect.

We have said enough to show that it is not ultimately the spear, but the idea of the spear, which is important, just as the clan-divinity is something more than its emblem. Masters of the fishing-spear usually have several spears which they use in invocations, and many have only comparatively modern spears, and say that their old spears have been lost. An 'old spear', however, represents the traditional legitimacy of its owners' claim to be masters of the fishing-spear, and hence all clans of spear-masters claim that at one time they had old spears. In a local descent-group of spear-masters of any span, it is always known how many 'spears' are held. This does not mean that it is known how many physical spears there are in existence, but how many old spears have been handed down, or would have been handed down if they had not been lost. When a master of the fishing-spear dies, he distributes his spears to his sons, usually giving the most important spear to the eldest son, though a junior son may be favoured if his father considers him more gifted than his elder brothers. Thus the most important lines of descent are those which have the most important spears, and minor lineages—that is, lineages of minor importance—may have no spear, though they are theoretically entitled to invoke with them. Consequently, in the genealogy of a master of the fishing-spear, the transmission and relative reputations of the 'spears' handed down form a number of points of genealogical reference of a kind lacking in warrior clans. Those who have the more important spears have also the more important shrines; and there can be no doubt that a factor in producing, in spear-master clans, a greater knowledge of the ramifications of their descent-groups than is found in most warrior clans, is the care with which knowledge of the transmission of 'spears' and location of shrines is passed on from generation to generation.

In addition to their spears, senior men of spear-master lineages often keep in their homesteads special gourds, 'gourds of the divinity'. A milk-gourd is reserved for the libations of milk which are poured over the peg to which the sacrificial victim is tethered, and over the mound-shrines. A half-gourd is reserved for water, blessed with the spittle of masters of the fishing-spear who happen to attend a sacrifice, and often with part of the chyme and urine of the sacrificial beast, from which those attending a sacrifice are asperged. Such gourds are carefully looked after, and frequently decorated with metal rings round the lip.

Spears and gourds are the most important of the objects of ceremonial use; but in addition to them, most masters of the fishing-spear have as it were private collections of relics to which more or less unspecified kinds of religious virtue are attached. Such relics may include the horns and skulls of beasts sacrificed at memorable ceremonies, and strips of their hide, along with a miscellaneous collection of old tethering-ropes from previous victims. In addition, one finds objects of various kinds which have at some time struck a master of the fishing-spear or one of his ancestors as being of possible religious significance.[1] Among them there will perhaps be old beads, small meteorites, a horn of thiang or cob containing medicine acquired at some time from a non-Dinka wizard, perhaps an ingot or two of metal and a collection of metal rings handed over by grateful mothers whose children have been cured, or for whom conception has been assured, by the prayers of a master of the fishing-spear or his ancestors. Such private collections, though indicating by their size, variety, and (for the Dinka) strangeness something of the prestige of the masters of the fishing-spear who own them, are very far from being of central religious importance.

In addition to these *materia sacra* and other small items which can best be mentioned where necessary in the description of ceremonies which follows, every Dinka homestead is likely to display, on a forked branch later described, one or two little sacred healing cucumbers, *kuoljok* (*cucumis prophetarum*). The rationale of the healing powers attributed to them is that they are intensely bitter (*kec*, like effective invocations) and that, when ripe, they turn a greenish-blue colour suggesting to the Dinka a stormy sky, and hence, Divinity. Sometimes if no beast is available for sacrifice, Dinka may split one of these sacred cucumbers and cast it aside. It is a temporary substitute for an animal victim, and an earnest of intention to provide one when possible.

The shrines which the Dinka construct in their homesteads are of various forms. Each homestead consists of one or more sleeping-huts and a cattle-byre,[2] arranged round a central unfenced courtyard of clean smoothed mud. In some convenient position in the courtyard its owner usually places a forked branch of any available wood, sometimes ebony or heglig. Near this branch, the *ghoro*, a fire may be kindled in the evening,

---

[1] Ibrahim Eff. Bedri, op. cit., 1948, mentions that the Northern Dinka have, in addition to the *materia sacra* here mentioned, sacred beads of the priestly office, sacred stools, ropes ornamented with gifts (beads and iron and brass rings) from every member of the political group associated with a master of the fishing-spear, a small (sacred) war spear, and a bunch of sacred axes. It appears to me that the formal aspect of priest-chieftainship is more developed there than among the Western Dinka, and some of its regalia and ceremonies are reminiscent of the neighbouring Shilluk.

[2] I speak here of the Rek Dinka and those to the west and north of them. Cattle-byres are not found in most of the homesteads of the Agar Dinka.

and those men who are at home sit round this fire. Occasionally they are joined by their womenfolk, whose usual place, however, is at their own cooking-fires near the sleeping-huts. The forked branch thus forms a kind of focus for the males of the homestead when they are outside, as does the cattle-byre when the weather is wet. Visitors support their spears on such a branch, and small items of household equipment such as gourds and ropes are hung upon it. Also, in cattle-camps, each distinct herding-group, consisting in the main of the men of a few families who are close agnatic kin, will erect a similar forked branch in its sector of the camp. There again it is erected for convenience, to serve as a place at which various possessions may be assembled.

The place marked by this forked branch, whether in the homestead or the camp, is referred to as 'the head of the cattle-hearth' (*gol nhom*). The *gol* is the hearth at which men gather, or the smudge fire which protects the cattle from insects. It is also the usual Western Dinka word for a herding-group within a cattle-camp, and which consists of a core of agnatic kin with such other kin and friends as wish to join them in looking after the family herds. By extension of this, *gol* is also the word for 'clan', and hence *gol nhom*, 'the head of the *gol*', is the place with which the agnatic solidarity of the males of a herding-group is associated. When a male child is born, and the father, according to the Dinka custom, asks his wife's attendant women what its sex is, they may reply, 'a boy stays at the head of his father's *gol*', that is, at his cattle-hearth. A female child is not announced in the same way. Only a senior wife, from whom a man's main line of descent will derive, is sometimes called 'the wife of the head of the *gol*'.

The cattle-hearth is also the place near which a stud bull, or any beasts which are not to be released to pasture or in marriage payments, in the ordinary way, are regularly tethered. Hence it is explicitly associated with beasts reserved for divinities. One may hear such a statement as 'DENG is our divinity—we reserve cattle at the hearth for DENG' (*DENG ee yahnda—ghok aa mac gol nhom tene DENG*). When the Dinka feel compelled to make a sacrifice, they therefore think first of some beast which, as they say, 'has stayed at the cattle-hearth for a long time'. In these ways, then, the cattle-hearth and the forked branch with which it is often marked represent the focus of agnatic values, and by a typical Dinka parallel stand for the male principle also in their herds; for the bull is tethered in the middle of his cows as the men gather centrally in the homestead with the women around them cooking at their separate fires.

The forked branch in a Western Dinka homestead is always potentially a shrine. It calls to mind the associations we have described, but also it is an obvious place to which to attach the first-fruits of the harvest, which the Dinka strictly but without ceremony offer there to Divinity and the clan-divinities. Upon it are hung sacred healing cucumbers for future use in case of some sickness in the family. At its foot are thrown small offerings of flesh from sacrificial victims, and occasional libations of beer and milk, and offerings of tobacco, may be made there, in a single act, to Divinity, clan-divinities, and ancestors. So it is that the *ghoro* tends to be used sometimes as a shrine, though some may originally have been erected for practical purposes as spear-rests and hangers for equipment.

The forked branch may or may not be part of the formal shrines which the Dinka call *yik*, and which might perhaps be more accurately called 'altars', though we adhere to the usual term. Formal shrines are of various kinds; but what defines them all, and distinguishes them from places where it is merely convenient to place occasional offerings and first-fruits, is that they are clearly marked places for animal sacrifice. Hence, most formal shrines of whatever construction include a cattle-peg, and sometimes several pegs, set permanently into the ground somewhere near to whatever additional erection may also be made.

In some cases such a peg, with no additional construction, is itself the shrine. If so, the ground immediately surrounding the base of the peg is kept clean from accumulations of rubbish, but otherwise allowed to remain in a natural state. Such grasses and grains as seed themselves naturally there are allowed to grow in moderation, and the shrine presents the appearance of a little rough patch in the carefully smoothed surrounding courtyard. If a peg alone forms the main shrine, a forked branch in some convenient position near by may serve for the exposition of the evidence of past sacrifice. On it will be found the ears of goats or sheep, bits of skin from sacrificed beasts, their jaw-bones or skulls and horns, and sometimes the tethering-rope and peg which had been theirs before sacrifice. In such a case the *ghoro* has been incorporated as part of the shrine, as a place of sacrifice and exposition of parts of the dead victim, though it may not have been erected specifically for that purpose.

In other cases a forked branch is erected specifically to serve as part of a shrine. This may be because the owner of the homestead or his family has been ill, and a diviner has attributed the sickness to some particular Power. The diviner himself then recommends the erection of a particular kind of shrine, and the forked branch is likely to form a part of it because of its general associations with divinities and ancestors. Again, the shrine or place of sacrifice may not include a forked branch at all, as with some of the shrines to GARANG earlier mentioned, which consist merely of a small rough area in the homestead surrounded by a thorn fence, and often with a small thorn-bush in the centre. Small parts of sacrificial victims are then attached to the thorn-bush, and their skulls and bones thrown or half-buried in the earth of the shrine. The shrines of the free-divinity LOI of the Agar Dinka consist merely of pegs, 3 or 4 ft. high, like enormous cattle-pegs from which undoubtedly they derive, and there seems to be no place in the homestead for the exposition of small parts of the victims sacrificed to this free-divinity. Whatever the form of such shrines erected for free-divinities or Powers of sickness, whether including a peg or a forked branch or both, the area immediately at the foot of the erection is often left in a more or less natural state. It is the place, not of men, but of a Power, and contrasts with the domestic neatness of the surrounding homestead. The range of materials available for marking a spot for sacrifice to the Powers, and therefore the range of suggestions which a diviner can make, are limited. In Anuakland, for example, I have seen what was recognized to be a unique shrine in which a long metal rod had been incorporated, and it is certainly not impossible that the same thing might occur among the Dinka were some striking material available, and the diviner sufficiently imaginative. Dinka themselves, visiting a strange Dinka homestead, will often not know what a particular shrine represents except that it has some connexion with Divinity. They know only that a forked branch within the homestead may be treated as a shrine to agnatic ancestors and the clan-divinity, which it calls to mind, and that any cattle-peg permanently set in the courtyard of a homestead is evidence of past sacrifice and earnest of future sacrifice there.

Shrines, along with sacred spears and invocations, are attributed originally to Aiwel Longar. Although there are several varieties of shrines now erected on the advice of diviners, and these are properly called *yik*, some Dinka suggest that the original *yik* was a construction of a rather different sort. The shrine which they particularly associate with Aiwel Longar is found mainly in the homesteads of some masters of the fishing-spear, though some of the more important families of warrior clans also, but less commonly, have similar shrines in their courtyards.

The traditional shrines of the spear-master clans (if we may regard them as traditional, in the absence of real historical evidence) are essentially small mounds of mud. There remains in the region of the Bahr-el-Zeraf, a mound which is said to have been the original *yik* of Aiwel Longar, and on this he is thought by some to have stood to spear in the head those who were following him across the river. Also, the famous 'pyramid' of Deng Kur, which is a man-made hill, is called by the Dinka a *yik*, and that word (which is not of Nuer origin) seems to be the one the Nuer use for it. Since the Nuer prophet Dengkur is also said to have been of Dinka origin, it has been suggested that the idea of building a mound or pyramid was itself a Dinka and not a Nuer idea.[1] The shrines which I now describe, are perhaps a type of such 'pyramids' in miniature.

Each consists of a small group of dome-shaped mounds of smooth mud. The largest mound in such a group may be up to 3 or 4 ft. high and similarly wide across the diameter at the base. The smaller mounds clustered at its base are perhaps a foot or so in height. In some cases the whole group is proportionately lower and smaller. Some shrines of this kind may have two larger mounds and three or four smaller ones; in another homestead there may be only a single small mound; in yet another there may be one large and two small mounds. The largest group of such mounds I have seen consisted of six altogether.

[1] See for example P. Coriat, 'Gwek the Witchdoctor and the Pyramid of Dengkur, *S.N. & R.*, vol. xxii, 1939, part 2, p. 223, and P. P. Howell, op. cit., 1948, pp. 52, 53.

These mound-shrines are normally found a little to one side of the centre of the courtyard of the home, and next to the hut of the senior wife, or of a senior wife of one of the ancestors of those now occupying the home. Their grouping is not, of course, a haphazard arrangement or combination, achieved as it were accidentally like some of the shrines erected on the advice of diviners. Each mound in the shrine signifies a particular ancestor or group of ancestors of the people living in the home. To describe one in particular, such a shrine in the home of a master of the fishing-spear in Pan Acier, in the Apuk Patuan tribe of the Rek Dinka, consisted of two larger and three smaller mounds, with a forked branch near by. The large mounds were said to represent the ancestor of the Paliecnguk lineage of the Paghol subclan in the subtribe which includes this village, and his son. The small mounds represented the one wife of the first ancestor, and the two wives of his son, from whom present lineages of the subclan there are descended. A *yik* of this sort thus indicates boldly the main genealogical points of reference of its owner; and since knowledge of the distribution of the *yik*, at least of spear-master clans, extends over the whole of a tribal territory, their relationship to each other is a representation of the correspondence between genealogy and territorial distribution of a clan. Masters of the fishing-spear in a tribe attend each other's ceremonies, and the most important ceremonies are held at the homesteads with the most important shrines. The senior shrine is the shrine of the most significant ancestors for the clan within the tribe, and the smaller ones represent ancestors of a narrower genealogical significance.

When members of spear-master clans go to live for some reason in a foreign territory, where they have no traditional links with the main body of the people, they build a shrine *inside* the cattle-byre, or *inside* the hut of the senior wife. The Dinka say that if such men prove themselves efficacious in invocation, and establish themselves as persons of local importance, their descendants may eventually move the shrine outside into the courtyard of the homestead, where everyone will see the claim thus made to an ancestral significance in the new home.

The mud shrine which we have described has sometimes been confused, at a superficial glance, with the woman's cooking-hearth (*buor*), where also there is a set of mud erections—a windscreen, and several mud humps to support the round-bottomed pots. The confusion is increased by the fact that the *buor* or woman's windscreen is the clan-divinity of one Western Dinka clan, who are said to have in one homestead a very large *buor* as a shrine. Also the *buor* may be a shrine among the Nuer. Among the Western Dinka, however, the significance of these two superficially similar constructions, the *yik* and the *buor*, is quite different.

The more elaborate mud shrines of the sort I have described are found in the homesteads of prominent masters of the fishing-spear; but smaller shrines, which the masters of the fishing-spear regard as imitations of their own, may be found in the homesteads of important members of warrior clans. Though members of these clans regard their shrines as shrines of their clan-divinities and their ancestors, the masters of the fishing-spear sometimes suggest that the warriors' shrines are little more than graves, at which offerings are made to the dead. I have not found that mud shrines are deliberately made to imitate the shape of bulls, though where the horns of a sacrifice are sunk, as often, at their base, they bear some resemblance to bulls in general outline. Professor and Mrs. Seligman, following Major G. W. Titherington and others whose experience was greater than mine, do say, however, that some such shrines are deliberately constructed as representations of bulls.[1]

The mound-shrines incorporate some of the earth of graves, but they are not, I think, made over graves.[2] The Dinka bury their dead either in the floor of the cattle-byre or somewhere near by outside it, and they do not seem to pay much attention to the grave itself. In fact I have never been shown a grave. The dead are remembered either at the forked branch, or at the mound-shrines. Since such shrines are the domestic localizations

[1] One is pictured in C. G. and B. Z. Seligman, op. cit., 1932, p. 201. In his privately circulated report on Totemism and Religion of the Dinka of the White Nile, Prof. Seligman wrote: 'The whole structure presents a certain resemblance to a bullock sunk in the earth so that only its back projects, but I could not learn that this resemblance was intentional, though a Dinka whom I met in Omdurman, where he had lived for a long time, said that in his country mud representations of cattle were erected over the graves of powerful men. Since writing the above Mr. A. B. Cook has shown me a photograph of a *buor* obviously modelled to represent a bullock, special care being devoted to the hump.'

[2] This also was the view taken by Prof. and Mrs. Seligman, op. cit., 1932, p. 203.

of Divinity, the clan-divinities, and the ancestors, from whom the Dinka beg life and vitality, it would in fact be inappropriate if they were sited upon graves, which bring to mind mortality. For at the shrine the dead are in some sense still living presences, accepting offerings there made to them.

I have never seen among the Western Dinka the cattle-byre shrines which are reported from other parts of Dinkaland. The appendix to Chapter II contributed by Dr. P. P. Howell describes the most famous of these. I did, however, visit the cattle-byre shrine of an important clan-divinity of which the emblem was a large drum in the territory of the Kongor tribe of the east bank Dinka. It was an ordinary cattle-byre, but with a large peg sunk into the centre, at the base of which was an elephant tusk, partly buried. Numerous small bulls made of mud hung by strings from the thatch, and outside the byre were several mud shrines, said to be shrines to the wife of the drum, at which black beasts were slaughtered. The drum itself, some 15 ft. long, which is much larger than the ordinary drum of the Dinka, was suspended from the roof-poles, and decorated with tassels and small bags made from the scrota of bulls. It was said that the guardian of the shrine sometimes became possessed by the divinity, which called for sacrifices, and there was evidence of many sacrifices outside the byre. By a curious coincidence, when I left the byre the vehicle in which I was passing through the village refused to start again. After much trouble had been taken with it, a Dinka travelling in it said that I had forgotten to make any offering to the guardian of the drum. I at once sent off a gift, and at the moment of its being placed in the hand of the guardian of the shrine, the vehicle started without difficulty.

Among the Agar Dinka there are cattle-byres of certain outstanding masters of the fishing-spear which have a tribal importance, and which are maintained and repaired by the members of the whole tribe, who also take beasts for sacrifice and offerings of first-fruits there. During my visit complaints were being made that such cattle-byres (called by the ordinary word for a byre, *luak*) were being neglected. The Agar Dinka, unlike the Rek, do not normally build cattle-byres in their homesteads, and their cattle are kept throughout the year in the open at some distance away from the village sites. Consequently, the only cattle-byres are those which are shrines to Divinity and the divinities of masters of the fishing-spear of outstanding importance.

It would be satisfying from an ethnographic and ethnological point of view to be able to produce a classified list of different sorts of Dinka shrine. To do so, however, would be to suggest formal demarcations between different sorts of erections which would quite falsify Dinka practice. The main differences between shrines are somewhat parallel to those between the shrines of the Roman *lars familiaris* and *lares praestites*—the domestic shrine which is important only for members of a family or a very small lineage, and the shrines which, while having this importance for the particular families in whose homesteads they are found, have also a wider importance for several lineages and through them for the whole territory within which those lineages are pre-eminent. It is to the latter kind that the mound-shrines and cattle-byre shrines of the masters of the fishing-spear belong. In addition, there are shrines made at the behest of a diviner in the case of individual sickness, which are eventually neglected and forgotten, and shrines made at places where some striking occurrence is remembered—for example, at a tree blasted by lightning. Any place where Divinity or divinities can be conceived as in some way localized is a kind of shrine; and any place where animal sacrifice has for some reason been made is a place where the Dinka tend to localize the divinity to which sacrifice has been made.

In turning now to several descriptions of Dinka rites, I emphasize that the centrally important property of these rites is the sacrificial victim. Shrines derive their importance from proximity to sacrifice; spears are valued because it is with them that the officiants project their intention upon an animal victim. These and other sacred properties are linked by the single theme of the death of a victim as a means towards the greater vitality of the people.

I

Though the main outlines of Dinka religious practice are as we now come to describe them, its measure of formality does not exclude the possibility of considerable local variation, change, and freedom. Sometimes indeed the Dinka themselves seem in doubt about how to proceed, or how it was customary to proceed in the past. The point is of some importance, for the presence of such uncertainties, and the absence of strict 'dogma' or rubric, make it easier for individual diviners and prophets to contribute their own original ideas to the general deposit of the Dinka faith.

At the time of the first ceremony I describe, when I knew little of the language, I was living in a village very near the boundary between two tribes of the Rek Dinka, the Agwok and the Apuk (Patuan). The boundary there ran through an area of settlement, and homesteads at one end of the village belonged to a master of the fishing-spear of a subtribe of the Agwok, while the main part of the village belonged to a subtribe of Apuk. The master of the fishing-spear of a subtribe of Agwok lived sometimes on the boundary in his late mother's home, now that of his senior wife, where his mound-shrine was. His main homestead was several miles farther into the territory of his own tribe. His presence on the boundary, with his kinsmen on both sides of it, was considered fortunate for the relations between the two tribes, who had had a history of hostility and were rivals for some of the better dry-season pastures.

The old Agwok master of the fishing-spear had a higher reputation for efficacy in his religious office than a comparatively junior master of the fishing-spear of Apuk, who lived in the Apuk part of the settlement. Consequently, he tended to draw towards him his affinal kin and others on the Apuk side, who had more faith in his invocation than in that of their own local master of the fishing-spear. The latter linked them into the genealogical structure of the spear-master clan with primacy in their own tribe; the former linked them more effectively with Divinity. His religious reputation thus partially elided political oppositions.

I left early in the morning, in January, with some people of the Apuk end of the village who said that they were attending a *yai* (a feast) in the Agwok home of the Agwok master of the fishing-spear, a few hours' walk across still flooded ground into Agwok territory proper. When we arrived a bull, an ox, and two goats had already been sacrificed—probably a significant fact, as it seemed that our visit had been timed to miss the climax of the sacrifice. As will be seen, even though close links may have been established between members of two different tribes, they have reason to avoid the moment of greatest social self-consciousness in each other's sacrifices.

Most of the following descriptions may be taken to represent what happens at any sacrifice of cattle. The girls and women, waving forked twigs and straked dancing-sticks, their bodies painted with ash and ochre and their hair blobbed with butter and reddened, were weaving their way in single file in and out of the buildings of the homestead. They made the high-pitched ululating sound of welcome and honour (*luor*), and from time to time broke into smaller groups which performed the women's dance (*dany*), with hand-clapping and jumping as in Plate III. The men, grouped roughly according to seniority in age but not with strict formality, were sitting in the shade of the huts and of a great sausage-tree which dominated the homestead. They drank beer and talked and laughed, while the old master of the fishing-spear and his eldest son wandered among their guests. The sausage-tree was the emblem of the clan-divinity of Pabuol, the clan of the master of the fishing-spear at whose home the sacrifice had taken place.

On the right-hand side of the entrance to the hut of the master of the fishing-spear's senior wife was a shrine consisting of one large mound of smooth mud, about 3 ft. high, with two smaller ones set close to its base. The bull and ox already sacrificed lay nose to tail in the centre of the homestead, near the shrine but not specially orientated towards it, and to the west of the sausage-tree. Between their legs lay sacrificed goats, the offering of the women. At this stage of the proceedings the victims were attracting little attention, and the guests and the family were enjoying beer and conversation.

The slaughtered ox was of a black and white configuration, and the whole bull a reddish brown. It was said that they had been killed in the early morning. They lay as the Dinka always allow beasts to lie for a short time after sacrifice, pointing to the east. The head of each was supported on a bough of a tree, as on a pillow. They thus lay in state, partly covered with the foliage of a tree called *dhot* (*Gardenia lutea*?) which is usually placed upon the carcasses of victims which, in their death, are 'respected'—that is, upon beasts sacrificed to divinities other than MACARDIT. *Dhot* is a tree of the dry-season pastures and river banks. The Dinka say that they use it 'for respect', and because it has a particularly sweet smell, and has no thorns. In their country, where so many trees and grasses are harsh and sharp, the soft and delicate plants have a value which they might lack were tender vegetation more common.

Both the ox and the bull had girls' skin skirts draped, as though worn, over their haunches. My companions explained to me that this was *rin athek*, out of respect, in order to cover the anus.[1] There was an uninterrupted passage between the sacrificed beasts and the sausage-tree. When later I stood between the tree and the victims, I was asked to move, for the victims were being exposed to the clan-divinity as represented in its emblem, the tree. Many new fishing-spears were thrust points downwards into the earth, in a rough semi-circle around the backs of the beasts, forming as it were a fence behind the animals, and leaving clear a space enabling them to be exposed directly to the east and to the sausage-tree.

People chatted and drank beer until just before noon, when a party of men began to gather around the beasts, and the women moved in and settled themselves upon the fringes of this male gathering. A young man in a leopard-skin, a prophet of GARANG, then took his place in the centre of the gathering near the sacrificed beasts, and began to sing a hymn which was taken up in chorus by those attending.

During the course of his song he took all the fishing-spears one by one and moved them to the other side of the beasts, that is, forming a fence between the beasts and the sausage-tree. When all had been moved, there was a brief intermission, during which the eldest son of the master of the fishing-spear, and several other young men, made mock demonstrations of hostility towards the animals, threatening them with brandished spears and parrying imaginary spear-thrusts and clubs, and sinking from time to time to one knee as the Dinka do when miming a battle or duel.

After another song the goats were removed to be cut up. The ox and the bull were left lying together, still covered by the sacred foliage. The eldest son of the master of the fishing-spear, a married man in the prime of life, then gave a sign for the next part of the proceedings, shouting out his ox-name

---

[1] For the Dinka, the most private part of the body. Men wear women's skirts when bending down to perform horticultural tasks in order to cover themselves.

(*myoc*) and making the shape of a bull's spreading horns with his arms. This is a gesture of pride and triumph. The shouting of the ox-name accompanies the throwing of the spear in battle. Men and women of the homestead, but none of the visitors with whom I had arrived, then approached the beasts and crouched in four groups around them, one group near the belly of each victim and one near the back.

Singing again in chorus and led by the prophet of GARANG, they took in their hands the leaves covering the carcasses and slowly began to move them between them, across the carcasses, thus gradually rolling away the covering to the rhythm of their song. When the beasts were completely exposed, several old women including two wives of the old master of the fishing-spear, and several wives of members of his lineage, came forward with a winnowing-tray which they all held. Bunched together, they approached the red-brown bull, and crouched near its hind legs. A man then came with a spear-head and, under the cover of the girl's skirt which still covered the beast's haunches, cut away the testicles and the pizzle, while the women pushed forward their winnowing-tray and together (with some altercation) groped for these parts as they became severed. They then placed them in the tray and covered them with the girl's skirt, and then with some appearance of urgency, respectfully stooping, they took them to the hut of the senior wife. The men of the homestead, under the supervision of the master of the fishing-spear and his son, then began to cut up and distribute the beast. A dance began near the homestead: I visited that for a time. When I returned, the beasts had both been skinned and the guests were preparing their shares to take home. The prophet of GARANG left for home, and as it was getting dark the party with whom I had attended also left.

The sacrifice was said to be for Divinity and the free-divinity DENG, for which the black and white ox (of DENG's colours) was intended, and for the clan-divinity (Sausage-Tree and Flesh), for which the red-brown bull had been killed. The fishing-spears were placed near the carcasses so that the clan-divinity might inform them; they were being consecrated, or reconse-crated, in the course of the ceremony. To have the prophet oi GARANG as officiant was said to be an innovation, and some thought that he ought not to have been invited to act as master of ceremonies, saying that this was properly and traditionally the task of the master of the fishing-spear and his eldest son. The pizzle and the testicles, which must be carefully severed from the carcass so that they are not separated from each other, are taken by the old women of the household, so that they and the old men of the sacrificing lineage only may eat the testicles privately at night, and the pizzle is split, dried, and twisted into a necklace for the master of the fishing-spear. The groping for and eating of the testicles by the old women is said to bring fertility to the people of the lineage. Since the old women, at least, were well beyond the age of child-bearing, we may see here how mistaken would be a too literal interpretation of this aspect of a Dinka rite. The effect of the consumption by the old of the symbol of a bull's fertility and vigour is transferred to the young members of the lineage.

This was a typical sacrifice to the clan-divinity, to Divinity, and to a free-divinity all in a single act. Parts of the ceremony which I then missed have already been described in the previous chapter—the reservation of the beasts (*mac*), the invocations over them (*lam*), the throwing (*wik piny*), the killing by cutting the throat (*nok*), and the intervals of hymns of honour (*rok*). The rolling away of the leaves is called *nuan*, and finally there is the sharing of the flesh, *tek*.

There was a sequel to this ceremony. Soon after the sacrifice I left the village in which I had been staying and did not return for some weeks. On my return I was told that the old master of the fishing-spear who had held the sacrifice had died suddenly, and that his funeral ceremonies were at that moment being held in his mother's homestead—that is, in the Agwok end of the village. It was now February, and many of the young people were away in the dry-season pastures. Many cattle were still tethered in mid-afternoon around the old man's homestead. It was said that his sudden death was the reason for a comparatively small gathering—had he lingered, many more people would have been brought in.

Some of the men were carrying large war shields (*kot*) made of tough hide, with which they from time to time made mock demonstrations of fighting and parrying. I was clearly unwelcome, and so sat silently with one or two visitors from the Apuk end of the village, who were taking no active part in the

proceedings. It was indicated that I must be quiet. The body of
the old man was said to be lying in the hut of his wife, which
was on the site of his mother's hut. I was not allowed to see it
or even to approach the hut. His wives, and the wives of some
of his sons, were sitting near the hut, silent and sad. Eventually
a group of men entered the hut and reappeared carrying the
body on a shield. It was surrounded by people and could not
be seen. (I was discouraged from trying to see it.) One of the
old man's wives began to sob and wail. At once those near her
tried to stop her, and one man brandished a cattle-rope at her,
in the gesture the Dinka use when threatening to punish a
child. The group of men with the shield entered the cattle-byre,
leaving the women and a few visitors outside, and I was refused
permission to enter.

One of my companions said that the eldest son was now
sitting by his father's grave. In time everyone except the eldest
son came out of the byre. He stayed there for a long time,
and eventually there was nothing to do but leave before
he reappeared. That night the cattle of the village were not
milked, and their bellowings of discomfort continued until
morning.

Several suggestions about the old man's death were made.
One said that it had been wrong for him to make his original
sacrifice in his own home, and not that of his mother. Another
said that it had been a mistake to call in the prophet of GARANG
to lead the ceremony. Others asserted that in the past the old
man had once bought the fetish MATHIANG GOK, which had
now turned upon him and killed him because he had for long
neglected it. This reasoning indicates that the Dinka see some
contradiction in the appearance of sudden death very soon after
a large sacrifice for life and vitality. The argument really was
that the sacrifice would have been effective, and all would have
been well, had it not been for some weakness or fault on the
old man's part. Belief in the sacrificial system is thus preserved
in spite of such apparent contradictions. In any case, though
the assistance of divinities is sometimes demanded as much as
requested, they cannot ultimately be coerced. *Nhialic aci kwec*,
'Divinity has refused', is the Dinkas' final answer to prayer
which seems not to have been answered.

The old master of the fishing-spear was entitled to the

ceremonial death of such priests—to be placed in his grave alive so that the fiction of his survival might be preserved.[1] This ceremonial burial alive is forbidden by the Government, and it is therefore difficult to make inquiries about any specific case. At first I was assured that the old man had died and been buried in the ordinary way; but a year later, when danger of exhumation was over and in any case I was better known, it was suggested to me that the old man might have been alive when he was placed in the grave, and that the long period his son spent at the graveside was an indication that his father was speaking his last words to him.

The sacrifice I have described was one of the regular sacrifices made after the harvest, in November or December. The season is then, in Dinka, *rut*, a time when the cool north winds blow, the flooded pastures are beginning to dry out, and grain and beer, in a good year, are plentiful. Most people are then living together in the permanent villages, before the main body move off to the dry-season pastures. It is for their protection during that move that prayers are offered and invocations made. The regular sacrifices of this period anticipate an approaching period of dispersion and danger but also of pleasure (for the Dinka enjoy their dry-season camps) at a time when social life is in the villages at its most concentrated and intense. People thus sacrifice for prosperity and strength just at the time when they are most experiencing the fullness of social life and, in the temporary abundance of the harvest, are at the peak of their physical well-being.

Sacrifices may be made on special occasions for some particular purpose. That which I now describe was made because, it was said, some years before a *deleib* palm had been struck by lightning near the homestead in which the ceremony took place, and this event had been followed by a number of cases of sickness, especially of the chest. Several women of the village were also showing no signs of bearing children. The sacrifice was intended to cure the sickness of the chest and to help these women to conceive.

A man of the spear-master clan Payi from a neighbouring village, who was said to 'have the creator in his body' (*lo gwop aciek*) also, had been called in to direct the proceedings. One

---

[1] The subject is discussed in the next chapter.

black and white bull had already been killed when I arrived.[1] It
was lying covered with the sweet *dhot* foliage as I have already
described. Another beast, a large white ox, was standing tethered
to a nearby tree, while as before everyone sat around chatting
and drinking beer, and the women from time to time gave their
little dances and cries of joy. Women and men sit and move
separately on the whole at these ceremonies. The children stand
or play in the background. When the main part of the sacrifice
is completed children begin to mingle with the gathering. The
tension is then over and, as is sung in one line of a hymn:

The feast becomes disordered by children, and the earth cools a
little. . . .

The bull which had already been sacrificed was the *muor yath*,
the bull of the clan-divinity. The white ox awaiting its turn was
the *muor nhialic*, the ox of Divinity, and I was told that Divinity
was given this ox so that his 'heart would fall' (*puou lony*) to the
people, keeping them well and permitting their women to
conceive.

In the background a sheep was tethered, later to be released.
This was what the Dinka call the 'wether of the ashes' (*nyong
arop*), and which may or may not figure in such ceremonies. It
had been rubbed with sacred ashes upon which oaths are
sworn, and then washed by the people. The purpose of this
ceremony, as earlier mentioned, is to free people from the
consequences of oaths they may have falsely sworn, in a symbolic act of which the nature is at once perceived.

At about midday the ox was tethered, not without some
difficulty as it could smell the blood of the beast already dead.
Eventually its hooves were loosely roped together to restrain it.
As it was being tethered to the sacrificial peg it urinated, and
somebody murmured 'Divinity has agreed' (*nhialic aci gam*).
This time no invocations were made. It was said that these had
already been completed. Men and women stood in a semicircle
around the beast, singing in chorus the responses to the officiant.
From time to time he menaced the ox, and crouched to the
ground preparing for a spring into the air, with the cries 'We
have greeted my father' (*ok aci wa muoth*) and 'We have greeted

---

[1] Though the Dinka, if they know one, suffer one's presence at their ceremonies,
they do not trouble to inform one about them.

the master (*beny*)' and 'We have greeted Divinity'. These greetings were repeated by the congregation.

In a little speech the officiant said that Divinity should support the life (*muk wei*) of men, of women, of the children, the life of the young, and the life of the old. Water and grain, in two separate gourds, were then brought and scattered in the air in all directions, and blessed water was poured over the tethering-peg. This was said to be for DENG, which had originally struck the *deleib* palm, after which misfortunes had followed. There were further songs and mimed fighting.

Here several young men began to become possessed, and staggered about the homestead, from time to time rushing at the tethered ox and slapping and thumping it. The ox became restive and had to be held for a while. Possessed young men then gently slapped some of the girls on the head and back, and several girls themselves became possessed. Men and women were now stumbling about, groaning and shrieking. Some fell to the ground and rolled about. Meanwhile the leader, and those who were not possessed, continued with the song and with their mimed skirmishes. Eventually people became calmer, and the ox was thrown and killed by a lateral cut in the throat, through which the wind-pipe was pierced with a fishing-spear. Women collected some of the blood in gourds, and the dogs were encouraged to lap up the rest.

Whilst the ox was in its last agonies the officiant cut away part of the dewlap, which he held and squeezed in a gourd of water. Those men and women who suffered from pains in the chest were called to him, and taking the water in his mouth, he blew it out over the dewlap and on to their chests, which were then wiped with the piece of skin and flesh. Their backs also were wiped, and finally the piece of dewlap was placed to the mouth of each in turn and they were told to blow upon it.

Meanwhile, the married women who wished to conceive had gathered round the bull. Some had been sitting on its carcass during the death agonies. Now, one by one, they were made to lean across the barrel of the ox, to bring their bellies into contact with it. One by one, they then went to the leader, who slapped and washed their bodies with water from the gourd. Each wife then returned to her husband, and the officiant approached each in turn, blew into their mouths and ears, and gave each instructions in a low voice, which they gravely repeated word for word after him.

All then '*wuuu*-ed' away illness to the country of those with their lower incisors and there followed a further interlude of beer-drinking, while some of the men covered this second ox with *dhot* leaves. A white ox of Divinity, and a black and white bull of the clan-divinity and DENG, were now lying as it were in state as described previously.[1] After a time the ceremonial rolling away of leaves from the carcass of the bull of the clan-divinity took place. The more recently killed ox was left until later. The testicles and pizzle of the bull were removed to a hut as in the previous sacrifice, but this time as many people as could do so followed them into the hut, the entrance was closed, and there was much singing and dancing by the people crammed together inside. This again was said to be in order to produce fertility. It was said also that small pieces of raw flesh had been saved for the masters of the fishing-spear of Payi to eat at night, to feed their divinity Flesh, but I did not see the collection of these. It was explained that the bull of the clan-divinity was to be eaten by the lineage to which the sacrificing homestead of the Payi clan belonged, while the ox of Divinity was for all comers, some of whom had travelled for considerable distances in order to take advantage of the officiant's reputation for overcoming barrenness. Consequently, the bull of the clan-divinity had been killed earlier in the morning, before the guests arrived, while the 'ox of Divinity' awaited the arrival of all guests.

Several features not so far mentioned appeared in the sacrifice for the sick master of the fishing-spear from which the texts of invocations given in Chapter VI (pp. 226–31) were taken. The ceremony began with the tethering of a small light brown bull-calf, and invocations by various masters of the fishing-spear, in mounting order of seniority. The sick master of the fishing-spear, a man of Aiwel's clan Pagong, was in the hut of one of his wives. The most important invocations were spoken by members of the Payi clan, which locally had the task of officiating at sacrifices for Pagong. This reciprocal officiation at sacrifices is found between clans in some parts of Dinkaland, but I think it is not (as among the Nuer) a regular and general

[1] pp. 267–9.

principle everywhere to call in such a traditional 'master of ceremonies'. Each set of invocations ended with a wild flourish of the spear across the back of the beast, and in the southerly direction where 'those with lower incisors' live. People became quieter, and sat down to listen to the later invocations. A few women—wives, I was told, of the sick man—wandered round the gathering sprinkling milk and water over the people, especially upon their feet. One man poured milk over the feet of the eldest son of the sick man.

Then, one after the other, all the married men among those attending, and some of the older women, went forward to the peg at which the calf was tethered, approaching it on their knees in an attitude of great respect. Each in turn took a gourd of milk which was near the peg (the gourd of the clan-divinity) and after kissing his own hands three times, poured a little milk over the peg.[1] He then kissed his own hands again, and gave way to another. The masters of the fishing-spear blew and spat slightly into the milk. I was told later (though I missed this) that in fact only members of the Pagong and Payi clans kissed their hands in this token of respect. Other masters of the fishing-spear present simply made a reverent libation.

Invocations proceeded. During one of them the calf urinated. 'He is very "biting",' said one man, referring to the master of the fishing-spear who at that time was invoking. At one point all raised their hands and gave a cry of 'Yo-yo-yo-yo' which, it was said, was made 'so that your cattle will be numerous'. People began to be possessed, as previously described, and the calf was slapped and pummelled.

Suddenly the calf was thrown, and a mob of young men raced towards it and slapped and kicked it. It was then impossible to see what was happening to the calf. In the first place it had been turned as far as possible with its belly upwards, and much of the attempt to touch it seemed to be aimed at the region of its genitals, but in a few seconds it was invisible under the mob. Strangers from other tribes (of whom there were one or two, since this ceremony took place very near a small administrative centre) took no part in these proceedings. It was not even clear whether the beast's throat was cut, or whether the trampling alone killed it. During the next few hours, in circumstances

[1] See Plate IV*a*.

irrelevant to the present account, there was government intervention. Later in the afternoon, after this, I visited the sick
man's homestead. The calf was still there, and still only partly
skinned and butchered. Much of its flesh had apparently not
been distributed, and the people had dispersed.

It was generally denied by many Dinka that this was a
ceremony preliminary to burial alive, but the arguments for
and against will appear in the next chapter, where we consider
what is known of this Dinka custom. Here I treat it as what the
main actors asserted it to be, a ceremony in order to make well
the sick master of the fishing-spear.

The verb here translated as 'make well' is in Dinka *koc*, and it
takes as its object the person or creature which is to be helped.
Thus one can *koc* a sick man (and, in doing so, those who are as
yet healthy) and one can *koc* cattle. It may also be used partly
intransitively. Fr. Nebel gives in his dictionary '*Koc, ghok a lo
koc*, the cattle are recovering (through a sacrifice)'. Although
most ceremonies for *koc*, as I understand, take place when there
is some sickness or misfortune, the essential meaning of the
word seems to be less 'to cure' than 'to strengthen', so that
when a master of the fishing-spear *koc* his people and their
cattle, he in fact strengthens them against future dangers. It is
a human act, not a divine one.

In this case, those who claimed that there had been no intention of burying the old man alive said that some months ago he
had first become sick, but that at that time nobody had any
beast to spare with which to make him well. Then his sickness
came again when the fishing-spear (see above, pp. 226 ff.) had
been found in his homestead, and people became really alarmed.
His sister's son, therefore, whose special duty it is to perform
this task, brought his little bull-calf, because, he said, a goat was
not big enough for the purpose. The old master of the fishing-
spear had himself suggested that unless this was done, the
cattle of his camp would die. In fact, after the administrative
intervention the man soon died under official medical care and
supervision, and was buried without much ceremony. Again,
in this intervention the Dinka had an explanation for the lack
of success which had conspicuously attended their sacrifice. I
leave other features until the next chapter.

I now describe briefly one or two other ceremonies of

comparatively minor importance. The invocations made to bring the fish back to the river, which are reported in the previous chapter, were accompanied by very simple acts. The people of the fishing-camp gathered on the river bank, and the women made their jumping and hand-clapping dance, while the officiants entered the river and, from a point downstream in the direction from which the fish were to come, walked slowly towards the crowd speaking their invocations. They drew after them a gourd containing water and the split sacred cucumbers, which was guided by a strand of *apac* grass. *Apac*, as we have said, is considered by the Dinka to be the best of the lush grasses of the swamps, and as the invocations show, it was from those swamps that the ceremony was intended to summon the fish. When the officiant approached the bank upon which the crowd was standing, one of them flung a little mud from the river-bed on the bank, in a gesture clearly indicating the taking of fish from the river which the ceremony was intended to assure. The crowd was then liberally asperged with water from the gourd.

The officiants here were kinsmen of the master of the fishing-spear who, in that place, was also known by the title *beny wir*, master of the river. All over Dinkaland at places chosen for major fish battues there are such masters of the river. They may come from spear-master clans or from warrior clans, and they may or may not be from spear-master lineages dominant in the subtribal area in which they function. They are traditionally controllers of the river, as their title implies, and their task it is to drown a bound beast (usually a kid) in the river before the fishing begins. This drowning is accompanied by prayers that the fishing may prosper. It is a minor and relatively informal ceremony.

Other minor experts are known as *bany rap*, masters of the grain. Like the masters of the river, they do not function for defined political groups, but for people in their neighbourhood who call them in if insects or birds are ruining the crops. They may belong to any clan which in a given locality traditionally performs this function. A master of the grain who is asked to protect people's crops from birds and insects takes a gourd in which water, milk, oil, and spittle are mixed and walks through the gardens asperging with this mixture, using a few leaves of *Tamarindus indicus* (the leaf of which has a pleasantly acid taste) for the purpose. While asperging the grain, he calls upon the birds and insects to leave the grain alone, conjuring them to do so in the name of his ancestors, his clan-divinity, Divinity, and any free-divinity his family may possess. He asks that the grain may ripen and whiten like the milk with which he asperges it. The children of the homesteads then take some of the affected grain and throw it away into the bush. Later, at the harvest, each family which has made use of his services will make him a present of a basket of grain.

The duties of such specialists, and the range of people they may serve, are not strictly limited or clearly defined. One master of grain, for example, had also a reputation for curing minor illnesses by praying over the patient and flourishing a stick as masters of the fishing-spear flourish spears, and then spitting upon the stick and drawing it several times across the body of the patient.

A non-sacrificial but clearly religious ceremony of some interest, and which displays some features characteristic of Dinka symbolic action, has been described by Mr. N. Nunn, who saw it among the Dinka of two villages near his mission station at Banjang in Upper Nile Province. I summarize the account of it which he published in *Sudan Notes and Records* under the title 'A Dinka Public Health Measure'.[1]

Mr. Nunn says that this ceremony is carried out annually, and was seen by him early in November. Then people from two neighbouring villages made their way to the river at 7 a.m. each carrying a head of *durra* (sorghum) and other stalks of the same grain which were to represent those members of their families which could not attend. A master of the fishing-spear (as I take him to be—Mr. Nunn writes of a 'rainmaker') stood in the centre of the semicircle of people. In his hand he carried a newly fashioned green gourd, into which all present, including the children, put grain, upon which he spat. The older people and the 'rainmaker' faced the river, chanting and moving their hands as though consigning something to the water. The 'rainmaker' then dashed into the river and submerged, followed rapidly and eagerly by all present, who splashed themselves and their children and carried into the river the stalks of *durra* representing their absent relations. The

[1] *S.N. & R.*, vol. xxv, part 1, 1942.

gourd seems to have remained in the river. Everyone took from the river the root of a reed, to be worn round the neck for a day. The purpose of this ceremony was to cure malaria. As Mr. Nunn points out, the rains had in fact stopped about a month previously, and it was to be expected, therefore, that malaria would soon abate in any case. He concludes with the following revealing paragraph:

I may add that people on the way home the same day seemed to feel no inconsistency in coming to us for medicine just as they had done the day before, and I suppose there is no one in the whole community who turns to us more quickly for help in case of sickness or accident than the old rain-maker himself who acted as high-priest on that day.

The circumstances thus recorded add support to the suggestion made earlier, that those symbolic acts which are regularly performed, like the sacrifices made after the harvest, take place at a time when people are already beginning to experience naturally (as we should say) something of the result which the ceremony is intended to bring about, or at least may soon expect to do so. Professor and Mrs. Seligman, writing about sacrifices performed during the droughts of spring, also indicate this in their comment:

It seemed that when rain was wanted, i.e. when the country is at its driest, but also (from the white man's standpoint) when the rainy season is approaching, the rain-maker is besought to seek rain from the particular spirit. . . .[1]

The Dinka themselves know, of course, when the rainy season is approaching; and, as Professor and Mrs. Seligman imply, the point is of some importance for the correct appreciation of the spirit in which the Dinka perform their regular ceremonies. In these their human symbolic action moves with the rhythm of the natural world around them, re-creating that rhythm in moral terms and not merely attempting to *coerce* it to conformity with human desires. To put the simplest interpretation upon their ritual, one may say that in the purely natural course of events, it always has a good chance of producing the effect which is intended and hoped for; but the most striking manifestation of religious authority in a man is that he should, on

[1] C. G. and B. Z. Seligman, op. cit., 1932, p. 198.

occasion, be able to produce effects parallel to our miracles, for which the 'natural' course of events provides no reasonable expectation.

A sacrifice, or collective ceremony even when no blood-sacrifice is offered, is called in Dinka *yai*, a word for which the word 'feast' is a not inappropriate translation. To perform and take part in such a ceremony is called 'to eat' (*cam*) a feast. This need not be taken too literally, since the food and drink which sacrificial ceremonies are accompanied by are a part only of the whole celebration of a joyful occasion. I emphasize that though the occasion of a sacrifice may be a sad one—the serious illness of a kinsman, for example, or the failure of women to conceive—the ceremony itself is regarded by the Dinka as essentially a happy one, and they behave at such ceremonies as though they enjoyed themselves, and indeed attend in order to do so. Every sacrifice has a festive atmosphere. People's 'hearts are sweet', as the Dinka say; and the idea which they sometimes express that, as a result of their offering, the 'hearts' of Divinity and divinities may be sweet towards them shows how they image in Divinity and divinities the experience which a sacrifice involves for them.

A sacrifice for life (which, ultimately, is what the Dinka seek) is also a demonstration of hostility to and strength against all enemies of life. Consequently, the expression *cam yai*, 'to make a feast or a sacrifice', often implies war. At the larger of such ceremonies the militant strength of a tribe or subtribe is assembled and in a sense made consciously present to those attending, and some of the skirmishes and mock duels which we have mentioned have as their object enemies from other tribes and peoples. Dinka often 'make a feast' against some-body, as may be seen in the following extracts from war-songs:

If a man has sharpened the buffalo's horns[1] who shall stop him?
They sharpen the horns of my tribe
We have spent the day at the feast of Kuot Dukbil and Magak[2]
The club strikes
Yauer Dit,[3] though late, I will revenge
I am insulted by the Abiem tribe

[1] The image conveys at once the superlative courage claimed by the singers, and the idea of preparation for war.
[2] Names of masters of the fishing-spear.
[3] A kinsman who had in the past been slain by their present enemies.

Daily they hold feasts against me. . . .
My tribe Awan Rup, let us make a feast, let us make a feast . . .

and

> Though the tribe holds a feast against me
> I shall not fear,
> Though all the people hold a feast against me
> I shall not fear,
> O my tribe, I am a bull with sharpened horns,
> I am a maddened bull. . . .

This connexion between religious action and war is further considered in relation to the mortuary ceremonies of the masters of
the fishing-spear described in the concluding chapter.

Animal sacrifice is the most complex, as it is the essential,
symbolic act of the Dinka; and in order to reach an understanding of what it means in their life, it is necessary to consider
it in the light of other acts which are simpler examples of
symbolism. From the great variety of these, I choose four. The
first is a small quasi-magical practice called in Dinka *thuic*,
which may have no overtly religious significance. The second is
the ceremony for cleansing people of incest, the third the ordinary mortuary ceremony, and the fourth the ceremony for
concluding peace. In the light of an understanding of these,
we may then turn to an analysis of the sacrificial rites earlier
described.

The practice called *thuic* involves knotting a tuft of grass to
indicate that the one who makes the knot hopes and intends to
contrive some kind of constriction or delay. In one of the texts
quoted (p. 222), for example, an enemy is to be 'knotted in
grass', meaning that it is desired that his freedom of action,
mental and physical, shall be restricted. One sometimes hears
that masters of the fishing-spear whose people have been
seriously troubled by lion will take a stone to represent the lion,
and, before their people, enclose it in a knot of grass. This action
is supposed to assist the people in their attempt to kill the lion
with spears. Further, and most commonly, when Dinka are
making a journey they often tie knots in the grass growing
beside the path with the intention that the preparation of food
at the end of the journey may be delayed until their arrival.[1]

---

[1] This is a common Nilotic practice. The Anuak do it even more frequently than
the Dinka, and their attitude towards it, at once hopeful and sceptical in a humorous

This is a simple example of what has been called 'imitative magic'; yet that expression does not adequately suggest the spirit in which the act is undertaken. No Dinka thinks that by performing such an action he has actually assured the result he hopes for. The framework of expectation within which such a symbolic act has meaning is not that appropriate for technical and practical acts. A Dinka who could send a message by the driver of some car going on ahead of him would not find it necessary to knot grass when hoping that supper might be kept for him. Further, the Dinka do not slacken their practical efforts to achieve their end because they have taken such 'mystical' action. The tying of a stone representing lion in a knot of grass is a prelude to serious hunting; the tying of knots of grass in the grass at the roadside is made as the traveller's mind, towards the end of his journey, dwells upon that end which his hastening footsteps bring rapidly nearer. This 'mystical' action is not a substitute for practical or technical action, but a complement to it and preparation for it. The man who ties such a knot has made an external, physical representation of a well-formed mental intention. He has produced a model of his desires and hopes, upon which to base renewed practical endeavour.

This action of *thuic* is in itself trivial, and among the Dinka themselves is not regarded in any way as an important ceremony. The objects which the Dinka have in mind when knotting grass as we have described might, were their circumstances different, be achieved in some purely technical way. The principle involved, however, is similar to that which obtains in symbolic action in situations which, by their very nature, preclude the possibility of technical or practical action as a complete alternative. In the ceremonies for cleansing people of incest, for death, and for peace-making which we now describe, what the symbolic action is intended to control is primarily a set of mental and moral dispositions, and hence in these ceremonies there is no purely technical alternative to the symbolic action taken.

In theory a Dinka may not marry any girl with whom he can

Anuak way, may be conveyed by the statement made by one of them that if you want to be quite sure of not being disappointed, you ought to tie two knots— one for porridge and one for sauce.

trace cognatic relationship unless it is agreed that this relationship has become extremely remote. Even then, again in theory, a ceremony should be performed to permit such a marriage. Where large clans have branched out in many parts of Dinkaland, and where even in a single tribe there is a large group of agnates whose distinct main lineages are but remotely linked, intermarriage between members is permissible; but this is always justified on the grounds that, since the relationship had become remote, a ceremony was once performed in order to make the intermarriage legitimate and free its partners from the results of incest. In such cases the Dinka sometimes say cynically that 'if a man has cattle, then he is my daughter's husband; if he has no cattle, then he is my clansman'. The rules of exogamy can in fact be manipulated either to permit or exclude a particular marriage unless the partners are so clearly unrelated, or so clearly related, that no question of the fitness of the marriage is raised.

In sexual intercourse outside marriage, however, the Dinka judge of whether incest has been effectively committed by results. Incest, *akeeth*, is supposed to result automatically in a serious skin disease, also *keeth*. The offence is thus, in a sense, the same thing as the result experienced. Incestuous congress also results in sterility, and where a woman appears to be barren, or dies in child-birth, one of the reasons likely to be adduced is the possibility that she has had incestuous relations with someone. I heard of a case in which a girl, bearing a child, was according to the Dinka custom reciting the names of her lovers: 'and she named ten of her father's clansmen, and ten of her mother's clansmen, and the child was not delivered. But she would not mention the last name, and so she died in childbirth.' The implication in this particular case was probably that she had once been seduced by her father, which, for the Dinka, is a horror too appalling to name. It is incestuous also for a man's son to have congress with any of his father's wives (his own mother, of course, is in any case excluded) unless his father has deputed him to do so.

When people fear or experience the results of incest, they perform a ceremony for 'separating' the partners to the incest and thus neutralizing the incest retroactively. I saw only one such ceremony, and it was for a comparatively minor case of incest, in which a man had slept with one of his father's junior wives and had for a time concealed the fact.[1] For serious cases a bull, or even a cow in calf, may have to be used to free the partners from the consequences of their sin. In this case only a ram was used. The ceremony was simple. A minor master of the fishing-spear made several short invocations with the guilty pair in front of him, and their kinsmen standing around, near a pool of rain-water. The ram was held near by. Then all went to the pool, and with a certain amount of joking and horseplay the partners to the incest were pulled into the water and ducked and washed by their kinsmen. While this was in progress the ram was also forced into the pool, and pushed under the water a few times. The intention of this, as is clear, was to cleanse the pair of their sin, and to transfer their condition to the ram. That this is conscious symbolism, and not a kind of materialist superstition that the sin in some way actually goes into the water, is shown by the fact that all the kin were also in the water. The sin was transferred only to the ram, according to the Dinkas' symbolic intention.

After the washing the ram was taken from the pool, led away some little distance, and cut in half alive, longitudinally. The first cut of the spear in the throat probably killed it, but I did not watch this performance very closely. I was told, however, that what was particularly important, whether the victim was male or female, was that the sexual organs should be cut clearly apart in two longitudinal halves. In this case all the meat was carried away, presumably to be eaten, but it is said that sometimes a beast thus killed is not eaten, and sometimes only half of it is used.

The important part of the symbolic act, however, is clearly the separation of the sexual organs, which obviously represent the single origin of the partners to the incest. This is negatively confirmed by those sacrifices in which it is particularly necessary that the sexual organs should *not* be divided or severed—sacrifices in which what is emphasized is the solidarity of the group of agnates performing the ceremony (see above, pp. 269–70). When it is thought that two branches of a clan have become

[1] An old father may permanently allot a junior wife to one of his sons, but without this understanding, it is possible that son and father may sleep with the same wife, and the father may further sleep with the mother of the son.

remote enough to make intermarriage safe, a beast is longitudinally divided as we have described. The sin of incest and its consequences are thus controlled by symbolic action; and it could not be otherwise, for incest is a fact of the moral and not of the physical universe.

For a peace-making ceremony, which I did not see, I rely upon an account given by G. W. T. (Major G. W. Titherington), who witnessed such a ceremony,[1] and on texts collected by myself. Major Titherington described how the two parties who had come together to make peace sat about 20 yards apart, on opposite sides of a dry water-course. The killer was not present, but was represented by his kin. The cattle to be paid in compensation for the homicide (*puk*) were driven between the parties, together with a small bull provided by the family of the killer. According to Titherington, the man who directs the ceremony may be 'either a chief or a kujur'—that is, either a master of the fishing-spear or a diviner or prophet—provided that he is not related to either party. When the leader of the ceremony indicated that they should do so, the people of the killer seized the forelegs of the bull, and the people of the killed man the hind legs. They turned it over on its back, and each side thrust a spear into its chest. The leader of the ceremony then at once cut the beast in half *across the belly*, the entrails were taken out and scattered over the two parties, and each party went off separately to divide its meat. After this the leader went to the spot where the bull had been slaughtered, and placed a spear among the remaining bits, thereafter taking some of the remains and throwing them over the two parties, who by this time had resumed their places. The parties then advanced in sixes, three from each side, and holding the spear between them in both hands bit into it, following this with spitting to the left, to the right, and downwards upon their own chests. They are said sometimes to spit upon each other. Ashes were then sprinkled over the knees of the parties, and this was the end of the ceremony. No form of words was spoken. It was believed that, after the conclusion of this ceremony, anyone who reopened the feud would surely die.

Here again the division of the beast is clearly made to

[1] G. W. T., 'Peace-Making Ceremony of Raik Dinka, Bahr-el-Ghazal Province', *S.N. & R.*, vol. vii, part 2, 1924, pp. 127–8.

represent the division of the relationship of feud between the parties, and it is significant that in this case the division of the animal, unlike that which takes place in incest ceremonies, should not involve the longitudinal division of the sexual organs which, in this situation, are not symbolically significant. The biting of the spear is almost certainly a form of oath to abide by the settlement, and (it is implied) involves the participants in crossing the watercourse which before (like the feud) had divided them. The spitting, scattering with entrails, and dusting with ashes, are all forms of purification and blessing. In this case it seems that gesture without speech was enough to confirm, in the external physical universe, an intention conceived interiorly in the moral.[1]

The following is a Dinka's account of what happens at a peace-making ceremony:

When a man has been killed in fighting, then very powerful [*kec*: effective in invocation] masters of the fishing-spear will meet together and the lineage of the clan-divinity will be present. And the people of the cattle-camp [subtribe] of the killer and of the cattle-camp of the man whom he killed will come and sit separately. And one master of the fishing-spear will tether a beast in the middle of the people [i.e., between the two groups].

And the masters of the fishing-spear will invoke, saying 'You camps of our ancestors of the distant past, our ancestors who created compensation (*puk*) among men, it is our custom of old: it is you [divinity] of my father, if you are called upon you will come to help us with that of the above [with affairs of Divinity], so that the camps shall not fight further. It is you who, if you stop a feud for us, [ensure] that there shall be no more trouble.'

All the masters of the fishing-spear invoke in this way, men from both camps. And one man is there, a man who stops feuds,[2] and when the words of the masters of the fishing-spear are finished, he stands with the ox between the parties. They have come with war shields and spears, and some people have come with *ambatch* shields.[3] And those people who were not at the original fight will seize the

---

[1] Though perhaps Major Titherington means merely that no form of words was used to conclude the ceremony, as is more likely.

[2] The man who stops feuds will be a master of the fishing-spear who stands in an equal relationship to both parties involved.

[3] This probably means that those people not closely involved in the feud carry the shields (which are really parrying-sticks, head-rests, stools, and containers for small possessions) made of this light wood.

bull, and the man who stops feuds will cut open the right leg of the ox so that half the flesh falls to one side and half to the other. Then he cuts out the bone at the hip joint and severs it at the hock, and places the bone in a winnowing-tray.[1] He anoints the bone with butter and strikes it with wood to break it in two. He puts one half on the side of the people who have killed a man, and one half on the side of the people whose man has been killed. The ox still has three legs, and one leg has had the bone cut out. And the master who has divided the bone invokes over half the bone, and throws that half at the people of the camp who have killed a man, and takes the other half of the bone and throws it at the people of the camp whose man has been killed.

The people of the camp from which the man has been killed will be heartbroken and will make a show of fighting with the camp which has killed their man and will threaten with their spears. Then the masters of the fishing-spear will sit between the camps and beat themselves upon the ground and cry out and break the shafts of war-spears and bend their blades, and even of fishing-spears also.

The fighting will stop, and both camps will return home. And those people who were not in the fight will skin the ox which stopped the feud, and eat it, and those camps which have fought will leave it alone. Thirty-one cows will be found for compensation so that the man who stops the feud may take one for stopping the feud. And compensation of thirty cows will be paid for the dead man, because they are the people of one camp (tribe or subtribe) which have fought.

Here again the symbolic act represents the separation between partners to a relationship (that of feud) which is to be ended. Included in it is a recognition of the hostility between the parties, whose display of bitterness is overcome by further symbolic acts of the masters of the fishing-spear (breaking spear-shafts and bending their points). The symbolic action, in fact, mimes the total situation in which the parties to the feud know themselves to be, including both their hostility and their disposition towards peace without which the ceremony could not be held. In this symbolic representation of their situation they control it, according to their will to peace, by transcending in symbolic action the only type of practical action (that is, continued hostilities) which for the Dinka follows from the situation of homicide.

[1] The winnowing-tray is the emblem of women, and of the *wen dyor* groups of clans related to Aiwel Longar who have a high reputation as peacemakers.

A final example of symbolic action, that which takes place at the death of ordinary people, emphasizes the special significance of those other mortuary rites which our concluding chapter describes. The Dinka do not talk much about death, and are not inclined to bring funeral ceremonies to one's attention. Consequently, I saw only two burials in Dinkaland, and both of them took place in circumstances which prevented the normal procedure as some Dinka may be persuaded to describe it. This account, therefore, comes largely from a few Dinka informants.

When a man dies he is stripped of his decorations and ornaments. His shallow grave is then dug (it is in fact an oval hole about 4 or 5 ft. deep) and after that his head is shaved and his body first washed with water and then anointed with oil. A skin, or preferably a hide shield, is then placed in the grave for him to be laid on. He is then placed on his side in the grave, with his head facing to the west (the direction of death associated with the setting of the sun), his knees flexed and his hands under his head, in a position of sleep. His exposed ear is covered with a skin so that earth shall not enter it. The burial party crouch round the grave, facing away from it, and push the earth into it backwards with their hands. Then they wash off the earth from their knees on the grave, and a close kinsman stays to cover the grave with a mat.

After three days the family of the deceased bring a little ram, a twin, to the graveside. They take straw from the roof of the dead man's hut, throw it near the grave, and set it alight. The smoke blows over the people, and the people, and the senior member of the family, or master of the fishing-spear if he has been called in, walks round the people beating the living kid upon the ground. He finally holds the bleating kid over the fire a little, and then makes an incision in its belly and takes out the entrails. Their contents are sprinkled over the people, and the carcass is thrown away for the vultures. This 'smoking' of the people is called *atol* (*tol*—smoke), and the kid is the *nyong atol*. The Dinka say that the offering is to please the deceased, and a twin animal is chosen because twins have a special relationship to Divinity.[1]

After another day a sheep or goat is sacrificed. This is called

---

[1] Twins, representing a divided unity, are particularly fitted to be closely associated with Divinity.

the *alok* (from *lok*, *lak* 'to wash'?) and it lifts the prohibition upon drinking milk from the dead man's family. Some time later a whole bull is sacrificed, and prayers are offered and invocations made by a master of the fishing-spear. This final sacrifice, called *apek*, propitiates the deceased, who without it would be likely to injure his people and kill their cattle.

There are some differences, though not large ones, between this ceremony and that for the death of a woman. A woman's skirts are placed about her, and tied up between her legs, for a woman's skirts are not ornaments. They are an essential part of her social personality. The period before 'the kid of the smoke' is brought out is said to be four days for a woman. Four is the number associated with females, though the Dinka have no explanation of this and sometimes even reverse the three/male, four/female connexion. The *alok* sacrifice, when performed for a woman, is to release her cooking-utensils for use, and the *apek* sacrifice is a female goat instead of a whole bull. In both cases the eating of this final sacrifice finally 'cleanses' the bereaved, who until that time still have the contamination of the dead about them.

The main principles behind these mortuary ceremonies we have described are easily understood. The mourners fill the grave without looking into it because they do not wish to experience the final interment. The suffering of 'the kid of the smoke' (and it is particularly stressed that it must bleat) represents that of the mourners, transferred here again to an animal victim and expressed thus in separation from, and 'outside', them. The other rites include *rites de séparation* and the eating of the final *apek* is also a *rite d'agrégation*. In suggesting that they represent and regulate the Dinka experience of death, we do not interpret them entirely differently from the Dinka themselves; for they assert that those who do not perform the mortuary ceremonies will be haunted by their dead. The ceremonies thus divide the dead from the living or (from our point of view) formally separate two different memories of the dead—the memory of them as they were in life, and the memory of them as dead. Hence, it is said, those killed in battle were left unburied, their presence above ground representing a reminder that they still claimed vengeance.

2

The symbolic actions described above thus re-create, and even dramatize, situations which they aim to control, and the experience of which they effectively modulate. If they do not change actual historical or physical events—as the Dinka in some cases believe them to do—they do change and regulate the Dinkas' experience of those events. Hence, in turning now to consider more generally animal sacrifice, the central symbolic act, we observe first that the objective of a sacrifice is achieved in the act itself, even though it may not at once, or at all, produce some change in external circumstances which the Dinka particularly hope for. For them also, a sacrifice involves *waiting* for some hoped-for amelioration in the condition which has occasioned it. They do not expect sacrifice automatically to achieve some specific result with the certainty of a well-tested technical procedure. So they will accept medical aid at the same time as performing sacrifices for the recovery of the sick. Medicine is not an alternative to sacrifice and prayer, but may complement it.

It is with this necessity for the symbolic as well as the technical act in mind that we end our discussion of symbolic action, and particularly the act of sacrifice which confirms and may accompany all other major symbolic acts. We ask ourselves what animal sacrifice may be observed to achieve for the Dinka, which technical action could not achieve. Why do they *both* sacrifice *and*, where possible, seek modern medical aid? And if sacrifice is made for the recovery of a sick man, for example, and he dies, why is sacrifice not regarded as ineffective, in the same way as a technical act which fails to produce its desired result?

The answer the Dinka give when faced with the failure of a sacrifice to produce the required result which is the proximate occasion of sacrifice is that 'Divinity has refused' or, more likely, that the Power which was really the grounds of the man's sickness was not correctly identified. So, what is required is another sacrifice, and not alternative action.

But even if a sacrifice has manifestly failed to achieve a specific end which it was part of the intention of those making the sacrifice to achieve, it has not therefore been without effect altogether; for any sacrifice involves ends which go quite beyond any particular end which may be its special proximate occasion. It is made not only and specifically for one sick man (to continue this example) and for his single sickness; it is made for and on behalf of the whole sacrificing community, for we have noted that the Dinka do not sacrifice individually, each for himself. A sick man does not make a sacrifice for his own recovery; his kin and community must be called together to sacrifice on behalf of their member. People provide the sacrificial victims for each other, and at the regular sacrificial ceremonies at the time of the harvest, members of different lineages take it in turn to provide for their masters of the fishing-spear the victims which he will sacrifice on behalf of and for the benefit of all.

No theory of sacrifice which neglects the fact that the act is primarily social can therefore be of service in interpreting the sacrifices of the Dinka. If sacrifice were merely, or essentially, a matter of exchanging the life of a beast for that of a man in a quasi-commercial traffic with supernatural persons, there would be no reason why a sick man should not take his own beast, kill it for himself, and ask divinities to accept its life in place of his. Such an act would be regarded as totally ineffective by the Dinka and, as I have pointed out, the importance of corporate action by a community of which the individual is really and traditionally a member is the reason for the fear which individual Dinka feel when they suffer misfortune away from home and kin. The individual whose sickness (in sacrifices for sickness) is the particular occasion of sacrifice derives benefit of some kind from his membership of the sacrificing community, whose sacrificial intention is partly, but only partly, focused upon him.

If we reduce to their main elements the actions which we have already described in our accounts of several sacrifices, they may be grouped consistently with the main elements of the oral rites as we have isolated them in the previous chapter. The victim is marked off from the other beasts of the herd by a special tethering or confinement (*mac*) and by invocations and gestures is made to stand in a special relationship to the human group which intends its death. To take a beast out of the herd and quickly kill it cannot be a sacrifice. The powerful gesturing with the spears in invocation, and the victimization of the beast first by a kind of imprisonment, which places it in human power, and then by the slapping, buffeting, and in some ceremonies more painful treatment to which it is subjected, are gestures complementary to what, in describing the oral rites, we referred to as statements of human power to prevail. The victim itself is made an object of displays of warlike hostility, which in gesture again complement the victimization of the oral rites, when the beast is made the vehicle of the *passiones* of men. This gesture, then, is correlative to the weakening of the victim which the oral part of the ceremony intends. Men manifest their strength in relation to the victim's weakness; and in this connexion it is interesting to note that the Dinka often show a theoretical preference for a strong victim, though they must often make the best of what they think they can afford. The stronger the victim, the more their own strength is emphasized by their ability to manipulate and finally kill it. For the young warriors, strength is primarily strength for battle with enemies; and hence their gestures of hostility at sacrifices represent at once the assertive repudiation of enemies, and of their own sufferings and misfortunes and sins which they have transferred to the victim. As we see in one set of invocations, the victim is to 'go' and take away with it various sicknesses and dangers (p. 227 above).

With these expressions of human strength are present also gestures by which weaknesses are admitted and then removed from the congregation. The effectiveness of a sacrifice requires, in fact, that those attending should already have disposed themselves in accordance with a part of the end which the sacrifice is intended to achieve. They intend that they shall be strong as a result of the sacrifice; they assert that they are so, both by claiming to wield the power which has enabled their ancestors to prevail in life and produce them, and by asserting, as they often do, the unity and peace of those attending. Quarrels weaken and divide the community. Hence, past quarrels are denied retroactively. Oaths falsely sworn create the confusion which the Dinka call *aliab*, and which particularly is singled out as destructive of the community itself. Hence, in some ceremonies, the 'wether of the ashes' is symbolically washed to remove the effects of those false oaths. In the more generally intended act of asperging, less articulate conditions of weakness are washed away (in Dinka *wac wei*), and the strength which is derived from the victim is applied, in its chyme and urine, to human beings. These gestures are correlative to what we have seen to be admissions of human weakness in the oral rites; but like those admissions, their function is to detach weakening from strengthening elements within the situation of the rite and the consciousness of the participants. By recognizing their weakness, the Dinka are able symbolically to act upon it, in a way parallel to their attempts to recognize, and detach from, an individual patient, the Power to which his suffering may be attributed.

The assertions of human strength and confessions of weakness are accompanied by gestures honouring the victim, except in sacrifices to MACARDIT. Sometimes the beast's horns are anointed with butter, and beer is put in its mouth. Honour is rendered finally to the victim, and to Divinity and divinities, when the carcass is covered with leaves and lies for a while thus, as earlier described. The removal of the pizzle and testicles by the old women is carried out with every show of respect, and the covering of the haunches with a girl's skirt is also, as the Dinka say, 'for respect'. Thus the victim and the divinities to which it is offered are honoured together. By the end of the ceremony the victim has become identified with those divinities, as was originally intended in the dedication of the animal to them. In victimizing a bull or an ox the Dinka are aware of using or manipulating something physically more powerful than themselves; and through the identification of the victim with the divinities they also control something spiritually more powerful. From this comes the blend of supplication and command exhibited in the manual and oral rites.

The honour and respect showed to the victim are to be understood in the wider social context of the sacrifice. A sacrifice is a feast, to which guests are bidden, and where they should be treated with courtesy and generosity. As the guests arrive in the homestead where the sacrifice takes place, they are met by the womenfolk with songs and dance. This welcome, which honours the guests, is called *luor*, which I think is also a term used on occasions for the movement of those taking part in a sacrifice towards the victim in its death agonies. Mutual respect among members of the sacrificing community is thus connected with the respect shown to the divinities and their victims. This mutual regard is a condition of corporate life, and at sacrifices is strongly emphasized and reinforced. It is with this in mind that we can understand why, in Dinka tradition, the establishment of a new community—a new 'cattle-camp' or section—is achieved by sacrifice, and the names of some Dinka subtribes today are explained as being derived from the colour-names of the beasts sacrificed to establish them. Similarly, the hymns sung in honour of clan-divinities and their victims evoke the notion of the communal strength of the clan. A good example is the following, sung in honour of the clan-divinity Gourd:

> . . . it is [for the enemy] bleeding of the belly
> It is coughing in the chest
> Bring these [upon the enemy]
> Come and work craftily
> Pray life from the container of seeds [the gourd]
> Great Gourd of my father will help me
> Even though I am left alone.
> A man who hates me, let him depart from me
> A man who loves me, let him come to me
> Great Gourd of my father will help me
> Great Gourd has filled the earth
> The cow of DENG is milked for libations
> The cow of my father is milked
> A huge gourd of milk
> Great Gourd of my father has filled the earth.

In such hymns the honouring of the clan-divinity is also an expression of the collective strength of the clansmen. The divinity is asked that enemies should depart, leaving only those who are bound together in mutual regard and who will help and not destroy each other.

It will have been obvious that the situation of sacrifice and the role of masters of the fishing-spear in it are in general prefigured in the myths of masters of the fishing-spear, and it is not necessary here to draw attention to such general correspondences between myth and rite, which a glance at the myths earlier recorded will make apparent. It remains, however, to make explicit the nature of the drama of life and death enacted in sacrificial rites, in relation to that drama as it is represented in myths.

In some of the myths, it will be remembered, the fishing-spear of the prototype of spear-masters is darted at the heads of men in the situation of a river-crossing. Men are being killed, until the spear of Aiwel Longar is deflected from them. Then Aiwel shares his life-giving power among the founders of those clans which are spear-masters at the present day, and in some versions is represented as making a feast, or a sacrifice, with animal victims, from which comes the divinity Flesh shared among the spear-masters. With the provision of animal victims, that is, Aiwel Longar hands on to the people his gift of life, when previously it was against the people themselves that his energies had been directed.

The darting of the spear which, in the myths, originally brings death to human beings, is re-enacted in the sacrificial rites but directed against an animal victim. It is amply clear that this beast dies in place of men, and its fitness thus to represent men has been suggested earlier in the book. In the boldest terms, then, both myth and rite represent the conversion of a situation of death into a situation of life. In the myth the spear is deflected from men and handed on to them as a source of life. In the rite the death of the victim is explicitly the source of life to the people. This conversion of death into life is particularly clear in the details of the rites we have described, especially in the removal of the sexual organs of the sacrificial victim by women and their consumption as a source of fertility to the lineage.

It is clear, then, that an important feature of sacrifice is that the people for whom it is made enact the death of a victim which in important respects represents themselves, in order to survive that death. In relation to this we may draw attention to one curious and, to the Dinka, inexplicable, feature of Aiwel's behaviour in a version of the myth (p. 180). There Aiwel places the carcass of an ox upon Adheou, and fixes him to the ground with a fishing-spear, and prays that he may die. But the carcass putrefies around Adheou, and yet he lives. The picture here presented is of the living man within the carcass of an ox, which decays about him, and leaves him still alive.

Every sacrificial rite thus anticipates the death (with its Dinka associations of sterility and finality) which the Dinka expect and fear, and by doing so demonstrates their own power of survival. Hence, it is not necessary for the validation of belief in sacrifice that a particular sickness which sacrifice is intended to avert should be immediately cured, or even cured at all. For when sacrifice is made, the victim dies while the patient still lives, and his life, however weak, remains life in relation to the death of the victim. A Dinka sacrifice is in part, therefore, a drama of human survival.

In some of the versions of the myth the darting of the spear of Aiwel Longar into the heads of men is made in the setting of a river-crossing, and we have earlier pointed out that 'to cross the river' means 'to survive'. This detail also has its parallel in the regular sacrificial rites of the autumn, for those rites are performed in anticipation of the movement to the dry-season pastures which is to come. Dinka giving a brief general account of the autumn sacrifices will often say something like 'and then the master of the fishing-spear will kill something to Divinity, and the people will go to the dry-season pastures'. As in some details of the myths, but with an animal victim, a death is a prelude to the river-crossing which ensures continued life.

I have pointed to the political significance of the fact that in some versions of the myth it is made explicit that the means by which Aiwel Longar's spear is deflected from men is a female symbol. In the sacrificial rites death is deflected from men by the provision of animal victims, ideally cattle. Cattle are in many ways substitutes for humans; but more specifically they are substitutes for women, who by the gift of cattle in bride-wealth are brought into the families of their husbands and produce new life in bearing children there. So the victim which deflects death from the people in the sacrificial rites is in a special sense representative of women, as in the myths Aiwel's death-dealing spear is deflected by female symbols. It will be remembered too that a girl's skirt is draped over the haunches of the victim. Again, though the Dinka do not normally sacrifice cows, the sacrifice of a cow, and even more of a cow-in-calf, is considered necessary to avert great calamities. Between the role of the female in the myths and in the sacrificial rites there are thus consistencies which, in a different account of the Dinka from that here attempted, might be examined more closely.

VIII

BURIAL ALIVE

I

IF any literate foreigner has seen the full mortuary ceremonies of a master of the fishing-spear, he has not, to my knowledge, described them. It is unfortunate, therefore, that our knowledge of these centrally important ceremonies must depend upon hearsay evidence,[1] even though it may be derived from Dinka who claim first-hand knowledge of the subject. There can be no doubt, however, that the ceremonies we now describe did, and perhaps do, actually occur; for although the ceremonies are now known to be officially forbidden, Dinka admit to having seen or heard of them, when they do not think it imprudent to admit to interest in a custom known to be illegal, and felt to be repugnant to foreigners whose knowledge of its meaning is superficial. During my stay in Dinkaland, but in another part of the country, one successful case attracted attention at a high official level, and in the discussions which followed the abortive ceremony already mentioned (pp. 275-7) those who tried to probe the intention of the participants were clearly aware, up to a point, of the general procedures which ought to accompany the full ceremonial burial of a master of the fishing-spear. During the course of these discussions I was told the names of several masters of the fishing-spear who had been put in the grave alive in comparatively recent times. Since the mystery which surrounds the custom gives rise to many misunderstandings which are to the disadvantage of the Dinka, I do not consider it a breach of confidence to represent the situation as it was represented to me, omitting only names and places which would identify the actors. In view of the ethnographical and theoretical interest of the ceremonies, I have added reports from others

---

[1] Similar doubt surrounds the manner of the deaths of the kings of the Shilluk, which has considerable bearing on theories of 'divine kingship' which we have borne in mind in the presentation of our account of the deaths of masters of the fishing-spear.

to the little evidence which I was able to collect, in face of the reticence induced partly by official prohibition of these practices. The burial of a master of the fishing-spear with full honour is called *dhor beny ke pir*, or *thiok (beny) ke pir*, or sometimes *beny aci lo thoc*. The *dhor*[1] of the first expression is a technical term of Dinka religion for which I can find no certain equivalent in English. Its object may be either a clan-divinity (*ok alo yanh wa dhor* means 'we are going to *dhor* the clan-divinity of my father') or a master of the fishing-spear, and I do not think that it is used outside these contexts. When used of the clan-divinity, it has the sense of serving, or giving homage to, the divinity, at a 'feast' with sacrifice and hymns of the kind we have described. People *dhor* the clan-divinity so that it may augment their strength, and in doing so satisfy a demand which it makes upon them. Similarly, as will appear, in placing their master of the fishing-spear in the grave while he yet lives, they think to augment their vitality and also, normally, to gratify his own desire. With these elements of the meaning of *dhor* in mind, we may perhaps translate *dhor beny ke pir* as 'to bury a master while he lives', which is its practical significance in ordinary Dinka usage. This also is the literal meaning of the second expression commonly used of the ceremony, *thiok ke pir*. The third, *beny aci lo thoc*,[2] means literally 'the master has gone to sit up' or 'the master has gone to his seat'. *Thoc* is to sit erect, and it is also something upon which one can sit erect, such as a saddle. Its implication here is that the subject is not lying prone in death as are the corpses of ordinary men, but is in some way propped up. It may be in fact that masters of the fishing-spear do recline when they are placed in the grave alive; but the expression used contradicts the impression of inert recumbence which is made by any mere corpse, and which is conveyed by the usual Dinka word *toc* which applies equally to the lying down of a corpse and the lying in sleep of the living. Similarly, the ceremonies now described contradict the customary configuration of ideas surrounding the deaths of ordinary men and women.

The following is a text typical of the accounts which Dinka friends may give of what happens at the deaths of masters of the

---

[1] A similar word also means 'to be tired of', but I do not think the meanings are related.

[2] Though *toc* means 'to rest'.

fishing-spear. The author did not claim to have witnessed such a ceremony, though he said that he knew of one which had been held in a tribe adjacent to his own. I have changed proper names, but the lineages actually mentioned were known to me.

When a master of the fishing-spear has fallen sick and is becoming weak, he will call all his people and tell them to bring his whole camp (tribe or subtribe) to his home to bury him whilst he lives. His people will obey him and quickly come, for if they delay and the master of the fishing-spear dies before they reach him, they will be most miserable.

They will come and drive their cattle-pegs into the ground by the side of the home of the master of the fishing-spear who is to be buried alive. When they have arrived, the master will talk to his people and tell them what they are to do with him. When his talk with the older people is finished, he will tell them to send the young men for *akoc* (*Cordia rothii*) branches, and the young men will be quickly sent to fetch *akoc*.

When they return, they clear a patch of ground so that nothing harmful remains in it;[1] and when they have prepared the ground they dig a grave and put the branches of *akoc* in it to make a platform. Then they will cut into strips the skin of a bull previously sacrificed, and make it like an *angareeb*[2] on the frame they have prepared. And they will take a living ram and tether it at the bottom of the hole (grave) at the side of the platform. They then lift up the master of the fishing-spear, and put him into the earth while he yet lives.

And he will not be afraid of death; he will be put in the earth while singing his songs. Nobody among his people will wail or cry because their man has died. They will be joyful because their master of the fishing-spear will give them life (*wei*) so that they shall live untroubled by any evil.

When they have placed the master of the fishing-spear on the platform on the ground, they make another platform above it, also with strips of hide, and put a gourd of milk in the earth with him. Then when all is completed, the young men and old men, girls, women and children, will all take cattle-dung and fling it upon the grave, until the grave is completely covered over with a heap of dung. For the grave of a master of the fishing-spear is not to be covered with earth. And they will sacrifice another bull and a cow-in-calf.

[1] That is, they clean the ground and remove any thorn-bushes.
[2] This is the bedstead of the Northern Sudan, made of strips of hide or rope laced across a wooden framework.

After this is finished, they cover the top of the grave with dung-ashes, and make a feast for the master of the fishing-spear. After another month, they will make beer and porridge, and kill two bulls, and remove the fence of *awar* grass with which the homestead of the master has been surrounded after the burial. And they will dance and sacrifice to all divinities so that they will be pleased with men.

The two texts which follow were dictated by a friend who claimed that, as a youth, he had been present at the ceremonies he here describes. His evidence, with proper names, was most circumstantial, and I have changed those names which might make the particular area recognizable; it was far from the country of the man who provided the text already quoted.

I first saw a master of the fishing-spear called Deng Deng buried alive in the land of the Majok tribe across the river. I was only a boy. The master's own home was called Malek, in the subtribe Magol, and he was the master of the fishing-spear of that subtribe. His clan was called Pakedang. They are few now but they are very strong in invocation, so that in my country we sometimes call them 'witches of the fishing-spear'.[1] There are other masters of the fishing-spear in that subtribe, but there are none to equal them.

The master of the fishing-spear Deng Deng was becoming very old, and when his years were finished and he was very old indeed, so that he could not see well and all his teeth had fallen out, he told his lineage that he wished to be buried alive, and that they should go and tell the people of the country and see if they agreed.

They prepared the ground for his burial at a very ancient cattle-camp site called Malwal, which was also hard by the homestead of Deng Deng and near his cattle-byre.[2] So it was at his very own original home [*panden nhom*, literally 'the head of his home']. The clan which cleared and dug the ground was Padiangbar; it is that clan which buries a master of the fishing-spear alive in my country.[3]

[1] In view of what we have earlier suggested, that there is on the whole a corre-spondence between religious reputation and political influence, which depends partly on the size of the spear-master clan, it is interesting to see here that their small numbers seen in relation to their religious reputation at once evokes the notion of something unnatural—witchcraft.

[2] This refers to a wet-season camping site, many of which are very near perma-nent villages.

[3] It is in this area particularly that the clan Padiangbar are regarded as having something of the strength of a spear-master clan (see pp. 145–6). Structurally, therefore, their role in the situation of the death of masters of the fishing-spear may be seen to have something in common with the reported role off the *ororo*, the demoted members of the royal clan of the Shilluk, at the death of the Shilluk king. See, for example, C. G. and B. Z. Seligman, op. cit., 1932, pp. 49–50.

They dug a very big hole on the highest point of the cattle-camp site, in the middle of the cattle. Next to it were two bulls, a big white one and a red one. They were the whole beasts of the clan-divinities *Mon* Grass and Flesh. When the hole had been dug, they made two platforms [frameworks] of *akoc* wood, which had been fetched by the young men of Padiangbar from far away in the forest, as much as a day's journey distant.

They worked for three days, and the old man was still above the ground. They honoured the bulls with songs for two days, speaking invocations each day in the morning and the evening. Then the masters of the fishing-spear of Pakedang, along with those of Paketoi and Pagong,[1] slit the throats of the bulls at about 10 o'clock. Deng Deng's mother was the daughter of a woman of Paketoi and his mother's father was of the clan Pagong. So they were all there together, to join together his father's and his maternal uncle's families (*bi panerden mat kek pan e wun*).

Deng Deng made invocations over the bulls, and the horns of the first bull, the white one, sank forwards to the ground. When the bull had been killed, they took its skin and cut it into strips, and made a bed from it on the framework. And every day they made a feast (*cam yai*) and danced inside the cattle-byre during the daytime, and outside at night. And men slept in the byre with other men's wives, and everyone agreed to this [literally 'and there was no bad word'].

They then placed a war-shield, made from the hide of a bull of the clan-divinity which had been killed in the past, on top of the bed. It was a war-shield which had for long been kept in the byre, and which the people had anointed with butter every spring and autumn, during the 'dividing months'.[2] They placed Deng Deng on the shield and lowered him into the grave.

The red (brown) bull remained. When Deng Deng had been lowered into the hole, they made a platform over him, and so arranged it that the top of the platform was level with the surface of the ground. They sang hymns, and after the singing was finished they made an enclosure of *dhot* wood around the grave. The enclosure was about twice the area of the surface of the grave, and of such a height that a man could just see over it if he tried. Then they took cattle-dung and partly covered over the top of the grave, leaving part uncovered so that his voice could be heard. From his grave, Deng Deng called the older men together outside the enclosure, and all the women and children, even his own wives, were sent away.

---

[1] I have retained the real clan-name here and in the case of Padiangbar.

[2] That is at the times between the seasons, when the Dinka move to and from the dry-season pastures.

The author of the text was therefore also sent away; but according to him, when the old master of the fishing-spear had finished speaking to the old men, they returned to the rest and reported to them what he had said. The text continues:

Deng Deng had died at the time of the harvest. He said that in the following dry season, in the month of Akanythii,[1] his tribe would fight with a neighbouring tribe, and that he was distressed because his people were not brave enough in war.

Two months later, this fight took place, and eight of his people were killed and two from the neighbouring tribe. That neighbouring tribe soundly beat his tribe and drove them off as far as Agar Dinka country. Eventually, the Government forces came and prevented thefts of cattle. But even then that neighbouring tribe made a feast near the river in the face of the dry-season pastures of his own tribe, which had been so harried that they could do nothing about it.

He added:

While the master of the fishing-spear still speaks, they do not cover the grave with dung. But when he no longer replies when they address him, they heap up the dung over him. And when it has all sunk in, they make a shrine.[2] Some people may then say 'The master of the fishing-spear has died', but they will usually say 'The master has been taken into the earth'. And nobody will say 'Alas, he is dead!' They will say 'It is very good.'

The same informant told me of the following case which he clearly preferred not to discuss at length as it had occurred much more recently. He spoke as follows:

Two masters of the fishing-spear known to you today are the sons of that master of the fishing-spear I saw buried. He was the master of the fishing-spear with supremacy in the whole tribe of Kwek, and was a man of the clan Pagong who are the chief masters of the fishing-spear in that tribe.

There follows a description which does not significantly differ from that previously given, and in which again it is made clear that the master of the fishing-spear was very old, though not sick, and asked that he might be buried. The site chosen was again an old cattle-camp site adjoining his homestead. The

---

[1] This is the height of the dry season.

[2] It is not clear whether this is actually on the site of burial, or near by. I have never seen or heard of a shrine of this type (the mud shrine) separated from a homestead.

following part of this text adds something to what has already
been described:

All the people of his tribe came, and the cattle were tethered
around. They made an enclosure, but this time they did not dance.
The young men were sent away when he was in the grave. The older
men later reported that he had spoken to them in this way: 'I am
going to see (deal with) in the earth the Powers of sickness which
kill people and cattle. And I am still displeased with my son Moror
because we quarrelled. I have nothing bad in my heart towards
other people.' After three months, there was no more cattle-plague,
and after three months also his son Moror died. His father had
fetched him (*aci wun lo dhiec*).

The following indication of the ground-plan of such a ceremony
was given:

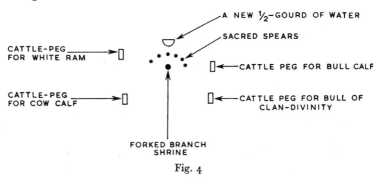

Fig. 4

  I include this simple plan because it represents what Dinka
themselves drew in the dust to explain such a ceremony, and
thus includes, one may suppose, a Dinka view of what is essential. The new gourd, to hold water for aspersions and the split
sacred cucumbers for drawing over the backs and chests of the
sick, was strongly marked in the plan. The sacred spears, for
consecration and reconsecration, are placed round the shrine.
At least four beasts are required. The bull-calf is tethered during
invocations, and then returned to the herd, where it becomes
the new 'bull of the clan-divinity'. The bull of the clan-divinity
is sacrificed, and provides the strips of hide for the burial-
platform. The cow-calf is tethered during the invocations, and
is then returned to the herd, to become later the dam of a new
'bull of the clan-divinity', of which the bull-calf will be the sire.

Beasts for sacrifice to the clan-divinity should be bred of consecrated stock, though this is not always possible, at least in routine sacrifices. The white ram was specifically stated to be the offering of the women, and those who provided the plan mentioned also that butter would be brought in gourds for anointing the horns and the testicles of the sacrificial victim. These accounts are typical of what one hears of the burial of masters of the fishing-spear in Western Dinkaland. I add to them some conclusions drawn from the inquiry into a suspected case of burial alive to which I have already referred, and which (if indeed it really was intended) was unsuccessful owing to official intervention. In the course of this inquiry it became apparent that certain activities were associated, in the minds of most of those present, with ceremonial burial. Naturally, since most of those who had attended the preliminaries of the trampling of the calf (already described) were implicated in the accusation that they intended to bury their chief alive, they were anxious to testify that their ceremony was intended only to strengthen the old man, and was therefore innocent in the eyes of the Government's law. The statements they made, however, reveal what for them would have been considered significant in suggesting that burial alive was intended. One emphasized that the old master of the fishing-spear was 'not an important master of the fishing-spear', rather minimizing his standing, because it is known that not everyone who is technically a master of the fishing-spear has sufficient standing to be treated in this manner. Others emphasized the frequency with which, in the ceremonies and in the preliminaries to them, people spoke of 'strengthening' the old man, and not of burying him. The son of the master of the fishing-spear said that his father had never told him that he wished to be buried, and it was in this case clear throughout the evidence and the reactions of those present to it that the desires of the master of the fishing-spear were considered relevant to the interpretation of the ceremony. Everyone seemed to take it for granted that such a burial would normally take place only at the initial instigation of the master of the fishing-spear concerned, and not against his will. The old master of the fishing-spear himself said that he had called his people to strengthen, and not to bury, him. One piece of evidence of innocence of intention which was strongly urged was that the young men of the camp had not been sent to cut the *akoc* wood from which the platform for the grave is made, and that when the people were making their sacrifice there was no *akoc* in the homestead. Further, the cattle had not been tethered outside around the home of the sick old man and, as his son insisted, there were several beasts in the cattle-byre. It is clear from this that the tethering of cattle outside around the place of burial is considered an important feature of the ceremony. The manner in which the calf was killed was said to be a quite normal procedure for the death of a beast sacrificed for the recovery of a master of the fishing-spear, as was the fact that some of the young men had brought gourds of milk for libations. But, it was pointed out, the young men were also drinking milk, whereas when a master of the fishing-spear was buried alive milk was not drunk, it was 'respected' (*thek*). Also, it was suggested, the sacrifice was not large enough for a burial alive, and the ceremony had not been mooted sufficiently long beforehand to make it possible for all those members of the sick man's clan who would have come to be informed. Only two days' preparation had been made. One man said also that if a burial of a master of the fishing-spear had been about to take place, all lineages in the subtribe would have produced beasts for sacrifice, that the young men would have gone into the woods and there slaughtered bulls and goats and left them for the birds to eat, and for Powers of sickness. Strangers, moreover, had been made welcome at the ceremony, but in a burial alive they would not have been encouraged to come near. It would also have been expected that the spear of an enemy should be taken and bent in the dust.

Some of this evidence was questioned by the Dinka elders who inquired into the case. It was pointed out, as a significant feature, that the young warriors and women of the whole subtribe were about the homestead, or near by in the cattle-camp, and that if only the strengthening ceremony had been intended the closer kin of the master of the fishing-spear would have been the only ones concerned. It was maintained that the trampling to death of the calf *was* a feature which suggested something more than the ordinary sacrificial act, and that, most importantly, some of the warriors were carrying war-shields. There was some disagreement about the situations in which it would be expected that the victim should be trampled to death (*kacic*), some saying that this would really be done in the forest, in order to free people from a serious pestilence, or as a preparation for war. We have remarked already upon the close connexion between religion and war among the Dinka. It was largely on these grounds, and on what was considered to be the untrustworthiness of some of the evidence of those accused—that, for example, though the cattle had not been tethered in the homestead, they had been brought to a cattle-camp near by—that the investigators decided that those who took part in the ceremony had a case to answer.

There are some differences between the substance of these accounts from Western Dinkaland, and what has been reported from other parts. Since evidence is unavoidably slender, I quote at length from the fullest published accounts of what happens at a burial alive, those of Professor and Mrs. Seligman, Major G. W. Titherington, and Ibrahim Eff. Bedri. The following is the information collected by Professor and Mrs. Seligman, whose visits to Dinkaland were made in 1909–10 and 1911–12. Professor and Mrs. Seligman write:[1]

In 1922 we found that Byordit [a rainmaker or master of the fishing-spear of a section of the Bor Dinka] was dead. Fear of the Government led to unwillingness to speak of the manner of his passing, but we understood that after he had several times requested that he might be killed his couch was at last placed in the midst of a cattle-hearth, i.e. upon a mass of dried and burnt dung, and his people danced round him until so much dust was raised that in a few hours the old man—a chronic bronchitic—was dead.

The rain-maker of the Niel tribe was also one of our informants; he told us that his father and paternal uncle had both been killed in the traditional manner, the Niel custom being to strangle their *bañ* in his own house, having first prepared his grave. They then wash the corpse and kill a bullock in front of the house, skinning it immediately and making a couch (*angareeb*) of its skin, which is placed in the grave and the body laid upon it; a cell should then be built over the couch so that the earth does not come in contact with the body. The Niel take every care to guard their *bañ* from accidental death, for should he die suddenly as a result of an accident some sickness would surely occur, even though his son or a close blood relative would immediately succeed him. If it was thought that the

[1] C. G. and B. Z. Seligman, op. cit., 1932, pp. 196–8.

bañ was seriously ill, he would be killed, even though he were quite young, for it would be a dangerous matter if he were to die of an illness, since as our informant pointed out, this would prevent any of his sons (i.e. presumably any relative) from becoming *bañ* in their turn. Actually this had never happened.

An Agar Dinka gave the following account of the slaying of their rainmaker. A wide grave is dug, and a couch is placed in it, upon which the rainmaker lies on his right side with a skin under his head. He is surrounded by his friends and relatives, including his younger children, but his elder children are not allowed near the grave, at any rate towards the end, lest in their despair they should injure themselves. The *bañ* lies upon his couch without food or drink for many hours, generally for more than a day. From time to time he speaks to his people, recalling the past history of the tribe, how he has ruled and advised them, and instructing them how to act in the future. At last he tells them he has finished, and bids them cover him up; earth is thrown into the grave and he is soon suffocated.

Captain J. M. Stubbs, writing of the Reik, informs us that the *bañ bith* is laid on a bier in a roofed-in cell built in the grave, and that his neck, elbows and knees are broken; sometimes he is first strangled with a cow-rope. According to another account, the *bañ* eats a little millet, drinks milk, and throws the remainder to the east, praying and affirming that he is going to his fathers but that the food he leaves to his children. A cow-rope is placed around his neck, his elbows and knees are broken, and one of the sacred spears is placed in his hand, which he is helped to raise. His son takes the spear, and the *bañ* is strangled. It appears that this is done in semi-privacy; then the drums beat, the people gather, and the grave is filled in. A shelter is built over it, which when it falls to pieces is not rebuilt, though the ground around is kept cleared lest bush fires should sweep across the tomb. It seems that certain species of trees are expected to grow on or near the grave, and there may be some connection between this and the initiation of sacrifice at the grave. Concerning the Bor, Archdeacon Shaw informs us that a rain-maker is buried in a *lwak* (cattle-byre) which continues to be used, the grave being fenced off with short poles. He is said to take the food of the community with him into the grave, so when the next season arrives a hole is dug at the side of the byre so that the food may come out again. This will ensure good crops, abundance of termites and other food. Dr. Tucker writes of the Cic that when the *bañ bith* is buried, milk is poured into his right hand, millet placed in his left and the hands closed over their contents, thus ensuring plenty until the new *bañ bith* is installed.

We believe that all tribes sprinkle milk on the graves of their rain-makers, and it is probable that all place some property in the grave, while perhaps some bury a bullock or a cow with their rainmaker.

I was not able to confirm the presence of any idea that the master of the fishing-spear took the food of the community with him into the grave, though undoubtedly most people say that he is buried with milk and perhaps with a beast, sometimes an ox and sometimes a ram. It is thought, among the Western Dinka, that the sick master of the fishing-spear may take some affliction of the community away with him into the grave.

There is one famous case in Western Dinkaland of a renowned master of the fishing-spear who entered the grave clutching in his hand a tsetse fly, and thereby removed the scourge of tsetse from his people. It may now happen also that a living beast is buried *in place of* a master of the fishing-spear. Shortly after the abortive ceremony already mentioned, it was reported that a burial alive was intended in a village of the same district. Police descended upon the village to find a new grave containing only a ram. Other discrepancies between my own accounts and those of Professor and Mrs. Seligman from other parts of Dinkaland are left for comment until other accounts have been considered, and a minimal measure of agreement between them all can be reached.

The account of 'Burial Alive among Dinka of Bahr-el-Ghazal Province' published in 1925 by G. W. T. (Major G. W. Titherington),[1] then a Sudan Political Officer in that Province, agrees substantially with what I myself was told. He says, however, that the custom was originally confined to the clans of Pagong and Parum, from whom it was copied by Payi. The various lineages represented among the people of a master of the fishing-spear are said to bring beasts to slaughter at the feast for his burial. Major Titherington also says that the burial takes place in a cattle-byre, which continues to be used as before until it falls into disrepair, when earth is taken from the grave and used to make a mound-shrine. There is no mention of strangulation or of other violence done to the master of the fishing-spear in Major Titherington's note, and it is made clear that his manner of meeting his death is voluntarily chosen by him. From the

[1] G. W. T., 'Burial Alive among Dinka of the Bahr-al-Ghazal Province', *S.N. & R.*, vol. viii, 1925, p. 196.

grave he eventually raises a spear to indicate that he wishes the grave to be filled in. Again, a platform is built over him, and he rests upon a 'pillow' under this platform, which is covered with grass. An ox, buried alive with him at the other end of this vast grave, is said to die in eight days, and he himself is covered in ten days unless he has given a sign that he wishes this to be done earlier. Major Titherington mentions that, once in the grave, the master of the fishing-spear does not usually come out again, but that he has heard of one successful case of change of mind.

Finally, though in this book not much attention has been paid to the Northern Dinka whom I never visited, we cannot omit the accounts of the deaths of their masters of the fishing-spear which Ibrahim Eff. Bedri has given. They have to be considered in relation to ceremonies for the installation of a master of the fishing-spear which, among the Northern Dinka, seem to be elaborate. These Dinka, in closer contact with the Shilluk than any of the others we have discussed, may have a development of ceremonial influenced by, but not modelled upon, that of the Shilluk kingship. In one article,[1] Ibrahim Eff. Bedri states briefly that generally the 'famous' rain-makers, when they become old or sick, should be killed in some way. Suffocation, he says, is the most common way. He continues:

Aiyong Dit, the famous Rain Maker of Danjol, was built into his barn with his first wife and favourite bull, and left to die of starvation.

Another way to kill a Beny Riem is to hold him standing, cover the whole body with thick cow butter, and vigorously stretch his legs, fingers, arms and privates and press the testicles. Then they break all the joints. Some people say they are broken before the death but others say after.

The question why the privates are stretched and the testicles pressed, is always an annoying one, and is simply answered by a shrug with a prompt 'I don't know.'

In a longer account[2] Bedri writes that 'When the elders of a section decide to kill their *Beny Rem*, or when he himself has made the request, all the warriors who were initiated by him are summoned.'[3] They are said to dance and sing in his honour,

[1] Ibrahim Eff. Bedri, op. cit., 1939.

[2] Ibrahim Eff. Bedri, op. cit., 1948.

[3] The *beny rem* or *beny riem* is described as a master of the fishing-spear who has been formally and ceremonially installed, as leader of his tribe or subtribe. I was not told of such formal installations among the Dinka I visited.

and finally to suffocate him. The treatment described in the last quotation is then given. The account continues:

He is buried secretly by night usually in the bed of a khor or in the forest so that nobody else may know his grave.[1] He is buried in a deep hole sitting on a bed made of *inderab*[2] stakes, and with stakes at his back bound with hide to keep him upright. His *mendyor* spear[3] is put in his hand pointing in the direction of the enemies of the tribe. The body is then covered with *Leyie* grass from the river bank, and the grave is filled in.

If an enemy interferes with the grave or the position of the body he brings misfortune to the section.

Further, it is said that all but children fast from the time of the master's death until his burial, that before the sunrise following his death people leave the village or the cattle-camp and stay in the sun until midday, that food which is cooked on fire is thrown away and all the fires in the village are put out, and that the grass around the village or cattle-camp is burnt and people return to their homes through the smoke. A sheep is sacrificed and thrown to the birds. On the third day, another sheep is killed and half of it boiled and eaten by those who have assisted in the burial, while half is thrown into the forest for the dead man. Meat, water, and charcoal from the cooking are thrown on the grave 'in order to release people from the spiritual keeping of the dead *Beny Rem* into which they had been symbolically delivered by placing a necklace of ostrich-egg beads round his neck at his installation'. At the first harvest after his death there is a big sacrifice attended by all the people of his section who dance and drink beer:

On the last day the heads of the sons of the *Beny Rem* are shaved and this signifies the end of the period of mourning, which is observed by his family only and not by the whole section. If for any reason the *Beny Rem* dies in another way, e.g. accidental drowning, a sheep is suffocated and buried with him in the same grave, and the rites are conducted in the same way.

---

[1] Professor Evans-Pritchard was told by a Dinka that the master of the fishing-spear was buried secretly so that his grave should not be found. I did not hear of this. [2] This is the *akoc* wood mentioned earlier.
[3] Among the Northern Dinka, those who claim descent from Aiwel Longar are called *mendyor* (pl. *dindyor*). This relates to the *wendyor* of the Western Dinka (pp. 108–9) but is clearly a much more important term among the Northern Dinka than among the Western.

It is not always necessary to kill a *Beny Rem* and it is generally sufficient if a sheep is killed and buried with him, but this ceremonial killing is essential in the case of a *Beny Nial* and there are always people accompanying him for this purpose.

By *Beny Rem* and *Beny Nial* Ibrahim Eff. Bedri refers to a distinction something like that we have already made between minor and major masters of the fishing-spear. In Northern Dinkaland, however, this distinction seems to be formally made by ceremonial action, in a way which I never encountered among the Western Dinka. It is said that the ordinary *Beny Rem* is the spiritual leader of a tribe, while a *Beny Nial* is an outstanding *Beny Rem* who seems to have a wider following. The ordinary *Beny Rem* is installed after sacrifice, from the bones of which a shrine is made, while the fire upon which the flesh is roasted is used for starting a special sacred fire in the new master's home. There are then other ceremonies which may be summarized as follows. The *Beny Rem* sits on a bed of *ambatch* (a very light wood which is of considerable ceremonial importance among the neighbouring Shilluk). He is washed by the elders, who then place special strings of ostrich egg-shell beads round his neck, and a circlet of roan antelope-hide round his head, and anoint him with butter. He then sits on an untrimmed bull-hide, and all those who had any right to his office cut bits from the hide, thereby renouncing their rights and reducing the hide to the usual, trimmed, oval shape. Other ceremonies expressive of promising allegiance are performed, and finally the sacred spear associated with the clan-divinity is placed in the master's hand. The warriors parade before him and he is sprinkled with blood and water. He then travels from village to village of his tribe with a few elders, carrying pieces of wood anointed with butter, which seem to represent life and fertility for his people. At each village the women come out to meet the *Beny Rem* 'and those without children touch the pieces of wood with their hands and then their stomachs and kiss their hands as a good omen for becoming pregnant'. This again is a much richer and more explicit ceremonial than I have found elsewhere among the Dinka, though to a large extent it simply presents overtly what the master of the fishing-spear means to the Dinka as, in a more latent way, that meaning may be found among the Western Dinka.

The installation of the *Beny Nial*, who is automatically destined for burial alive, is thus described:[1]

A Dindyor member who is deemed of exceptional character and shows interest in his people's affairs, is carried (in order to evince their feelings) in an *ambach* bed on the shoulders of elders who run with him towards the four directions singing, while the chorus repeats '*beny aci jaj, beny aci riak kany*' (The Chief has been carried, the Chief destroys things). I do not know whether they mean their own or their enemies' things. Such a *Beny Riem* must not be left to die a natural death, otherwise some evil, such as famine, will fall on the country.

Elsewhere, Bedri writes: 'The people . . . lower the ambach bed and before it reaches the ground the *Beny Rem* jumps from it as though returning to life again.'

2

The information assembled above indicates that there is some variety in the practice described for different parts of Dinkaland, but that, except for the elaborate ceremonies of the Northern Dinka which I have not found elsewhere, these varieties can scarcely be ordered on a regional basis. Details from ceremonies described for one part are repeated in another, while considerable differences may appear in different accounts of the ceremonies performed in one area. It is safe for one who knows the Dinka to say that nothing in any of the accounts given above would surprise Dinka anywhere, even though it might not be part of their actual practice. A characteristically Dinka symbolism is integral to all.

The fundamental principle, clear in all accounts, is that certain masters of the fishing-spear must not or should not be seen to enter upon physical death and the debility which precedes it in the same way as ordinary men or domestic animals. Their deaths are to be, or are to appear, deliberate, and they are to be the occasion of a form of public celebration. It is with this point that we may start a consideration of the material presented above.

First, it is necessary to make clear that the ceremonies described in no way prevent the ultimate recognition of the ageing

[1] Ibrahim Eff. Bedri, op. cit., 1939, p. 130.

and physical death of those for whom they are performed. This death is recognized; but it is the public experience of it, for the survivors, which is deliberately modified by the performance of these ceremonies. It is clear also that this is the Dinka intention in performing the rites. They do not think that they have made their masters of the fishing-spear personally immortal by burying them before they have become corpses or, in some accounts, by anticipating their deaths by ritual killing. The expressions used for the deaths of masters of the fishing-spear are euphemisms for an event which is fully admitted. In my experience they are not even inevitably used, though a Dinka would prefer to say gently 'The master has gone to the earth' or 'The master has gone to sit', rather than 'The master has died', particularly at the time of death. These euphemisms replace the involuntary and passive connotations of the ordinary verb for 'to die' (*thou*) by expressions suggesting a positive act. Similarly (though this point is not specifically made in any of the accounts) when we hear that the people 'bury their master of the fishing-spear' it is as an alternative to 'letting him die'. In other words, the deliberately contrived death, though recognized as death, enables them to avoid admitting in this case the involuntary death which is the lot of ordinary men and beasts. Further, it is not the master of the fishing-spear who 'kills' himself, though he requests or receives a special form of death. The action to avoid, for him, the mere deprival of life which death represents for ordinary Dinka, is action taken by his people. And, as we see in most of the accounts given, their intention is not primarily to undertake the special ceremonies for *his* sake, but for their own.

If we regard the ceremonies so far described in this way, we do not need to make much of the variations which seem to contradict each other with regard to the part played, in the ceremony, by the master of the fishing-spear's own volition. It *is* possible for the Dinka to conceive of the burial of a master of the fishing-spear alive against his will, though it must be said that, in the case of the Western Dinka, I have never heard that this has been done within the limits of what might be considered real historical tradition. The account which these Dinka will give of the custom almost invariably begins with the request of the old master of the fishing-spear himself, and his securing of the agreement of his people. There is, however, a story which tells of the burial of one master of the fishing-spear against his will, and I doubt if it would surprise any Dinka. It is told as follows among the Agar Dinka:

Jokom was a person of long ago. Long ago he thought that he would build a cattle-byre with people, with some people standing and then others standing on their heads and other people on their backs. And he built for two days and the cattle-byre collapsed. And his son called Macot thought about this, and acted craftily, and spoke with the people of his father's camp, and said 'The camp of my father is being finished [killed]. Better that we bury my father alive.' The people of the camp agreed.

A clan called Pabuong brought out a *mangok* (blue-grey) bull to bury their master Jokom. Jokom did not know they were going to bury him alive, even when they had dug the earth out. When they had finished digging, they brought out the bull and deceived the master of the fishing-spear into coming to the grave. When he came, they seized him and pushed him in, and pushed the bull in with him, and covered the grave with wood and covered it with earth and then cleared the ground around it.

They stayed there by the grave for about five days and after that the master of the fishing-spear and the bull died. And while they yet lived, the bull bellowed and the master answered it.

His son Macot remained. When people fought with spears he took a rod and went between the people and spoke, that the fighting might end, and people were afraid [to continue]. And if a man had been killed Macot said that compensation must be paid [rather than revenge taken] and people listened to him because they feared his word.

The cruel master of the fishing-spear who 'tried to build a cattle-byre with living people' figures in the lore of many Dinka;[1] and in this story his death against his will is clearly intended to follow from his cruelty. Even here, however, though he does not consult his people, his son must. We do not have to go further than a consideration of the communal labour involved, however, to conclude that in such ceremonies the will of the people of the master of the fishing-spear is what is primarily significant for the Dinka. Their purpose, in burying the master alive, is served whatever may be his intentions in

---

[1] P. P. Howell, op. cit., 1948, reports that, according to some legends, it was thus that the 'pyramid' of Aiwel Longar at Puom was built.

the situation, though it is usually supposed that he takes the initiative, and this is expected of him.

We have earlier discussed the Dinka belief that the master of the fishing-spear 'carries the life' of his people. It appears from the account of Ibrahim Eff. Bedri that, among the Northern Dinka, this belief is symbolically represented by the ostrich shell beads, which stand for his people, which a master keeps in his possession. Among the Western Dinka, at least, it is this belief which is invoked when one asks why it is necessary to bury a master of the fishing-spear alive. If he 'dies' like ordinary men, the 'life' of his people which is in his keeping goes with him. It may be that the frequent references to strangulation and suffocation which we find in other accounts relate also to this belief; for, as we have shown, for the Dinka 'life', *wei*, is recognized particularly in breath, and these forms of killing involve, above all, the retention within him of the master's breath. He is not, in our idiom, allowed to 'breathe his last' or 'expire'. This situation should not be interpreted too materialistically or literally. The Dinka know, as we have said, that the master dies. What they represent in contriving the death which they give him is the conservation of the 'life' which they themselves think they receive from him, and not the conservation of his own personal life. The latter, indeed, is finally taken away from him by his people so that they may seem to divide it from the public 'life' which is in his keeping, and which must not depart from them with his death.

The action by which this separation is achieved is clearly shown in some of the accounts which we have given. In my own discussions with the Western Dinka, one feature of their reaction to the death of a master of the fishing-spear was very marked; it was that people should not mourn, but rather should be joyful. It is conceded to the man's close kin—those for whom his own personality has been most significant—that they may indeed break down under the strain imposed, by custom, upon them, in having to control the expression of the sadness they may feel. It is said also, by some, that the closest kin may observe some of the customs of mourning. This is clearly felt to be a concession to their sense of personal bereavement, a recognition by the Dinka indeed of the artifice by which, in a collective act of will and control of sentiment, they repudiate the contradiction in experience which the inevitability of personal death would otherwise here represent. For the rest of the master's people (and even for the close kin in that they are also his people) the human symbolic action involved in the 'artificial' burial must be seen to transform the experience of a leader's death into a concentrated public experience of vitality and, in the Dinka world, aggressiveness. It is sometimes said that the cattle of his people, bellowing because they have not been milked, alone mourn his death with their cries; but also, since the crying of cattle heavy with milk is one of the most joyful sounds a Dinka can wish to hear, their cries simultaneously call to mind the plenty with which the master of the fishing-spear has always in life been ideally associated—the fecundity of cattle and the watered pastures upon which they depend. To confirm this impression, and re-create the whole configuration of experience which, in a previous chapter (Chap. V, pp. 194–6), we have seen to be associated with the master of the fishing-spear, we find in some accounts that the materials necessary for the burial have riverain associations, or are connected with the dry-season pastures which represent for the Dinka much of the 'life' which they hope to ensure for themselves. In some accounts the fence round a grave is made with *awar* grass, the grass of the riverain pastures which appears and gives sustenance to the cattle before others in a protracted dry season, as we have earlier described. It is also, it will be remembered, the grass from beneath which the prototype of spear-masters, Aiwel Longar, watered his cattle in a time of famine and drought. In another account (p. 302) it is said that *dhot* wood is required. This again is associated with the dry-season pastures, and, it may be remembered, is the tree with branches of which sacrificial victims are covered as they lie in state immediately after death. Finally, it is fairly consistently stated that the wood from which the framework of the platform on which the master reclines is made is *akoc* (*Cordia rothii*), a wood which is renowned for its sappy moistness, and which, in putting forth its leaves before other trees, is associated with moisture and persistence through the most arid and difficult period of the dry season.

If the burial is thus associated by a wide range of associations with a social triumph over death and the factors which bring death in Dinkaland, this association is reinforced by the militant display which the ceremony involves. Fighting was for the Dinka often a condition of survival, and it still has something of the value attached to it which must have made it a serious necessity in the time of their complete autonomy. One of the functions of masters of the fishing-spear was to open and close age-sets; and though the age-sets seem never to have had in themselves specific regimental functions, their pride and reputation were and are still connected with their military prowess. Consequently, a renowned master of the fishing-spear was himself at the centre of the military organization of his people, and the inspiration of the most active fighting men. So, though every public sacrifice involves warlike display, at the burial of a master of the fishing-spear the fighting power of his people is particularly emphasized. Members of groups other than those rallied by the ceremony are in danger if they approach it; the young men are fully armed for war; and the cattle are tethered during the day, not taken out in their separate herding groups which are weak in the face of attack.

In other ways also the ceremony emphasizes the unity, and equivalence, of those taking part. The lineages represented in the community should all contribute victims to the feast; and, very characteristically of Dinka thought, it is specifically said in one text that the master's maternal kin are 'put together' with his paternal kin. His daughters and their families also bring their offerings to the grave at his burial. He is recognized as 'the maternal uncle of the camp' (*nar wut*), which such a leader is often called. A further indication of the solidarity which such a ceremony ideally creates is the statement, in one of the texts, that after the burial men and women may sleep promiscuously together. I do not know if in fact this happens; but that it should be thought to do so is significant, not only in its similarity to orgiastic behaviour at critical periods elsewhere, but in that such an abandonment of personal rights which would normally be strongly asserted is a measure of the common interests and equivalence of members of the community.

In his death, then, the Dinka master of the fishing-spear is made to represent to his people the survival with which masters of the fishing-spear are associated in myth and present-day ritual. Nor, in one sense, are the Dinka deceiving themselves in maintaining that the death of an old master of the fishing-spear produces a renewal of life in his people. His burial ceremonies do create a militant self-consciousness, as we have seen. The masters of the fishing-spear who are the principal repositories of their tribal and subtribal traditions, are said to recall these traditions when they lie in the grave. They cannot die like ordinary men, for the traditions and beliefs which they embody, reaching back to the myth of Aiwel, live on. Notions of individual personal immortality mean little to non-Christian Dinka, but the assertion of collective immortality means much, and it is this which they make in the funeral ceremonies of their religious leaders.

INDEX